Infant and
Toddler Health
SOURCEBOOK

Health Reference Series

First Edition

Infant and Toddler Health SOURCEBOOK

Basic Consumer Health Information about the Physical and Mental Development of Newborns, Infants, and Toddlers, Including Neonatal Concerns, Nutrition Recommendations, Immunization Schedules, Common Pediatric Disorders, Assessments and Milestones, Safety Tips, and Advice for Parents and Other Caregivers:

Along with a Glossary of Terms and Resource Listings for Additional Help

Edited by
Jenifer Swanson

Omnigraphics

615 Griswold Street • Detroit, MI 48226

Bibliographic Note

Because this page cannot legibly accommodate all the copyright notices, the Bibliographic Note portion of the Preface constitutes an extension of the copyright notice.

Each new volume of the *Health Reference Series* is individually titled and called a "First Edition." Subsequent updates will carry sequential edition numbers. To help avoid confusion and to provide maximum flexibility in our ability to respond to informational needs, the practice of consecutively numbering each volume will be discontinued.

Edited by Jenifer Swanson

Health Reference Series

Karen Bellenir, *Series Editor*
Peter D. Dresser, *Managing Editor*
Joan Margeson, *Research Associate*
Dawn Matthews, *Verification Assistant*
Jenifer Swanson, *Research Associate*

EdIndex, Services for Publishers, *Indexers*

Omnigraphics, Inc.

Matthew P. Barbour, *Vice President, Operations*
Laurie Lanzen Harris, *Vice President, Editorial Director*
Kevin Hayes, *Production Coordinator*
Thomas J. Murphy, *Vice President, Finance and Comptroller*
Peter E. Ruffner, *Senior Vice President*
Jane J. Steele, *Marketing Consultant*

Frederick G. Ruffner, Jr., Publisher

© 2000, Omnigraphics, Inc.

Library of Congress Cataloging-in-Publication Data

Infant and toddler health sourcebook : basic consumer health information about the physical and mental development of newborns, infants, and toddlers ... / edited by Jenifer Swanson.— 1st ed.
    p. cm. — (Health reference series)
  Includes bibliographical references and index.
  ISBN 0-7808-0246-2
  1. Infants—Care. 2. Toddlers—Care. 3. Infants—Health and hygiene. 4. Toddlers—Health and hygiene. 5. Infants—Development. 6. Consumer education. I. Swanson, Jenifer. II. Health reference series (Unnumbered)

RJ101 .I535 2000
618.92—dc21
                                         00-042784

∞

Table of Contents

Part III: Well-Baby Care

Part IV: Tips for Parents

Part V: Common Medical Concerns during Early Childhood

Part VI: Safety and First Aid

Part VII: Additional Help and Information

Preface

About This Book

The first few years of a child's life are filled with wonder as he or she grows and discovers the world. Although infancy and toddlerhood can be exciting, they can also be confusing. New parents often have questions and concerns about health issues, including nutrition, immunizations, and common childhood illnesses. They may wonder if their child is progressing through developmental stages at a normal rate or if perceived delays signify potential problems.

This *Sourcebook* presents information for parents about the health and development of newborns, infants, and toddlers up to the age of three. It includes neonatal concerns, nutrition recommendations, immunization schedules, common pediatric disorders, developmental assessments and milestones, and safety tips. A glossary of important terms will help readers better communicate with pediatricians and a directory of resources will provide guidance to parents seeking additional help and information.

How to Use This Book

This book is divided into parts and chapters. Parts focus on broad areas of interest. Chapters are devoted to single topics within a part.

Part I: The Newborn introduces the newborn infant, describes routine screening examinations, and provides information about concerns specific to young infants.

Part II: Nutrition offers information about food choices for infants and toddlers. Facts about breast feeding and formula feeding, introducing solid foods, evaluating nutrition labels, and food safety are included. A chapter discussing the special needs of young children on vegetarian diets is also provided.

Part III: Well-Baby Care offers parents information about what to expect at routine health check-ups. It also describes important developmental milestones, discusses vaccination recommendations, and provides information about vision and hearing screening.

Part IV: Tips for Parents includes practical advice for common concerns, including caring for a newborn's navel, bathing an infant, fighting diaper rash, taking a temperature, suctioning the nose, understanding crying, coping with colic, recognizing sleep problems, and dealing with temper tantrums. For parents considering the adoption of an infant prenatally exposed to alcohol or other drugs, a chapter addressing these concerns is also included.

Part V: Common Medical Concerns during Early Childhood presents basic facts about some of the most commonly encountered health problems in infants and toddlers, including allergies, asthma, birthmarks, colds, constipation, croup, ear infections, fevers, impetigo, roseola, scarlet fever, strep throat, and thrush.

Part VI: Safety and First Aid offers advice on keeping children safe at home, in the car, and with caretakers.

Part VII: Additional Help and Information includes a glossary of important terms and a directory of resources.

Bibliographic Note

This volume contains documents and excerpts from publications issued by the following U.S. government agencies: Agency for Health Care Policy and Research (AHCPR); Centers for Disease Control and Prevention (CDC); National Highway Traffic Safety Administration; National Institute of Allergy and Infectious Disease (NIAID); National Institute of Child Health and Human Development (NICHD); National Institute of Dental and Craniofacial Research (NIDCR); National Institute of Mental Health (NIMH); National Institute of Neurological Disorders and Stroke (NINDS); U.S. Consumer Product Safety Commission; U.S. Department of Health and Human Services (DHHS);

U.S. Food and Drug Administration (FDA); and the U.S. Public Health Service (PHS), Office of Disease Prevention and Health Promotion; and from the New York State Department of Health.

In addition, this volume contains copyrighted documents from the following organizations and individuals: American Academy of Dermatology; American Academy of Family Physicians; American Academy of Pediatrics; BabyCenter; BabyWorld; Channing L. Bete Co., Inc.; Children's Hospital Research Foundation; Clinical Reference Systems; The Evan B. Donaldson Adoption Institute; Drs 4 Kids; Dr. Paula Elbirt; Dr. Alan Greene; Institute of Food and Agricultural Sciences; Vicki Lansky; Kaiser Permanente; KidsDoctor; National Healthy Mothers, Healthy Babies Coalition; National Safe Kids Campaign; Nemours Foundation; New York Online Access to Health (NOAH); Norton Healthcare; Barton Schmidt; University of Virginia Health Sciences; Vegetarian Society; and Zero to Three. Copyrighted articles from *Parenting Magazine* and *Pediatrics* are also included.

Full citation information is provided on the first page of each chapter. Every effort has been made to secure all necessary rights to reprint the copyrighted material. If any omissions have been made, please contact Omnigraphics to make corrections for future editions.

Acknowledgements

Thanks go to researcher Joan Margeson, verification assistant Dawn Matthews, permissions specialist Maria Franklin, and to everyone else who contributed to this book—and most especially to my husband, Matt, and my daughter, Devon.

Note from the Editor

This book is part of Omnigraphics' *Health Reference Series*. The series provides basic information about a broad range of medical concerns. It is not intended to serve as a tool for diagnosing illness, in prescribing treatments, or as a substitute for the physician/patient relationship. All persons concerned about medical symptoms or the possibility of disease are encouraged to seek professional care from an appropriate health care provider.

Our Advisory Board

The *Health Reference Series* is reviewed by an Advisory Board comprised of librarians from public, academic, and medical libraries. We would like to thank the following board members for providing guidance to the development of this series:

Health Reference Series *Update Policy*

The inaugural book in the *Health Reference Series* was the first edition of *Cancer Sourcebook* published in 1992. Since then, the *Series* has been enthusiastically received by librarians and in the medical community. In order to maintain the standard of providing high-quality health information for the lay person, the editorial staff at Omnigraphics felt it was necessary to implement a policy of updating volumes when warranted.

Medical researchers have been making tremendous strides, and it is the purpose of the *Health Reference Series* to stay current with the most recent advances. Each decision to update a volume will be made on an individual basis. Some of the considerations will include how much new information is available and the feedback we receive from people who use the books. If there is a topic you would like to see added to the update list, or an area of medical concern you feel has not been adequately addressed, please write to:

Editor
Health Reference Series
Omnigraphics, Inc.
615 Griswold Street
Detroit, MI 48226

The commitment to providing on-going coverage of important medical developments has also led to some format changes in the *Health Reference Series*. Each new volume on a topic is individually titled and called a "First Edition." Subsequent updates will carry sequential edition numbers. To help avoid confusion and to provide maximum flexibility in our ability to respond to informational needs, the practice of consecutively numbering each volume has been discontinued.

Part One

The Newborn

Chapter 1

The Normal Newborn

Appearance

Even after your child's physician assures you that your baby is normal, you may find that he or she looks a bit odd. Your baby does not have the perfect body you have seen in baby books. Be patient. Most newborns have some peculiar characteristics. Fortunately they are temporary. Your baby will begin to look normal by 1 to 2 weeks of age.

This discussion of these transient newborn characteristics is arranged by parts of the body. A few minor congenital defects that are harmless but permanent are also included. Call your physician if you have questions about your baby's appearance that this list does not address.

Head

Molding

Molding refers to the long, narrow, cone-shaped head that results from passage through a tight birth canal. This compression of the head can temporarily hide the fontanel. The head returns to a normal shape in a few days.

Reprinted with permission of Barton Schmitt from *Clinical Reference Systems*, December 1997, p1566. © 1997 Clinical Reference Systems Ltd.

Caput

This refers to swelling on top of the head or throughout the scalp due to fluid squeezed into the scalp during the birth process. Caput is present at birth and clears in a few days.

Cephalohematoma

This is a collection of blood on the outer surface of the skull. It is due to friction between the infant's skull and the mother's pelvic bones during the birth process. The lump is usually confined to one side of the head. It first appears on the second day of life and may grow larger for up to 5 days. It doesn't resolve completely until the baby is 2 or 3 months of age.

Anterior Fontanel

The "soft spot" is found in the top front part of the skull. It is diamond-shaped and covered by a thick fibrous layer. Touching this area is quite safe. The purpose of the soft spot is to allow rapid growth of the brain. The spot will normally pulsate with each beat of the heart. It normally closes with bone when the baby is between 9 and 12 months of age.

Eyes

Swollen Eyelids

The eyes may be puffy because of pressure on the face during delivery. They may also be puffy and reddened if silver nitrate eye drops are used. This irritation should clear in 3 days.

Subconjunctival Hemorrhage

A flame-shaped hemorrhage on the white of the eye (sclera) is not uncommon. It's harmless and due to birth trauma. The blood is reabsorbed in 2 to 3 weeks.

Iris Color

The iris is usually blue, green, gray, or brown, or variations of these colors. The permanent color of the iris is often uncertain until your baby reaches 6 months of age. White babies are usually born with blue-gray eyes. Black babies are usually born with brown-gray eyes. Children who will have dark irises often change eye color by 2 months of age; children who will have light-colored irises usually change by 5 or 6 months of age.

Tear Duct, Blocked

If your baby's eye is continuously watery, he or she may have a blocked tear duct. This means that the channel that normally carries tears from the eye to the nose is blocked. It is a common condition, and more than 90% of blocked tear ducts open up by the time the child is 12 months old.

Ears

Folded Over

The ears of newborns are commonly soft and floppy. Sometimes one of the edges is folded over. The outer ear will assume normal shape as the cartilage hardens over the first few weeks.

Earpits

About 1% of normal children have a small pit or dimple in front of the outer ear. This minor congenital defect is not important unless it becomes infected.

Nose Flattened

The nose can become misshapen during the birth process. It may be flattened or pushed to one side. It will look normal by 1 week of age.

Mouth

Sucking Callus or Blister

A sucking callus occurs in the center of the upper lip from constant friction at this point during bottle or breast-feeding. It will disappear when your child begins cup feedings. A sucking callus on the thumb or wrist may also develop.

Tongue-Tie

The normal tongue in newborns has a short tight band that connects it to the floor of the mouth. This band normally stretches with time, movement, and growth. Babies with symptoms from tongue-tie are rare.

Epithelial Pearls

Little cysts (containing clear fluid) or shallow white ulcers can occur along the gumline or on the hard palate. These are a result of blockage of normal mucous glands. They disappear after 1 to 2 months.

Teeth

The presence of a tooth at birth is rare. Approximately 10% are extra teeth without a root structure. The other 90% are prematurely erupted normal teeth. The distinction can be made with an x-ray. The extra teeth must be removed by a dentist. The normal teeth need to be removed only if they become loose (with a danger of choking) or if they cause sores on your baby's tongue.

Breast Engorgement

Swollen breasts are present during the first week of life in many female and male babies. They are caused by the passage of female hormones across the mother's placenta. Breasts are generally swollen for 4 to 6 months, but they may stay swollen longer in breast-fed and female babies. One breast may lose its swelling before the other one by a month or more. Never squeeze the breast because this can cause infection. Be sure to call your physician if a swollen breast develops any redness, streaking, or tenderness.

Genitals, Girls

Swollen Labia

The labia minora can be quite swollen in newborn girls because of the passage of female hormones across the placenta. The swelling will resolve in 2 to 4 weeks.

Hymenal Tags

The hymen can also be swollen due to maternal estrogen and have smooth 1/2-inch projections of pink tissue. These normal tags occur in 10% of newborn girls and slowly shrink over 2 to 4 weeks.

Vaginal Discharge

As the maternal hormones decline in the baby's blood, a clear or white discharge can flow from the vagina during the latter part of the first week of life. Occasionally the discharge will become pink or blood-tinged (false menstruation). This normal discharge should not recur once it stops.

Genitals, Boys

Hydrocele

The newborn scrotum can be filled with clear fluid. The fluid is squeezed into the scrotum during the birth process. This painless collection of clear fluid is called a "hydrocele." It is common in newborn males. A hydrocele may take 6 to 12 months to clear completely. It is harmless but can be rechecked during regular visits. If the swelling frequently changes size, a hernia may also be present and you should call your physician during office hours for an appointment.

Undescended Testicle

The testicle is not in the scrotum in about 4% of full-term newborn boys. Many of these testicles gradually descend into the normal position during the following months. In 1-year-old boys only 0.7% of all testicles are undescended; these need to be brought down surgically.

Tight Foreskin

Most uncircumcised infant boys have a tight foreskin that doesn't allow you to see the head of the penis. This is normal and the foreskin should not be retracted.

Erections

Erections occur commonly in a newborn boy, as they do at all ages. They are usually triggered by a full bladder. Erections demonstrate that the nerves to the penis are normal.

Bones and Joints

Tight Hips

Your child's physician will test how far your child's legs can be spread apart to be certain the hips are not too tight. Upper legs bent outward until they are horizontal is called "90 degrees of spread." (Less than 50% of normal newborn hips permit this much spreading.) As long as the upper legs can be bent outward to 60 degrees and are the same on each side, they are fine. The most common cause of a tight hip is a dislocation.

Tibial Torsion

The lower legs (tibia) normally curve in because of the cross-legged posture your baby was confined to while in the womb. If you stand your baby up, you will also notice that the legs are bowed. Both of these curves are normal and will straighten out after your child has been walking for 6 to 12 months.

Feet Turned Up, In, or Out

Feet may be turned in any direction inside the cramped quarters of the womb. As long as your child's feet are flexible and can be easily moved to a normal position, they are normal. The direction of the feet will become more normal between 6 and 12 months of age.

Long Second Toe

The second toe is longer than the great toe as a result of heredity in some ethnic groups that originated along the Mediterranean, especially Egyptians.

"Ingrown" Toenails

Many newborns have soft nails that easily bend and curve. However, they are not truly ingrown because they don't curve into the flesh.

Hair

Scalp Hair

Most hair at birth is dark. This hair is temporary and begins to shed by 1 month of age. Some babies lose it gradually while the permanent hair is coming in; others lose it rapidly and temporarily become bald. The permanent hair will appear by 6 months. It may be an entirely different color from the newborn hair.

Body Hair or Lanugo

Lanugo is the fine downy hair that is sometimes present on the back and shoulders. It is more common in premature infants. It is rubbed off with normal friction by 2 to 4 weeks of age.

Skin

Acne of Newborn

More than 30% of newborns develop acne of the face: mainly small, red bumps. This neonatal acne begins at 3 to 4 weeks of age and lasts until 4 to 6 months of age. The cause appears to be the transfer of maternal androgens (hormones) just prior to birth. Since it is temporary, no treatment is necessary. Baby oil or ointments will just make it worse.

Drooling Rash

Most babies have a rash on the chin or cheeks that comes and goes. Often, this rash is caused by contact with food and acid that have been spit up from the stomach. Some of this can be helped by placing an absorbent diaper under your baby's face during naps. Also, rinse your baby's face with water after all feedings.

Other temporary rashes on the face are heat rashes in areas held against the mother's skin during nursing (especially in the summertime). Change your baby's position more frequently and put a cool washcloth on the area that has a rash.

No baby has perfect skin. The babies in advertisements wear makeup.

Erythema Toxicum

More than 50% of babies get a rash called erythema toxicum on the second or third day of life. The rash is composed of ½ to 1-inch-size red blotches with a small white lump in the center. They look like insect bites. They can be numerous, keep occurring, and be anywhere on the body surface (except palms and soles). The cause of this rash is unknown and it is harmless. The rash usually disappears by the time an infant is 2 weeks old, but sometimes not until a child is 4 weeks old.

Forceps or Birth Canal Trauma

If your baby's delivery was difficult, a forceps may have been used to help him through the birth canal. The pressure of the forceps on the skin can leave bruises or scrapes or can even damage fat tissue anywhere on the head or face.

Pressure from the birth canal can damage the skin overlying bony prominences (such as the sides of the skull) even without a forceps delivery. Fetal monitors can also cause scrapes and scabs on the scalp.

You will notice the bruises and scrapes 1 or 2 days after birth. They will disappear in 1 to 2 weeks.

Injury to fat tissue won't be apparent until the fifth or sixth day after birth. A thickened lump of skin with an overlying scab is what you usually see. This may take 3 or 4 weeks to heal. If it becomes tender to the touch or soft in the center or shows other signs of infection, call your physician.

Milia

Milia are tiny white bumps that occur on the faces of 40% of newborn babies. The nose and cheeks are most often involved, but milia are also seen on the forehead and chin. Although they look like pimples, they are smaller and not infected. They are blocked-off skin pores and will open up and disappear by 1 to 2 months of age. Do not apply ointments or creams to them.

Any true blisters (little bumps containing clear fluid) or pimples (little bumps containing pus) that occur during the first month of life (especially on the scalp) must be examined and diagnosed quickly. If they are caused by the herpes virus, they must be treated right away. If you suspect blisters or pimples, call your child's physician immediately.

Mongolian Spots

A Mongolian spot is a bluish-gray, flat birthmark that is found in more than 90% of American Indian, Oriental, Hispanic, and black babies. They occur most commonly over the back and buttocks, although they can be present on any part of the body. They vary greatly in size and shape. Most fade away by 2 or 3 years of age, although a trace may persist into adult life.

Stork Bites or Pink Birthmarks

Flat pink birthmarks (also called capillary hemangiomas) occur over the bridge of the nose, the eyelids, or the back of the neck in more than 50% of newborns. The birthmarks on the bridge of the nose and eyelids clear completely by 1 to 2 years of age. Most birthmarks on the nape of the neck also clear, but 25% can persist into adult life.

Behavior

Some findings in newborns that concern parents are not signs of illness. Most of the following harmless reflexes are due to an immature nervous system and will disappear in 2 or 3 months:

- chin trembling

- lower lip quivering

- hiccups

- irregular breathing (This is normal if your baby is content, the rate is less than 60 breaths per minute, any pauses are less than 6 seconds long, and your baby doesn't turn blue. Occasionally infants take rapid, progressively deeper, stepwise breaths to completely expand their lungs.)

- passing gas (not a temporary behavior)

- sleep noise from breathing and moving

- sneezing

- spitting up or belching

- brief stiffening of the body after a noise or movement (also called the startle reflex, the Moro reflex, or the embrace reflex)

- straining with bowel movements

- throat clearing (or gurgling sounds of secretions in the throat)

- trembling or jitteriness of arms and legs during crying (Jittery babies are common. Convulsions are rare. During convulsions babies also jerk, blink their eyes, rhythmically suck with their mouths, and don't cry. If your baby is trembling and not crying, give her something to suck on. If the trembling doesn't stop when your baby is sucking, call your physician's office immediately.)

- yawning

—by B.D. Schmitt, M.D., author of
Your Child's Health, *Bantam Books.*

Chapter 2

Newborn Screening

Virtually all states require screening of newborns for congenital hypothyroidism and phenylketonuria (PKU). Testing for galactosemia and hemoglobinopathies is required in a majority of states, and some states require screening of newborns for maple syrup urine disease, homocystinuria, biotinidase deficiency, tyrosinemia, congenital adrenal hyperplasia, cystic fibrosis, and toxoplasmosis. Table 2.1 provides a state-by-state listing of newborn screening policies.

Hypothyroidism

Most children with congenital hypothyroidism who are not identified and treated promptly suffer the irreversible mental retardation, growth failure, deafness, and neurologic abnormalities characteristic of the syndrome of cretinism. The incidence of this disorder is 1 per 3600 to 1 per 5000 live births. Infants who receive adequate treatment with thyroxine within the first weeks of life have normal or near-normal intellectual performance at 4 to 7 years of age.

Phenylketonuria (PKU)

Phenylketonuria is an autosomal recessive aminoacidopathy that leads to severe, irreversible mental retardation (IQ below 50) if it is not treated during infancy. The incidence of this disorder is 1 per

Excerpted from *Clinician's Handbook of Preventive Services*, U.S. Department of Health and Human Services, 1998.

10,000 to 1 per 15,000 live births. Most children who undergo early screening, diagnosis, and optimal treatment with dietary restriction of phenylalanine will be in the normal range of intelligence.

Galactosemia

Galactosemia presents following milk feeding with vomiting, diarrhea, failure to thrive, and Escherichia coli septicemia (which is often fatal). Continued exposure to galactose results in liver disease (manifested by hepatomegaly, jaundice, and cirrhosis), cataracts, and irreversible mental retardation. The incidence of galactosemia is 1 per 60,000 to 1 per 80,000 live births. Treatment is directed to the elimination of dietary lactose by avoiding galactose in breast milk, cow's milk, and infant formulas. Treatment can lead to dramatic improvement in all clinical features except for central nervous system dysfunction.

Hemoglobinopathies

Sickle cell disease and other hemoglobinopathies, such as thalassemia and hemoglobin E, are most common in persons of African, Mediterranean, Asian, Caribbean, and South and Central American ancestry. Affected individuals may have overwhelming sepsis, chronic hemolytic anemia, episodic vascular occlusive crises, hyposplenism, periodic splenic sequestration, and bone marrow aplasia. Carriers (genetic heterozygotes) do not suffer significant morbidity. Early detection of sickle cell disease in newborns allows prophylactic use of penicillin to prevent septicemia and prompt clinical intervention for infection and sequestration crises.

Recommendations of Major Authorities

American Academy of Pediatrics and **Bright Futures**—Newborn screening should be performed according to each state's regulations.

National authorities have made recommendations for the following specific conditions:

Hypothyroidism

American Academy of Family Physicians—Neonatal screening for thyroid function abnormalities is recommended.

American Academy of Pediatrics (AAP), American Thyroid Association (ATA), Canadian Task Force on the Periodic

Health Examination (CTFPHE), and US Preventive Services Task Force (USPSTF)—All neonates should be screened for congenital hypothyroidism between 2 and 6 days of life. Care should be taken to assure that infants born at home, ill at birth, or transferred between hospitals in the first week of life are screened before 7 days of life. According to the CTFPHE, it is better to obtain a specimen within 24 hours of birth than no specimen at all. According to the AAP and ATA, blood should be obtained from infants before discharge from the hospital or after 48 hours of age.

Phenylketonuria (PKU)

American Academy of Family Physicians—Neonatal screening for PKU is recommended.

Canadian Task Force on the Periodic Health Examination (CTFPHE) and US Preventive Services Task Force (USPSTF)— All infants should be screened for PKU before discharge from the nursery. Premature infants and those with illness should be tested at or near 7 days of age. Infants tested before 24 hours of age should receive a repeat screening. According to the CTFPHE, this should occur between 2 and 7 days of age; according to the USPSTF, this should occur by 2 weeks of age.

Hemoglobinopathies

American Academy of Family Physicians—Neonatal screening for hemoglobinopathies is recommended.

Canadian Task Force on the Periodic Health Examination and US Preventive Services Task Force (USPSTF)—Neonatal screening for sickle hemoglobinopathies is recommended. Whether such screening should be universal or targeted to high-risk groups will depend on the proportion of high-risk individuals in the screening area. All screening must be accompanied by comprehensive counseling and treatment services. There is insufficient evidence to recommend for or against screening for hemoglobinopathies in adolescents and young adults in order to help them make informed reproductive decisions. According to the USPSTF, such screening may be justified on the basis of burden of suffering and patient preference.

Sickle Cell Disease Guideline Panel of the Agency for Health Care Policy and Research, US Public Health Service—Universal screening for sickle cell disease should be conducted on all newborns.

This recommendation has been endorsed by the **American Academy of Pediatrics, the American Nurses Association, and the National Medical Association.**

Basics of Newborn Screening

Schedule[1]

1. For the full-term, well neonate, obtain the specimen as close as possible to the time of discharge from the nursery and in no case later than 7 days of age. If the initial specimen is obtained earlier than 24 hours after birth, obtain a second specimen at 1 or 2 weeks of age to decrease the probability that PKU and other disorders with metabolite accumulation will be missed.

2. For any premature infant, any infant receiving parenteral feeding, or any neonate being treated for illness, obtain a specimen for screening at or near the seventh day of life if a specimen has not been obtained before that time, regardless of feeding status. For infants requiring transfusion or dialysis before the standard time for obtaining a specimen, obtain the sample for screening before transfusion or dialysis, if the neonate's condition is amenable. If a sample cannot be obtained beforehand, ensure that an adequate specimen is obtained at a time when the plasma or red blood cells, or both, will again reflect the child's own metabolic processes or phenotype.

Collection Technique[2]

1. Apply the same standards and techniques for the collection of blood specimens for neonatal screening programs for all of the congenital diseases. State screening agencies hold individual hospitals accountable for instituting policies that assure proper collection of filter-paper blood samples.

2. Enter the required information on the specimen collection kit with a ballpoint pen, not a soft-tip pen or typewriter.

3. Universal precautions: Use all appropriate precautions, including wearing gloves, when handling blood, and dispose of used lancets in a biohazard container for sharp objects.

4. Site Selection: The source of blood must be the most lateral surface of the plantar aspect (walking surface) of the infant's

heel. Skin punctures to obtain blood specimens must not be performed on the central area of the newborn's foot (area of the arch) or on the fingers of newborns. Puncturing the heel on the posterior curvature will permit blood to flow away from the puncture, making proper spotting difficult. Do not lance a previous puncture site.

5. Site Preparation: Warm the puncture site to increase blood flow. Place a warm, moist towel at a temperature no higher than 42° C (108° F) on the site for 3 minutes. Holding the infant's leg in a position lower than the heart will increase venous pressure.

6. Cleaning the Site: Clean the infant's heel with 70% isopropyl alcohol (rubbing alcohol). Wipe away excess alcohol with a dry sterile gauze or cotton ball, and allow the heel to air-dry thoroughly. Failure to wipe off alcohol residue may dilute the specimen and adversely affect test results.

7. Puncture: To ensure sufficient blood flow, puncture the plantar surface of the infant's heel with a sterile lancet to a depth of 2.0 to 2.4 mm or with an automated lancet device. Wipe away the first drop of blood with sterile gauze. In small premature infants, the heel bone may be no more than 2.4 mm beneath the plantar heel skin surface and half this distance at the posterior curvature of the heel. Puncturing deeper may risk bone damage. Do not milk or squeeze the puncture site, as this may cause hemolysis and admixture of tissue fluids with the specimen.

8. Filter Paper Handling and Application: Avoid touching the area within the printed circle on the filter paper before collection. Gently touch the filter paper against a large drop of blood and, in one step, allow a sufficient quantity of blood to soak through to completely fill the circle on the filter paper. Do not press the paper against the puncture site on the heel. Apply blood to only one side of the filter paper. Examine both sides of the filter paper to assure that the blood penetrates and saturates the paper. Do not layer successive drops of blood within the circle. If blood flow diminishes so that the circle is incompletely filled, repeat the sampling steps at a different site. Do not touch the blood sample after collection; do not allow water, feeding formulas, antiseptic solutions, or any

other contaminant to come into contact with the sample. Allow the sample to dry thoroughly before insertion into the envelope. Insufficient drying can adversely affect test results.

9. Hemostasis: After blood has been collected from the heel of the newborn, elevate the foot above the body and press a sterile gauze pad or cotton ball against the puncture site until the bleeding stops.

Documentation

Ensure that children receive proper newborn screening and that test results are reviewed. Be aware of patients who are at increased risk for not being screened. Such patients include sick or premature neonates, neonates undergoing adoption or being transferred within or between hospitals, infants born at home, children of transient or homeless families, and infants born outside the United States and Canada. Document newborn screening results in an easily accessible part of the patient record for future reference.

Follow-up

Confirm all abnormal results with retesting. With certain rare exceptions (e.g., galactosemia and maple syrup urine disease), do not initiate treatment until a confirmatory test result has been obtained. Prompt physical examination of patients with abnormal results is important. Start all patients with sickle cell disease on penicillin prophylaxis as soon as the diagnosis is confirmed.

Counseling

Provide appropriate counseling to all parents of children with abnormal test results. Provide information about the significance of the results and the need for retesting, the implications for the child's health, treatment regimens, symptoms to be alert for, and genetic issues for future childbearing.

[1]Adapted from: American Academy of Pediatrics, Committee on Genetics. Issues in newborn screening. *Pediatrics*. 1992;89:345-349. Reproduced by permission of Pediatrics; copyright © 1992.

[2]Adapted from: National Committee for Clinical Laboratory Standards. *Blood Collection on Filter Paper for Neonatal Screening Programs-Second Edition; Approved Standard*. Villanova, Pa: National

Committee for Clinical Laboratory Standards; 1992, Permission to use portions of NCCLS document LA4-A2 has been granted by the National Committee for Clinical Laboratory Standards; copyright © 1992.

Table 2.1. Newborn Screening by State (continued on next page)

STATE	MANDATED	BIO	CAH	CF	GAL	HGB	HCU	HYPO	MSUD	PKU	TOXO	TYR
ALABAMA	•		•		•	•		•		•		
ALASKA	•	•	•		•			•	•	•		
ARIZONA	•	•			•	•	•	•	•	•		
ARKANSAS	•				•	•		•		•		
CALIFORNIA	•				•	•		•		•		
COLORADO	•	•		•	•	•		•		•		
CONNECTICUT	•	•		•	•	•	•	•	•	•		
DELAWARE	•	•			•	•		•		•		
FLORIDA	•		•		•	•		•		•		
GEORGIA	•		•		•	•	•	•	•	•		•
HAWAII	•							•		•		
IDAHO	•	•			•			•	•	•		
ILLINOIS	•	•	•		•	•		•		•		
INDIANA	•				•	•	•	•	•	•		
IOWA	•		•		•	•		•		•		
KANSAS	•				•	•		•		•		
KENTUCKY	•				•	•		•		•		
LOUISIANA	•					•		•		•		
MAINE	•				•	•	•	•	•	•		
MARYLAND	•	•			•	•	•	•	•	•		•
MASSACHUSETTS	•	•	•		•	•	•	•	•	•	•	
MICHIGAN	•	•	•		•	•		•	•	•		
MINNESOTA	•		•		•	•		•		•		
MISSISSIPPI	•				•	•		•		•		
MISSOURI	•				•	•		•		•		
MONTANA	•			•	•			•		•		•
NEBRASKA	•	•			•	•		•		•		
NEVADA	•	•			•	•		•	•	•		
NEW HAMPSHIRE	•				•	•	•	•	•	•	•	
NEW JERSEY	•				•	•		•		•		
NEW MEXICO	•	•			•	•		•		•		
NEW YORK	•	•			•	•	•	•	•	•		
NORTH CAROLINA	•		•		•	•		•		•		

Table 2.1. Newborn Screening by State (continued)

STATE	MANDATED	BIO	CAH	CF	GAL	HGB	HCU	HYPO	MSUD	PKU	TOXO	TYR
NORTH DAKOTA	•		•		•			•		•		
OHIO	•				•	•	•	•		•		
OKLAHOMA	•				•	•		•		•		
OREGON	•	•			•	•		•	•	•		
PENNSYLVANIA	•					•		•	•	•		
RHODE ISLAND	•	•	•		•	•	•	•	•	•		
SOUTH CAROLINA	•		•		•			•		•		
SOUTH DAKOTA	•				•			•		•		
TENNESSEE	•				•	•		•		•		
TEXAS	•		•		•	•		•		•		
UTAH	•				•			•		•		
VERMONT	•	•			•	•	•	•	•	•		
VIRGINIA	•	•			•	•	•	•	•	•		
WASHINGTON	•		•		•			•		•		
WASHINGTON, DC	•				•	•	•	•	•	•		
WEST VIRGINIA	•				•	•		•		•		
WISCONSIN	•	•	•	•	•	•		•		•		
WYOMING	•	•		•	•	•		•		•		

Key

BIO	Biotinidase Deficiency	HYPO	Congenital Hypothyroidism
CAH	Congenital Adrenal Hyperplasia	MSUD	Maple Syrup Urine Disease
CF	Cystic Fibrosis	PKU	Phenylketonuria
GAL	Galactosemia	TOXO	Toxoplasmosis
HGB	Hemoglobinopathies	TYR	Tyrosinemia
HCU	Homocystinuria		

Adapted from: Illinois Department of Public Health. An Overview of Newborn Screening Programs in the United States and Canada. Springfield, Ill, Illinois Department of Public Health; 1996.

Patient Resources

Sickle Cell Disease: Guide for Parents. Agency for Health Care Policy and Research Publications Clearinghouse, PO Box 8547, Silver Spring, MD 20907; (800)358-9295.

Sickle Cell Anemia (New Hope for People With). FDA Office of Consumer Affairs HFE 88 Room 1675, 5600 Fishers Ln, Rockville, MD 20857; (800)532-4440.

Understanding PKU. PKU Clinic, Children's Hospital Medical Center, 300 Longwood Ave, Boston, MA 02115; (617)355-6394.

Selected References

American Academy of Family Physicians. *Summary of Policy Recommendations for Periodic Health Examination*. Kansas City, Mo: American Academy of Family Physicians; 1997.

American Academy of Pediatrics, Committee on Genetics. Health supervision for children with sickle cell diseases and their families. *Pediatrics*. 1996;98:467-472.

American Academy of Pediatrics, Committee on Genetics. Health supervision for children with fragile X syndrome. *Pediatrics*. 1996; 98:297-300.

American Academy of Pediatrics, Committee on Genetics. Health supervision for children with Marfan syndrome. *Pediatrics*. 1996; 98: 978-982.

Illinois Department of Public Health. *An Overview of Newborn Screening Programs in the United States and Canada*. Springfield, Ill: Illinois Department of Public Health; 1996.

US Preventive Services Task Force. Screening for congenital hypothyroidism. In: *Guide to Clinical Preventive Services. 2nd ed*. Washington, DC: US Department of Health and Human Services; 1996: chap 45.

US Preventive Services Task Force. Screening for hemoglobinopathies. In: *Guide to Clinical Preventive Services. 2nd ed*. Washington, DC: US Department of Health and Human Services; 1996: chap 43. US Preventive Services Task Force. Screening for phenylketonuria. In: *Guide to Clinical Preventive Services. 2nd ed*. Washington, DC: US Department of Health and Human Services; 1996: chap 44.

Chapter 3

Hospital Stay for Healthy Term Newborns

The timing of discharge of the mother and infant after birth was, until recently, a mutual decision between the physician and the mother. Discharge soon after birth began as a consumer-initiated movement and as an alternative to home delivery in the 1980s. Today, financial rather than family or medical considerations frequently drive the decision. Increasingly, insurers are refusing payment for a hospital stay that extends beyond 24 hours after an uncomplicated vaginal delivery,[1] which has placed increasing pressure on physicians to discharge infants shortly after birth.

Few scientific data support the insurer's mandate. Several clinical studies have examined the effects of short hospital stay on infant outcomes.[2-24] Unfortunately, these studies have methodologic flaws that make it difficult to draw definite conclusions,[25] including their 1) retrospective nature, 2) lack of comparison groups, 3) insufficient sample sizes, and 4) study design.

The pediatrician's primary role is to ensure the health and well-being of the baby in the context of the family. It is within this context that this statement addresses the short hospital stay (<48 hours of age) for healthy term newborns.

The hospital stay of the mother-infant dyad should be long enough to allow identification of early problems and to ensure that the family is

"Hospital Stay for Healthy Term Newborns," in *Pediatrics*, October 1995, Vol. 96, No. 4, p. 788(3). © 1995 American Academy of Pediatrics; used with permission of the American Academy of Pediatrics.

able and prepared to care for the baby at home. Many cardiopulmonary problems related to the transition from an intrauterine to an extrauterine environment usually become apparent during the first 12 hours after birth.[26] However, other problems, such as jaundice, ductal-dependent cardiac lesions, and gastrointestinal obstruction, may require a longer period of observation by skilled and experienced personnel. Furthermore, the length of stay should be based on the unique characteristics of each mother-infant dyad, including the health of the mother, the health and stability of the baby, the ability and confidence of the mother to care for her baby, the adequacy of support systems at home, and access to appropriate follow-up care. All efforts should be made to keep mothers and infants together to ensure simultaneous discharge.

It is recommended that the following minimum criteria are met before newborn discharge. It is unlikely that fulfillment of these criteria and conditions can be accomplished in less than 48 hours. Furthermore, the timing of discharge of the newborn from the hospital should be the decision of the physician caring for the baby, not by arbitrary policy established by third-party payors.

- The antepartum, intrapartum, and postpartum courses for both mother and baby are uncomplicated.

- Delivery is vaginal.

- The baby is a single birth at 38 to 42 weeks' gestation and the birth weight is appropriate for gestational age according to appropriate intrauterine growth curves.

- The baby's vital signs are documented as being normal and stable for the 12 hours preceding discharge, including a respiratory rate below 60/min, a heart rate of 100 to 160 beats per minute, and an axillary temperature of 36.1 degrees C to 37 degrees C in an open crib with appropriate clothing.

- The baby has urinated and passed at least one stool.

- The baby has completed at least two successful feedings, with documentation that the baby is able to coordinate sucking, swallowing, and breathing while feeding.

- Physical examination reveals no abnormalities that require continued hospitalization.

- There is no evidence of excessive bleeding at the circumcision site for at least 2 hours.

- There is no evidence of significant jaundice in the first 24 hours of life. (Use of noninvasive means of detecting jaundice may be useful.)

- The mother's knowledge, ability, and confidence to provide adequate care for her baby are documented by the fact that they have received training sessions regarding:

  - Breastfeeding or bottle-feeding. The breastfeeding mother-infant dyad should be assessed by trained staff regarding nursing position, latchon, adequacy of swallowing, and mother's knowledge of urine and stool frequency.

  - Cord, skin, and infant genital care.

  - Ability to recognize signs of illness and common infant problems, particularly jaundice. Proper infant safety (e.g., proper use of a car seat and positioning for sleeping).

  - Family members or other support person(s), including health care providers, such as the family pediatrician or his/her designees, familiar with newborn care and knowledgeable about lactation and the recognition of jaundice and dehydration are available to the mother and the baby for the first few days after discharge.

- Laboratory data are available and reviewed, including: Maternal syphilis and hepatitis B surface antigen status. Cord or infant blood type and direct Coombs' test result as clinically indicated.[27]

- Screening tests are performed in accordance with state regulations. If the test is performed before 24 hours of milk feeding, a system for repeating the test must be assured during the follow-up visit.

- Initial hepatitis B vaccine is administered or a scheduled appointment for its administration has been made within the first week of life.

A physician-directed source of continuing medical care for both the mother and the baby is identified. For newborns discharged in less than 48 hours after delivery, a definitive appointment has been made for the baby to be examined within 48 hours of discharge. The follow-up visit can take place in a home or clinic setting, as long as the personnel examining the infant are competent in newborn assessment and the results of the follow-up visit are reported to the infant's physician, or his designees, on the day of the visit.

- Family, environmental and social risk factors should be assessed. These risk factors may include but are not limited to 1) untreated parental substance abuse/positive urine toxicology results in the mother or newborn; 2) history of child abuse or neglect; 3) mental illness in a parent who is in the home; 4) lack of social support, particularly for single, first-time mothers; 5) no fixed home; 6) history of untreated domestic violence, particularly during this pregnancy; or 7) teen mother, particularly if other conditions above apply. When these or other risk factors are present, the discharge should be delayed until they are resolved or a plan to safeguard the infant is in place.

It is essential that all infants having a short hospital stay be examined by experienced health care providers within 48 hours of discharge. If this cannot be assured, then discharge should be deferred until a mechanism for follow-up evaluation is identified.

The purpose of the follow-up visit is to:

- Assess the infant's general health, hydration, and degree of jaundice; identify any new problems; review feeding pattern and technique, including observation of breastfeeding for adequacy of position, latch-on, and swallowing; and historical evidence of adequate stool and urine patterns.

- Assess quality of maternal-infant interaction and details of infant behavior.

- Reinforce maternal or family education in infant care, particularly regarding infant feeding.

- Review the outstanding results of laboratory tests performed before discharge.

- Perform screening tests in accordance with state regulations and other tests that are clinically indicated.

- Identify a plan for health care maintenance, including a method for obtaining emergency services, preventive care and immunizations, periodic evaluations and physical examinations, and necessary screening.

The follow-up visit should be considered an independent service to be reimbursed as a separate package and not as part of a global fee for maternity-newborn labor and delivery services.

In summary, the fact that a short hospital stay (<48 hours of age) for term healthy infants can be accomplished does not mean that it is appropriate for every mother and infant. Each mother-infant dyad should be evaluated individually to determine the optimal time of discharge. The timing of the discharge should be the decision of the physician caring for the infant and not by arbitrary policy established by third-party payors. Local institution of these guidelines is best accomplished through the collaborative efforts of all parties concerned. Institutions should develop guidelines through their professional staff in collaboration with appropriate community agencies, including third-party payors, to establish hospital stay programs for healthy term infants that implement these recommendations. State and local public health agencies should also be involved in the oversight of existing hospital stay programs for quality assurance and monitoring. Further research to evaluate the various issues of short-stay programs is strongly encouraged.

References

1. Hospital stays continue 10-year decline. *Am J Public Health*. 1992;82:54

2. Arthurton MW, Bamford FN. Pediatric aspects of the early discharge of maternity patients. *Br Med J*. 1967;3:517-520

3. Avery MD, Fournier LC, Jones PL, Sipovic CP. An early postpartum hospital discharge program: implementation and evaluation. *J Obstet Gynecol Neonatal Nurs*. 1982;11:233-235

4. Beck CT, Reynolds MA, Rutowski P. Maternity blues and postpartum depression. *J Obstet Gynecol Neonatal Nurs*. 1992;21:287-293

5. Britton HL, Britton JR. Efficacy of early newborn discharge in a middle-class population. *AJDC*. 1984;138:1041-1046

6. Britton JR, Britton HL, Beebe SA. Early discharge of the term newborn: a continued dilemma. *Pediatrics*. 1994;94:291-295

7. Brooten D, Roncoli M, Finkler S, Arnold L, Cohen A, Mennuti M. A randomized trial of early hospital discharge and home follow-up of women having cesarean birth. *Obstet Gynecol*. 1994;84:832-838

8. Carty EM, Bradley CF. A randomized, controlled-evaluation of early postpartum hospital discharge. *Birth*. 1990;17:199-204

9. Conrad PD, Wilkening RB, Rosenberg AA. Safety of newborn discharge in less than 36 hours in a indigent population.*AJDC*. 1989;143:98-101

10. Cottrell DG, Pittala LJ, Hey DJ. One-day maternity care: a pediatric viewpoint. *J Am Osteopath Assoc*, 1983;83:216-221

11. Craig GA, Muirhead JM. Obstetric aspects of the early discharge of maternity patients. *Br Med J*. 1967;3:520-522

12. Guerriero WF. A maternal welfare program for New Orleans. *Am J Obstet Gynecol*. 1943;46:312-313

13. James ML, Hudson CN, Gebski VJ, et al. An evaluation of planned early postnatal transfer home with nursing support. *Med J Aust*. 1987;147: 434-435; 437-438

14. Jansson P. Early postpartum discharge. *Am J Nurs*. 1985;85:547-550

15. Lemmer CM. Early discharge: outcomes of primiparas and their infants. *J Obstet Gynecol Neonatal Nurs*. 1987;16:230-236

16. Nabors GC, Herndon ET. Home puerperal care following hospital delivery. *Obstet Gynecol*. 1956;7:211-213

17. Norr KF, Nacion KW, Abramson R. Early discharge with home follow-up: impacts on low-income mothers and infants. *J Obstet Gynecol Neonatal Nurs*. 1989;18:133-141

18. Pittard WB III, Geddes KM. Newborn hospitalization: a closer look. *J Pediatr*. 1988;112:257 261

19. Rhodes MK. Early discharge of mothers and infants following vaginal childbirth at the United States Air Force Academy: a three-year study. *Mil Med*, 1994;159:227-230

20. Strong TH, Brown WL Jr, Brown WL, Curry CM. Experience with early postcesarean hospital dismissal. *Am J Obstet Gynecol*. 1993;169:116-119

21. Waldenstrom U, Sundelin C, Lindmark G. Early and late discharge after hospital birth: health of mother and infant in the postpartum period. *Ups J Med Sci*. 1987;92:301-314

22. Welt SI, Cole JS, Myers MS, Sholes DM Jr, Jelovsek FR. Feasibility of postpartum rapid hospital discharge: a study from a community hospital population. *Am J Perinatol*. 1993;10:384-387

23. Williams LR, Cooper MK. Nurse-managed postpartum home care. *J Obstet Gynecol Neonatal Nurs*. 1993;22:25-31

24. Yanover MJ, Jones D, Miller MD. Perinatal care of low-risk mothers and infants: early discharge with home care. *N Engl J Med*. 1976;294:702-705

25. Braveman P. Early discharge of newborn and mother: a critical review of the literature. *Pediatrics*. 1995;96:716-726

26. Desmond MM, Rudolph AJ, Phitaksphraiwan P. The transitional care nursery: a mechanism for preventive medicine in the newborn. *Pediatr Clin North Am*. 1966;13:651 668

27. American Academy of Pediatrics, Provisional Committee on Quality Improvement. Management of hyperbilirubinemia in the healthy term newborn. *Pediatrics*. 1994;94:358-565

The recommendations in this statement do not indicate an exclusive course of treatment or procedure to be followed. Variations, taking into account individual circumstances, may be appropriate.

Chapter 4

Treating Jaundice in Healthy Newborns

Guidelines for Parents

You may have been told that your child has "jaundice" and you probably have many questions about this condition. Jaundice is a common condition in newborn infants that usually shows up shortly after birth. In most cases, it goes away on its own. If not, it can be treated easily. This information has been developed by the American Academy of Pediatrics to help you understand this common condition and how it is treated.

What is jaundice?

A baby has jaundice when bilirubin, which is produced naturally by the body, builds up faster than a newborn's liver can break it down and get rid of it in the baby's stool. This happens because of one or more of the following reasons:

- The baby's developing liver is not yet able to remove the bilirubin from the blood

- More bilirubin is being made than the liver can handle

- Too much of the bilirubin is reabsorbed from the intestines before the baby gets rid of it in the stool

From www.aap.org © 1999 American Academy of Pediatrics; used with permission of the American Academy of Pediatrics.

Too much bilirubin makes a jaundiced baby's skin look yellow. This yellow color will appear first on the face, then on the chest and stomach, and, finally, on the legs.

What is bilirubin?

Everyone's blood contains hemoglobin found in red blood cells. Red blood cells live only a short time and, as they die, the oxygen-carrying substance (hemoglobin) is changed to yellow bilirubin. Normal newborns have more bilirubin because their liver is not efficient at removing it. Older babies, children, and adults get rid of this yellow blood product quickly, usually through bowel movements.

Can jaundice hurt my baby?

Jaundice can be dangerous if the bilirubin reaches too high a level in the blood. The level at which it becomes dangerous will vary based on a child's age and if there are other medical conditions. A small sample of your baby's blood can be tested to measure the bilirubin level. Other tests may be needed to see if your baby has a special reason to make extra bilirubin that is causing the jaundice.

How do I know if my baby has jaundice?

Parents should be aware of any changes in their newborn's skin color or the coloring in the whites of their child's eyes. Look at the baby under natural daylight or in a room that has fluorescent lights. A quick and easy way to test for jaundice is to press gently with your fingertip on the tip of your child's nose or forehead. If the skin looks white (this is true for babies of all races), there is no jaundice. If you see a yellowish color, contact your pediatrician to check your baby to see if significant jaundice is present.

How is jaundice treated?

Mild to moderate levels of jaundice do not require any treatment. If high levels of jaundice do not clear up on their own, your baby may be treated with special lights or other treatments. These special lights help get rid of the bilirubin by altering it to make it easier for your baby's liver to get rid of it. This treatment may require that your baby stay in the hospital for a few days. Some pediatricians treat babies with these lights at home. If your baby needs light therapy, talk to your pediatrician about how long the treatment lasts and where it will be done.

Another treatment is more frequent feedings of breastmilk or formula to help pass the bilirubin out in the stools. Increasing the amount of water given to a child is not sufficient to pass the bilirubin because it must be passed in the stools. Rarely, babies may require treatment of their blood to remove bilirubin. For example, in a few cases of very high bilirubin levels, a blood exchange is done to give a baby fresh blood and remove the bilirubin. Your pediatrician will give you more details if other treatments are necessary. Once your child's bilirubin level goes down, it is unlikely that it will increase again. However, if your child continues to look yellow after 3 weeks of life, talk to your pediatrician as other tests may need to be done.

What effect does breastfeeding have on jaundice?

Most breastfed babies do not have a problem with jaundice that requires interruption of breastfeeding. However, if your baby develops jaundice that lasts a week or more, your pediatrician may ask you to temporarily stop breastfeeding for a day or two. If you must temporarily stop breastfeeding, talk to your pediatrician about pumping your breasts so you can keep producing breast milk and can restart nursing easily.

If your baby has jaundice, do not be alarmed. Remember that jaundice in a healthy newborn is not serious and usually clears up easily. If your baby has a very serious case of jaundice and other medical problems, your pediatrician will talk to you about other treatments.

Chapter 5

Pediatric Acquired Immunodeficiency Syndrome (AIDS)

Overview

The National Institute of Allergy and Infectious Diseases (NIAID) has a lead role in research devoted to children infected with the human immunodeficiency virus (HIV), the virus that causes the acquired immunodeficiency syndrome (AIDS).

NIAID-supported researchers are developing and refining treatments to prolong the survival and improve the quality of life of HIV-infected infants, children and adolescents. Many promising therapies are being tested in the Pediatric AIDS Clinical Trials Group (ACTG), a nationwide clinical trials network jointly sponsored by NIAID and the National Institute of Child Health and Human Development (NICHD). Scientists also are improving tests for diagnosing HIV infection in infants soon after birth so that therapy can begin as soon as possible.

Epidemiologic studies are examining risk factors for transmission as well as the course of HIV disease in pregnant women and their babies in an era of antiretroviral therapy. Researchers have helped illuminate the mechanisms of HIV transmission as well as the distinct features of pediatric HIV infection and how the course of disease and the usefulness of therapies can differ in children and adults.

Researchers also are studying ways to prevent transmission of HIV from mother to infant. Notably, Pediatric ACTG investigators have demonstrated that a specific regimen of zidovudine (AZT) treatment,

National Institute of Allergy and Infectious Disease (NIAID), NIH, April 1997.

given to an HIV-infected woman during pregnancy and to her baby after birth, can reduce maternal transmission of HIV by two-thirds. Many consider this finding to be one of the most significant research advances to date in the fight against HIV and AIDS.

The Scope of the Problem

UNAIDS and the World Health Organization (WHO) estimate that by late 1996, 2.6 million children worldwide had been infected with HIV and 1.3 million had died as a result. By 2000, the WHO projects that 5 to 10 million children will have been infected with HIV, with another 5 to 10 million children orphaned by the HIV/AIDS pandemic.

In the United States, through December 1996, 7,629 cases of AIDS in children younger than 13 and 2,754 cases in those aged 13 through 19 had been reported to the Centers for Disease Control and Prevention (CDC). Many other children are currently infected with HIV but have not yet developed AIDS.

HIV infection ranks seventh among the leading causes of death for U.S. children 1 to 14 years of age. In many cities in the northeastern United States, HIV disease is the leading cause of death among children ages 2 to 5.

Transmission

Almost all HIV-infected children acquire the virus from their mothers before or during birth, a process called perinatal transmission. In the United States, approximately 25 percent of pregnant HIV-infected women not receiving AZT therapy have passed on the virus to their babies.

Most perinatal transmission, causing an estimated 50 to 80 percent of infections in children, probably occurs late in pregnancy or during birth. Although the precise mechanisms are unknown, scientists think HIV may be transmitted when maternal blood enters the fetal circulation, or by mucosal exposure to virus during labor and delivery. The role of the placenta in maternal-fetal transmission is unclear and the focus of ongoing research.

The risk of perinatal transmission is significantly increased if the mother has advanced HIV disease, increased levels of HIV in her bloodstream, or fewer numbers of the immune system cells—CD4+ T cells—that are the main targets of HIV.

Other factors that may increase the risk of perinatal transmission are maternal drug use, severe inflammation of fetal membranes, or a prolonged period between membrane rupture and delivery. A recent study sponsored by NIAID and others found that HIV-infected women who gave birth more than four hours after the rupture of the fetal membranes were nearly twice as likely to transmit HIV to their infants, as compared to women who delivered within four hours of membrane rupture.

HIV also may be transmitted from a nursing mother to her infant. Recent studies suggest that breast-feeding introduces an additional risk of HIV transmission of approximately 14 percent among women with chronic HIV infection. The WHO recommends that all HIV-infected women be advised as to both the risks and benefits of breast-feeding of their infants so that they can make informed decisions. In countries where safe alternatives to breast-feeding are readily available and economically feasible, this alternative should be encouraged. In general, in developing countries where safe alternatives to breast-feeding are not readily available, the benefits of breast-feeding in terms of decreased illness and death due to other infectious diseases greatly outweigh the potential risk of HIV transmission.

Prior to 1985 when screening of the nation's blood supply for HIV began, some children were infected through transfusions with blood or blood products contaminated with HIV. A small number of children also have been infected through sexual or physical abuse by HIV-infected adults.

Preventing Perinatal HIV Transmission

In 1994, a landmark study conducted by the Pediatric ACTG demonstrated that AZT, given to HIV-infected women who had very little or no prior antiretroviral therapy and CD4+ T cell counts above 200/mm^3, reduced the risk of maternal-infant transmission by two-thirds, from 25 percent to 8 percent.

In the study, known as ACTG 076, AZT therapy was initiated in the second or third trimester and continued during labor, and infants were treated for six weeks following birth. AZT produced no serious side effects in mothers or infants; long-term follow-up of the infants and mothers is ongoing.

Researchers have subsequently shown that this AZT regimen has reduced perinatal transmission in other populations in which it has been used. Several recent observational studies in the United States and Europe indicate that similar reductions in perinatal HIV transmission can be achieved by using this regimen in regular clinical care settings.

Following up on the success of ACTG 076, the Pediatric ACTG has begun new perinatal HIV prevention trials that build on the AZT regimen. These trials include additional antiretrovirals in an attempt to reduce perinatal HIV transmission even more than that achieved by AZT alone.

The AZT regimen used in ACTG 076 is not always available because of cost and logistical demands. Therefore, NIAID is pursuing a global strategy that assesses whether simpler and less costly regimens for preventing mother-to-infant HIV transmission can be effective in various settings.

Because a significant amount of perinatal HIV transmission occurs around the time of birth, and the risk of maternal-fetal transmission depends, in part, on the amount of HIV in the mother's blood, it may be possible to reduce transmission using drug therapy only around the time of birth.

NIAID has planned other studies that will assess the effectiveness of this approach as well as the role of new antiretrovirals, microbicides and other innovative strategies in reducing the risk of perinatal transmission.

Diagnosis

HIV infection is often difficult to diagnose in very young children. Infected babies, especially in the first few months of life, often appear normal and may exhibit no telltale signs that would allow a definitive diagnosis of HIV infection. Moreover, all children born to infected mothers have antibodies to HIV, made by the mother's immune system, that cross the placenta to the baby's bloodstream before birth and persist for up to 18 months. Because these maternal antibodies reflect the mother's but not the infant's infection status, the test is not useful in newborns or young infants.

In the past few years, investigators have demonstrated the utility of highly accurate blood tests in diagnosing HIV infection in children 6 months of age and younger. One laboratory technique called polymerase chain reaction (PCR) can detect minute quantities of the virus in an infant's blood. Another procedure allows physicians to culture a sample of an infant's blood and test it for the presence of HIV.

Currently, PCR assays or HIV culture techniques can identify at birth about one-third of infants who are truly HIV-infected. With these techniques, approximately 90 percent of HIV-infected infants are identifiable by 2 months of age, and 95 percent by 3 months of age. One innovative new approach to both RNA and DNA PCR testing uses dried blood spot specimens, which should make it much simpler to gather and store specimens in field settings.

Progression of HIV Disease in Children

Researchers have observed two general patterns of illness in HIV-infected children. About 20 percent of children develop serious disease in the first year of life; most of these children die by age 4 years.

The remaining 80 percent of infected children have a slower rate of disease progression, many not developing the most serious symptoms of AIDS until school entry or even adolescence.

A recent report from a large European registry of HIV-infected children indicated that half of the children with perinatally acquired HIV disease were alive at age 9. Another study, of 42 perinatally HIV-infected children who survived beyond 9 years of age, found about one-quarter of the children to be asymptomatic with relatively intact immune systems.

The factors responsible for the wide variation observed in the rate of disease progression in HIV-infected children are a major focus of the NIAID pediatric AIDS research effort. The Women and Infants Transmission Study, a multisite perinatal HIV study funded by NIH, has found that maternal factors including Vitamin A level and CD4 counts during pregnancy, as well as infant viral load and CD4 counts in the first several months of life, can help identify those infants at risk for rapid disease progression who may benefit from early aggressive therapy.

Signs and Symptoms of Pediatric HIV Disease

Many children with HIV infections do not gain weight or grow normally. HIV-infected children frequently are slow to reach important milestones in motor skills and mental development such as crawling, walking and speaking. As the disease progresses, many children develop neurologic problems such as difficulty walking, poor school performance, seizures, mental retardation and cerebral palsy.

Like adults with HIV infection, children with HIV develop life-threatening opportunistic infections (OIs), although the incidence of various OIs differs in adults and children. For example, toxoplasmosis is seen less frequently in HIV-infected children than in HIV-infected adults, while serious bacterial infections occur more commonly in children than in adults. Also, as children with HIV become sicker, they may suffer from chronic diarrhea due to opportunistic pathogens.

Pneumocystis carinii pneumonia (PCP) is the leading cause of death in HIV-infected children with AIDS. PCP, as well as cytomegalovirus (CMV) disease, usually are new infections in children, whereas in adults these diseases result from the reactivation of latent infections.

A lung disease called lymphocytic interstitial pneumonitis (LIP), rarely seen in adults, also occurs frequently in HIV-infected children. This condition, like PCP, can make breathing progressively more difficult and often results in hospitalization.

Children with HIV suffer the usual childhood bacterial infections—only more frequently and more severely than uninfected children. These bacterial infections can cause seizures, fever, pneumonia, recurrent colds, diarrhea, dehydration and other problems that often result in extended hospital stays and nutritional problems.

HIV-infected children frequently have severe candidiasis, a yeast infection that can cause unrelenting diaper rash and infections in the mouth and throat that make eating difficult.

Treatment of HIV-Infected Children

Anti-HIV Therapies. NIAID investigators are defining the best treatments for pediatric patients. Largely due to studies in the Pediatric ACTG, four anti-HIV agents are currently approved for use in children. In addition, two protease inhibitors are now approved for children with HIV disease. Most doctors consider giving anti-HIV therapy to children who have HIV-related symptoms or who have laboratory evidence of immunosuppression.

NIAID-supported researchers have demonstrated that two treatment regimens—ddl alone or in combination with AZT—are each superior to AZT alone in children who have had little or no previous antiretroviral therapy. Many other promising new antiretroviral regimens are being assessed for use in children in the Pediatric ACTG, including various combinations of nevirapine, d4T, lamivudine (3TC), and 1592U89. The Institute also is undertaking clinical trials of new protease inhibitors in pediatric patients, as well as novel treatment approaches such as gene therapy. The overall trend in both adult and pediatric HIV disease management is for early and aggressive use of combination antiretroviral therapy to keep HIV virus replication at as low a level as possible.

Opportunistic Infections. Many medications used to treat adults with opportunistic infections are effective in children when given in appropriate doses. For example, 85 percent of HIV-infected children are able to tolerate trimethoprim/sulfamethoxazole (TMP/SMX) for

PCP. This drug is extremely effective in preventing new or recurrent PCP in children and is the first choice for pediatric patients, as it is in adult patients. NIAID studies are assessing alternative treatments to prevent PCP in children who do not benefit from or cannot tolerate TMP/SMX.

NIAID investigators are developing pediatric formulations of other agents commonly used against OIs, and to understand how children absorb and metabolize these drugs.

Immune Product Studies. Clinical trials sponsored by NIAID and NICHD have demonstrated that intravenous immunoglobulin (IVIG), a preparation containing many types of antibodies, can reduce bacterial infections frequent in children with AIDS. However, the NIAID study suggested that the benefits of IVIG are confined to those patients who had not received TMP/SMX as preventive therapy for PCP. Studies are now underway to assess whether specially made immune globulin products with extra antibodies to HIV can further improve the health status of children with HIV.

AIDS in Adolescents

Adolescents account for a rapidly growing percentage of the reported AIDS cases in the United States. Although less than 1 percent of AIDS patients in the United States are between 13 and 19 years of age, this figure underestimates the significance of HIV transmission during adolescence.

Since the average period of time from HIV infection to the development of AIDS is 10 years, the majority of people in their twenties with AIDS were likely infected as adolescents. Approximately 20 percent of all reported cases of AIDS in the United States have occurred in young adults between the ages of 20 and 29.

Several recent studies have found that increasing numbers of teenagers are becoming infected with HIV, especially in poor, urban areas as well as in rural areas of the South. Surveys of military recruits and Job Corps participants as well as blinded seroprevalance studies indicate that as many as one in 20 individuals aged 15 to 20 years from certain populations in the northeastern and southern United States are HIV-infected.

Psychosocial Issues

A disproportionate number of children with AIDS belong to minority groups: 84 percent of children reported with AIDS in 1996 in the

United States were black or Hispanic. Most live in inner cities, where poverty, illicit drug use, poor housing and limited access to and use of medical care and social services add to the challenges of HIV disease. A mother and child with HIV usually are not the only family members with the disease. Often, the mother's sexual partner is infected, and other children in the family may be infected as well. Frequently, a mother with AIDS does not survive to care for her HIV-infected child.

Management of the complex medical and social problems of families affected by HIV requires a multidisciplinary case management team, integrating medical, social, mental health and educational services. NIAID provides special funding to many of its clinical research sites to provide for services, such as transportation, day care, and the expertise of social workers, crucial to families devastated by HIV.

Resources

AIDS Clinical Trials Information Service. For information about pediatric and adult AIDS clinical trials open to enrollment, call (800) TRIALS-A, 9 a.m. to 7 p.m. Eastern Time, Monday through Friday. World Wide Web address: http://www.actis.org

National AIDS Hotline. Staffed 24 hours a day, seven days a week. (800) 342-AIDS.

The National Pediatric HIV Resource Center. (800) 362-0071.

The Pediatric AIDS Foundation. (415) 883-1796.

The Pediatric Branch of the National Cancer Institute conducts clinical trials for HIV-infected children on the NIH campus in Bethesda, Md. (301) 402-0696.

Chapter 6

Risk Factors for Infants Most Likely to Be Homicide Victims

An infant's chances of becoming a homicide victim during the first year of life are greatest if he or she is the second or later born child of a teenage mother, according to an analysis of birth and death certificates by researchers at the National Institute of Child Health and Human Development (NICHD). Homicide is the leading cause of infant death due to injury.

In the study appearing in the October 22 issue of *The New England Journal of Medicine*, the authors also found that the likelihood of being killed was greatest for infants whose mothers were less than 15 years old, had less than 12 years of school, or did not have prenatal care. One half of the infants killed were dead by the fourth month of life.

The authors noted, however, that other studies of nonfatal child abuse suggest that a program to have home nurses visit expectant teenage mothers regularly could reduce the infant homicide rate.

"To a large extent, very young teens aren't ready to be either pregnant or parents," said the leader of the NICHD research team, Mary Overpeck, DrPH, a researcher with NICHD's Division of Epidemiology, Statistics, and Prevention Research. "Since these needless, tragic deaths occur early in a child's life, the key to preventing them is to reach the mothers early in pregnancy, before the child is born."

National Institute of Child Health and Human Development (NICHD), NIH News Alert, undated.

Other NICHD members of the research team were Ruth Brenner, MD, MPH, Ann C. Trumble, PhD, Lara B. Trifiletti, MA, and Heinz W. Berendes, MD, MPH.

Dr. Overpeck added that visiting home nurse programs that have reduced the incidence of child abuse have focused on helping teenage mothers gain behavioral skills and support.

"Most of these girls don't feel as if they're in control of their environment," Dr. Overpeck said. "The visiting health care professionals can help the girls develop their options—to finish school and take care of themselves and their babies."

In the article, Dr. Overpeck and her co-authors noted that a study of the most successful intervention to prevent child abuse was conducted in Elmira, New York, by researcher David Olds.

Dr. Overpeck explained that the intervention strategies used in the Olds study probably would reduce the infant homicide rate as well. Earlier studies, she said, have shown that more than 80 percent of infant homicides are due to abuse. The Olds study, of low-income, primarily white, unmarried, pregnant teenage girls, found that visits by trained nurses during the girls' pregnancies and the first two years of the children's lives reduced the incidence of child abuse and neglect among first born children. The girls who took part in the program also had fewer subsequent child births and were more likely to complete their education than were teenage mothers who did not take part in the study. Dr. Overpeck said this finding was extremely important, as the risk of infant homicide is higher for second or later born children of teenage mothers. A follow-up study of these girls, conducted 15 years later, showed that they were also less likely to abuse alcohol and drugs. She stressed, too, that since most infant homicides are committed by fathers or other males who are left to care for the infants, the resultant educational and behavior modifications learned by the girls may allow the infants to be cared for in a safer environment.

She added that 8 states account for about 50 percent of the total births to girls below the age of 17: California, Texas, Florida, Georgia, Illinois, New York, Ohio, and Michigan. Visiting nurse programs targeted to these areas would probably reduce the infant homicide toll significantly.

In *The New England Journal of Medicine* article, the researchers compared birth certificate data from all 34,895,000 births that occurred in the U.S. from 1983 to 1991 to data from death certificates completed during the same period. After analyzing the data, they determined that 2,776 infants died from homicide. An additional 52 deaths, caused by neglect, abandonment, or exposure to severe weather (but not considered intentional) were not included in the analysis.

Over all, second or later children born to mothers younger than 19 were 10 times more likely to be killed than the first child of the oldest mothers. The risk of death to children born to mothers with less than 12 years of education was 8.4 times that of children born to mothers who had completed 16 years of education. The researchers added, however, that it was difficult to separate the risk of death to infants born to mothers younger than 17 from the risk to infants born to mothers with less than 12 years of education, because many mothers under 17 years of age have not had the time to complete 12 years of education.

Still, when the researchers excluded girls younger than 17 from their analysis, the risk of homicide among children born to mothers who were old enough to complete 12 years of education but had not done so was still greater than for mothers who had completed additional years of school. In fact, children whose mothers were older than 17 but had not completed 12 years of school had 8 times the risk of death as did infants born to mothers who had 16 years of education.

The researchers also found that 1 out of 4 homicides occurred by the second month of life, one half occurred by the fourth month, and two-thirds by the sixth month. The investigators noted that they were able to obtain little information from death certificates about the circumstances surrounding the death. For example, only 10 percent of the available certificates listed the relationship of the infant to the person identified with killing him or her. One third of the certificates listed the cause of death as "battering or other maltreatment." About 28 percent listed the cause of death as "assault from unspecified means."

The authors noted, however, that other studies have reported that most infant homicides are carried out by either parents or stepparents, and a slight majority are carried out by males. Other studies have also found that most homicides of children older than two years of age are carried out by someone who is unrelated to the child.

Still other studies, the authors added, have found that when the child is killed during the first week of life, the homicide was usually conducted by the mother. The authors also reported that 5 percent of infant homicides occurred during the first day of life; of these, 95 percent were not born in a hospital. One explanation for these cases, the authors wrote, is that the mother committed the homicide to hide the pregnancy and birth.

The researchers also noted, however, that infant homicides are probably under reported. For example, some homicides committed on the day of the child's birth may be so well hidden that they simply go undetected. In addition, other homicides may have been attributed to death due to accidental injury or some other cause. In fact, other studies have shown that from 7 to 27 percent of deaths attributed to unintentional injuries actually may have been due to child abuse or neglect.

To remedy this situation, the researchers recommended that reviews of child deaths be conducted not just from death certificates and records of medical examiners, but also abuse registries, crime reports, hospitals, and ambulatory care records. The researchers added that one such review of the records from several agencies indicated that the number of deaths from abuse and neglect for children up to four years of age were double the rate reported by medical examiners' records.

The researchers also uncovered a disturbing trend: the number of homicides increased from 7.2 for every 100,000 births from 1983 to 1987, to 8.8 homicides for every 100,000 births from 1988 to 1991. The authors added that this increase is probably not due to better detection and reporting of infant homicide cases and most probably represents an increase in infant homicides. In fact, from 1988 through 1991, an average of 351 infant homicides were committed each year—almost one each day. Based on studies of the under reporting of infant homicides, the authors surmise that about twice the amount of infant homicides actually may have been committed during the same time period.

Dr. Overpeck said that no studies have been conducted to determine why the infant homicide rate has risen. She theorized, however, that the increase coincides with an increasing need for mothers to enter the work force, combined with a shortage of affordable child care for infants.

The NICHD is one of the Institutes of the National Institutes of Health, the world's premier biomedical research organization, located in Bethesda, Maryland. NICHD supports and conducts basic, clinical, and epidemiological research on the reproductive, developmental, and behavioral processes that determine and maintain the health of children, adults, families, and populations.

Chapter 7

Infant Mortality Statistics

Introduction

This report presents infant mortality data from the 1997 period linked file. In the linked file the information from the death certificate is linked to information from the birth certificate for each infant under 1 year of age who died in the 50 States, the District of Columbia, Puerto Rico, the Virgin Islands, or Guam during 1997. The purpose of the linkage is to use the many additional variables available from the birth certificate to conduct more detailed analyses of infant mortality patterns. This report presents infant mortality data by race and Hispanic origin of the mother, birthweight, period of gestation, sex of infant, plurality, trimester of pregnancy prenatal care began, maternal age, maternal educational attainment, live-birth order, marital status, mother's place of birth, maternal smoking during pregnancy, age at death, and underlying cause of death for the 50 States and the District of Columbia. Other variables that are available on the linked file data tapes, but which are not discussed in this report include: father's age, race, and Hispanic origin; Apgar score; birth attendant; place of delivery; alcohol use during pregnancy; weight gain during pregnancy; medical risk factors; method of delivery; obstetric procedures; complications of labor/delivery; and abnormal conditions of newborn.

Excerpted from "Infant Mortality Statistics from the 1997 Period Linked Birth/Infant Death Data Set," by Marian F. MacDorman, Ph.D., and Jonnae O. Atkinson, M.S., *National Vital Statistics Reports*, Vol. 47, No. 23, July 30, 1999.

Methods

Data shown in this report are based on birth and infant death certificates registered in all States and the District of Columbia. As part of the Vital Statistics Cooperative Program (VSCP), each State provided matching birth and death certificate numbers for each infant under 1 year of age that died in the State in 1997. When the birth and death occurred in different States, the State of death was responsible for contacting the State of birth identified on the death certificate to obtain the original birth certificate number. NCHS used the matching birth and death certificate numbers provided by the States to extract final edited data from the NCHS natality and mortality statistical files. These data were linked to form a single statistical record, thereby establishing a national linked record file.

After the initial linkage, NCHS returned computer lists of unlinked infant death records and records with inconsistent data between the birth and death certificates to each State. State additions and corrections were incorporated, and a final national linked file was produced. In 1997, 97.9 percent of all infant death records were successfully matched to their corresponding birth records.

Data by Maternal and Infant Characteristics

This report presents descriptive tabulations of infant mortality data by a variety of maternal and infant characteristics. These tabulations are useful for understanding the basic relationships between risk factors and infant mortality, unadjusted for the possible effects of other variables. In reality, women with one risk factor often have other risk factors as well. Thus, teenage mothers are more likely to also be unmarried and of a low-income status. Mothers who do not receive prenatal care are more likely to be of a low-income status and uninsured. The preferred method for disentangling the multiple inter-relationships among risk factors is multivariate analysis; however, an understanding of the basic relationships between risk factors and infant mortality is a necessary precursor to more sophisticated types of analysis, and is the aim of the current report.

Race and Hispanic origin data—Infant mortality rates are presented for detailed race and Hispanic origin groups. The linked file is particularly useful for computing accurate infant mortality rates for this purpose because the race of the mother from the birth certificate is used in both the numerator and denominator of the infant mortality rate. Race information reported on the birth certificate is generally considered to be more accurate than that on the death certificate because on the birth certificate, race of each parent is usually reported by the mother at the time of delivery, whereas on the death certificate, race of the deceased infant is reported by the funeral director based on information provided by an informant or on observation.

Infant mortality rates for five detailed Asian and Pacific Islander groups, including Vietnamese, Asian Indian, Korean, Samoan, and Guamanian, are presented for an eight-State reporting area: California, Hawaii, Illinois, Minnesota, New Jersey, New York, Texas, and Washington. In 1990, more than 60 percent of the U.S. population for each of these additional Asian and Pacific Islander groups lived in the eight-State reporting area: Asian Indian, Korean, and Vietnamese, 64–68 percent; Guamanian, 75 percent; and Samoan, 85 percent.

Race and Hispanic origin of mother are reported as separate items on the birth certificate; thus, a mother of Hispanic origin may be of any race. Although the overwhelming majority of Hispanic-origin births are to white women (97 percent in 1997), there are notable differences in infant mortality trends between Hispanic and non-Hispanic white women. Therefore, race-specific data for non-Hispanic mothers are presented for comparison in tables showing data for Hispanic mothers. Race and ethnic differentials in infant mortality rates may reflect differences in income, educational levels, access to health care, health insurance, and other factors.

Statistical significance—Text statements have been tested for statistical significance, and a statement that a given infant mortality rate is higher or lower than another rate indicates that the rates are significantly different.

Results and Discussion

Infant Mortality by Race and Hispanic Origin of Mother

In 1997, the overall infant mortality rate from the linked file was 7.2 infant deaths per 1,000 live births, compared with 7.3 in 1996. Infant mortality rates varied considerably by race of mother. Mortality rates were lowest for infants born to Chinese (3.1), Japanese (5.3), Filipino (5.8), and White (6.0) mothers. Rates were considerably higher for American Indian (8.7), Hawaiian (9.0), and black (13.7) mothers. When these differentials are examined by age at death, it is

49

apparent that the high mortality rate for infants of American Indian mothers is due primarily to a post-neonatal mortality rate, which is twice that for infants of white mothers. For infants of Hawaiian mothers, the neonatal mortality rate was 1.6 times that for white mothers. There were not sufficient numbers of post-neonatal deaths to compute an accurate post-neonatal mortality rate for Hawaiian mothers. For infants of black mothers, both neonatal and post-neonatal mortality rates are more than twice those for infants of white mothers.

Among the more detailed Asian groups enumerated in the eight-State reporting area, the infant mortality rate was 3.1 for Korean mothers, 4.8 for Asian Indian mothers, and 4.9 for Vietnamese mothers. Among the Pacific Islander groups, it was not possible to compute reliable infant mortality rates for infants of Samoan and Guamanian mothers because of the small number of infant deaths.

Mortality rates for infants born to Hispanic origin mothers ranged from 5.5 for Cuban and Central and South American mothers to 7.9 for Puerto Rican mothers. The infant mortality rate for Puerto Rican mothers was the highest of any of the Hispanic origin groups, 36 percent higher than the rate for Mexican mothers, and 44 percent higher than the rate for Cuban and Central and South American mothers. The higher rate for infants of Puerto Rican mothers was primarily due to a neonatal mortality rate which was 38–42 percent higher than that for Mexican or Central and South American mothers.

Infant Mortality by Selected Infant and Maternal Characteristics

Infant mortality rates by a variety of infant and maternal characteristics are presented in Table 7.4 for infants of white, black, American Indian, and Asian or Pacific Islander mothers and in Table 7.5 for infants of Hispanic mothers.

Sex of infant—In 1997 the infant mortality rate for all races combined was 7.9 for male infants, 18 percent higher than the rate of 6.5 for female infants. Similar to previous years, infant mortality rates were higher for male than for female infants for each race and Hispanic origin group, although differences were not statistically significant for infants of American Indian, Asian and Pacific Islander, Puerto Rican, Cuban, and Central and South American mothers.

Multiple births—For all races combined, the infant mortality rate for plural births was about five times the rate of 6.4 for single births.

Table 7.1. Infant, neonatal, and post-neonatal deaths and mortality rates by specified race or national origin of mother: United States, 1997 linked file.

Race of mother	Live births	Number of deaths			Mortality rate per 1,000 live births		
		Infant	Neonatal	Postneonatal	Infant	Neonatal	Postneonatal
All races	3,880,894	27,968	18,507	9,461	7.2	4.8	2.4
White	3,072,640	18,578	12,250	6,328	6.0	4.0	2.1
Black	599,913	8,210	5,536	2,673	13.7	9.2	4.5
American Indian[1]	38,572	335	173	162	8.7	4.5	4.2
Asian or Pacific Islander	169,769	845	548	298	5.0	3.2	1.8
Chinese	28,434	87	59	28	3.1	2.1	1.0
Japanese	8,890	47	27	20	5.3	3.0	2.2
Hawaiian	5,687	51	36	15	9.0	6.3	*
Filipino	31,501	183	112	72	5.8	3.6	2.3
Other Asian or Pacific Islander	95,257	477	314	163	5.0	3.3	1.7

* Figure does not meet standard of reliability or precision.
[1] Includes Aleuts and Eskimos.

Table 7.2. Infant, neonatal, and post-neonatal deaths and mortality rates by race or national origin of mother: Total of 8 States, 1997 linked file.

Race of mother	Live births	Number of Deaths			Mortality rate per 1,000 live births		
		Infant	Neonatal	Postneonatal	Infant	Neonatal	Postneonatal
All races	1,570,216	10,126	6,627	3,500	6.4	4.2	2.2
Total Asian or Pacific Islander	118,921	583	373	209	4.9	3.1	1.8
Chinese	22,233	59	38	22	2.7	1.7	1.0
Japanese	6,901	35	19	16	5.1	*	*
Filipino	25,499	146	85	60	5.7	3.3	2.4
Vietnamese	12,685	62	44	18	4.9	3.5	*
Asian Indian	17,550	84	67	17	4.8	3.8	*
Korean	8,282	26	12	13	3.1	*	*
Hawaiian	5,186	45	32	13	8.7	6.2	*
Samoan	1,602	9	3	6	*	*	*
Guamanian	533	2	1	1	*	*	*
Remaining Asian or Pacific Islander	18,450	114	72	42	6.2	3.9	2.3
White	1,247,464	6,999	4,589	2,410	5.6	3.7	1.9
Black	195,607	2,483	1,633	849	12.7	8.3	4.3
American Indian[1]	8,224	62	31	31	7.5	3.8	3.8

* Figure does not meet standard of reliability or precision.
[1] Includes Aleuts and Eskimos.
NOTE: States included are California, Hawaii, Illinois, Minnesota, New Jersey, New York, Texas, and Washington.

Table 7.3. Infant, neonatal, and post-neonatal deaths and mortality rates by Hispanic origin of mother and by race of mother for mothers of non-Hispanic origin: United States, 1997 linked file.

Hispanic origin and race of mother	Live births	Number of deaths			Mortality rate per 1,000 live births		
		Infant	Neonatal	Postneonatal	Infant	Neonatal	Postneonatal
All origins[1]	3,880,894	27,968	18,507	9,461	7.2	4.8	2.4
Total Hispanic	709,767	4,226	2,806	1,421	6.0	4.0	2.0
Mexican	499,024	2,908	1,908	1,000	5.8	3.8	2.0
Puerto Rican	55,450	436	299	138	7.9	5.4	2.5
Cuban	12,887	71	52	19	5.5	4.0	...
Central and South American	97,405	531	381	150	5.5	3.9	1.5
Other and unknown Hispanic	45,001	280	166	114	6.2	3.7	2.5
Non-Hispanic total[2]	3,115,174	23,141	15,225	7,916	7.4	4.9	2.5
Non-Hispanic white	2,333,363	14,046	9,181	4,865	6.0	3.9	2.1
Non-Hispanic black	581,431	7,978	5,358	2,620	13.7	9.2	4.5
Not stated	55,953	600	477	124	...	...	...

... Category not applicable.
1 Origin of mother not stated included in "All origins" but not distributed among origins.
2 Includes races other than white or black.

53

Table 7.4. Infant mortality rates, live births, and infant deaths by selected characteristics and specified race of mother: United States, 1997 linked file. (continued on next page)

Characteristics	All races	Race of mother			
		White	Black	American Indian[1]	Asian/ Pacific Islander
		Infant mortality rates per 1,000 live births in specified group				
Total	7.2	6.0	13.7	8.7	5.0
Age at death:					
Total neonatal	4.8	4.0	9.2	4.5	3.2
Early neonatal (< 7 days)	3.8	3.1	7.7	3.4	2.5
Late neonatal (7-27 days)	0.9	0.8	1.6	1.1	0.7
Postneonatal	2.4	2.1	4.5	4.2	1.8
Sex:					
Male	7.9	6.7	14.9	9.9	5.4
Female	6.5	5.4	12.4	7.4	4.5
Plurality:					
Single births	6.4	5.3	12.4	8.1	4.4
Plural births	33.8	29.8	52.5	34.6	34.9
Birthweight:					
Less than 1,500 grams	252.8	245.5	270.1	241.4	218.8
1,500-2,499 grams	16.7	17.0	15.9	25.6	13.7
2,500 grams or more	2.7	2.4	4.1	4.6	1.9
Period of gestation:					
Less than 32 weeks	184.6	179.3	197.9	145.9	162.0
32-36 weeks	9.9	9.5	11.4	12.1	8.2
37-41 weeks	2.8	2.6	4.2	4.8	2.0
42 weeks or more	3.5	3.2	5.0	6.2	2.2
Trimester of pregnancy prenatal care began:					
First trimester	6.3	5.5	12.3	7.5	4.4
After first trimester or no care	9.4	7.8	14.7	10.0	6.3
Second trimester	7.6	6.6	11.1	8.9	5.7
Third trimester	6.6	5.9	8.8	*	*
No prenatal care	35.6	28.0	50.3	28.0	22.5
Age of mother:					
Under 20 years	10.4	9.0	14.2	10.4	9.4
20-24 years	8.0	6.7	13.4	8.1	6.0
25-29 years	6.2	5.2	13.2	7.5	4.4
30-34 years	5.8	5.0	13.6	9.8	3.6
35-39 years	6.8	5.9	14.4	8.5	5.3
40-54 years	8.7	7.7	15.6	*	9.7
Educational attainment of mother:					
0-8 years	7.6	6.9	16.2	13.0	4.9
9-11 years	9.8	8.4	14.4	9.5	6.4
12 years	7.6	6.4	13.4	8.7	5.9
13-15 years	6.0	4.9	11.7	6.6	4.5
16 years and over	4.6	4.2	10.6	7.7	3.7
Live-birth order:					
1	7.1	6.0	13.6	8.3	4.7
2	6.5	5.5	12.8	7.6	4.4
3	7.0	5.8	12.7	9.4	5.4
4	8.6	7.2	14.4	9.7	6.0
5 or more	11.2	8.7	18.3	9.9	10.5
Marital status:					
Married	5.6	5.2	11.5	7.5	4.5
Unmarried	10.5	8.5	14.6	9.5	7.3
Mother's place of birth:					
Born in the 50 States and D.C.	7.4	6.1	13.7	8.6	6.7
Born elsewhere	5.6	5.3	9.9	*	4.6
Maternal smoking during pregnancy:[2]					
Smoker	10.8	9.4	19.9	13.2	11.5
Nonsmoker	6.8	5.5	12.8	7.3	4.8

See footnotes at end of table.

Infant mortality rates for plural births were significantly higher than rates for single births for all race and Hispanic-origin groups. From 1996–97, infant mortality rates for plural births increased for most

Table 7.4. (continued) Infant mortality rates, live births, and infant deaths by selected characteristics and specified race of mother: United States, 1997 linked file. (continued on next page)

Characteristics	All races	Race of mother			
		White	Black	American Indian[1]	Asian/ Pacific Islander
		Live births			
Total	3,880,894	3,072,640	599,913	38,572	169,769
Sex:					
Male	1,985,596	1,573,622	304,530	19,627	87,817
Female	1,895,298	1,499,018	295,383	18,945	81,952
Plurality:					
Single births	3,770,020	2,984,532	581,394	37,763	166,331
Plural births	110,874	88,108	18,519	809	3,438
Birthweight:					
Less than 1,500 grams	55,659	34,962	18,432	464	1,801
1,500-2,499 grams	236,410	164,019	59,775	2,147	10,469
2,500 grams or more	3,587,099	2,872,582	521,347	35,933	157,237
Not stated	1,726	1,077	359	28	262
Period of gestation:					
Less than 32 weeks	74,403	46,530	24,776	788	2,309
32-36 weeks	362,197	264,313	79,376	3,876	14,632
37-41 weeks	3,103,295	2,489,555	445,747	29,727	138,266
42 weeks or more	302,541	243,494	44,745	3,705	10,597
Not stated	38,458	28,748	5,269	476	3,965
Trimester of pregnancy prenatal care began:					
First trimester	3,119,693	2,545,590	414,251	25,452	134,400
After first trimester or no care	660,509	460,349	158,935	11,937	29,288
Second trimester	512,228	363,139	117,343	8,719	23,027
Third trimester	102,041	69,505	25,356	2,431	4,749
No prenatal care	46,240	27,705	16,236	787	1,512
Not stated	100,692	66,701	26,727	1,183	6,081
Age of mother:					
Under 20 years	493,341	343,293	133,251	8,012	8,785
20-24 years	942,048	720,546	182,600	12,316	26,586
25-29 years	1,069,436	871,636	135,529	9,168	53,103
30-34 years	886,798	735,571	94,123	5,812	51,292
35-39 years	409,710	337,423	45,069	2,694	24,524
40-54 years	79,561	64,171	9,341	570	5,479
Educational attainment of mother:					
0-8 years	224,911	196,441	17,272	1,616	9,582
9-11 years	620,586	451,023	145,147	10,786	13,630
12 years	1,257,946	969,727	229,003	15,209	44,007
13-15 years	848,379	670,870	134,490	7,611	35,408
16 years and over	872,733	745,496	61,868	2,589	62,780
Not stated	56,339	39,083	12,133	761	4,362
Live-birth order:					
1	1,573,768	1,252,047	230,724	13,696	77,301
2	1,254,354	1,012,916	174,612	10,596	56,230
3	628,579	498,451	101,843	6,579	21,706
4	241,418	182,633	47,865	3,616	7,304
5 or more	162,167	110,873	41,244	3,846	6,204
Not stated	20,608	15,720	3,625	239	1,024
Marital status:					
Married	2,623,450	2,279,438	184,859	15,932	143,221
Unmarried	1,257,444	793,202	415,054	22,640	26,548
Mother's place of birth:					
Born in the 50 States and D.C.	3,124,817	2,528,268	533,038	37,162	26,349
Born elsewhere	746,928	538,829	63,691	1,324	143,084
Not stated	9,149	5,543	3,184	86	336
Maternal smoking during pregnancy:[2]					
Smoker	406,484	344,666	51,891	6,609	3,318
Nonsmoker	2,671,200	2,063,713	480,773	25,176	101,538
Not stated	46,426	36,608	6,493	1,240	2,085

See footnotes at end of table.

race and Hispanic-origin groups (except for infants of black, American Indian, and non-Hispanic white mothers), although the differences were not statistically significant. This increase is primarily due

Table 7.4. (continued) Infant mortality rates, live births, and infant deaths by selected characteristics and specified race of mother: United States, 1997 linked file. (continued on next page)

Characteristics	All races	Race of mother			
		White	Black	American Indian[1]	Asian/ Pacific Islander
		Infant deaths			
Total	27,968	18,578	8,210	335	845
Age at death:					
Total neonatal	18,507	12,250	5,536	173	548
Early neonatal (< 7 days)	14,827	9,673	4,596	130	428
Late neonatal (7-27 days)	3,680	2,576	940	44	120
Postneonatal	9,461	6,328	2,673	162	298
Sex:					
Male	15,729	10,519	4,543	194	473
Female	12,239	8,059	3,667	141	372
Plurality:					
Single births	24,225	15,956	7,236	307	726
Plural births	3,743	2,622	973	28	120
Birthweight:					
Less than 1,500 grams	14,068	8,584	4,978	112	394
1,500-2,499 grams	3,944	2,794	952	55	143
2,500 grams or more	9,615	7,020	2,130	167	298
Not stated	341	180	150	1	10
Period of gestation:					
Less than 32 weeks	13,736	8,344	4,903	115	374
32-36 weeks	3,583	2,508	908	47	120
37-41 weeks	8,672	6,381	1,866	142	283
42 weeks or more	1,046	779	223	23	23
Not stated	930	565	310	9	46
Trimester of pregnancy prenatal care began:					
First trimester	19,762	13,886	5,096	191	589
After first trimester or no care	6,221	3,574	2,344	119	184
Second trimester	3,904	2,392	1,304	78	131
Third trimester	670	408	224	19	19
No prenatal care	1,647	775	816	22	34
Not stated	1,985	1,118	769	25	73
Age of mother:					
Under 20 years	5,149	3,085	1,898	83	83
20-24 years	7,559	4,856	2,444	100	159
25-29 years	6,598	4,501	1,794	69	234
30-34 years	5,174	3,647	1,282	57	187
35-39 years	2,793	1,993	647	23	130
40-54 years	695	495	146	2	53
Educational attainment of mother:					
0-8 years	1,699	1,352	280	21	47
9-11 years	6,096	3,811	2,095	103	87
12 years	9,621	6,168	3,060	133	260
13-15 years	5,052	3,272	1,568	50	161
16 years and over	4,003	3,095	655	20	233
Not stated	1,497	880	552	8	56
Live-birth order:					
1	11,149	7,542	3,129	114	364
2	8,177	5,616	2,232	81	249
3	4,370	2,891	1,298	62	118
4	2,079	1,313	687	35	44
5 or more	1,821	965	753	38	65
Not stated	372	250	111	5	5
Marital status:					
Married	14,771	11,866	2,134	120	651
Unmarried	13,197	6,712	6,076	215	194

See footnotes at end of table.

to an increase in the number of higher order multiple births (the number of triplet, quadruplet, and quintuplet and other higher order multiple births), since the risk of infant death increases with the

Table 7.4. (continued) Infant mortality rates, live births, and infant deaths by selected characteristics and specified race of mother: United States, 1997 linked file.

Characteristics	All races	Race of mother			
		White	Black	American Indian[1]	Asian/ Pacific Islander
		Infant deaths			
Mother's place of birth:					
Born in the 50 States and D.C.	23,096	15,321	7,277	321	177
Born elsewhere	4,179	2,878	633	10	659
Not stated	693	379	300	3	10
Maternal smoking during pregnancy:[2]					
Smoker	4,392	3,237	1,031	87	38
Nonsmoker	18,118	11,296	6,153	183	487
Not stated	711	466	212	17	16

* Figure does not meet standard of reliability or precision.
1 Incudes Aleuts and Eskimos.
2 Excludes data for California, Indiana, New York State (but includes New York City), and South Dakota, which do not report tobacco use on the birth certificate.

NOTE: Infant deaths are weighted so numbers may not exactly add to totals due to rounding. Not stated responses were included in totals but not distributed among groups for rate computations.

increasing number of infants in the pregnancy. Higher order multiple birth rates have more than doubled from 1991–97 (from 81.4 per 100,000 live births in 1991 to 173.6 per 100,000 live births in 1997). In 1997, the infant mortality rate for triplet and higher order births (69.0) was more than double the rate for twin births (31.5), and 10 times the rate for single births (6.4).

Factors associated with the rapid increase in multiple births include an increase in births to older women (older women are more likely to have a multiple birth even without the use of fertility therapy), and the more widespread use of fertility-enhancing therapies (fertility drugs and techniques such as in vitro fertilization).

Multiple pregnancy can lead to an accentuation of maternal risks and complications associated with pregnancy. Multiple births are much more likely to be born preterm and at low birthweight, and thus are at higher risk for infant death.

Birthweight and period of gestation—Birthweight and period of gestation are the two most important predictors of an infant's subsequent health and survival. In 1997, 65 percent of all infant deaths occurred to the 7.5 percent of infants born at low birthweight (less than 2,500 grams). Infants born too small and too soon have a much greater risk of death and both short term and long term disability than those born at term (37–41 weeks of gestation) or with birthweights

Table 7.5. Infant mortality rates, live births, and infant deaths by selected characteristics and Hispanic origin of mother and by race of mother for mothers of non-Hispanic origin: United States, 1997 linked file. (continued on next page)

Characteristics	All origins[1]	Hispanic						Non-Hispanic			Not stated
		Total	Mexican	Puerto Rican	Cuban	Central and South American	Other and unknown Hispanic	Total[2]	White	Black	
		Infant mortality rates per 1,000 live births in specified group									
Total	7.2	6.0	5.8	7.9	5.5	5.5	6.2	7.4	6.0	13.7	...
Age at death:											
Total neonatal	4.8	4.0	3.8	5.4	4.0	3.9	3.7	4.9	3.9	9.2	...
Early neonatal (< 7 days)	3.8	3.1	2.9	4.5	2.8	3.1	3.0	3.9	3.1	7.6	...
Late neonatal (7-27 days)	0.9	0.9	0.9	0.9	*	0.8	0.7	1.0	0.8	1.6	...
Postneonatal	2.4	2.0	2.0	2.5	*	1.5	2.5	2.5	2.1	4.5	...
Sex:											
Male	7.9	6.4	6.3	8.7	5.8	5.6	6.9	8.2	6.7	15.0	...
Female	6.5	5.5	5.4	7.0	5.2	5.3	5.5	6.6	5.3	12.4	...
Plurality:											
Single births	6.4	5.4	5.3	7.1	4.5	4.9	6.1	6.6	5.3	12.5	...
Plural births	33.8	31.1	31.7	39.3	*	30.9	*	33.7	29.0	52.5	...
Birthweight:											
Less than 1,500 grams	252.8	250.2	255.4	242.0	227.3	266.7	195.4	250.8	240.7	268.9	...
1,500-2,499 grams	16.7	16.9	18.5	12.7	*	11.5	17.6	16.6	17.0	15.8	...
2,500 grams or more	2.7	2.3	2.4	2.6	*	1.8	2.6	2.8	2.5	4.1	...
Period of gestation:											
Less than 32 weeks	184.6	163.1	161.1	179.0	191.1	170.5	132.9	186.4	181.6	196.9	...
32-36 weeks	9.9	8.4	8.7	8.8	*	5.9	9.4	10.2	9.8	11.4	...
37-41 weeks	2.8	2.4	2.5	2.5	*	2.0	2.9	2.9	2.6	4.2	...
42 weeks or more	3.5	3.2	3.3	*	*	3.2	*	3.5	3.2	5.0	...
Trimester of pregnancy prenatal care began:											
First trimester	6.3	5.6	5.5	7.0	4.9	5.2	5.7	6.5	5.4	12.4	...
After first trimester or no care	9.4	6.2	6.1	8.3	*	5.2	6.5	10.5	8.6	14.8	...
Second trimester	7.6	5.2	5.2	6.8	*	4.8	5.1	8.5	7.3	11.2	...
Third trimester	6.6	4.8	5.1	*	*	*	*	7.3	6.6	8.9	...
No prenatal care	35.6	21.6	19.4	35.4	*	23.5	*	39.5	31.0	50.2	...
Age of mother:											
Under 20 years	10.4	7.3	7.2	7.8	*	6.5	8.5	11.4	9.8	14.3	...
20-24 years	8.0	5.7	5.5	8.8	*	4.8	5.9	8.6	7.1	13.5	...
25-29 years	6.2	5.2	4.8	7.3	*	5.8	5.8	6.3	5.1	13.3	...
30-34 years	5.8	5.5	5.7	6.1	*	4.8	5.6	5.8	4.8	13.6	...
35-39 years	6.8	7.0	7.4	8.8	*	5.7	5.8	6.7	5.7	14.2	...
40-54 years	8.7	10.1	11.2	*	*	8.7	*	8.5	7.2	15.4	...
Educational attainment of mother:											
0-8 years	7.6	5.8	5.5	7.5	*	7.5	6.0	11.4	10.7	16.9	...
9-11 years	9.8	6.4	6.3	8.4	*	5.2	6.8	11.4	9.9	14.6	...
12 years	7.6	5.8	5.6	8.2	5.8	5.2	6.0	8.0	6.5	13.4	...
13-15 years	6.0	5.1	5.2	6.3	*	4.2	5.0	6.1	4.9	11.7	...
16 years and over	4.6	4.4	4.6	6.0	*	4.2	4.3	4.6	4.1	10.7	...
Live-birth order:											
1	7.1	6.1	6.0	7.5	5.7	5.4	6.8	7.2	5.9	13.6	...
2	6.5	5.4	5.3	7.0	4.3	5.1	5.8	6.7	5.5	12.9	...
3	7.0	5.2	5.2	7.8	*	4.3	4.9	7.3	6.0	12.7	...
4	8.6	6.2	5.5	11.7	*	6.5	7.6	9.3	7.6	14.3	...
5 or more	11.2	8.6	8.7	7.5	*	10.8	*	12.0	8.7	18.2	...
Marital status:											
Married	5.6	5.3	5.3	6.8	4.4	4.7	5.3	5.6	5.1	11.6	...
Unmarried	10.5	6.9	6.6	8.6	8.9	6.5	7.4	11.5	9.2	14.7	...
Mother's place of birth:											
Born in the 50 States and D.C.	7.4	6.7	6.7	7.7	5.2	6.3	6.5	7.4	6.0	13.7	...
Born elsewhere	5.6	5.3	5.2	8.0	5.7	5.4	4.1	5.9	5.4	10.3	...
Maternal smoking during pregnancy:[3]											
Smoker	10.8	9.1	9.5	11.0	*	*	*	10.8	9.4	19.8	...
Nonsmoker	6.8	6.0	5.9	7.5	5.6	5.2	6.1	6.9	5.3	12.9	...

See footnotes at end of table.

of 2,500 grams or more. The percent of infants born at low birthweight ranged from a low of 5 percent for births to Chinese mothers to a high of 13 percent for births to black mothers. The percent of preterm births

Table 7.5. (continued) Infant mortality rates, live births, and infant deaths by selected characteristics and Hispanic origin of mother and by race of mother for mothers of non-Hispanic origin: United States, 1997 linked file. (continued on next page)

Characteristics	All origins[1]	Hispanic						Non-Hispanic			Not stated
		Total	Mexican	Puerto Rican	Cuban	Central and South American	Other and unknown Hispanic	Total[2]	White	Black	
						Live births					
Total	3,880,894	709,767	499,024	55,450	12,887	97,405	45,001	3,115,174	2,333,363	581,431	55,953
Sex:											
Male	1,985,596	361,868	254,230	28,384	6,580	49,693	22,981	1,595,040	1,196,537	295,134	28,688
Female	1,895,298	347,899	244,794	27,066	6,307	47,712	22,020	1,520,134	1,136,826	286,297	27,265
Plurality:											
Single births	3,770,020	695,430	489,525	54,101	12,487	95,301	44,016	3,020,563	2,260,786	563,436	54,027
Plural births	110,874	14,337	9,499	1,349	400	2,104	985	94,611	72,577	17,995	1,926
Birthweight:											
Less than 1,500 grams	55,659	8,130	5,156	1,033	176	1,151	614	46,527	26,407	17,961	1,002
1,500-2,499 grams	236,410	37,489	24,692	4,182	698	4,957	2,960	195,574	125,012	58,455	3,347
2,500 grams or more	3,587,099	663,973	469,083	50,205	12,012	91,281	41,392	2,871,842	2,181,273	504,709	51,284
Not stated	1,726	175	93	30	1	16	35	1,231	671	306	320
Period of gestation:											
Less than 32 weeks	74,403	11,675	7,530	1,408	225	1,654	858	61,577	34,449	24,172	1,151
32-36 weeks	362,197	66,244	45,354	6,115	1,191	9,119	4,465	291,254	196,143	77,361	4,699
37-41 weeks	3,103,295	560,079	393,513	43,197	10,495	77,460	35,414	2,498,873	1,905,396	431,630	44,343
42 weeks or more	302,541	57,582	40,902	4,326	913	7,709	3,732	240,687	183,691	43,296	4,777
Not stated	38,458	14,187	11,725	404	63	1,463	532	22,783	13,684	4,972	1,488
Trimester of pregnancy prenatal care began:											
First trimester	3,119,693	506,442	351,737	39,942	11,487	70,583	32,693	2,570,400	2,014,137	401,994	42,851
After first trimester or no care	660,509	180,884	135,825	12,261	1,218	21,260	10,320	471,755	277,991	154,396	7,870
Second trimester	512,228	138,218	103,078	9,445	1,027	16,628	8,040	368,063	223,753	113,971	5,947
Third trimester	102,041	31,283	23,886	1,996	125	3,653	1,623	69,555	38,205	24,502	1,203
No prenatal care	46,240	11,383	8,861	820	66	979	657	34,137	16,033	15,923	720
Not stated	100,692	22,441	11,462	3,247	182	5,562	1,988	73,019	41,235	25,041	5,232
Age of mother:											
Under 20 years	493,341	120,955	88,529	12,343	951	10,224	8,908	367,356	222,097	129,956	5,030
20-24 years	942,048	216,152	159,304	17,192	2,520	23,992	13,144	715,227	500,928	177,494	10,669
25-29 years	1,069,436	188,669	133,465	13,337	3,609	27,144	11,114	865,694	674,498	130,942	15,073
30-34 years	886,798	121,539	78,891	8,357	3,835	22,710	7,746	749,555	603,304	90,637	15,704
35-39 years	409,710	51,601	32,026	3,515	1,697	10,930	3,433	350,343	280,393	43,434	7,766
40-54 years	79,561	10,851	6,809	706	275	2,405	656	66,999	52,143	8,968	1,711
Educational attainment of mother:											
0-8 years	224,911	155,599	129,076	3,349	274	19,262	3,638	68,291	41,659	15,872	1,021
9-11 years	620,586	194,592	147,123	16,855	1,483	18,477	10,654	420,240	256,605	140,790	5,754
12 years	1,257,946	205,465	137,369	17,952	4,129	30,403	15,612	1,036,873	757,734	222,692	15,608
13-15 years	848,379	93,925	54,712	11,340	3,380	15,945	8,548	743,146	570,573	131,000	11,308
16 years and over	872,733	46,973	21,970	5,026	3,569	11,309	5,099	811,079	686,483	60,248	14,681
Not stated	56,339	13,213	8,774	928	52	2,009	1,450	35,545	20,309	10,829	7,581
Live-birth order:											
1	1,573,768	266,392	182,542	21,778	5,633	37,931	18,508	1,286,028	974,855	223,429	21,348
2	1,254,354	214,352	147,737	17,024	4,621	31,083	13,887	1,022,467	788,759	169,163	17,535
3	628,579	127,872	92,294	9,180	1,898	17,100	7,400	492,203	366,267	98,781	8,504
4	241,418	56,782	42,598	3,929	486	6,729	3,040	181,452	124,488	46,602	3,184
5 or more	162,167	40,123	30,973	2,951	219	4,085	1,895	119,514	69,726	40,228	2,530
Not stated	20,608	4,246	2,880	588	30	477	271	13,510	9,268	3,228	2,852
Marital status:											
Married	2,623,450	419,330	304,976	22,515	9,744	56,734	25,361	2,163,526	1,830,743	177,895	40,594
Unmarried	1,257,444	290,437	194,048	32,935	3,143	40,671	19,640	951,648	502,620	403,536	15,359
Mother's place of birth:											
Born in the 50 States and D.C.	3,124,817	277,118	195,285	35,038	4,995	8,791	33,009	2,797,591	2,214,861	524,853	50,108
Born elsewhere	746,928	431,150	303,024	20,318	7,885	88,505	11,418	311,117	115,136	53,834	4,661
Not stated	9,149	1,499	715	94	7	109	574	6,466	3,366	2,744	1,184
Maternal smoking during pregnancy:[3]											
Smoker	406,484	18,092	7,989	5,459	500	1,172	2,972	383,905	323,821	50,840	4,487
Nonsmoker	2,671,200	422,425	269,246	44,081	11,352	65,718	32,028	2,225,854	1,638,023	466,061	22,921
Not stated	46,426	4,888	2,407	1,014	54	679	734	38,280	29,148	6,097	3,258

See footnotes at end of table.

(those born before 37 completed weeks of gestation) ranged from a low of 7 percent for births to Chinese mothers to a high of 18 percent for births to black mothers.

Table 7.5. (continued) Infant mortality rates, live births, and infant deaths by selected characteristics and Hispanic origin of mother and by race of mother for mothers of non-Hispanic origin: United States, 1997 linked file. (continued on next page)

Characteristics	All origins[1]	Hispanic						Non-Hispanic			Not stated
		Total	Mexican	Puerto Rican	Cuban	Central and South American	Other and unknown Hispanic	Total[2]	White	Black	
						Infant deaths					
Total	27,968	4,226	2,908	436	71	531	280	23,141	14,046	7,978	600
Age at death:											
Total neonatal	18,507	2,806	1,908	299	52	381	166	15,225	9,181	5,358	477
Early neonatal (< 7 days)	14,827	2,168	1,448	248	36	303	133	12,240	7,271	4,440	417
Late neonatal (7-27 days)	3,680	638	460	51	16	78	33	2,985	1,910	918	59
Postneonatal	9,461	1,421	1,000	138	19	150	114	7,916	4,865	2,620	124
Sex:											
Male	15,729	2,319	1,597	246	38	280	158	13,089	8,034	4,425	321
Female	12,239	1,907	1,311	190	33	251	122	10,052	6,013	3,552	279
Plurality:											
Single births	24,225	3,780	2,607	383	56	466	268	19,953	11,942	7,033	491
Plural births	3,743	446	301	53	15	65	12	3,188	2,104	945	109
Birthweight:											
Less than 1,500 grams	14,068	2,034	1,317	250	40	307	120	11,669	6,357	4,830	365
1,500-2,499 grams	3,944	632	456	53	14	57	52	3,237	2,123	926	76
2,500 grams or more	9,615	1,520	1,105	129	17	163	106	7,966	5,449	2,079	129
Not stated	341	41	29	5	-	4	3	270	117	143	30
Period of gestation:											
Less than 32 weeks	13,736	1,904	1,213	252	43	282	114	11,481	6,257	4,759	351
32-36 weeks	3,583	555	395	54	10	54	42	2,964	1,923	885	64
37-41 weeks	8,672	1,355	975	110	16	153	101	7,195	4,972	1,819	123
42 weeks or more	1,046	187	137	10	2	25	13	849	590	218	10
Not stated	930	227	188	11	-	17	11	651	303	297	52
Trimester of pregnancy prenatal care began:											
First trimester	19,762	2,822	1,931	279	56	369	187	16,620	10,900	4,973	319
After first trimester or no care	6,221	1,116	826	102	10	111	67	4,970	2,392	2,292	136
Second trimester	3,904	721	532	64	5	79	41	3,111	1,641	1,273	72
Third trimester	670	149	122	9	1	9	8	509	254	219	11
No prenatal care	1,647	246	172	29	4	23	18	1,349	497	800	52
Not stated	1,985	289	151	56	5	51	26	1,551	754	713	145
Age of mother:											
Under 20 years	5,149	885	637	96	10	66	76	4,184	2,185	1,853	81
20-24 years	7,559	1,232	877	151	12	115	77	6,179	3,547	2,390	147
25-29 years	6,598	973	635	98	19	157	64	5,473	3,439	1,746	153
30-34 years	5,174	668	446	51	18	110	43	4,376	2,904	1,235	128
35-39 years	2,793	359	237	31	9	62	20	2,357	1,594	615	76
40-54 years	695	110	76	10	2	21	1	569	376	138	15
Educational attainment of mother:											
0-8 years	1,699	904	711	25	2	144	22	776	447	268	18
9-11 years	6,096	1,255	932	142	13	96	72	4,775	2,544	2,053	65
12 years	9,621	1,196	772	148	24	158	94	8,269	4,909	2,986	157
13-15 years	5,052	483	283	71	19	67	43	4,517	2,775	1,538	51
16 years and over	4,003	209	101	30	9	47	22	3,732	2,841	642	62
Not stated	1,497	176	109	19	3	18	27	1,073	529	492	247
Live-birth order:											
1	11,149	1,630	1,103	164	32	205	126	9,281	5,780	3,046	238
2	8,177	1,167	790	120	20	157	80	6,870	4,376	2,180	141
3	4,370	670	476	72	13	73	36	3,614	2,192	1,254	86
4	2,079	352	235	46	4	44	23	1,686	943	668	41
5 or more	1,821	346	268	22	1	44	11	1,439	609	732	36
Not stated	372	60	36	12	-	8	4	251	146	98	60
Marital status:											
Married	14,771	2,217	1,620	153	43	267	134	12,220	9,413	2,061	334
Unmarried	13,197	2,010	1,288	284	28	264	146	10,920	4,633	5,916	267

See footnotes at end of table.

Infant mortality rates were much higher for low birthweight infants than for infants with birthweights of 2,500 grams or more for all race and ethnic groups studied. Overall, the infant mortality rate for very low birthweight infants (those with birthweights of less than

Table 7.5. (continued) Infant mortality rates, live births, and infant deaths by selected characteristics and Hispanic origin of mother and by race of mother for mothers of non-Hispanic origin: United States, 1997 linked file.

Characteristics	All origins[1]	Hispanic						Non-Hispanic			Not stated
		Total	Mexican	Puerto Rican	Cuban	Central and South American	Other and unknown Hispanic	Total[2]	White	Black	
		Infant deaths									
Mother's place of birth:											
Born in the 50 States and D.C.	23,096	1,870	1,305	269	26	55	215	20,806	13,189	7,167	420
Born elsewhere	4,179	2,305	1,576	163	45	474	47	1,831	617	557	44
Not stated	693	53	28	5	*	2	18	503	240	254	137
Maternal smoking during pregnancy:[3]											
Smoker	4,392	164	76	60	3	7	18	4,158	3,041	1,005	70
Nonsmoker	18,118	2,519	1,591	330	64	339	195	15,369	8,733	6,000	230
Not stated	711	66	35	13	*	9	9	560	341	192	85

* Figure does not meet standard of reliability or precision.
- Quantity zero.
.. Category not applicable.
[1] Origin of mother not stated included in "All origins" but not distributed among origins.
[2] Includes races other than black or white.
[3] Excludes data for California, Indiana, New York State (but includes New York City), and South Dakota, which do not report tobacco use on the birth certificate.

NOTE: Infant deaths are weighted so numbers may not exactly add to totals due to rounding. Not stated responses were included in totals but not distributed among groups for rate computations.

1,500 grams) was 252.8, over 90 times the rate of 2.7 for infants with birthweights of 2,500 grams or more. The rate for moderately low birthweight infants (those with birthweights of 1,500–2,499 grams) was 16.7, about six times the rate for infants with birthweights of 2,500 grams or more. Similarly, the infant mortality rate for very preterm infants (those born at less than 32 weeks of gestation) was 184.6, 66 times the rate of 2.8 for infants born at term (37–41 weeks of gestation). The infant mortality rate for moderately preterm infants (those born at 32–36 weeks of gestation) was 9.9, almost four times the rate for term births.

Infant mortality rates for more detailed birthweight categories are presented in Table 7.6. About 9 out of 10 infants with birthweights of less than 500 grams die within the first year of life—most within the first few days of life. An infant's chances of survival increase rapidly with increasing birthweight. At birthweights of 1,250–1,499 grams, about 95 out of 100 infants now survive the first year of life. Infant mortality rates are lowest at birthweights of 4,000–4,499 grams, with small increases among the heaviest infants. Infant mortality rates are lower for black than for white infants at individual birthweight categories under 2,000 grams, but are higher at birthweights of 2,000

Table 7.6. Life births, infant, neonatal, and post-neonatal deaths and mortality rates by race of mother and birthweight: United States, 1997 linked file, and percent change in birthweight-specific infant mortality, 1996-97 linked file.

Race and birthweight	Number				Mortality rate per 1,000 live births			Percent change in infant mortality rate 1996-97
	Live births	Infant deaths	Neonatal deaths	Postneonatal deaths	Infant	Neonatal	Postneonatal	
All races[1]	3,880,894	27,968	18,507	9,461	7.2	4.8	2.4	-1.4
Less than 2,500 grams	292,069	18,012	14,697	3,315	61.7	50.3	11.4	-1.9
Less than 1,500 grams	55,659	14,068	12,456	1,612	252.8	223.8	29.0	-2.5
Less than 500 grams	5,994	5,298	5,210	88	883.9	869.2	14.7	-0.6
500-749 grams	10,853	5,249	4,661	588	492.7	437.5	55.2	-3.8
750-999 grams	11,341	1,829	1,388	441	161.3	122.4	38.9	-3.5
1,000-1,249 grams	12,735	966	684	282	75.9	53.7	22.1	-1.7
1,250-1,499 grams	14,936	726	513	213	48.6	34.3	14.3	-7.8
1,500-1,999 grams	56,899	1,720	1,071	649	30.2	18.8	11.4	-0.3
2,000-2,499 grams	179,511	2,224	1,170	1,054	12.4	6.5	5.9	-7.5
2,500 grams or more	3,587,099	9,615	3,486	6,129	2.7	1.0	1.7	-3.6
2,500-2,999 grams	642,394	3,158	1,261	1,897	4.9	2.0	3.0	-3.9
3,000-3,499 grams	1,435,825	3,685	1,274	2,411	2.6	0.9	1.7	-3.7
3,500-3,999 grams	1,117,955	2,079	670	1,409	1.9	0.6	1.3	*
4,000-4,499 grams	331,020	564	220	344	1.7	0.7	1.0	*
4,500-4,999 grams	53,963	105	45	60	1.9	0.8	1.1	-5.0
5,000 grams or more	5,942	24	16	8	4.0	*	*	-35.5
Not stated	1,726	341	324	17	...	...	...	...
White	3,072,640	18,578	12,250	6,328	6.0	4.0	2.1	-1.6
Less than 2,500 grams	198,981	11,378	9,350	2,028	57.2	47.0	10.2	-0.5
Less than 1,500 grams	34,962	8,584	7,659	924	245.5	219.1	26.4	-1.4
Less than 500 grams	3,315	2,962	2,909	53	893.5	877.5	16.0	0.2
500-749 grams	6,265	3,228	2,901	328	515.2	463.0	52.4	-2.4
750-999 grams	7,048	1,221	967	254	173.2	137.2	36.0	-2.1
1,000-1,249 grams	8,355	647	494	154	77.4	59.1	18.4	-2.4
1,250-1,499 grams	9,979	526	389	136	52.7	39.0	13.6	-5.2
1,500-1,999 grams	39,047	1,239	813	426	31.7	20.8	10.9	4.3
2,000-2,499 grams	124,972	1,556	878	678	12.5	7.0	5.4	-6.0
2,500 grams or more	2,872,582	7,020	2,731	4,289	2.4	1.0	1.5	-4.0
2,500-2,999 grams	459,862	2,193	952	1,240	4.8	2.1	2.7	-2.0
3,000-3,499 grams	1,123,860	2,652	1,000	1,652	2.4	0.9	1.5	-4.0
3,500-3,999 grams	944,629	1,619	549	1,070	1.7	0.6	1.1	*
4,000-4,499 grams	291,289	455	182	273	1.6	0.6	0.9	6.7
4,500-4,999 grams	47,812	87	39	49	1.8	0.8	*	*
5,000 grams or more	5,130	13	9	4	*	*	*	*
Not stated	1,077	180	169	11	...	...	...	...
Black	599,913	8,210	5,536	2,673	13.7	9.2	4.5	-2.8
Less than 2,500 grams	78,207	5,930	4,796	1,134	75.8	61.3	14.5	-3.7
Less than 1,500 grams	18,432	4,978	4,351	627	270.1	236.1	34.0	-3.7
Less than 500 grams	2,484	2,174	2,139	34	875.2	861.1	13.7	-1.2
500-749 grams	3,990	1,823	1,581	242	456.9	396.2	60.7	-5.9
750-999 grams	3,831	538	371	167	140.4	96.8	43.6	-3.6
1,000-1,249 grams	3,831	277	163	114	72.3	42.5	29.8	1.0
1,250-1,499 grams	4,296	167	97	70	38.9	22.6	16.3	-16.3
1,500-1,999 grams	15,163	404	212	192	26.6	14.0	12.7	-9.5
2,000-2,499 grams	44,612	548	233	315	12.3	5.2	7.1	-10.9
2,500 grams or more	521,347	2,130	596	1,534	4.1	1.1	2.9	-2.4
2,500-2,999 grams	139,692	816	254	562	5.8	1.8	4.0	-3.3
3,000-3,499 grams	227,482	850	213	637	3.7	0.9	2.8	*
3,500-3,999 grams	122,133	356	88	268	2.9	0.7	2.2	-14.7
4,000-4,499 grams	27,343	83	28	55	3.0	1.0	2.0	-6.3
4,500-4,999 grams	4,167	14	5	9	*	*	*	*
5,000 grams or more	530	10	6	4	*	*	*	*
Not stated	359	150	144	5	...	...	...	...

* Figure does not meet standard of reliability or precision.
... Category not applicable.
[1] Includes races other than white or black.
NOTE: Infant deaths are weighted so numbers may not exactly add to totals due to rounding.

grams or more. From 1996–97, infant mortality rates declined most rapidly for infants with birthweights of 1,250–1,499 grams, 2,000–2,499 grams, and 5000 grams or more at birth, although the differences were not statistically significant.

Prenatal care—Although difficult to measure, the timing and quality of prenatal care received by the mother during pregnancy can be important to the infant's subsequent health and survival. Early comprehensive prenatal care can promote healthier pregnancies by providing health behavior advice and early detection and treatment of maternal complications that may influence the infant's subsequent health and survival. In general, infant mortality was higher for women who began prenatal care after the first trimester of pregnancy or not at all than for those who began care in the first trimester. For all race and Hispanic-origin groups combined, infants of mothers who began prenatal care after the first trimester of pregnancy or not at all had an infant mortality rate, which was 49 percent higher than those who began care in the first trimester (9.4 and 6.3, respectively). For each race and Hispanic-origin group, infant mortality rates were higher for mothers who began prenatal care after the first trimester or not at all, although differences were not statistically significant for mothers of Hispanic-origin (Mexican, Puerto Rican, and Central and South American mothers).

Similar to 1995–96, the infant mortality rate for mothers who began prenatal care in the first trimester continued to decline from 1996 to 1997. The rate in 1997 (6.3) was 3 percent lower than the rate in 1996 (6.5) and 4.5 percent lower than in 1995 (6.6). Reasons for the decrease in infant mortality rates among mothers who begin care in the first trimester may include earlier detection of adverse pregnancy conditions, improvements in the delivery of care, and greater utilization of health behavior services.

Maternal age—Infant mortality exhibits a curvilinear relationship with maternal age with rates being highest for teenage mothers, lowest for mothers in their late twenties and early thirties, and again higher for mothers in their forties and over. The percent of births to teenage mothers was lowest for Chinese mothers (1 percent) and highest for black and Puerto Rican mothers (22 percent).

For the total population, white, and non-Hispanic white mothers, infant mortality rates were higher for teenage mothers than for mothers 40–54 years of age. For black, Asian and Pacific Islander, total Hispanic, and Mexican mothers, infant mortality rates were higher for mothers 40–54 years of age than for teenagers, although the difference was not statistically significant for black and Asian and Pacific Islander mothers. For American Indian, Puerto Rican, and Cuban mothers, there were not enough infant deaths for mothers 40–54 years of age to be able to compute reliable rates.

Infant mortality rates were higher for infants of teenaged mothers than for infants of mothers 25–29 years of age for all race and

Hispanic origin groups, although differences were only statistically significant for infants of white, Mexican, and Asian and Pacific Islander mothers. For Cuban mothers there were not enough infant deaths to teenage mothers to be able to compute reliable rates. Infant mortality rates were higher for women 40–54 years of age than for women 25–29 years of age for all race and Hispanic origin groups that rates could be computed for, although differences were only statistically significant for white and Mexican mothers. Recent studies suggest that the higher mortality risk for younger mothers may be related to the preponderance of teenage mothers who are from disadvantaged backgrounds, while for older mothers, both biological and sociological factors may play a role.

Maternal education—The percent of births to mothers who had completed high school or more ranged from a low of 44 percent for Mexican mothers to a high of 98 percent for Japanese mothers. Infant mortality rates generally decreased with increasing educational level. This pattern may reflect in part socioeconomic differences because women with more education tend to have higher family income levels.

Among infants of black, American Indian, Central and South American, and non-Hispanic white mothers, infant mortality rates declined steadily with increasing educational level with the highest mortality rates occurring among infants of mothers with 0–8 years of education. In contrast, for Asian and Pacific Islander, total Hispanic, Mexican, and Puerto Rican mothers (and by extension for total white and the total population), mortality rates were lower for infants of mothers with 0–8 years of education than for infants of mothers with 9–11 years of education, although the differences were only statistically significant for white mothers. This may be due in part to the very different population composition of women with 0–8 years of education, most of whom were born outside the 50 States and the District of Columbia. In general, infants of women born outside the 50 States and the District of Columbia have lower infant mortality rates than infants of women born in the 50 States and the District of Columbia.

Live birth order—Overall, infant mortality rates were slightly higher for first births than for second births, and thereafter increased with increasing birth order. Compared with the infant mortality rate for second births (6.5), the rate for first births was 9 percent higher (7.1), the rate for fourth births (8.6) was 32 percent higher, and the rate for fifth and higher order births (11.2) was 72 percent higher. The proportion of women with fourth and higher order births ranged from a low of 2 percent for Chinese mothers to a high of 20 percent for American Indian mothers.

Marital status—Marital status interacts with a wide variety of other factors, such as the degree of economic and social support for the mother and child; whether or not the pregnancy was wanted; as well as maternal age, educational level, and prenatal care attendance. For all races combined, there was a decrease in infant mortality rates for married mothers in 1997. The infant mortality rate for married mothers was 5.6 in 1997 compared with 5.8 in 1996. The rate for unmarried mothers in 1997 (10.5) did not change and was 1.9 times the rate for married mothers. For each race and Hispanic-origin group studied, infant mortality rates were higher for unmarried mothers than for married mothers, although differences were not significant for American Indian and Puerto Rican mothers.

The percent of births to unmarried women ranged from a low of 7 percent for Chinese mothers to a high of 69 percent for black mothers.

Nativity—For all races combined, the infant mortality rate for mothers born in the 50 States and the District of Columbia (7.4) was nearly one-third (32 percent) higher than the rate for those born outside of the 50 States and the District of Columbia (5.6). For each race and Hispanic origin group, infant mortality rates were higher for mothers born in the 50 States and the District of Columbia than for those born elsewhere, although the differences were not statistically significant for Puerto Rican, Cuban, and Central and South American mothers. The infant mortality rate for American Indian mothers born outside the 50 States and the District of Columbia could not be computed because of insufficient numbers. The percent of births to mothers born in the 50 States and the District of Columbia ranged from a low of 9–10 percent for Central and South American and Chinese mothers to a high of 97–98 percent for American Indian and Hawaiian mothers.

A variety of different hypotheses has been advanced to account for the lower infant mortality rate among mothers born outside the 50 States and the District of Columbia, including possible differences in the level of familial integration and social support for new mothers. Also, women born outside the 50 States and the District of Columbia have been shown to have different characteristics than women born within the 50 States and the District of Columbia with regard to socioeconomic and educational status, and risk behaviors such as smoking and alcohol use.

Maternal smoking—The infant mortality rate for smokers was 10.8 in 1997, nearly 60 percent higher than the rate for nonsmokers (6.8). The percentage of women who smoked during pregnancy ranged from a low of 1 percent for Chinese mothers to a high of 21 percent for American Indian mothers. For each race and Hispanic-origin group, the infant mortality rate for smokers was higher than for nonsmokers, although the difference was not statistically significant for Puerto Rican mothers. Reliable rates for smokers could not be calculated for Cuban and Central and South American mothers due to an insufficient number of infant deaths.

Tobacco use during pregnancy causes the passage of substances such as nicotine, hydrogen cyanide, and carbon monoxide from the placenta into the fetal blood supply. These substances restrict the growing infant's access to oxygen and can lead to adverse pregnancy and birth outcomes such as low birthweight, preterm delivery, intrauterine growth retardation, and infant mortality.

Leading Causes of Infant Death

Infant mortality rates for the five leading causes of infant death are presented in Table 7.7 by race of mother and in Table 7.8 for selected Hispanic origin groups and for non-Hispanic white mothers. The three leading causes of infant death—congenital anomalies; disorders relating to short gestation and unspecified low birthweight (low birthweight); and sudden infant death syndrome (SIDS) taken together accounted for nearly one-half (47 percent) of all infant deaths in the United States in 1997.

Rankings of leading causes of infant death varied by race and Hispanic origin of the mother. For all races combined, white, Hispanic total, Mexican, and Central and South American mothers, congenital anomalies was the leading cause of infant death in 1997, followed by low birthweight, SIDS, respiratory distress syndrome (RDS), and new-born affected by maternal complications of pregnancy (maternal complications). For infants of black mothers, low birthweight was the leading cause of infant death, followed by congenital anomalies, and SIDS. For infants of American Indian mothers, congenital anomalies was the leading cause of death, followed by SIDS and low birthweight. For infants of Puerto Rican mothers, the order of the first three causes

Table 7.7. Infant deaths and mortality rates for the five leading causes of infant death by race of mother, United States, 1997 linked file.

[Rates per 100,000 live births in specified group]

Cause of death (Ninth Revision International Classification of Diseases, 1975)	All races			White			Black			American Indian			Asian and Pacific Islander		
	Rank	Number	Rate	Rank	Number	Rate	Rank	Number	Rate	Rank	Number	Rate	Rank	Number	Rate
All causes	...	27,968	720.7	...	18,578	604.6	...	8,210	1368.5	...	335	868.5	...	845	497.7
Congenital anomalies (740-759)	1	6,187	159.4	1	4,793	156.0	2	1,100	183.4	1	64	165.9	1	230	135.5
Disorders related to short gestation and unspecified low birthweight (765)	2	3,917	100.9	2	2,099	68.3	1	1,704	284.0	3	26	67.4	2	88	51.8
Sudden infant death syndrome (798.0)	3	2,996	77.2	3	1,991	64.8	3	859	143.2	2	60	155.6	3	87	51.2
Respiratory distress syndrome (769)	4	1,303	33.6	4	797	25.9	4	453	75.5	10	8	*	4	44	25.9
Newborn affected by maternal complications of pregnancy (761)	5	1,234	31.8	5	791	25.7	5	407	67.8	4	13	*	7	23	13.5

*   Figure does not meet standard of reliability or precision.
... Category not applicable.

NOTE: For American Indians, Newborn affected by complications of placenta, cord and membranes was the 5th leading cause of infant death, however, with only 12 deaths, a reliable infant mortality rate could not be computed. For Asian and Pacific Islanders, Infections specific to the perinatal period was the 5th leading cause of infant death, with 25 deaths and a rate of 14.5.

67

Table 7.8. Infant deaths and mortality rates for the five leading causes of infant death by Hispanic origin of mother and for non-Hispanic White mothers: United States, 1997 linked file.

[Rates per 100,000 live births in specified group]

Cause of death (Ninth Revision International Classification of Diseases, 1975)	Hispanic[1]			Mexican			Puerto Rican			Central and South American			Non-Hispanic White		
	Rank	Number	Rate	Rank	Number	Rate	Rank	Number	Rate	Rank	Number	Rate	Rank	Number	Rate
All causes	...	4,226	595.4	...	2,908	582.7	...	436	786.3	...	531	545.1	...	14,046	602.0
Congenital anomalies (740-759)	1	1,194	168.2	1	884	177.1	1	79	142.5	1	147	150.9	1	3,536	151.5
Disorders related to short gestation and unspecified low birthweight (765)	2	504	71.0	2	321	64.3	2	60	108.2	2	82	84.2	3	1,528	65.5
Sudden infant death syndrome (798.0)	3	330	46.5	3	234	46.9	3	33	59.5	3	39	40.0	2	1,649	70.7
Respiratory distress syndrome (769)	4	187	26.3	4	127	25.4	5	19	*	4	29	29.8	5	596	25.5
Newborn affected by maternal complications of pregnancy (761)	5	148	20.9	5	91	18.2	4	20	36.1	5	25	25.7	4	624	26.7

* Figure does not meet standard of reliability or precision.
† Category not applicable.
[1] Includes Cuban and other and unknown Hispanic.

of infant death was the same as for the total population, but maternal complications was ranked fourth, and RDS fifth. For non-Hispanic white mothers, congenital anomalies was the leading cause of infant death, followed by SIDS, low birthweight, maternal complications, and RDS.

Mortality rates were higher for black than for white mothers for all of the five leading causes of infant death. For infants of black mothers, mortality rates from congenital anomalies were 18 percent higher than for infants of white mothers. For low birthweight, the mortality rate was 284.0 for infants of black mothers, over four times the rate of 68.3 for infants of white mothers. For SIDS, RDS, and maternal complications, rates were 2.2–2.9 times higher for infants of black than for infants of white mothers.

For infants of American Indian mothers, the SIDS rate was 155.6, 2.4 times that for infants of white mothers. As most SIDS deaths occur during the post-neonatal period, the high SIDS rate for infants of American Indian mothers accounts for much of their elevated risk of post-neonatal mortality. For infants of Asian and Pacific Islander mothers cause-specific mortality rates were significantly lower than those for white mothers for low birthweight and maternal complications.

For Mexican mothers, the infant mortality rate for congenital anomalies was 177.1, 17 percent higher than the rate of 151.5 for non-Hispanic white mothers. The SIDS rate of 46.9 was one-third lower than the rate of 70.7 for non-Hispanic white mothers. The rate for maternal complications was also nearly one-third lower for Mexican than for non-Hispanic white mothers.

For Puerto Rican mothers, the most notable finding was the much higher infant mortality rate for low birthweight. The rate of 108.2 was 65 percent higher than the rate of 65.5 for non-Hispanic white mothers. For Central and South American mothers, the most notable finding was the much lower SIDS rate. The SIDS rate of 40.0 was 43 percent below the rate for non-Hispanic white mothers.

An examination of cause-specific differences in infant mortality rates between race and Hispanic origin groups can help the researcher to understand overall differences in infant mortality rates between these groups. For example, more than one-third (34 percent) of the elevated infant mortality rate for American Indian mothers when compared with white mothers can be accounted for by their higher SIDS rates. In other words, if American Indian SIDS mortality could be made equal to white SIDS mortality, the difference in the infant mortality rate between American Indian and white mothers would be reduced by one-third.

For black mothers, more than one-fourth (28 percent) of their elevated infant mortality rate, when compared with white mothers, can be accounted for by their higher infant mortality rate due to low birthweight and a further 10 percent can be accounted for by differences in SIDS. If black infant mortality rates for low birthweight and SIDS could be reduced to white levels, the difference in the infant mortality rate between black and white mothers would be reduced by 38 percent. In addition to helping to explain differences in infant mortality rates between various groups, comparisons such as these can be helpful in targeting prevention efforts.

Chapter 8

Sudden Infant Death Syndrome (SIDS)

Sudden Infant Death Syndrome (SIDS) is the diagnosis given for the sudden death of an infant under one year of age that remains unexplained after a complete investigation, which includes an autopsy, examination of the death scene, and review of the symptoms or illnesses the infant had prior to dying and any other pertinent medical history. Because most cases of SIDS occur when a baby is sleeping in a crib, SIDS is also commonly known as crib death.

SIDS is the leading cause of death in infants between 1 month and 1 year of age. Most SIDS deaths occur when a baby is between 1 and 4 months of age. African American children are two to three times more likely than white babies to die of SIDS, and Native American babies are about three times more susceptible. Also, more boys are SIDS victims than girls.

What are the risk factors for SIDS?

A number of factors seem to put a baby at higher risk of dying from SIDS. Babies who sleep on their stomachs are more likely to die of SIDS than those who sleep on their backs. Mothers who smoke during pregnancy are three times more likely to have a SIDS baby, and exposure to passive smoke from smoking by mothers, fathers, and others in the household doubles a baby's risk of SIDS. Other risk factors include mothers who are less than 20 years old at the time of their

National Institute of Child Health and Human Development (NICHD), April 1997.

first pregnancy, babies born to mothers who had no or late prenatal care, and premature or low birthweight babies.

What causes SIDS?

Mounting evidence suggests that some SIDS babies are born with brain abnormalities that make them vulnerable to sudden death during infancy. Studies of SIDS victims reveal that many SIDS infants have abnormalities in the *arcuate nucleus*, a portion of the brain that is likely to be involved in controlling breathing and waking during sleep. Babies born with defects in other portions of the brain or body may also be more prone to a sudden death. These abnormalities may stem from prenatal exposure to a toxic substance, or lack of a vital compound in the prenatal environment, such as sufficient oxygen. Cigarette smoking during pregnancy, for example, can reduce the amount of oxygen the fetus receives.

Scientists believe that the abnormalities that are present at birth may not be sufficient to cause death. Other possibly important events occur after birth such as lack of oxygen, excessive carbon dioxide intake, overheating or an infection. For example, many babies experience a lack of oxygen and excessive carbon dioxide levels when they have respiratory infections that hamper breathing, or they rebreathe exhaled air trapped in underlying bedding when they sleep on their stomachs. Normally, infants sense such inadequate air intake, and the brain triggers the babies to wake from sleep and cry, and changes their heartbeat or breathing patterns to compensate for the insufficient oxygen and excess carbon dioxide. A baby with a flawed arcuate nucleus, however, might lack this protective mechanism and succumb to SIDS. Such a scenario might explain why babies who sleep on their stomachs are more susceptible to SIDS, and why a disproportionately large number of SIDS babies have been reported to have respiratory infections prior to their deaths. Infections as a trigger for sudden infant death may explain why more SIDS cases occur during the colder months of the year, when respiratory and intestinal infections are more common.

The numbers of cells and proteins generated by the immune system of some SIDS babies have been reported to be higher than normal. Some of these proteins can interact with the brain to alter heart rate and breathing during sleep, or can put the baby into a deep sleep. Such effects might be strong enough to cause the baby's death, particularly if the baby has an underlying brain defect.

Some babies who die suddenly may be born with a metabolic disorder. One such disorder is medium chain acylCoA dehydrogenase deficiency, which prevents the infant from properly processing fatty acids. A build-up of these acid metabolites could eventually lead to a rapid and fatal disruption in breathing and heart functioning. If there is a family history of this disorder or childhood death of unknown cause, genetic screening of the parents by a blood test can determine if they are carriers of this disorder. If one or both parents is found to be a carrier, the baby can be tested soon after birth.

What might help lower the risk of SIDS?

There currently is no way of predicting which newborns will succumb to SIDS; however, there are a few measures parents can take to lower the risk of their child dying from SIDS.

Good prenatal care, which includes proper nutrition, no smoking or drug or alcohol use by the mother, and frequent medical check-ups beginning early in pregnancy, might help prevent a baby from developing an abnormality that could put him or her at risk for sudden death. These measures may also reduce the chance of having a premature or low birthweight baby, which also increases the risk for SIDS. Once the baby is born, parents should keep the baby in a smoke-free environment.

Parents and other caregivers should put babies to sleep on their backs as opposed to on their stomachs. Studies have shown that placing babies on their backs to sleep has reduced the number of SIDS cases by as much as a half in countries where infants had traditionally slept on their stomachs. Although babies placed on their sides to sleep have a lower risk of SIDS than those placed on their stomachs, the back sleep position is the best position for infants from 1 month to 1 year. Babies positioned on their sides to sleep should be placed with their lower arm forward to help prevent them from rolling onto their stomachs.

Many parents place babies on their stomachs to sleep because they think it prevents them from choking on spit-up or vomit during sleep. But studies in countries where there has been a switch from babies sleeping predominantly on their stomachs to sleeping mainly on their backs have not found any evidence of increased risk of choking or other problems.

In some instances, doctors may recommend that babies be placed on their stomachs to sleep if they have disorders such as gastroesophageal reflux or certain upper airway disorders which predispose them to choking or breathing problems while lying on their backs. If a parent is unsure about the best sleep position for their baby, it is always a good idea to talk to the baby's doctor or other health care provider.

A certain amount of tummy-time while the infant is awake and being observed is recommended for motor development of the shoulder. In addition, awake-time on the stomach may help prevent flat spots from developing on the back of the baby's head. Such physical signs are almost always temporary and will disappear soon after the baby begins to sit up.

Parents should make sure their baby sleeps on a firm mattress or other firm surface. They should avoid using fluffy blankets or covering as well as pillows, sheepskins, blankets, or comforters under the baby. Infants should not be placed to sleep on a waterbed or with soft stuffed toys.

Recently, scientific studies have demonstrated that bed-sharing, between mother and baby, can alter sleep patterns of the mother and baby. These studies have led to speculation that bed-sharing, sometimes referred to as co-sleeping, may also reduce the risk of SIDS. While bed-sharing may have certain benefits (such as encouraging breast feeding), there are no scientific studies demonstrating that bed-sharing reduces SIDS. Some studies actually suggest that bed-sharing, under certain conditions, may increase the risk of SIDS. If mothers choose to sleep in the same beds with their babies, care should be taken to avoid using soft sleep surfaces. Quilts, blankets, pillows, comforters, or other similar soft materials should not be placed under the baby. The bed-sharer should not smoke or use substances such as alcohol or drugs which may impair arousal. It is also important to be aware that unlike cribs, which are designed to meet safety standards for infants, adult beds are not so designed and may carry a risk of accidental entrapment and suffocation.

Babies should be kept warm, but they should not be allowed to get too warm because an overheated baby is more likely to go into a deep sleep from which it is difficult to arouse. The temperature in the baby's room should feel comfortable to an adult and overdressing the baby should be avoided.

There is some evidence to suggest that breast feeding might reduce the risk of SIDS. A few studies have found SIDS to be less common in infants who have been breast fed. This may be because breast milk can provide protection from some infections that can trigger sudden death in infants.

Parents should take their babies to their health care provider for regular well-baby check-ups and routine immunizations. Claims that immunizations increase the risk of SIDS are not supported by data, and babies who receive their scheduled immunizations are less likely to die of SIDS. If an infant ever has an incident where he or she stops breathing and turns blue or limp, the baby should be medically evaluated for the cause of such an incident.

Although some electronic home monitors can detect and sound an alarm when a baby stops breathing, there is no evidence that such monitors can prevent SIDS. A panel of experts convened by the National Institutes of Health in 1986 recommended that home monitors not be used for babies who do not have an increased risk of sudden unexpected death. The monitors are recommended, however, for infants who have experienced one or more severe episodes during which they stopped breathing and required resuscitation or stimulation, premature infants with apnea, and siblings of two or more SIDS infants. If an incident has occurred or if an infant is on a monitor, parents need to know how to properly use and maintain the device, as well as how to resuscitate their baby if the alarm sounds.

How does a SIDS baby affect the family?

A SIDS death is a tragedy that can prompt intense emotional reactions among surviving family members. After the initial disbelief, denial, or numbness begins to wear off, parents often fall into a prolonged depression. This depression can affect their sleeping, eating, ability to concentrate, and general energy level. Crying, weeping, incessant talking, and strong feelings of guilt or anger are all normal reactions. Many parents experience unreasonable fears that they, or someone in their family, may be in danger. Over-protection of surviving children and fears for future children is a common reaction.

As the finality of the child's death becomes a reality for the parents, recovery occurs. Parents begin to take a more active part in their own lives, which begin to have meaning once again. The pain of their child's death becomes less intense but not forgotten. Birthdays, holidays, and the anniversary of the child's death can trigger periods of intense pain and suffering.

Children will also be affected by the baby's death. They may fear that other members of the family, including themselves, will also suddenly die. Children often also feel guilty about the death of a sibling and may feel that they had something to do with the death. Children may not show their feelings in obvious ways. Although they may deny being upset and seem unconcerned, signs that they are disturbed include intensified clinging to parents, misbehaving, bed wetting, difficulties in school, and nightmares. It is important to talk to children about the death and explain to them that the baby died because of a medical problem that occurs only in infants in rare instances and cannot occur in them. The National Institute of Child Health and Human Development (NICHD) continues to support research aimed at uncovering what causes SIDS, who is at risk for the disorder, and ways to lower the risk of sudden infant death. Inquiries regarding research programs should be directed to Dr. Marian Willinger, 301-496-5575.

Families with a baby who has died from SIDS may be aided by counseling and support groups. Examples of these groups include the following:

Association of SIDS and Infant Mortality Programs
630 West Fayette Street
Room 5-684
Baltimore, MD 21201
(410) 706-5062

National SIDS Resource Center
2070 Chain Bridge Road
Suite 450
Vienna, VA 22181
(703) 821-8955

SIDS Alliance (a national network of SIDS support groups)
1314 Bedford Avenue
Suite 210
Baltimore, MD 21208
(800) 221-7437 or
(410) 653-8226

Part Two

Nutrition

Part Two

Chapter 9

Breast Milk or Formula

New parents want to give their babies the very best. When it comes to nutrition, the best first food for babies is breast milk.

More than two decades of research have established that breast milk is perfectly suited to nourish infants and protect them from illness. Breast-fed infants have lower rates of hospital admissions, ear infections, diarrhea, rashes, allergies, and other medical problems than bottle-fed babies.

"There are 4,000 species of mammals, and they all make a different milk. Human milk is made for human infants, and it meets all their specific nutrient needs," says Ruth Lawrence, M.D., professor of pediatrics and obstetrics at the University of Rochester School of Medicine in Rochester, N.Y., and spokeswoman for the American Academy of Pediatrics.

Health experts say increased breast-feeding rates would save consumers money, spent both on infant formula and in health-care dollars. It could save lives as well.

"We've known for years that the death rates in Third World countries are lower among breast-fed babies," says Lawrence. "Breast-fed babies are healthier and have fewer infections than formula-fed babies."

Although breast-feeding is still the best nourishment for infants, infant formula is a close enough second that babies not only survive but thrive.

Commercially prepared formulas are regulated by the Food and Drug Administration.

FDA Consumer, 98-2307, updated September, 1998.

The nutritional adequacy of commercially prepared formula is also ensured by the agency's nutrient requirements and its safety by strict quality control procedures that require manufacturers to analyze each batch of formula for required nutrients, to test samples for stability during the shelf life of the product, to code containers to identify the batch, and to make all records available to FDA investigators.

The composition of infant formula is similar to breast milk, but it isn't a perfect match, because the exact chemical makeup of breast milk is still unknown.

Human milk is very complex, and scientists are still trying to unravel and understand what makes it such a good source of nutrition for rapidly growing and developing infants.

More than half the calories in breast milk come from fat, and the same is true for today's infant formulas. This may be alarming to many American adults watching their intake of fat and cholesterol, especially when sources of saturated fats, such as coconut oil, are used in formulas. (In adults, high intakes of saturated fats tend to increase blood cholesterol levels more than other fats or oils.) But the low-fat diet recommended for adults doesn't apply to infants.

The reason is that infants have a high energy requirement, and they have a restricted volume of food that they can ingest. The way to meet these energy requirements in a restricted amount of food is to have a high amount of fat.

While greater knowledge about human milk has helped scientists improve infant formula, it has become "increasingly apparent that infant formula can never duplicate human milk," wrote John D. Benson, Ph.D, and Mark L. Masor, Ph.D., in the March 1994 issue of *Endocrine Regulations*. "Human milk contains living cells, hormones, active enzymes, immunoglobulins and compounds with unique structures that cannot be replicated in infant formula."

Benson and Masor, both of whom are pediatric nutrition researchers at infant formula manufacturer Abbott Laboratories, believe creating formula that duplicates human milk is impossible. "A better goal is to match the performance of the breastfed infant," they wrote. Performance is measured by the infant's growth, absorption of nutrients, gastrointestinal tolerance, and reactions in blood.

Human Milk for Human Infants

The primary benefit of breast milk is nutritional. Human milk contains just the right amount of fatty acids, lactose, water, and amino acids for human digestion, brain development, and growth.

Cow's milk contains a different type of protein than breast milk. This is good for calves, but human infants can have difficulty digesting it. Bottle-fed infants tend to be fatter than breast-fed infants, but not necessarily healthier.

Breast-fed babies have fewer illnesses because human milk transfers to the infant a mother's antibodies to disease. About 80 percent of the cells in breast milk are macrophages, cells that kill bacteria, fungi and viruses. Breast-fed babies are protected, in varying degrees, from a number of illnesses, including pneumonia, botulism, bronchitis, staphylococcal infections, influenza, ear infections, and German measles. Furthermore, mothers produce antibodies to whatever disease is present in their environment, making their milk custom-designed to fight the diseases their babies are exposed to as well.

A breast-fed baby's digestive tract contains large amounts of *Lactobacillus bifidus*, beneficial bacteria that prevent the growth of harmful organisms. Human milk straight from the breast is always sterile, never contaminated by polluted water or dirty bottles, which can also lead to diarrhea in the infant.

Human milk contains at least 100 ingredients not found in formula. No babies are allergic to their mother's milk, although they may have a reaction to something the mother eats. If she eliminates it from her diet, the problem resolves itself.

Sucking at the breast promotes good jaw development as well. It's harder work to get milk out of a breast than a bottle, and the exercise strengthens the jaws and encourages the growth of straight, healthy teeth. The baby at the breast also can control the flow of milk by sucking and stopping. With a bottle, the baby must constantly suck or react to the pressure of the nipple placed in the mouth.

Nursing may have psychological benefits for the infant as well, creating an early emotional attachment between mother and child. At birth, infants see only 12 to 15 inches, the distance between a nursing baby and its mother's face. Studies have found that infants as young as 1 week prefer the smell of their own mother's milk. When nursing pads soaked with breast milk are placed in their cribs, they turn their faces toward the one that smells familiar.

Many psychologists believe the nursing baby enjoys a sense of security from the warmth and presence of the mother, especially when there is skin-to-skin contact during feeding. Parents of bottle-fed babies may be tempted to prop bottles in the baby's mouth, with no human contact during feeding. But a nursing mother must cuddle her infant closely many times during the day. Nursing becomes

81

more than a way to feed a baby; it's a source of warmth and comfort.

Benefits to Mothers

Breast-feeding is good for new mothers as well as for their babies. There are no bottles to sterilize and no formula to buy, measure and mix. It may be easier for a nursing mother to lose the pounds of pregnancy as well, since nursing uses up extra calories. Lactation also stimulates the uterus to contract back to its original size.

A nursing mother is forced to get needed rest. She must sit down, put her feet up, and relax every few hours to nurse. Nursing at night is easy as well. No one has to stumble to the refrigerator for a bottle and warm it while the baby cries. If she's lying down, a mother can doze while she nurses.

Nursing is also nature's contraceptive—although not a very reliable one. Frequent nursing suppresses ovulation, making it less likely for a nursing mother to menstruate, ovulate, or get pregnant. There are no guarantees, however. Mothers who don't want more children right away should use contraception even while nursing. Women who are breast-feeding can use barrier methods of birth control, such as condoms and diaphragms. Hormone-containing methods are not first choice. These include injections (such as Depo-Provera), implants (such as Norplant), and birth control pills. A woman who breast-feeds should consult her doctor about which type of contraception is appropriate for her until the baby is weaned.

Breast-feeding is economical also. Even though a nursing mother works up a big appetite and consumes extra calories, the extra food for her is less expensive than buying formula for the baby. Nursing saves money while providing the best nourishment possible.

When Formula Is Necessary

There are very few medical reasons why a mother shouldn't breast-feed, according to Lawrence.

Most common illnesses, such as colds, flu, skin infections, or diarrhea, cannot be passed through breast milk. In fact, if a mother has an illness, her breast milk will contain antibodies to it that will help protect her baby from those same illnesses.

A few viruses can pass through breast milk, however. HIV, the virus that causes AIDS, is one of them. Women who are HIV positive should not breast-feed.

A few other illnesses—such as herpes, hepatitis, and beta strepto-coccus infections—can also be transmitted through breast milk. But that doesn't always mean a mother with those diseases shouldn't breast-feed, Lawrence says.

"Each case must be evaluated on an individual basis with the woman's doctor," she says.

Breast cancer is not passed through breast milk. Women who have had breast cancer can usually breast-feed from the unaffected breast. Studies have shown, however, that breast-feeding a child reduces a woman's chance of developing breast cancer later.

Silicone breast implants usually do not interfere with a woman's ability to nurse, but if the implants leak, there is some concern that the silicone may harm the baby. Some small studies have suggested a link between breast-feeding with implants and later development of problems with the child's esophagus. Further studies are needed in this area. But if a woman with implants wants to breast-feed, she should first discuss the potential benefits and risks with her child's doctor.

Tough but Worthwhile

For all its health benefits, breast-feeding isn't always easy. In the early weeks, it can be painful. A woman's nipples may become sore or cracked. She may experience engorgement more than a bottle-feeding mother, when the breasts become so full of milk they're hard and pain-ful. Some nursing women also develop clogged milk ducts, which can lead to mastitis, a painful infection of the breast. While most nurs-ing problems can be solved with home remedies, mastitis requires prompt medical care (see "Tips for Breast-Feeding Success" towards end of chapter).

Women who plan to go back to work soon after birth will have to plan carefully if they want to breast-feed. If her job allows, a new mother can pump her breast milk several times during the day and refrigerate or freeze it for the baby to take in a bottle later. Some women alternate nursing at night and on weekends with daytime bottles of formula.

In either case, a nursing mother is physically tied to her baby more than a bottle-feeding mother. The baby needs her for nour-ishment, and she needs to nurse regularly to avoid getting uncom-fortably full breasts. But instead of feeling it's a chore, nursing mothers often cite this close relationship as one of the greatest joys of nursing.

If a woman is unsure whether she wants to nurse, she can try it for a few weeks and switch if she doesn't like it. It's very difficult to switch to breast-feeding after bottle-feeding is begun.

If she plans to breast-feed, a new mother should learn as much as possible about it before the baby is born. Obstetricians, pediatricians, childbirth instructors, nurses, and midwives can all offer information about nursing. But perhaps the best ongoing support for a nursing mother is someone who has successfully nursed a baby.

La Leche League, an international support organization for nursing mothers, has chapters in many cities that meet regularly to discuss breast-feeding problems and offer support.

Most La Leche League chapters allow women to come to a few meetings without charge. League leaders offer advice by phone as well. To find a convenient La Leche League chapter, call 1-800-LA-LECHE (1-800-525-3243) or contact the organization's world wide web site at http://www.lalecheleague.org.

Formula Choices

If the mother cannot or chooses not to breast-feed, normal, full-term infants should get a conventional cow's-milk-based formula, according to John N. Udall Jr., M.D., chief of nutrition and gastroenterology at Children's Hospital of New Orleans. However, adverse reactions to the protein in cow's milk formula or symptoms of lactose intolerance (lactose is the carbohydrate in cow's milk) may require switching to another type of formula, he says.

Symptoms that may indicate an adverse reaction to cow's milk protein include vomiting, diarrhea, abdominal pain, and rash. With lactose intolerance, the most common symptoms are excessive gas, abdominal distension and pain, and diarrhea. Since some of the symptoms overlap, a stool test may be necessary to determine the culprit. Usually, lactose intolerance will produce acidic stools that contain glucose. If the protein is the problem, stools will be nonacidic and have flecks of blood.

The main alternative to cow's milk formula is soy formula.

The carbohydrates in most soy formulas are sucrose and corn syrup, which are easily digested and absorbed by infants. However, soy is not as good a protein source as cow's milk. Also, babies don't absorb some minerals, such as calcium, as efficiently from soy formulas. Therefore, according to the American Academy of Pediatrics, "Healthy full-term infants should be given soy formula only when medically necessary."

For a child who can't tolerate cow's milk protein, William J. Klish, M.D., a Baylor College of Medicine pediatrician and former chairman of the American Academy of Pediatrics Committee on Nutrition recommends the use of hydrolyzed-protein formula. Although hydrolyzed-protein formulas are made from cow's milk, the protein has been broken up into its component parts. Essentially, it's been predigested, which decreases the likelihood of an allergic reaction.

Iron

The infant formulas currently available in the United States are either "iron-fortified" —with approximately 12 milligrams of iron per liter—or "low iron" —with approximately 2 milligrams of iron per liter.

"There should not be a low-iron formula on the market for the average child because a low-iron formula is a nutritionally deficient formula," says Klish. "It doesn't provide enough iron to maintain proper blood cell counts or proper hemoglobin." (Hemoglobin is a blood protein that carries oxygen from the lungs to the tissues, and carbon dioxide from the tissues to the lungs.)

In addition, studies have shown that school children who had good iron status as infants because they were fed iron-fortified formula performed better on standardized developmental tests than children with poor iron status. However, FDA has permitted marketing of low-iron formulas because some pediatricians prefer to use them.

Why is there low-iron formula on the market? "In the past there have been a lot of symptoms that have been attributed to iron, including abdominal discomfort, constipation, diarrhea, colic, and irritability," says Klish. "Also there was some concern about too much iron interfering with the immune system. All of those concerns and questions have been laid to rest with appropriate studies."

Another reason for originally producing low-iron formulas was that human milk contains low amounts of iron—less than a milligram per liter. However, it is now understood that an infant absorbs virtually 100 percent of the iron from human milk, but considerably less from infant formula.

Cooking Lessons

Both milk and soy formulas are available in powder, liquid concentrate, or ready-to-feed forms. The choice should depend on whatever the parents find convenient and can afford.

Whatever form is chosen, proper preparation and refrigeration are essential. Opened cans of ready-to-feed and liquid concentrate must be refrigerated and used within the time specified on the can. Once the powder is mixed with water, it should also be refrigerated if it is not used right away. The exact amount of water recommended on the label must be used. Under-diluted formula can cause problems for the infant's organs and digestive system. Over-diluted formula will not provide adequate nutrition, and the baby may fail to thrive and grow.

In the past, the American Academy of Pediatrics felt that municipal water supplies were safe enough without boiling the water before mixing with the formula. But because of the contamination of Milwaukee's water with the parasite *Cryptosporidium* in 1993, "the whole business of boiling water has come up again," says Klish. "The academy is now again recommending boiling water for infant formulas."

Klish advises heating the water until it reaches a rolling boil, continue to boil for one to two minutes, and then let it cool. "That should take care of all the bacteria and parasites that might be in the water," he explains.

The American Academy of Pediatrics does not have any recommendations about bottled water. Klish says bottled water is fine, but it still needs to be boiled. "There's no reason to think that bottled water is any safer than city water," he says.

Bottled water must meet specific FDA quality standards for contaminants. These are set in response to requirements that the Environmental Protection Agency has established for tap water.

A regulation published in the Nov. 13, 1995, *Federal Register* sets standard definitions for different types of bottled waters, helping resolve possible confusion about what different terms mean.

The regulation also requires accurate labeling of bottled waters marketed for infants. If a product is labeled "sterile," it must be processed to meet FDA's requirements for commercial sterility. Otherwise, the labeling must indicate that it is not sterile and should be used as directed by a physician or according to infant formula preparation instructions.

What about sterilizing the bottles and nipples? "Dishwashers tend to sterilize bottles and nipples fairly well," says Klish. They can also be sterilized by placing them in a pan of boiling water for five minutes.

Warming the formula before feeding isn't necessary for proper nutrition, but most infants prefer the formula at least at room temperature. The best way to warm a bottle of formula is by placing the bottle in a pot of water and heating the pot on the stove.

Don't Try This at Home

Homemade formulas should not be used. Homemade formulas based on cow's milk don't meet all of an infant's nutritional needs, and cow's milk protein that has not been cooked or processed is difficult for an infant to digest. In addition, the high protein and electrolyte (salt) content of cow's milk may put a strain on an infant's immature kidneys. Substituting evaporated milk for whole milk may make the homemade formula easier to digest because of the effect of processing on the protein, but the formula is still nutritionally inadequate and still may stress the kidneys.

Today's infant formula is a very controlled, high-tech product that can't be duplicated at home, says Udall.

—by Rebecca D. Williams and Isadora Stehlin

Rebecca D. Williams is a writer in Oak Ridge, Tenn. Isadora Stehlin is a member of FDA's public affairs staff.

Tips for Breast-Feeding Success

It's helpful for a woman who wants to breast-feed to learn as much about it as possible before delivery, while she is not exhausted from caring for an infant around-the-clock. The following tips can help foster successful nursing:

- Get an early start: Nursing should begin within an hour after delivery if possible, when the infant is awake and the sucking instinct is strong. Even though the mother won't be producing milk yet, her breasts contain colostrum, a thin fluid that contains antibodies to disease.

- Proper positioning: The baby's mouth should be wide open, with the nipple as far back into his or her mouth as possible. This minimizes soreness for the mother. A nurse, midwife, or other knowledgeable person can help her find a comfortable nursing position.

- Nurse on demand: Newborns need to nurse frequently, about every two hours, and not on any strict schedule. This will stimulate the mother's breasts to produce plenty of milk. Later, the baby can settle into a more predictable routine. But because breast milk is more easily digested than formula, breast-fed babies often eat more frequently than bottle-fed babies.

- No supplements: Nursing babies don't need sugar water or formula supplements. These may interfere with their appetite for nursing, and that can lead to a diminished milk supply. The more the baby nurses, the more milk the mother will produce.

- Delay artificial nipples: It's best to wait a week or two before introducing a pacifier, so that the baby doesn't get confused. Artificial nipples require a different sucking action than real ones. Sucking at a bottle could also confuse some babies in the early days. They, too, are learning how to breast-feed.

- Air dry: In the early postpartum period or until her nipples toughen, the mother should air dry them after each nursing to prevent them from cracking, which can lead to infection. If her nipples do crack, the mother can coat them with breast milk or other natural moisturizers to help them heal. Vitamin E oil and lanolin are commonly used, although some babies may have allergic reactions to them. Proper positioning at the breast can help prevent sore nipples. If the mother's very sore, the baby may not have the nipple far enough back in his or her mouth.

- Watch for infection: Symptoms of breast infection include fever and painful lumps and redness in the breast. These require immediate medical attention.

- Expect engorgement: A new mother usually produces lots of milk, making her breasts big, hard and painful for a few days. To relieve this engorgement, she should feed the baby frequently and on demand until her body adjusts and produces only what the baby needs. In the meantime, the mother can take over-the-counter pain relievers, apply warm, wet compresses to her breasts, and take warm baths to relieve the pain.

- Eat right, get rest: To produce plenty of good milk, the nursing mother needs a balanced diet that includes 500 extra calories a day and six to eight glasses of fluid. She should also rest as much as possible to prevent breast infections, which are aggravated by fatigue.

Medicines and Nursing Mothers

Most medications have not been tested in nursing women, so no one knows exactly how a given drug will affect a breast-fed child. Since very few problems have been reported, however, most over-the-counter and prescription drugs, taken in moderation and only when necessary, are considered safe.

Even mothers who must take daily medication for conditions such as epilepsy, diabetes, or high blood pressure can usually breast-feed. They should first check with the child's pediatrician, however. To minimize the baby's exposure, the mother can take the drug just after nursing or before the child sleeps. In the January 1994 issue of Pediatrics, the American Academy of Pediatrics included the following in a list of drugs that are usually compatible with breast-feeding:

- acetaminophen

- many antibiotics

- anti-epileptics (although one, Primidone, should be given with caution)

- most antihistamines

- alcohol in moderation (large amounts of alcohol can cause drowsiness, weakness, and abnormal weight gain in an infant)

- most antihypertensives

- aspirin (should be used with caution)

- caffeine (moderate amounts in drinks or food)

- codeine

- decongestants

- ibuprofen

- insulin

- quinine

- thyroid medications

Drugs That Are NOT Safe While Nursing

Some drugs can be taken by a nursing mother if she stops breast-feeding for a few days or weeks. She can pump her milk and discard it during this time to keep up her supply, while the baby drinks previously frozen milk or formula.

Radioactive drugs used for some diagnostic tests like Gallium-69, Iodine-125, Iodine-131, or Technetium-99m can be taken if the woman stops nursing temporarily.

Drugs that should never be taken while breast-feeding include:

- Bromocriptine (Parlodel): A drug for Parkinson's disease, it also decreases a woman's milk supply.

- Most Chemotherapy Drugs for Cancer: Since they kill cells in the mother's body, they may harm the baby as well.

- Ergotamine (for migraine headaches): Causes vomiting, diarrhea, convulsions in infants.

- Lithium (for manic-depressive illness): Excreted in human milk.

- Methotrexate (for arthritis): Can suppress the baby's immune system.

- Drugs of Abuse: Some drugs, such as cocaine and PCP, can intoxicate the baby. Others, such as amphetamines, heroin and marijuana, can cause a variety of symptoms, including irritability, poor sleeping patterns, tremors, and vomiting. Babies become addicted to these drugs.

- Tobacco Smoke: Nursing mothers should avoid smoking. Nicotine can cause vomiting, diarrhea and restlessness for the baby, as well as decreased milk production for the mother. Maternal smoking or passive smoke may increase the risk of sudden infant death syndrome and may increase respiratory and ear infections.

Whole Milk for First Birthday

The American Academy of Pediatrics recommends that babies be breast-fed for at least 12 months and thereafter for as long as mutually desired. The only acceptable alternative to breast milk is infant formula iron fortified and solid foods can be introduced gradually when the baby is 6 months old, but a baby should drink breast milk or formula, not regular cow's milk, for a full year.

"There aren't any rules about when to stop breast-feeding," says Ruth Lawrence, M.D., professor of pediatrics and obstetrics at the University of Rochester School of Medicine in Rochester, N.Y., and spokeswoman for the academy. "As long as the baby is eating age-appropriate solid foods, a mother may nurse a couple of years if she wishes. A baby needs breast milk for the first year of life, and then as long as desired after that." Formula, however, should not be continued after the first birthday. That's the time to introduce milk. For all babies the milk, however, should be whole milk. Low-fat and skim milk do not have enough fat and calories to supply the nutritional needs of a 1-year-old, explains John Udall, chief of nutrition and gastroenterology at Children's Hospital of New Orleans. At that age, "the child is growing so quickly, and the fat is so important for brain and central nervous system development," he says. "The recommendation that our daily intake of fat should compose less than 30 percent of our caloric intake does not apply to children under 2 years of age."

New on the market are special toddler formulas that claim to be better than milk. The formulas are good nutritionally, says Udall, but they're not necessary. "A well-balanced diet with milk and juices would be just as good in a healthy, normally active, normally growing child," says Udall.

William Klish, former chairman of the American Academy of Pediatrics Committee on Nutrition, says that if a child needs to take a vitamin supplement, the toddler formula, fortified with a full range of vitamins and minerals, including iron, can serve that purpose. In addition, the toddler formulas don't need refrigeration, making them a convenient choice for snacks away from home.

Chapter 10

Working and Breastfeeding

The Truth about Working and Breastfeeding

Here are some things that are true about breastfeeding and working:

- Breastfeeding can reduce the amount of sick time you have to take off because breastfed infants are more protected from infections than formula fed infants.

- Breastfeeding offers convenience. You don't have to buy, prepare, or warm infant formula when you breastfeed.

- Breastfeeding makes you feel special because you are giving your baby something only you can provide.

- Removing breastmilk by hand or with a breast pump (often called expressing or pumping) at work can be easy and painless.

- Many working mothers, like you, have successfully combined breastfeeding and bottle feeding.

- With a little practice, babies will accept a bottle close to the time when you return to work. It's not necessary to introduce a bottle in your baby's first two weeks.

- Child care providers will feed your baby breastmilk. Just ask.

The text in this chapter was produced by the National Healthy Mothers, Healthy Babies Coalition, 409 12th Street, SW, Washington, DC 20024-2118; (202) 863-2458. Reprinted with permission.

- Co-workers and bosses will be more supportive of breastfeeding if they know it is important to you.

- Breastfeeding takes commitment and some planning. Working moms say, "It's worth it."

Planning during Pregnancy

Deciding to Breastfeed Your Baby

Can you really do it? If you say "Yes" to at least one of these questions, then breastfeeding is for you—even if you will be returning to work soon after your baby is born.

- Do you want to feed your baby the best food and at low cost?

- Do you want to protect your baby against illnesses and allergies?

- Do you want to have a special feeling of closeness with your baby?

- Do you want to do something for your baby that no one else can do?

It Helps to Plan Ahead

Breastfeeding is a natural process, but you need to know how to do it. Contact a breastfeeding expert to learn about how breastfeeding works. The more comfortable you feel with breastfeeding, the easier it will be for you to continue breastfeeding when you return to work.

Before your baby is born, talk with your supervisor, personnel manager, or union steward about your employer's policy on family leave—with or without pay. It's easier to combine work and breastfeeding when your baby is at least six weeks old.

Some questions to ask your employer:

- Can you return to work on a part-time or flexible schedule, especially at the beginning? This may help you and your baby adjust.

- Can your baby come to work with you or come in for feedings?

- Is there a place where you can breastfeed your baby or express your milk?

- Ask for a quiet, private, clean place with a comfortable chair. If you plan to use an electric pump, look for a room with an electrical outlet. It helps if you can use a refrigerator on site. You can also store milk in a small cooler with ice packs.

- Is there good child care on-site or nearby? If so, could you go there to breastfeed your baby once or more during the work day?

Get tips from mothers who have continued to breastfeed after returning to work.

Talk to other pregnant women at your work site, and figure out ways to help each other combine work and breastfeeding.

Talk with your partner or family members about your plans to work and breastfeed. Dads and grandmothers can be very helpful to a working mother.

Doing these things makes it easier to continue breastfeeding when you return to work. If you didn't have a chance to do them when pregnant, it's still not too late. Call your employer from home or make a special trip to work to discuss your plans. Breastfeeding is a great experience that you and your baby won't want to miss.

After Delivery

Getting Started

Rest, relax and focus on getting breastfeeding off to a good start. Allow only a few visitors in the beginning so you can breastfeed your baby frequently. This will help develop and maintain a good milk supply.

Breastfeeding takes practice. It may feel awkward or uncomfortable at first. Seek help from a breastfeeding expert if you have questions or concerns.

Remember, the more you breastfeed, the more milk you make. The less you breastfeed, the less milk you make. Supplementing with infant formula may keep your body from making enough milk.

If you plan to use a bottle or cup, introduce it to your baby about two weeks before you go back to work. Then offer the bottle or cup every once in a while so the baby learns how to drink from it. If your baby will not take a bottle or cup from you, have someone else give it.

Choose a child care provider who is willing to support your plans for breastfeeding. The provider should know how to handle breastmilk safely and to feed your baby the way you have requested.

Keep track of the times your baby usually wants to breastfeed. You can try to express milk or breastfeed about those same times once you've gone back to work. This will keep your breasts feeling comfortable and less likely to leak.

Express your breastmilk every time the baby takes a bottle or cup feeding so you keep up your own supply.

Breastfeed in different places. This will help you feel more comfortable later when breastfeeding or expressing milk at work or at the child care site.

Getting Ready to Return to Work

You will need to decide how you want your baby fed while you are at work:

- Use your breaks for lunch or dinner and in between to go to the child care site to breastfeed; or

- Take breaks to express your breastmilk so your child care provider can feed it to your baby another day; or

- Have your child care provider give infant formula to your baby. You can still breastfeed your baby before and after child care, and on your days off.

Leave your baby with your child care provider for short periods before you return to work. This lets you, the child care provider and the baby get used to each other. Tell your provider your baby's usual feeding times so she can feed then.

Usually these initial feedings go more smoothly if your provider knows the baby's feeding times. She can offer a bottle before the baby is frantic with hunger. You may want to make a whole-day trial run a few days before you go back to work to see how things go.

Expressing Milk

If you want your baby to be fed breastmilk while you are working, start to collect your breastmilk about two weeks before you return to work. This gives you a chance to learn how to express milk, how long it will take, and how your body feels. It will also help you build up an extra supply of stored breastmilk. Try these tips:

- Express milk about 1 hour after you breastfeed in the morning or between feedings. Freeze the milk you express in hard plastic bottles with 2-4 ounces in each.

- Don't be frustrated if you don't get much milk at first. You will slowly build up your supply.

- Being relaxed will help you express more milk. It takes time to get into a routine.

- To help with milk expression, place a warm wash cloth on your breasts and massage them before you begin pumping.

Your health care provider or other breastfeeding expert, such as a nurse, nutritionist, lactation consultant or La Leche League leader can help you with questions about expressing milk and using pumps. Choose the method of expressing milk that best meets your needs:

- Hand-express your milk without using a pump. Some women express as much milk by hand as they can by using a pump. Hand expression costs nothing and needs no special equipment.

- Rent or buy an electric pump. This is the most efficient type of pump. You can pump each breast separately or both breasts at the same time. If you do both breasts at the same time, expressing takes about 10-15 minutes. You can share a pump with other mothers, but you must each have your own pumping kit.

- Buy a mini-electric, battery-operated or manual pump. These are less expensive and more portable, but not as efficient. Most of them will pump only one breast at a time, taking about 30 minutes to pump both sides.

Returning to Work

When you return to work, if possible, keep a light schedule or work shorter hours. Consider returning to work mid-week or late in the week. This will make you less tired and less worried about being away from your baby as you adjust to your new routine.

Organize lunches, diaper bag and clothes the night before so your morning is less hectic.

Get up a little early so you can breastfeed the baby (even if you are both half asleep). Then the baby will he happy while you get yourself ready for the day.

Wear two-piece outfits or clothes that button in the front to make expressing milk or breastfeeding easier.

Express your breastmilk at least twice a day, once in the morning and once in the afternoon. When your baby starts eating solid foods, you may not need to express milk as often.

Any private space where you feel comfortable can be used for collecting milk. Wash your hands before beginning to express milk.

Look at pictures of your baby to make it easier for you to express milk.

Keep breastmilk cool in a refrigerator or cooler with ice packs. Store it in small amounts, 2 to 4 ounces, for a young baby. Label each bottle with the baby's name and the date. Then your child care provider knows who the milk is for and how fresh it is.

Use refrigerated breastmilk within 2 days. Use frozen milk (from a freezer with a separate door from the refrigerator) within 3 months. Use thawed frozen milk within 24 hours. Use oldest milk first. To thaw milk, place frozen container in a pan of warm water. Never use a microwave to thaw or warm milk.

Table 10.1. Guidelines for Storing Breastmilk

Refrigerated 40º F or below	Use Within 2 days
Frozen (freezer with a separate door from the refrigerator) 0º F or below	Use Within 3 Months
Thawed (from frozen) and refrigerated 40º F or below	Use Within 24 hours

Express milk more often if your breasts leak. You can also use nursing pads inside your bra and press gently against your nipples to stop the leak. Keep a sweater or a jacket at work in case you need to cover leak marks.

Breastfeed when you pick up your baby from child care or when you get home. Relaxing together for the first 30 minutes can refresh you and give you some quiet time with your baby.

Breastfeed whenever you're with the baby to keep up your milk supply—mornings, evenings, and days off. You don't need to use bottles or infant formula when you're with your baby.

Give employers feedback on how it is going. Let them know how happy you are with their support. Encourage them to keep helping you. Tell them how healthy your baby has been.

Other Tips

Expect many areas in your life to change now that you have a new baby. Learning to breastfeed and returning to work are just some of those changes. Once you set up a routine, it's easier. Don't be too hard on yourself. Give yourself and your family time to settle in to your new life.

All new mothers are tired. Give yourself time to rest or take a nap when you get home. Ask other family members or friends to help make meals, clean house, or do laundry. Focus on the things that really need to get done. You and your baby are most important—let other people take care of you.

Have the dad or grandmother cuddle and comfort the baby while you do other things.

No matter how successful you are at breastfeeding and in your job, there will still be times when you need someone to talk to. Find people at work and in the community who understand and support what you are doing.

Remember that a working mother on the go still needs to eat three meals plus snacks each day. Choose healthful foods that are quick and easy. Try cooking foods in larger quantities on your days off. Store these foods in smaller portions that can be used during the week.

If you have questions about breastfeeding, call your health care provider, WIC agency, lactation consultant, or La Leche League (1-800-LA-LECHE). Check your library or bookstore for other resources.

To help gain the support of your employer, you can get a free copy of *What Gives These Businesses a Competitive Edge?—Worksite Support for Breastfeeding Employees* by writing to:

National Healthy Mothers, Healthy Babies Coalition
409 12th Street, SW
Washington, DC 20024-2188
(202) 863-2458

Chapter 11

Introduction to Solid Foods

The introduction of solid foods usually occurs between 3-5 months of age. Check with your baby's pediatrician for his recommendation on when to introduce solid foods to your baby's diet. Starting solids too early may cause allergies or an overweight baby. The following tips can be used when starting solid foods.

General Guide

- Introduce one new food at a time. Give for 3-4 days before introducing another one.
- In the beginning, use jars of one kind of fruit or vegetable rather than mixed fruits/vegetables.

Cereals (3-5 months)

- Use the dry form of cereal from the box rather than from the jar.
- Use single cereals rather than mixed cereals.
- Begin using rice cereal (rather than barley, oatmeal, or corn cereals). Start by using two teaspoonfuls twice a day and slowly increase the quantity up to a maximum of 12 teaspoonfuls.
- Feed cereal only from a spoon. Never mix cereal in baby's bottle.

Children's Hospital Medical Center (Cincinnati), Patient Education Program, July 1987, revised February 1996. Used with permission of Children's Hospital Medical Center—Cincinnati.

Vegetables (4-6 months)—Introduce Before Fruits

- Feed vegetables only from a spoon. Never mix vegetables in baby's bottle. Use of an infant "feeder" is not recommended because baby won't develop proper feeding skills.

- Introduce vegetables about 2-3 weeks after starting cereals.

- Introduce only one vegetable at a time (again using single vegetable servings before mixed vegetables).

- Suggested vegetables to begin with are squash, sweet potato, green beans, or carrots.

Fruits (4-6 months)

- Feed fruits only from a spoon. Never mix fruits in baby's bottle. Use of an infant "feeder" is not recommended because baby won't develop proper feeding skills.

- About 2-3 weeks after your baby has started vegetables—a single fruit may be added. Start with pears, applesauce, bananas, or peaches.

Meats (5 months and over)

- Meats may be added 2-3 weeks after fruits.

- A meat and vegetable mix may be used instead of a single vegetable.

- Begin with chicken or turkey and vegetable, then add other kinds.

- Do not use dinners. They contain very little meat and much starch.

Egg Yolks (6 months and over)

- Egg yolks are only introduced after 6 months of age. The white of the egg is more apt to cause an allergic reaction, so do not start it until after your child's first birthday.

Table Foods (8-12 months)

- Table foods have no nutritional advantage over baby foods.

- Table foods should be given while the child is sitting at the table with the family.

- If table food is started too early, the child may not be able to chew it well and might choke.

- Offer soft bland foods at first. Good choices are mashed potatoes, noodles, rice, soft vegetables.

- Cut or mash foods into bite sized pieces appropriate for child's age.

- Things to avoid because of choking risk:
  - peanuts or nuts
  - popcorn
  - whole grapes
  - hot dogs

Chapter 12

Labeling Rules for Young Children's Food

How much fat should we eat to stay healthy? For adults, the answer is clear: The *Dietary Guidelines for Americans* tell us to restrict fat to no more than 30 percent of our total calorie intake.

But for infants and toddlers, the answer is less straightforward; the *Dietary Guidelines* don't apply to children under 2. In fact, health experts advise against restricting fat in young children's diets because they need the calories and nutrients fat provides to grow and develop properly.

For this reason, FDA and the U.S. Department of Agriculture's Food Safety and Inspection Service have established special rules to govern the labeling of foods for children under 4. (USDA regulates labeling of meat and poultry products. FDA oversees labeling of all other foods.)

Just as for other foods, the regulations require labels for foods for young children to include information about nutrients important to health—for example, fat, sodium, carbohydrate, protein, vitamins, and minerals. This is to help parents choose foods that contain the appropriate kinds and amounts of nutrients their children need.

But the new regulations forbid labels for foods for children under 2 to carry certain nutrition information because the presence of the information may lead parents to wrongly assume that certain nutrients should be restricted in young children's diets, when, in fact, they should not.

Reprinted from *FDA Consumer Magazine*, March 1995 with revisions made in May 1995, Publication No. (FDA) 95-2292.

In addition, the labels for foods for children under 4 cannot show how the amounts of some nutrients correspond to Daily Values—recommended daily intakes. The reason is because Daily Values for some nutrients, such as fat, fiber and sodium, have not been established for children under 4. This is because current dietary recommendations do not specify appropriate levels for young children. FDA has set Daily Values only for vitamins, minerals and protein for this age group because the National Academy of Sciences has established appropriate levels of these nutrients for this age group in the Recommended Dietary Allowances. FDA incorporated those recommendations in the Daily Values.

Up-to-Date Label

These labeling requirements stem from the Nutrition Labeling and Education Act of 1990, which, among other things, requires labels of most foods—including those for children under 4—to carry nutrition information.

The children's nutrition labeling rules apply to most foods whose labels suggest that the food is intended for infants and toddlers. This includes infant cereals, infant strained meats, vegetables and fruits, "junior" foods, teething biscuits, and infant and "junior" juices. The regulations do not apply to infant formula, which has special nutrition labeling requirements.

Many foods for infants and toddlers have carried some nutrition information since at least the 1970s, when voluntary nutrition labeling went into effect. But now, for many such foods, the information is required and more pertinent to today's health concerns.

Importance of Fat

Concerns about excessive fat and cholesterol intake for most of the population don't apply to children under 2, however. Fat is one of six nutrient categories essential for proper growth and development. (The others are protein, carbohydrate, water, vitamins, and minerals.) At no other age does fat play such an important role as in infancy and early childhood, a period of rapid growth and development. Dietary fat serves as:

- a source of energy (infants and toddlers have the highest energy needs per kilogram of weight of any age group)

- a carrier for the fat-soluble vitamins A, D, E, and K and as an aid in their absorption in the intestine

- the only source of linoleic acid, an essential fatty acid.

Fat also gives taste, consistency, stability, and palatability to foods and converts to body fat, which is necessary to hold organs in place, absorb shock, and insulate the body from temperature changes.

Some parents fail to realize fat's importance for young children. According to a Gerber Products Co.'s telephone survey of 1,076 adults, nearly one in five respondents said they reduce the amount of fat in their baby's diet.

Yet, according to Virginia Wilkening, a registered dietitian and consumer safety officer in FDA's Office of Food Labeling, case reports have shown that limiting fat intakes in very young children can cause them to "fail to thrive."

"Babies need fat and cholesterol in their diets for proper growth and development," Wilkening said. "Parents should be aware of this and avoid reducing fat in their young children's diets."

Restrictions

For foods for children under 2, the amount of saturated fat, poly-unsaturated fat, monounsaturated fat, cholesterol, calories from fat, and calories from saturated fat in the food cannot be listed on the label.

Labels of foods for children under 2 also cannot carry most of the claims about a food's nutritional content—such as "low-fat" and "low-cholesterol" —that labels of other foods can. And, they cannot carry the eight FDA-approved health claims about the relationship between a nutrient or food and a health problem—for example, dietary fat and cancer—that other labels can.

Allowed Facts

What information is allowed? The following is a list of dietary components about which information is allowed on the Nutrition Facts panel on the labels of foods for children under 2. Information usually appears on the side or back of the package and is mandatory for underlined components.

- total calories
- total fat
- sodium
- potassium

- total carbohydrate
- dietary fiber
- soluble fiber
- insoluble fiber
- sugars
- sugar alcohol
- protein
- vitamin A
- vitamin C
- calcium
- iron
- other essential vitamins and minerals. (Information about them is mandatory only when they are added to enrich or fortify a food, or when a claim is made about them on the label.)

Labels for foods for children 2 to 4 also must give the amount of cholesterol and saturated fat per serving. They can voluntarily provide the calories from fat and calories from saturated fat, and the amount of polyunsaturated and monounsaturated fat per serving.

The %Daily Values for protein and vitamins and minerals present in significant amounts must be listed. This helps parents see how a serving of food fits into their child's total daily diet. The amount of other nutrients is given in grams or milligrams.

Serving Size

The serving size, under "Nutrition Facts," is the basis on which manufacturers declare the nutrient amounts and %Daily Values on the label. It is the amount of food customarily eaten at one time—not necessarily the amount recommended by dietary guidelines.

The serving size is based on FDA- and USDA-established lists of "Reference Amounts Customarily Consumed Per Eating Occasion." FDA has established 11 groups of foods specially intended for children under 4. USDA has four such groups.

The serving size must be stated in both common household units and metric measures—for example, for dry instant cereal, "¼ cup (15 g)."

These standardized serving sizes make it easier to compare the nutritional quality of similar foods.

Nutrient and Health Claims

FDA and USDA's regulations also extend to label claims.

Among the few allowed in children's nutrition labeling are claims that describe the percentage of vitamins or minerals in the food as they apply to the Daily Values for children under 2—for example, "provides 50 percent of the Daily Value for vitamin C." This type of claim also is allowed in the labeling of dietary supplements for children under 2.

Also allowed for foods for children under 2 are the claims "unsweetened" and "unsalted." FDA believes that for foods for this age group, these claims refer to taste and not nutrition.

Two claims— "no sugar added" and "sugar free" —are approved only for use on dietary supplements for children under 2 because they often contain added sugar.

If presented with sound evidence, however, FDA will consider allowing other nutrient content claims, as well as health claims, in the labeling of foods for children under 2.

These and other rules are intended to help consumers select the best foods for children. The absence of some information allowed in labeling for other foods can help them do that.

—by Paula Kurtzweil

Paula Kurtzweil is a member of FDA's public affairs staff.

Chapter 13

Keep Your Infant's Food Safe

Bacteria and other germs can make foods unsafe. You cannot see or smell germs. If they contaminate food, this can cause a foodborne illness.

Your infant has a greater risk for a foodborne illness than you do. This is because your infant is smaller, with an immune system that is still developing.

You can help prevent your infant from getting a foodborne illness by handling foods safely.

You can keep your infant's food safe by following certain rules when buying, storing and preparing foods. This chapter will tell you how to:

- Buy safe foods for your infant
- Keep your infant's foods safe at home
- Prepare your infant's foods safely
- Keep and prepare leftovers safely

Buying Your Infant's Foods

Be aware of certain foods that should not be fed to your infant.

This text is from document number FCS-8543, Department of Family, Youth and Community Sciences, Institute of Food and Agricultural Sciences, P.O. Box 110365, University of Florida, Gainesville, Florida 32611-0310. The National Food Safety Database can be found online at www.foodsafety.org.

Harmful germs that can make your infant sick can get into foods through cracks and openings in food packages. So, only buy baby foods in undamaged packages. Do not buy cans that have dents or bulges, packages that are torn or damaged, or glass jars that are cracked or have loose lids.

Baby food jars have a safety button on the lid. Check each jar to be sure the button is down. Do not buy or use jars if the safety button is popped up.

While you shop, keep raw meat packages away from other foods. Raw meats and other their juices contain germs that can make your baby sick. Put raw meats in plastic bags at the store so that juices do not touch vegetables and fruits. Check that the person who bags your food at the checkout counter keeps the meats away from vegetables and fruits.

Infant formula and infant foods have dates printed on the cans or jars. These expiration dates tell how long the foods are still safe. It is important to check the dates on the jars at the store, and at home, to make sure they are still safe. Do not use any food or formula after the expiration date has passed.

How to Safely Store Your Infant's Food

- Store unopened formula and infant foods in a dry, cool area.

- Do not store your infant's food next to any appliance that heats up.

- Check the expiration dates and safety buttons before feeding.

- Perishable foods should never be kept at room temperature for more than 2 hours.

- Finger foods for your infant should be stored properly.

- If you have any doubts about food or formula...THROW IT OUT!

Be Clean...Be Safe

Make sure that you and your kitchen are clean before you prepare any baby food. Always wash your hands with soap and warm water. Also, use hot water and soap to wash any utensils used to prepare food.

- Avoid spreading germs in your kitchen. Plastic cutting boards are easier to clean than wooden boards.

- Remove germs by cleaning counters, cutting boards and sinks before and after your prepare food. Use clean sponges and hot soapy water.

- Also, wash the tops of cans and the can opener you will use before preparing infant foods and formula.

Preparing Infant Formula

- Let chlorinated tap water run for 2 minutes before using.
- Bring non-tap water to a rolling boil, or use bottled water.
- Fill bottle with just enough formula for one feeding.
- Never leave prepared formula out of the refrigerator for more than 2 hours.
- Throw out any formula left in the bottle after feeding.
- Always wash bottles with hot, soapy water after each use.

Preparing Baby Foods

Solid food should be given to babies after they are 4 to 6 months old. Before this age, breast milk or formula is the only food your infant needs.

Do not serve infant food directly from a jar. Put a small amount in a dish and feed from the dish. The food left in the jar should be labeled with the date it was opened, stored in the refrigerator and used within 2 days.

Do not feed your infant raw or undercooked meats. Cook table foods until they are steaming hot (165°F)—this will kill germs. Be sure to cool the food before feeding it to your child.

You can grind table foods to make them soft for your infant to chew. However, do not chew your infant's food to soften it. Your mouth could have germs that might make your infant sick.

Handling Leftovers

Infant formula should be labeled and kept covered in the refrigerator after it is mixed. Unused opened formula should be thrown out after 2 days. Breast milk can be stored in the refrigerator for 5 days or frozen for 2-3 months.

Leftover infant food should be labeled with the date it was opened or prepared, then stored in the refrigerator. If it is still unused after 2 days, THROW IT OUT!

Partially eaten foods always should be thrown away. Do not return them to the refrigerator—they contain germs.

Hazardous Foods

Some foods are more likely to cause your infant to get sick if improperly handled. Raw honey should never be fed to your infant.

Other foods like meats, poultry and seafood need to be cooked thoroughly before feeding them to your infant. Meats and poultry should not be pink inside. Fish should be flaky.

Keep Your Infant's Food Safe

It is difficult to tell if your infant's food is unsafe because it may look and smell the same as other foods. So, be safe when shopping and preparing foods.

If you think food might be unsafe, do not taste it. THROW IT AWAY. It is better to be safe than sorry.

If you have any questions about infant food safety: 1.Call your local county extension office. 2.Contact your local WIC office. 3.Contact your infant's physician. 4.Write to the Food & Drug Administration. 5.Call the USDA hotline at 1-800-535-4555.

— by Mark L. Tamplin, Ph.D., Brenda Somes, and Carrie West

Mark L. Tamplin, Ph.D., Associate Professor and Food Safety Specialist, Department of Family, Youth and Community Sciences; Brenda Somes, Art and Publications Specialist, Department of Family, Youth and Community Sciences; Carrie West, Graduate Student, Department of Food Science and Human Nutrition; Institute of Food and Agricultural Sciences, P.O. Box 110365, University of Florida, Gainesville, Florida 32611-0310.

Chapter 14

Vegetarian Nutrition for Children

Introduction

Childhood nutrition has a significant influence on health and development throughout life. As children grow, their nutritional needs are much greater than those of adults and the consequences of a poor diet will be long lasting. A good diet will protect against everyday illness and ensure the development of strong bones and teeth, firm muscles and healthy tissues.

Choosing to bring up your child as a vegetarian is a positive step towards a healthy and morally sound diet for your child. Nutritional research has shown that a vegetarian diet can provide all the nutrients necessary for a child's growth and development. Well-informed dietitians, doctors and other health professionals now accept that vegetarianism is a healthy option for infants and children of all ages.

The Pre-School Child (Age 1-5)

The pre-school child, whether vegetarian or not, is almost totally dependent on others for its food. The eating habits of parents and other carers will be the ones that the child imitates and acquires. Some pre-school children are naturally sensitive to the use of animals for food and occasionally refuse all meats even if their parents aren't vegetarian.

Text from the Vegetarian Society, Parkdale, Dunham Rd., Altrincham, Chesire WA14 4QG, UK; reprinted with permission. Website at www.vegsoc.org.

Whether vegetarian or not, it is vital that children have a well balanced diet. This is particularly important during the pre-school years, as this is a time of rapid growth and development. The nutrients to particularly watch are calcium, iron, zinc, protein, vitamin B_{12} and vitamin D.

Children should be offered a variety of foods which they can enjoy and should not be forced to eat anything if they are determined to resist. Food and eating should not be allowed to become an issue as children can be very fussy at this age.

Good eating habits should begin now, as likes and dislikes will be influenced by what is offered in these early years. High fiber, low fat diets, recommended for adults, are not suitable for children of this age, as explained below. The emphasis should be on family eating habits that are healthy and sensible. Foods containing a lot of sugar and salt should be avoided.

As they are growing very rapidly, young children need a lot of dietary energy (calories) relative to their small size. A diet that is too high in fiber or very low in fat will not provide sufficient concentrated energy or nutrients. Frequent meals containing food of relatively high nutrient and energy density are important, although young children often have marked fluctuations in appetite.

Nutritious snacks between meals will help ensure that enough food is eaten. Try and avoid shop-bought sweets, biscuits and cakes, sweetened fizzy drinks, and salty snacks such as crisps. Offer sandwiches, fruit, scone or malt bread, and home-made cake or biscuit instead. Sweets given occasionally as a special treat will not do any harm.

Unless your child is prone to being overweight you can try to increase the energy density of foods. Vegetable oil can be added to foods like mashed lentils or beans. Include nut and seed purées such as tahini and smooth peanut butter, cheese, yogurt, soy products, such as tofu and veggie-burgers, and if liked, avocado. Try to include as wide a variety of foods as possible, bearing in mind that children may be fussy or find some foods too strong in taste. Consumption of fresh, frozen, or juiced fruit and vegetables should be encouraged.

Assessment of a child's growth should be made over a period of time, as growth at this age is often very uneven and interspersed with sudden increases in height and weight.

Sugar and Teeth

Children naturally like the taste of sugar and sweet foods. Though sugary foods do provide calories, they have little else of nutritional value and are a major cause of tooth decay. Whilst it may not be practical to ban sugar altogether, it should be limited. It is better to discourage the development of a sweet tooth now. A small amount of sugar with otherwise healthy desserts such as yogurt, soy puddings, and rice pudding is fine and better than using artificial additives for sweetness.

Milk

Children under two should not be given semi-skimmed milk and children under five should not be given skimmed milk because it lacks the fat soluble vitamins A and D. Young children also need the energy from fat. Soy milks should be fortified with calcium, vitamin B_{12} and vitamin D if used as an alternative to cow's milk for young children.

Salt

Salt should be avoided in the diet of young children as their kidneys are not mature enough to cope with large amounts. Many common foods such as cheese, manufactured soup, packet meals, and bread are quite high in added salt. Avoid too many salty snacks, such as crisps and other snack foods. Spread yeast extract thinly or use the low salt varieties.

Nuts

Whole nuts and seeds must be avoided until the age of five as young children can easily choke on them. Ground or puréed nuts and seeds are fine and nutritious, for example smooth peanut butter, tahini (sesame seed paste) or ground almonds.

Part Three

Well-Baby Care

Chapter 15

Choosing the Right Pediatrician

Expectant parents are often overwhelmed with decisions: What to name the baby, which crib to purchase, whether to breast or bottle feed and how much visiting from the grandparents will be just enough. Often the very important decision of who will care for the baby's medical health is left to the last minute and maybe even left to the obstetrician to choose. This choice will have a huge impact on the birth experience and should be made with an eye towards establishing a long-term relationship. The pediatrician should be a vital part of your new family's life, not only as the guardian of your child's health but also as a guide and a resource as you inevitably muddle your way through the process of becoming a family.

There are several guideposts to keep in mind as you make this conscious choice.

But first and foremost, of course, is to make sure your child will receive the highest quality care.

Is your prospective doctor well trained?

- Generally, board certification in pediatrics is good assurance, but if the doctor is not fresh out of school you might want to ask what recertification or updating criteria does s/he use to stay current. (The Physician's Recognition Award renewed every few years by the AMA for physicians who complete a minimum

---

number of hours of current education and evaluation is one way to make this judgment.)

- Another way to check out your doctor is to contact the local medical society and ask for the public record of complaints or citations for the physician in question. Although this may not be an accurate indication of quality of care, if there are many complaints it would cast some doubt on your choice.

- Another measure of quality of care is the hospital affiliations of the doctor and what, if any, teaching positions s/he holds. Generally, teaching hospitals only permit the very best practitioners to participate in student and resident education. Where there are no local teaching hospitals, doctors who participate in local health concerns and regional medical boards are usually those who are keeping most abreast of the progress in the field.

Recipients of teaching commendations or community service awards are often the most committed to excellence in care.

Is your prospective doctor available and affable—is s/he easy to reach and easy to deal with?

- What are the doctor's usual hours and what is the procedure for getting help after hours?

- Are there other doctors involved in the "on-call" system for the doctor's office and if so how available are they?

- Do you have access to your doctor for questions of non-urgent matters and if not, what is the training of the person who is designated to answer these questions? Often a busy pediatrician will train a nurse practitioner or medical assistant to answer the common, non-urgent day to day questions about infant care and as long as there is close communication between these professionals this is usually very satisfactory.

- If you specifically need to speak with your pediatrician can s/he be reached even if only later in the day; and if your questions are more pressing how soon will your doctor call you back?

- Is the pediatrician relaxed in her answers or do you feel that your questions are not really welcome? Can you see yourself asking a "silly" question or does the style of the doctor intimidate you?

- Do you sense that the doctor sincerely likes children and enjoys the work of caring for children? Would you feel safe letting this doctor hold your baby?

What are the office rules for emergencies?

- Where would you be expected to take your child in an emergency and is the doctor able to attend to your child at that facility?

- Is the office equipped to handle common pediatric emergencies and can the office arrange easily for expert outside consultations?

- Does the office have a laboratory and if so which tests can be run there? At a minimum any pediatrician should to be able to do routine urine analysis, urine and throat cultures and check blood for anemia and glucose.

How are messages taken and is the staff friendly and inviting?

- Does the office feel safe and clean, a place you would let your child crawl around in assuming, of course, no one nearby was sick?

- Is there a method for separating very sick children from well visitors?

- Is there a triage system for very sick children to get priority and does the staff make an effort to contact well visitors about possible lengthy waits when sick children overrun the schedule as often happens in the winter time and just after school starts in the Fall?

- What is the usual wait time when there are no emergencies?

- Are there weekend and evening appointments for well care or only for sick visits? (If you are a working family this can be a very important consideration.)

Is the office a good source of information and networking?

- Is this pediatrician interested in developmental pediatrics and can you rely on this doctor to help guide you through the times your child may need assistance that is not limited to prescription writing and medical instructions?

- Is the pediatrician a child advocate with vocal opinions about children and drug use, violence, media influences, etc and if so do his opinions match your own beliefs or are they radically different in ways that might make communication difficult?

Try to make an appointment to meet the pediatrician—or if the office policy does not allow for that—at least make a visit to the office that includes 15-30 minutes in the waiting room. You can learn a lot about a practice this way including how other parents feel about the doctor. You will get a first hand view of how the staff handles children, (who may be irritable), parents, (who may be equally irritable), and you may even see the pediatrician if s/he routinely accompanies a child either to or from the examination—sometimes a picture is worth a thousand questions and answers. Don't assume that the doctor is mean or uncaring if some children refuse to leave the toys in the waiting room to be examined or emerge from the examination crying. Pediatrics is tricky business, as is parenting, and much of what happens in the doctor's office is a lot less than pleasant from the receiver's viewpoint—you might recall your own childhood vaccinations and understand things haven't changed much when it comes to needles! The key to recovery for children is in how the parents manage the visit and is determined by the general mood of the office—the staff's sympathetic manner, and the presence of rewards such as stickers and "high-fives" from the nursing professionals. Put yourself behind your child's eyes and ears and evaluate the environment for kid friendliness—are the toys "fun" and are there enough trucks and blocks to go around?

Picking a pediatrician can be an intense and challenging task but it can also be an educational and enlightening one. Often parents, after visiting in my office, tell me how much more excited they are about the upcoming birth, now that they have seen the "in-living color" version of being a parent; and nowhere is being a parent more deeply felt than when bringing your precious child to the doctor's office. Evaluate carefully but also look to enjoy the experience. Instincts do count in choosing a pediatrician, and if possible both parents should feel equally as comfortable with the choice since this is a very long-term relationship. You are creating a long-term partnership with all members aimed at one goal—the healthy and happy development of your new family.

Chapter 16

Baby's First Year

This text provides basic information about your baby's first year. It is not intended as a comprehensive manual on safety or heath issues, nor is it a substitute for pediatric care from a qualified health-care provider.

During the First Weeks

Drink

- Breast milk (or formula) is the only food your baby needs until 6 months. Health-care providers recommend breast milk over formula.

- If you breastfeed, it's especially important that you not smoke, drink alcohol, or use other drugs. Ask your baby's healthcare provider about any medications you take.

- If you decide to use formula, ask your baby's health-care provider what kind to buy. Follow label directions exactly.

- Do not give your baby cow's milk until your baby is 1 year old.

Sleep

Most newborns should sleep on their backs. Ask the health-care provider how to position your baby.

From *Baby's First Year: A Calendar of Tips for Parents*, Kosair Children's Hospital, ©1993 Channing L. Bete Co., Inc. 1998 edition; reprinted with permission.

Cry

- Babies cry because they're hungry, hot, cold, or uncomfortable in other ways. In time, you'll understand your baby's cries.

- Responding promptly helps your baby feel loved and secure—it won't "spoil" him or her.

Keep Your Baby Healthy and Safe

Right from the Start

- Schedule regular checkups and immunizations Your child may be given a hepatitis B vaccine between birth and 2 months.

- Use an approved rear-facing infant car carrier (or convertible infant/toddler car seat) every time you drive. Buckle it in the center of the back seat, never in a seat with an air bag in front of it. (If your vehicle has no back seat or you are absolutely unable to avoid transporting child in the front seat, see a dealer or mechanic about an air bag on/off switch.) IMPORTANT: Not all seatbelts are compatible with all safety seats. Check your automobile owner's manual. It will tell you if modifications are needed to ensure safe operation.

- Support baby's head and neck when lifting and carrying baby.

- Never shake baby—it can cause brain damage.

- Keep objects smaller than 1½ inches across away from baby, to prevent choking.

- Don't leave baby alone in a room with pets or small children.

- Never leave baby in a bath or on a changing table or counter top—even for a second.

- Don't drink hot liquids while holding baby.

- Don't smoke around baby.

- Never prop baby up with a bottle—or put baby to bed with one.

As Your Baby Becomes More Active

- Call the health department if cracked or peeling paint is in your home. Ask for information about having your home tested for lead paint.

- Replace any plastic miniblinds made outside the United States with a type that is lead-free.

- Remove toys hung across a crib or playpen when baby starts to push self up with arms.

- Supervise baby closely near a bath, toilet, wading pool, bucket or other things containing water.

- Remove hazards (breakables, heavy or sharp objects, etc.) within 3 feet of the floor.

- Cover unused outlets with tape or safety caps. Put cords out of reach.

- Put gates at the top and bottom of stairs, to prevent falls.

- Remove the bumper and stuffed animals from the crib when baby starts to pull up with hands.

- Store medicine, alcohol, cleansers, etc., out of baby's reach. Lock them up.

Weeks 1-5

Your newborn is precious—and unique. Each baby develops at his or her own rate. If your baby's timetable is different than the one described here, talk with your health-care provider. Everything's probably just fine.

Physical Development

- Is alert only a few minutes at a time.

- Can best see things 8-12 inches away (such as parent's face at feeding time).

- May feed every 1-4 hours in the first 2 weeks.

- Will lose stump of umbilical cord in 2-3 weeks.

- Has blackish-green bowel movements the first 4-5 days. Later, a breastfed baby's stools resemble yellow applesauce; a bottle-fed baby's range from yellow to black, and are firmer. (Baby may not have a bowel movement every day. But if you're worried, ask baby's health-care provider.)

Mental and Social Development

- Knows Mom's voice.

- Enjoys watching faces.
- Likes black-and-white patterns.
- Needs to be cuddled.

Tips for Weeks 1-5

- Limit visitors. You need to rest.
- Try to nap when baby naps.
- Feeling overwhelmed? So is every other new parent.
- List all the things you "have" to do. Then, cross off a few! Baby needs you most.
- Change diapers often—when wet or soiled, and before or after feedings.

Weeks 6-9

Physical Development

- Waves arms and kicks legs to exercise.
- Has more predictable feeding and sleeping times.
- May lift head slightly when lying on belly.

Mental and Social Development

- Can gurgle and coo.
- May begin to enjoy baths.
- Turns face away when there's too much activity or talking.
- Smiles back when you smile.

Immunizations

Immunizations that may be given at 2 months:

- DTaP or DTP (diphtheria, tetanus and pertussis)
- Hib (*Haemophilus influenzae* type b)
- Polio
- Hep B (hepatitis B), at 1-4 months

Tips for Weeks 6-9

- Tobacco smoke in the air can make baby sick. Keep your home smoke-free.
- When you do chores let baby watch you from an infant seat on the floor.
- Attach an unbreakable mirror to the changing table or playpen for baby to enjoy.
- A walk outdoors or a car ride soothes some crying babies.

Weeks 10-14

Physical Development

- Stays awake for longer stretches.
- Studies his or her hands and fingers, and brings hands together.
- May hold head upright when lying on belly.

Mental and Social Development

- Likes to laugh.
- Shows signs of having a memory—recognizes different family members, for example.
- Likes batting at objects hung from a mobile or toy bar.
- "Talks" to toys.
- Will carry on a "conversation" with you, if you repeat baby's sounds.
- Cries much less often!

Tips for Weeks 10-14

- Ask a friend to stay with baby while you take a break.
- Read a book to baby. Point to the pictures as you read.
- Talk to baby as you do things: "Now Mommy (or Daddy) will wash the dishes."
- Baby will need a crib soon. Make sure the slats are no more than 2 3/8 inches apart.
- Let baby feel the textures of different fabrics.

Weeks 15-18

Physical Development

- Probably takes 2 or 3 naps a day.
- Holds head steady when pulled upright.
- Is losing the hair he or she had at birth; new hair is coming in.
- Can push self up with arms.
- Can roll to one side.
- Reaches for objects.
- May sleep through the night! (By 6 months most babies do.)

Mental and Social Development

- Pays attention to small objects squeals in delight.
- Likes to shake rattles.
- Investigates objects by putting them in his or her mouth. (Try to keep these objects clean.)

Immunizations

Immunizations that may be given at 4 months:

- DTaP or DTP
- Hib
- Polio

Tips for Weeks 15-18

- Prop baby into a sitting position in the carriage or stroller.
- If you wake and feed baby before you go to bed, baby may skip that 2 am snack.
- Offer baby just a few toys at a time to avoid overwhelming him or her.
- While you bathe or dress baby, name the parts of his or her body.

Weeks 19-23

Physical Development

- Baby rolls over easily.

- Can bear weight on legs if someone "stands" baby up.

- Wakes earlier in the morning.

- May suck on toes.

Mental and Social Development

- Looks for a dropped object.

- Puts vowel and consonant sounds together "ah-goo," for example.

- Discovers his or her genitals.

- Imitates sounds and movements.

- Enjoys rhythm.

- Likes it when you play peek-a-boo (but can't yet "peek" back).

Tips for Weeks 19-23

- Baby is more demanding now and that requires more patience.

- Get down on the floor and see your home from baby's point of view.

- Lower crib mattress to bottom position to keep baby safely inside.

- Arrange to have time for yourself.

- Sing to your baby. Read nursery rhymes.

Weeks 24-27

Physical Development

- Is probably ready for "solid" foods (rice cereal is usually the first—ask baby's health-care provider for advice).

- Can briefly sit without support.

- Gets around on belly by pushing with legs (may go backward before going forward).

- May be teething (some babies teethe earlier).
- May sleep through the night.

Mental and Social Development

- Changes mood suddenly.
- Smiles at him- or herself in mirror.
- Studies objects for a long time.
- Explores parent's face, hair, ears, etc., with hands.
- Is interested in cause-and-effect—how a light goes on when you flip a wall switch, for example.

Immunizations

Immunizations that may be given:

- At 6 months—DTaP or DTP, and Hib
- At 6-18 months—Hep B and Polio

Tips for Weeks 24-27

- Offer a teething baby a hard teething ring or a cold wash-cloth.
- When you first offer cereal, let baby suck it off the spoon.
- Use the safety straps when you put baby in a shopping cart.
- Give a new food 5 days before offering another. If there's an allergy, you'll know the cause.

Weeks 28-32

Physical Development

- Gets up on hands and knees and rocks back and forth.
- May start to crawl.
- Moves objects from hand to hand.
- Is ready to digest puréed, ground, or finely minced meat.
- Drinks from a cup with help.

Mental and Social Development

- Babbles ("ga-ga-ga-ga," for example).

- Shows a sense of humor.

- Understands "no" (from tone of voice).

- Protests if you try to take away a toy.

- Likes to bang and shake things.

- May become anxious around strangers.

- "Dances" (wiggles) to music.

Tips for Weeks 28-32

- Let baby hold a short-handled spoon while you feed with a long-handled spoon.

- Let baby out of the playpen to explore—while you watch closely.

- Use caution when you push open a door—baby may be behind it.

- If baby still wakes at night, respond more slowly. Then rock baby, instead of feeding.

- Use of baby walkers leads to many injuries. It's safest to avoid them.

Weeks 33-37

Physical Development

- Probably crawls (but some babies never crawl—later, they just start walking).

- May carry an object while crawling.

- Stands by pulling up on furniture (but can't get back down).

- May resume night waking (this, too, shall pass).

Mental and Social Development

- Can be very stubborn.

- Likes following a parent around the house.

- Pushes away unwanted toys—or unwanted food.

Tips for Weeks 33-37

- Carry some infant sunscreen in your diaper bag. Choose sunscreen that's at least SPF 15.

- Give baby age-appropriate toys that nest inside each other.

- A crawling baby means clutter. Lower your neatness standards (but keep floors clean).

- If you go to another room, call out to let baby know where you are.

- Distract baby from unwanted activities by offering something else.

Weeks 38-42

Physical Development

- May wean him- or herself from breast or bottle between now and 12 months.

- Can get into sitting position without help.

- Picks up small objects with finger and thumb.

- Can make a "tower" of 2 blocks.

Mental and Social Development

- Understands simple instructions: "Come here," "Wave bye-bye," etc.

- Likes simple games, such as raising arms in answer to, "How big is baby? So-o big!"

- Is more curious than ever.

- Can find a toy if he or she sees you hide it.

Tips for Weeks 38-42

- Turn pot handles inwards when cooking.

- Give baby a kitchen cabinet filled with sturdy plastic containers, lightweight pots, lids, etc.

- Get down on all fours and pretend to chase baby.

- Check to be sure your baby hasn't outgrown his or her infant car seat.
- Encourage baby's attempts to feed him- or herself.

Weeks 43-47

Physical Development

- Can get down after standing.
- May nap only in the afternoon.
- Climbs on chairs—and stairs (watch baby closely).

Mental and Social Development

- Loves to play with water.
- Likes to help with getting dressed.
- Anticipates events—for example, getting a coat means going outside.
- May resist going to bed.
- May say "mama" or "da-da" —and mean you!

Tips for Weeks 43-47

- Baby doesn't need shoes. Allow bare feet indoors.
- When you say no, offer an alternative: "You can play with this. Don't play with that."
- Babies are curious. Never scold or punish baby for wanting to explore.
- Establish a quiet evening routine: a bath, a book, then bed, for example.
- When you talk to baby, pause and give baby time to "answer."

Weeks 48-52

Physical Development

- Can play patty-cake.
- Gets around a room by holding on to furniture.

- Practices standing on one foot.
- May stand briefly without support.
- May start to walk.

Mental and Social Development

- Studies sizes and shapes.
- Likes to put things in containers—and take them out.
- Understands much of what you say.
- May like to undress self (indoors or out).

Immunizations

Immunizations that may be given:

- At 12-15 months—Hib and MMR (measles, mumps and rubella)
- At 12-18 months—Var (chickenpox)

Tips for Weeks 48-52

- Let baby turn the pages as you read a picture book.
- Use "please" and "thank you" when talking to baby—baby will learn to say them, too.
- Baby will need more immunizations in the months/years to come. Ask baby's health-care provider for details.
- Planning birthday party # 1? Keep it simple to avoid stressing out the guest of honor.
- Happy Birthday! Your baby made it through the first year—and so have you!

Chapter 17

Your Child's Growth: A Checklist

Guidelines for Parents

Watching a young child grow is a wonderful and unique experience for a parent. Learning to sit up, walk, and talk are some of the more major developmental "milestones" your child will achieve. But your child's growth is a complex and ongoing process. Young bodies are constantly going through a number of physical and mental changes.

Although no two children develop at the same rate, they should be able to do certain things at certain ages. As a parent, you are in the best position to note your child's development, and you can use the milestones described below as guidelines.

At the ages noted, observe your child for one month. (This lets you take into account any days when your child may be acting differently because he or she is sick or upset.) Use the milestones listed for each age to see how your child is developing.

Remember a "no" answer to any of these questions does not necessarily mean that there is a problem. Every child develops at his or her own pace and may sometimes develop more slowly in certain areas than other children the same age. Keep in mind these milestones should be used only as guidelines.

Plan to talk about these guidelines with your pediatrician during your next office visit if you note the following:

From www.aap.org © 1998 American Academy of Pediatrics; used with permission of the American Academy of Pediatrics.

- major differences between your child's development and the "milestones"

- your child does not yet do many of the things usually done at his or her age

3 Months

- When your baby is lying on his back, does he move each of his arms equally well? Answer "No" if your child makes jerky or un-coordinated movements with one or both of his arms or legs, or uses only one arm all the time.

- Does your child make sounds such as gurgling, cooing, babbling, or other noises besides crying?

- Does your baby respond to your voice?

- Are your child's hands frequently open?

- When you hold your child in the upright position, can he support his head for more than a moment?

6 Months

- Have you seen your baby play with her hands by touching them together?

- Does your child turn his head to sounds that originate out of his immediate area?

- Has your baby rolled over from her stomach to her back or from back to stomach?

- When you hold your baby under his arms, can he bear some weight on his legs? Answer "Yes" only if he tries to stand on his feet and supports some of his weight.

- When your child is on his stomach, can he support his weight on outstretched hands?

- Does your baby see small objects such as crumbs?

9 Months

- When your child is playing and you come up quietly behind him, does he sometimes turn his head as though he hears you? (Loud sounds do not count.) Answer "Yes" only if you have seen him respond to quiet sounds or whispers.

- Can your child sit without support and without holding up her body with her hands?

- Does your baby crawl or creep on her hands and knees?

- Does your baby hold his bottle?

12 Months

- When you hide behind something or around a corner and then reappear again, does your baby look for you or eagerly plan for you to reappear?

- Does your baby make "ma-ma" or "da-da" sounds? Check "Yes" if she makes either sound.

- Does your baby pull up to stand?

- Does your baby say at least one word?

- Does your baby walk holding on to furniture?

- Is your baby able to locate sounds by turning her head?

18 Months

- Can your child hold a regular cup or glass without help and drink from it without spilling?

- Can your child walk all the way across a large room without falling or wobbling from side to side?

- Does your child walk without support or help?

- Does your child say at least two words?

- Does your child take off his shoes by himself?

- Does your child feed himself?

2 Years

- Can your child say at least three specific words, other than "da-da" and "ma-ma," that mean the same thing each time they are said?

- Can your child take off clothes such as pajamas (tops or bottoms) or pants? (Diapers, hats, and socks do not count.)

- Does your child run without falling?

- Does your child look at pictures in a picture book?

- Does your child tell you what she wants?
- Does your child repeat words others say?
- Does your child point to at least one named body part?

3 Years

- Can your child name at least one picture when you look at animal books together?
- Can your child throw a ball overhand (not sidearm or underhand) toward your stomach or chest from a distance of 5 feet?
- Can your child answer simple questions?
- Does your child help put things away?
- Can your child answer the question, "Are you a boy or girl?"
- Can your child name at least one color?

4 Years

- Can your child pedal a tricycle at least 10 feet forward?
- Does your child play hide-and-seek, cops-and-robbers, or other games where he takes turns and follows rules?
- Can your child name pictures in books or magazines?
- Can your child tell you what action is taking place in a picture?
- Does your child use action words (verbs)?
- Does your child play pretend games, such as with toys, dolls, animals, or even an imaginary friend?

5 Years

- Can your child button some of his clothing or his doll's clothes? (Snaps do not count.)
- Does your child react well when you leave him with a friend or sitter?
- Can your child name at least three colors?
- Can your child walk down stairs alternating her feet?
- Can your child jump with her feet apart (broad jump)?

- Can your child point while counting at least three different objects?

- Can your child name a coin correctly?

6 Years

- Can your child tie his shoes?

- Can your child dress herself completely without help?

- Can your child catch a small bouncing ball, such as a tennis ball, using only her hands? (Large balls do not count.)

- Can your child copy a circle?

- Can your child tell his age correctly?

- Can your child repeat at least four numbers in the proper sequence?

- Can your child skip with both feet?

Summary

As a parent, you are in the best position to note these subtle aspects of your child's behavior. These clues signal that your child's development is on schedule or that something might be wrong. A "no" answer to any of the questions may be a warning sign; make sure to bring it to your pediatrician's attention. Remember, these milestones are an aid, and not a test.

If you have any questions, plan to discuss them with your pediatrician. Pediatricians are trained to detect and treat developmental problems in children. Many problems, if detected early, can be treated by your pediatrician and successfully managed.

Chapter 18

Developmental Assessments

Introduction

If you are reading this chapter, chances are that you have some questions or concerns about your baby or young child's development. You may want to understand more about how your child learns best. You may be puzzled about your baby's behavior. You, a relative, your doctor or child care provider, or someone else who knows young children well may have noticed that your child seems to be developing differently from other children his age. To help answer your questions, you may want an assessment of your child's development.

A developmental assessment is a process in which you, as parents, can observe your child carefully and discuss your child with professionals who are experienced in working with very young children and their families. What you learn from the assessment should answer many of your questions, but may also raise some questions, too. The assessment should give you ideas about things you can do at home to help your child learn and grow, how to choose learning environments to meet the needs of your child, and ways of finding any special services your child may need.

Excerpted from "A Letter to Parents about Developmental Assessment of Babies and Very Young Children," "New Visions: A Parent's Guide to Understanding Developmental Assessment," "Planning and Preparing for Your Child's Developmental Assessment," and "List of Terms: Terms Frequently Used in Developmental Assessment," © ZERO TO THREE, 734 15th St., N.W. Suite 1000, Washington, DC 20005-1013, (202) 638-114; reprinted with permission. Full text available at www.zerotothree.org.

You should know that ideas about the best way to understand very young children's development have changed a great deal during the last 10 years. For example, professionals now realize that it is just as important in a developmental assessment to learn about a baby or young child's special strengths as it is to understand his or her difficulties. Doctors and other experts in child development also realize that parents usually know the most about their own child and should be, as much as possible, active partners in the assessment process.

A Parent's Guide to Understanding Developmental Assessment

As the parent of a baby or toddler, you know that very young children are quite different from children of elementary school age or even preschoolers. This is why an assessment of a baby's or toddler's development needs to be different from the assessment of an older child. You also know that every baby and every family is unique. This is why an assessment of a baby's or toddler's development should not be "standard," but should be planned with your child, your family, and your individual questions in mind.

Guidelines for the Developmental Assessment of Infants and Young Children

The following nine guidelines for the developmental assessment of a baby or young child have been adapted from ZERO TO THREE's book, *New Visions for the Developmental Assessment of Infants and Young Children*, published in 1996. We offer these following principles of assessment to help parents recognize what is appropriate and what they should expect from this process. We believe that following these guidelines will help make the process of developmental assessment more productive, effective and comfortable for everyone involved.

1. Assessment means working together to learn about the child. Professionals and parents need to work together from beginning to end of the assessment process. Everyone has a great deal to contribute. You know more about your child than anyone else. Professionals with special training have important expertise to offer. And by working together, parents and professionals will complete a thorough look at the child and his strengths. Other adults who know you and your child well may have helpful information. You can help to decide the role you wish to play in the assessment and who else should be part of the assessment team.

2. An assessment should take into account all aspects of the baby or young child's development. Many factors influence how a baby or young child grows and learns. Some examples are the child's health; his temperament; his daily family life; his experiences outside the home; and the family's values, beliefs, and traditions. All of these affect the way your child plays, moves, eats, talks, listens, watches, and develops in every way.

How your child "organizes" experience is important, too—for example, how long does the baby pay attention to you or an interesting toy? How does he get what he wants or get you to help him? How does your child show her feelings? Thinking together about all of these questions will help you and the professionals with whom you are working understand your child's development.

3. An assessment should give a picture of the child in different settings, and gather information from many people. An assessment is a chance to learn about everything a child can already do, what she is interested in and enjoys, and where she is having difficulties. Professionals and parents can learn most by observing the child in several familiar settings (playing at home and in child care, for example), with familiar people. In addition (or when it is not possible to observe the child in the home), parents, relatives, and others who know the child well should offer professionals on the assessment team as much information as they can about the child's development. They can do this in words, through written reports (like baby books or health records) or with snapshots and home videos.

Your description of what your child does at home is as important as what the examiner observes directly. There is no single test that provides all of the information and no test is complete without parent (your) input.

4. Steps in the assessment of a baby or young child's development should follow in order.

- The assessment begins with a conversation with a child development professional, who asks parents about the child's strengths and challenges and the questions they hope the assessment will answer.

- Parents are encouraged to tell the story of their baby and family, in their own words, and professionals should listen carefully.

- The child is observed playing with parents or familiar caregivers at home, or in a way that is as much like ordinary play at home as possible. The familiar setting is intended to make your child comfortable and bring out her best.

- Parents observe the interactions and the relationship between the child and the person conducting the assessment, in order to see whether the child's response is typical.

- Specific areas of development (for example, hearing or communication), are assessed as needed, depending on the nature of what questions parents and professionals want answered.

- The professional or the team of professionals takes responsibility for pulling together information obtained from conversations with parents, direct observation, and other sources. The information is discussed with parents and presented in a written report in order to answer parents' original questions and other questions that may have come up during the assessment. Possibilities for treatment or intervention are considered by the complete team, of which parents are an integral part.

5. Watching a baby or young child do something he or she enjoys with someone he or she trusts should be the most important part of a developmental assessment. A developmental assessment is the time to learn about how a child uses his or her abilities to interact with people and objects in the environment. Children usually function at their best with the people they are most comfortable with and in places where they feel at ease. An examiner can learn a great deal by observing what a child and parent (or other trusted caregiver) do on their own. The examiner may also coach you to try a certain kind of game or other interaction in order to give your child a chance to show a specific ability. Before an examiner interacts directly with a baby or young child, he or she must take time to get to know the child and must be sure that the child feels secure and comfortable in the interaction.

6. Any professional who assesses the development of an infant or toddler should understand the sequences, timetables, and variations of development that are typical of children in this age group. The period from birth to three years is one of rapid physical growth and change. There is considerable range in what can be considered "normal" or "typical" development. Each child develops at a different pace. A professional who assesses the development of an infant or toddler should know the order in which skills emerge and the age range in which they are usually seen.

Experienced clinicians and professionals in many fields have studied and observed a wide range of infants and toddlers in order to understand both the sequence and timetable of development. This allows them to make an informed judgment, based on their experiences in the past, as to what may be happening with your child.

Making an informed judgment involves more than administering and scoring a standardized test. Parents should expect that the examiner will not rely on tests alone to assess a child's development.

7. The assessment process should identify the child's current strengths and abilities, as well as competencies that will help the child develop further. In development, one capacity builds on another. It is important to help the professional understand what your child can do already and what is important in the context of your family and your family's interests and needs. For example, if your child can now use some simple gestures to let you know what she wants, you can think about how to help her progress to more complex games, then to "pretend" play, and on to using words. If holding hands would be important in your family, perhaps to walk with you or grandpa to enjoy the park together, then working on that skill should be a priority, because it will bring your child new opportunities to enjoy being with people and learn about the world. Think about what is important in your family. What skills could help make the time spent with your child more satisfying. Plan to build on your child's current strengths and capabilities to make those dreams a reality.

8. An assessment should feel like help! You may have been advised to seek a developmental assessment as a first step in the process of deciding whether your child might benefit from treatment or early intervention and creating an Individualized Family Service Plan (IFSP). In some communities, assessment or evaluation must be completed before publicly funded intervention can begin. Many parents and professionals believe, however, that a well-done assessment is itself an extremely helpful "intervention" —whether or not it marks the beginning of a longer treatment program. Many parents say that they learn new ideas, feel a sense of relief, and realize that they are not alone with their questions when they have the chance to observe and talk about their child's development with experienced infant/toddler professionals. You and your child deserve a positive relationship with professionals and a developmental assessment that "feels like help."

9. Reassessment of your child's development should occur in familiar settings and should involve typical daily activities. Young children grow and develop so rapidly during the first years of life that ongoing monitoring and frequent reassessment of the child's capacities are important. Like a first developmental assessment, a reassessment should include careful observation of your child in several settings that are familiar to him or her, on multiple occasions. This process will provide a rich picture of your child's strengths and challenges and help you plan next steps. If your child participates in an early intervention or child care program, observing and recording his or her day-to-day experiences in that familiar setting over time may help you measure your child's developmental progress more meaningfully than a formal structured assessment.

Warning Signals in a Developmental Assessment of Infants and Young Children

Some current practices have no place in an assessment process that is designed to be an ongoing, collaborative effort between professionals and parents to understand a baby or young child's competencies and resources. We believe that the following "don'ts" are as important as the preceding positive guidelines for developmental assessment.

1. Young children should not be challenged by being separated from their parents during the assessment. This seems like common sense, but professionals who are not accustomed to working with infants and toddlers may forget how stressful a separation can be on both the child and the parent. One mother made her point by asking, "Do you want to test my son's hearing ability, or do you want to find out what a frightened two-year-old will do if you ask him to leave his mother and follow a stranger into a cubicle?"

2. Young children should never be assessed by an examiner who is a complete stranger to them. Unfortunately, in many settings where assessments take place, very young children are introduced to examiners who are strangers. The children are expected, after only a brief "warm-up" period, to demonstrate their highest abilities to one or more of these examiners. This practice represents an unnecessary challenge to the child and is highly unlikely to yield meaningful information about the child's true capacities. Assessment by an unfamiliar examiner with the parent allowed only to observe, rather than participate actively, also represents an unnecessary challenge to the child.

3. Young children's abilities should not be assessed based on a test that focuses solely on one or two aspects of development. The story of an infant or toddler's development is truly "more than the sum of its parts." You and the professionals with whom you are working may have questions about an area of your child's development which can be answered through the use of a specialized assessment tool, but it is important first of all to understand your child's overall abilities and behavior.

4. Young children's abilities should not be measured solely on the basis of tests and tools. Structured tests look at what a child can do when you or the examiner present him or her with a specific task (for example, making a tower of blocks after you have shown him how). But many babies and young children have difficulty paying attention to directions, many are not particularly interested in following directions (especially from a stranger), and many test items have little or nothing to do with the child's daily life. Observations of you and your child in a comfortable, familiar setting and discussions with you about your experiences, hopes, and day-to-day life with your child are the most reliable "tools" a professional can use in assessing your infant or toddler's development.

Steps to Take When You Encounter a "Warning Signal"

It is in everyone's best interest to work collaboratively as a team—parents and professionals—in order to meet the needs of you, your family and especially, your child. If you have concerns about the way in which an assessment is taking place, trust your instincts. Talk with the professional or "team" that is working with you and your family. Share your concerns. Offer suggestions about ways in which you all can work toward resolving the problem.

Gather support from parent support groups, friends and family. Link up with a parent of a child with similar concerns. Discuss what worked for that family. Would it work for yours? Feel free to share articles, information, and materials with the team. Talk freely about your concerns. And if all else fails, seek a second opinion.

Planning and Preparing for Your Child's Developmental Assessment

An assessment of your child's development can be a valuable experience. You can expect to learn more about how your child plays, moves, eats, talks, listens, watches, and develops in every way. An assessment can have a profound, positive impact on the growth of your child by giving you and others the information you need to help your child. But at times, developmental assessments can be confusing, scary, and overwhelming.

Remember that different families may choose to be more or less involved during the whole assessment process or at different stages of the process. How involved you choose to be may depend on your child's needs and other life circumstances. Your decision to become more or less involved should be accepted by the professionals with whom you are working.

These suggestions are arranged in the order that an assessment process usually follows.

The Referral Process

Your child will probably be referred by her doctor, a Child Find screening team in your community, or another professional, to go to a center, clinic, or private professional for assessment of your child's development. Here are some of the ways you can prepare:

- Talk with the person making the referral about the type of evaluation or assessment that is being recommended. Why are they making this referral? What questions does the referring professional hope the developmental assessment will answer? Are these questions similar to your own? Will the assessment that is being recommended follow the guidelines described above? What kinds of professionals will be involved in the assessment? Will there be a medical and/or a neurological examination?

- Get as much information as you can in advance of the assessment. More information is likely to help you feel more comfortable. Knowing what is going to happen will help you talk to your child about what he or she will be asked to do during the assessment—for example, "play with toys," "listen to sounds in your ears," or "meet a new doctor who will want to examine you."

If you are seeking a developmental assessment because of your own questions or concerns ("self-referring"), here are some options to consider:

- Your pediatrician's office or Health Maintenance Organization (HMO);

- Your local health department or Maternal and Child Health Agency;

- Your public school (ask for "Child Find");

- Your local Infants and Toddlers Program (also has a "Child Find"), your local Early Intervention program (the same as the Infants and Toddlers program, but may be called "Early Intervention,") or a Central Directory or Resource and Referral Agency to help you find sources of services;

- Your community mental health center; and

- Child and family service agencies in your community.

Planning Your Child's Developmental Assessment

- Call the individual professional or developmental assessment center to arrange an office appointment or home visit. Use this opportunity to make sure that the professionals with whom you will be working understand your questions, concerns, and goals for the assessment, and take them seriously.

- A "team" of professionals representing multiple disciplines (such as, speech and language pathology, psychology, etc.) will be assigned to you. Many professions should be represented in order to get a complete picture of your child's strengths and areas of concern.

- If you decide to continue with the process and professionals are planning a time to observe your child (at home, in a familiar child care facility, or in an office or clinic), think about the following:

  - Consider your child's sleeping and eating schedules when you make an appointment. You know your child best and should try to schedule an observation time when he or she will be most alert and active.

  - Find out if the examiner will permit or encourage brothers and sisters to be part of the assessment. If so, decide if you

151

want your other children to be at the assessment or not.
Will you be more comfortable with them there, or will their
presence interfere.

- Find out if you will be expected to separate from your child
  during any part of the assessment. If so, decide if this is acceptable to you. If not, tell the assessment professionals that
  you will remain with your child throughout the process so
  that he or she will not be stressed unnecessarily.

- Consider inviting a spouse, friend or relative to accompany
  you to the assessment. This person can attend to your child
  (or your other children) when needed, help take notes, keep
  track of information, and lend support to help ease any
  anxiety you may feel.

- Find out how assessment findings will be shared with you. Will
  this happen immediately following the observation or in a separate appointment? Will you have a chance to review a draft of a
  written report?

- Ask who will be paying for the assessment. Check with your
  own private insurance company, if need be.

Gathering Information for the Assessment

- Ask about what information would be useful to send in advance,
  bring with you, or have available during a home visit to help
  the assessment professional(s) learn about your child. Some
  suggestions are:

  - photographs or home videos of your child and family;

  - notes from your journal or baby book;

  - your child's health records;

  - descriptions of your child by family friends and relatives;

  - reports from professionals and programs that know you and
    your child;

  - information from books or magazines that seems to describe
    your child's pattern of development;

  - any other personal items or information that will help pro-
    fessionals know your child as an individual; and

  - Social Security and health insurance cards.

- Gather together your questions and concerns, preferably in writing. You may want to list questions that your doctor or others (for example, grandparents, child care workers, and friends) have raised about your child's development.

Note: Don't mail valuables, personal items, or your only copy of important records.

The Observation/Assessment

- Have ready, or bring to the office or clinic some of your child's favorite toys, snacks, books, and "loveys" —whatever will make your child feel relaxed and comfortable.

- Your child may be asked to play with toys, blocks and puzzles, move, jump and do things, look at pictures, talk and even color, depending on their age.

- You may be surprised by your child's performance or behavior during the observation. Share your impressions, such as, "She usually doesn't protest when we hold her that way" or "He's making a new sound!"

- Don't be afraid to disagree with an examiner. You are the expert on your child and know him or her much better than anyone else.

- Feel free to be responsive to your child during the observation or examination. If necessary, ask for a break for nursing, a snack, or diapering/toileting.

Talking with Professionals about Your Child and Family

- You don't need to learn technical terms. Ask for a definition of any term you don't understand. (The list of terms below may be helpful.)

- Explain in your own words how you see your child. Your observations are an important part of the assessment and should be taken seriously by all involved.

- You may be asked questions about family strengths (for example, how you make decisions or cope with problems), relationships, ways of communicating, and religious, cultural, or personal beliefs. These questions are not intended to be intrusive. Family characteristics contribute to a child's growth and development, so professionals need to understand your family in order to understand your child.

Reviewing Assessment Findings

As a part of the assessment process, the professional or team who has talked with you, observed your child, and reviewed other materials will take some time to consider all this information. A summary of findings will be prepared that will note both strengths and concerns. You may be able to discuss assessment findings with the assessment professionals on the day of the observation or may need to schedule a separate appointment.

- You can't always know in advance how you will react to hearing the assessment findings. Some parents will be reassured, some dismayed, and some surprised. Some parents may be relieved to find out that their child's challenges are not as severe as they feared. Other parents may be glad that someone else now understands why they have been worried about their child and can think with them about next steps.

- You may not get satisfying answers to all your questions. Young children's development is complicated. It is not always possible to know, for example, why a child is having a specific difficulty or set of problems. It is very risky to try to predict a child's future on the basis of an assessment.

- You may not agree that the assessment findings describe your child accurately. It may be that the examiner or the type of assessment did not bring out the best in your child.

- It is in everyone's best interest to work collaboratively—parents and professionals—in order to meet the needs of you, your family and especially, your child. The team can serve as a forum for support, feedback, information gathering and sharing and discussion. If you have concerns, talk with the team. Share articles, ideas and ways in which the problem can be resolved.

- Gather support from other parents in a similar situation. Find them by contacting parent support groups (parent-to-parent) and parent training and information centers.

- If all else fails, consider seeking a second opinion.

- You have a right to all information about your child. Find out what type of written report of the assessment you will receive, including results of any developmental tests. Many professionals send parents a draft to review before the final report is prepared. Keep your own notes. Keep all of the information together. Service providers may wish to see some of these reports in the future.

Determination of Eligibility for Services

One source of funding for early intervention and preschool special education services is the Individuals with Disabilities Education Act (IDEA), Public Law 103-382. Eligibility guidelines for services under the program vary from state to state. The process for determining eligibility may involve standardized tests and should permit the person conducting the test to use "informed clinical opinion" (see list of terms below). Other funding sources, such as private health insurance or Medicaid, also may require some kind of evaluation of your child before services are authorized.

You should be aware that, despite their limitations, standardized developmental tests are a required part of the process to determine eligibility for the Infants and Toddlers portion of IDEA in many states. In administering a standardized test, the practitioner must follow test guidelines exactly.

Planning Next Steps

- Take time to think about what you are hearing. You may hear a diagnosis and recommendations for treatment, and be eager to begin right away. You may want to know about next steps that are needed, whatever they may be. You may hear information about your child that is not what you expected. All parents need time to think about what they have heard, ask questions, and call back to discuss questions that occur to them later.

- Take time to recall the reasons you began the process of assessing your child's development. What have you learned? What questions still remain? Does there seem to be a need for further assessment now? Or are you likely to learn more by trying some new ways to help your child, within the family or working with professionals?

- Talk about possible next steps with people you trust. These may include the professionals with whom you planned and carried out the developmental assessment, your child's health care or child care providers, family and friends, and/or perhaps parents whose children's development is similar to your child's.

- Use what you learned through the process of developmental assessment to plan realistic, meaningful ways to help your child reach his or her full potential.

List of Terms Frequently Used in Developmental Assessment

Assessment: The ongoing process by which qualified professionals, together with families, through standardized tests and observation, look at all areas of a child's development: motor, language, intellectual, social/emotional and self-help skills, including dressing, toileting, etc. Both areas of strength and those requiring support and intervention are identified. Types of assessments include:

- *Developmental assessment:* An ongoing process of observing and thinking about a child's current competencies (including knowledge, skills, and personality), and the best ways to help the child develop further.

- *Family assessment:* A systematic process of learning from family members their ideas about a child's development and their strengths, priorities, and concerns as they are related to the child's development.

- *Multidisciplinary assessment:* A form of developmental assessment (see above) in which a group of professionals with different kinds of training and experience works with a child and family, directly or indirectly. This type of assessment can be helpful because professionals with different kinds of training are skilled in observing and interpreting different aspects of a child's development and behavior.

- *Play-based assessment:* A form of developmental assessment that involves observation of how a child plays alone, with peers, or with parents or other familiar caregivers, in free play or in special games. This type of assessment can be helpful because play is a natural way for children to show what they can do, how they feel, how they learn new things, and how they behave with familiar people.

Audiologist: A professional trained in assessing a child's hearing. In a developmental assessment of an infant or young child, an audiologist would look for signs of whether or not there are any hearing impairments or loss, usually by placing earphones on a child through which sounds are transmitted at various frequencies. Audiologists often work closely with speech and language specialists to address problems in communication.

Child and Adolescent Psychiatrist: A psychiatrist who, in addition to medical and adult psychiatric training (social, emotional and behavioral concerns), has been trained and certified in working with children and adolescents and can prescribe medication.

Child and Adolescent Psychologist: A psychologist who has specialized training in working with children and adolescents. In a developmental assessment of an infant or toddler, the child and adolescent psychologist would assess a child's social, emotional and intellectual development. She would likely administer some standardized tests that consist of presenting a variety of tasks, ranging from very easy to very challenging, in order to determine the full range of the child's skills. She may also observe the child during free play with herself and/or her caregivers as part of her assessment.

Child Development Specialist: A professional who is trained in infant/toddler development and in identifying developmental delays and disabilities. In a developmental assessment, a child development specialist would help identify a child's strengths and areas of concern, and suggest strategies to promote optimal social, emotional and intellectual development.

Child Find: A publicly funded program under IDEA (see below) intended to identify, locate, and evaluate/assess infants and toddlers with potential developmental delays or disabilities. The program may have different names in different communities (for example, "Community Screening") and may include public education about child development and parenting.

Clinical: Related to direct observation and treatment of an individual child, adult, or family. For example, a "clinical interview" is a face-to-face conversation. An "informed clinical opinion" is the judgment of a qualified professional, based on direct contact with a child, adult, or family.

Development: The process of how a child acquires skills in the areas of social, emotional, intellectual, speech and language and physical development including fine and gross motor skills. Developmental stages refer to the expected, sequential order of acquiring skills that children typically go through. For example, most children crawl before they walk, or use their fingers to feed themselves before they use utensils.

Developmentally Delayed/Disabled: A term used to describe infants and toddlers who need early intervention services because they:

- are experiencing developmental delays, a term used when a child has not achieved skills and abilities which are expected to be mastered by children of the same age. Delays can be in any of the following areas: physical, social, emotional, intellectual, speech and language and/or adaptive development, sometimes called self-help skills, which include dressing, toileting, feeding, etc.; or

- have a diagnosed physical or mental condition which has a high probability of resulting in a developmental delay. Some examples include: chromosomal abnormalities; genetic or congenital disorders; severe sensory impairments, including hearing and vision; inborn errors of metabolism; disorders reflecting disturbance of the development of the nervous system; congenital infections; disorders secondary to exposure to toxic substances, including fetal alcohol syndrome; and severe attachment disorders.

Caution: The term developmental delay may be used loosely and occasionally is used incorrectly, giving a false impression that the child will "catch up."

Developmental Domains: Term used by professionals to describe areas of a child's development, for example: "gross motor development" (large muscle movement and control); "fine motor development" (hand and finger skills, and hand-eye coordination); speech and language/ communication; the child's relationship to toys and other objects, to people and to the larger world around them; and the child's emotions and feeling states, coping behavior and self-help skills.

Developmental History: Term used by many professionals for the story of a child's development, beginning before birth.

Developmental Milestone: Term frequently used to describe a memorable accomplishment on the part of a baby or young child—

for example, rolling over, sitting up without support, crawling, pointing to get an adult's attention, walking.

Developmental Pediatrician: A pediatrician with specialized training in children's social, emotional, and intellectual development as well as health and physical growth.

Diagnosis: Term used to describe the critical analysis of a child's development in all the developmental domains, after reviewing all the assessment results, and the conclusion reached by such analysis. From this diagnosis, professionals should offer parents a precise and detailed description of the characteristics of a child's development, including strengths and the ways in which a child learns.

Early Childhood Special Educator: A professional trained in young children's typical and atypical development. An early childhood special educator would assist with developing plans and implementing intervention services based on the outcomes of the evaluation/assessment. In a developmental assessment of an infant or young child, the early childhood educator might administer developmental tests looking at the child's developmental domains.

Early Intervention: Refers to the range of services designed to enhance the development of infants and toddlers with disabilities or at risk of developmental delay. These services should be offered, to the maximum extent possible, in a natural environment, such as the home or in community settings, in which children without disabilities participate. Early intervention services that are under public supervision, must be given by qualified personnel and require the development of an individualized family service plan (*see* Individual Family Service Plan), developed in conjunction with the family, to guide the early intervention or therapeutic services given to a child.

Early intervention services should also enhance the capacity of families to meet the needs of their infants and toddlers with disabilities. Services may include but are not limited to: speech and language therapy, physical and/or occupational therapy, special education, and a range of family support services.

Early intervention is sometimes used to refer to any systematic effort to improve developmental outcomes for young children.

Early Interventionist: General term used for a person who works with infants and young children who have developmental delays, disabilities, or are at risk of developmental problems and their families. Early Interventionists may have different kinds of professional training (for example, in speech/language pathology or nursing), but they all have work experience and special training in helping young children and their families.

Eligibility: Specific criteria of developmental delay that meets the eligibility level needed for publicly funded services. This criteria is unique to each state's definition. Children who have a diagnosed physical or mental condition or are experiencing developmental delays are "eligible" for services. In addition, states may choose to serve children who are "at risk" of developmental delay by making them eligible for publicly funded early intervention services. Children who may be "at risk" of a developmental delay may be provided services in some states. Risk factors include:

- *Established risk:* a diagnosed physical or mental condition that has a high probability of resulting in developmental delay;

- *Biological / medical risk:* significant biological or medical conditions or event that give a child a greater chance of developing a delay or a disability than children in the general population; and

- *Environmental risk:* caregiving circumstances and current family situations that may place children at a greater risk for delay than the general population. Examples include: parental substance abuse, family social disorganization, poverty, parental developmental disability, parent age, parental educational attainment, and child abuse or neglect.

Etiology: The cause or origin of a disabling condition.

Evaluation: Term that is often used interchangeably with "assessment." However, in the context of services supported by the Individuals with Disabilities Education Act (IDEA) (see below), evaluation refers to a procedure that is used to determine a child's eligibility for early intervention services.

IDEA: An acronym for the Individuals with Disabilities Education Act which provides grants to states and jurisdictions to support the planning of service systems and the delivery of services, including evaluation and assessment, for young children who have or are at risk of developmental delays/disabilities. Funds are provided through the

Infants and Toddlers Program (known as part C of IDEA) for services to children birth through 2 years of age, and through the Preschool Program (known as Part B-Section 619 of IDEA) for services to children 3 through 5 years of age.

Incidence: The frequency of occurrence of a problem at a particular point in time.

Individualized Family Service Plan (IFSP): A statement of the family's strengths and needs related to enhancing the development of the family's child, including specific statements about outcomes, criteria, and timelines regarding progress, specific services, provisions for service coordination, and dates for initiation, duration and reevaluation process.

Informed Clinical Opinion: A term that describes professionals' use of qualitative and quantitative information to assess a child's development, especially if there are not standardized measures, or if the standardized procedures are not appropriate for a given age or development area. Informed clinical opinion makes use of a practitioner's training, previous experience with evaluation and assessment, previous experience with children, sensitivity to cultural needs, and the ability to gather and include family perceptions as important elements in order to make a judgment.

Interview: In-depth conversation between a professional and a parent or family. In a developmental assessment, a clinical interview may be a time in which parents or other family members have an opportunity to talk about their child, what it is like to care for him or her, and what their hopes and worries are, with the professional asking questions as needed in order to understand more clearly. A structured interview includes a series of specific questions—for example, about developmental history.

Multidisciplinary Team: A group of people with different kinds of training and experience working together, usually on an ongoing basis. Professionals often use the word "discipline" to mean a "field of study," such as medicine, social work, or education; Therefore, a multidisciplinary team might include a pediatrician, an occupational therapist, a social worker, and an early childhood educator.

Norms: A pattern or average regarded as typical for a specific group.

Occupational Therapist (OT): A professional who has specialized training in helping an individual develop mental or physical skills that aid in daily living activities, with careful attention to enhancing fine motor skills (hand and finger skills, eye-hand coordination and sensory integration). In a developmental assessment, the occupational therapist would assess the child's fine motor skills, coordination, and age-appropriate self-help skills (eating with utensils, dressing, etc.). She would also look at how the child responds to and uses what he sees, hears, feels, tastes and smells.

Pediatric Nurse Practitioner (PNP): A registered nurse with specialized, post-graduate training in providing ongoing care for the child/patient in both health (well-child visits) and illness. Their training often includes significant attention to child behavior and development.

Pediatrician: A medical doctor who has specialized training in caring for the physical health and development of children.

Physical Therapist (PT): A professional trained in assessing and providing therapy to treat developmental delays, disease and injury using methods such as exercise, heat, light and massage. In a developmental assessment, the physical therapist would assess the ability and quality of the child's use of her legs, arms, and complete body by encouraging the display of specific motor tasks as well as observing the child in play.

Prevalence: The number or proportion of individuals in a community or population with a given condition or problem.

Public Health Nurse: Nurses who are specially trained to provide care, usually in the home, to families. They often have a strong background in social work skills and child and family development.

Referral: The process of helping a child or family to access a service — for example, a more in-depth assessment, or an organization that provides child care or early intervention.

Reliability: The extent to which a test is consistent in measuring whatever it measures.

Sensory Integration: The process of how a child (person) takes in information and processes it based on their senses (touch, taste, smell, sound, sight). This may include how a child perceives his body or the world around him, or how a child adapts himself to his world. According to the theory of sensory integration, the many parts of the nervous system work together so that a child can interact with the environment effectively and experience appropriate satisfaction. Having poor sensory integration may interfere with many activities necessary for daily functioning, such as brushing teeth, playing on play equipment or even hugging.

Screening: A brief assessment procedure designed to identify children who should receive more intensive assessment. Screening is designed to identify children who are at risk for health problems, developmental problems, and/or disabling conditions, who may need to receive helpful intervention services as early as possible.

Speech/Language Pathologist: A professional who is trained in assessing and treating problems in communication including: articulation (pronunciation of sounds), receptive language (understanding and processing what is communicated by others), expressive language (the ability to communicate to others), fluency (including stuttering), and voice problems (including pitch and intonation.) A speech and language pathologist also is trained to work with oral/motor problems, such as swallowing, and other feeding difficulties.

Tests

- *Achievement test:* A test that measures the extent to which an individual has acquired certain information or mastered certain skills.

- *Criterion-referenced test:* A test that measures a specific level of performance or a specific degree of mastery.

- *Psychometric test:* Quantitative assessments of an individual's psychological and other developmental traits or abilities.

- *Readiness test:* A test that measures the extent to which a child has acquired certain skills for successfully undertaking some new learning activity.

- *Standardized test:* A systematic sample of performance obtained under prescribed conditions, scored according to definite rules, which allows professionals to compare your child's performance to every other child who takes the same test.

163

Validity: The extent to which a test or observation measures what it is intended to measure.

Chapter 19

Child Health Guide

Check-Up Visits

Check-up visits are important because they allow your health care provider to review your child's growth and development, perform tests or give shots. To help your provider get a complete picture of your child's health status, be sure to bring your child's health record and a list of any medications your child is taking to each visit.

Check-up visits are a time for parents to ask questions. Bring a list of concerns you have. For example: "My child is not sleeping through the night yet"; "I don't think my child is eating enough"; or, "My child seems uncoordinated and is always walking into things."

Some authorities recommend check-up visits at the following ages: 2-4 weeks; 2, 4, 6, 9, 12, 15 and 18 months; 2, 3, 4, 5, 6, 8, 10, 12, 14, 16 and 18 years. Some children may need to be seen more often, others less. Ask your clinician how often your child will need to be seen.

Immunizations

Your child needs immunizations. Immunizations (shots) protect your child from many serious diseases. Table 19.1 provides a list of immunizations and the ages when your child should receive them. Immunizations should be given at the recommended ages—even if your child has a cold or illness at the time. Ask your health care provider

Excerpted from *Child Health Guide*, U.S. Department of Health and Human Services, Office of Disease Prevention and Health Promotion, September 1997 and April 1998.

about when your child should receive these important shots. Ask also if your child needs other immunizations.

Periodically, the recommended timing for immunizations changes. For the latest immunization schedule, check this website: http://www.ecbt.org/immsche.htm or call Every Child By Two at (202) 651-7226.

Growth Record

Your child's health care provider will measure your child's height and weight regularly. Your child's head size will also be measured

Table 19.1. Immunizations

Type	Age
Hepatitis B (3 doses)	Birth-2 months 1-4 months 6-18 months
Polio (4 doses)	2 months 4 months 6-18 months 4-6 years
Haemophilus Influenzae Type B (Hib) (4 doses)	2 months 4 months 6 months 12-15 months
Diphtheria, Tetanus, Pertussis (DTaP) (5 doses)	2 months 4 months 6 months 15-18 months 4-6 years
Tetanus (Td) (1 dose)	11-16 years
Measles, Mumps, Rubella (MMR) (2 doses)	12-15 months 4-6 years **or** 11-12 years
Varicella (chicken pox) (1 dose)	1-12 years

during the first 2 years of life. These measurements will help you and your health care provider know if your child is growing properly.

Newborn Screening

These blood tests should be done before your baby is 7 days old. They are usually done just before your baby leaves the hospital. If the blood tests were done earlier than 24 hours after birth, a repeat test at 1 to 2 weeks of age is recommended. Common newborn screening tests include those for PKU, thyroid and sickle cell disease.

Table 19.2. Recommended Screening Tests

Age	Screening Test	How Often
Newborn	Newborn screening (PKU, sickle cell, hemoglobinopathies, hypothyroidism)	Once
Newborn	Hearing	Once
Birth-2 months	Head circumference	Periodically
Birth-18 years	Height and weight	Periodically
1 year	Lead	Once
3-4 years	Eye screening	Once
3-18 years	Blood pressure	Periodically
3-18 years	Dental	Periodically
11-18 years	Alcohol use	Periodically

Blood Pressure

Your child should have blood pressure measurements regularly, starting at around 3 years of age. High blood pressure in children needs medical attention. It may be a sign of underlying disease and, if not treated, may lead to serious illness.

Check with your child's health care provider about blood pressure measurements.

Lead

Lead can harm your child, slowing physical and mental growth and damaging many parts of the body. The most common way children get lead poisoning is by being around old house paint that is chipping or peeling. Some authorities recommend lead tests at 1 and 2 years of age.

"Yes" answers to any of the following questions may mean that your child needs lead tests earlier and more often than other children.

Has Your Child

- Lived in or regularly visited a house built before 1950? (this could include a day care center, preschool, the home of a babysitter or relative, etc.)

- Lived in or regularly visited a house built before 1978 (the year lead-based paint was banned for residential use) with recent, ongoing, or planned renovation or remodeling?

- Had a brother or sister, housemate, or playmate followed or treated for lead poisoning?

Vision and Hearing

Your child's vision should be tested before starting school, at about 3 or 4 years of age. Your child may also need vision tests as he or she grows. Some authorities recommend hearing testing beginning at 3 to 4 years of age. If at any age your child has any of the vision or hearing warning signs listed below, be sure to talk with your health care provider.

Vision Warning Signs

- Eyes turning inward (crossing) or outward

- Squinting

- Headaches

- Not doing as well in school work as before

- Bluffed or double vision

Hearing Warning Signs

- Poor response to noise or voice
- Slow language and speech development
- Abnormal sounding speech

Special Warning: Listening to very loud music, especially with earphones, can permanently damage your child's hearing.

Additional Tests

Your child may need other tests to prevent health problems. Some common tests are:

Anemia (Blood) Test. Your child may need to be tested for anemia ("low blood") when he or she is still a baby (usually around the first birthday). Children may also need this test as they get older. Some children are more likely to get anemia. Ask your health care provider about anemia testing.

Cholesterol (Blood) Test. Children (2 years and older) may need this test especially if they have a parent with high cholesterol or a parent or grandparent with heart disease before age 55. If a family history is not available, testing may be needed if your child is obese or has high blood pressure.

Tuberculosis (TB) Skin Test. Children may need this test if they have had close contact with a person who has TB, live in an area where TB is more common than average (such as a Native American reservation, a homeless shelter, or an institution) or have recently moved from Asia, Africa, Central America, South America, the Caribbean or the Pacific Islands.

Nutrition

What your child eats is very important for his or her health. Follow the nutrition guidelines below.

0-2 Years Old

- Breast milk is the best single food for infants from birth to six months of age. It provides good nutrition and protects against infection. Breast feeding should be continued for at least the first year, if possible. If breast feeding is not possible or not desired, iron-enriched formula (not cow's milk) should be used during the first 12 months of life. Whole cow's milk can be used to replace formula or breast milk after 12 months of age.

- Breast-fed babies, particularly if dark-skinned, who do not get regular exposure to sunlight may need to receive Vitamin D supplements.

- Begin suitable solid foods at 4-6 months of age. Most experts recommend iron-enriched infant rice cereal as the first food. Start new foods one at a time to make it easier to identify problem foods. For example, wait one week before adding each new cereal, vegetable, or other food. Use iron-rich foods, such as grains, iron-enriched cereals, and other grains and meats.

- Do not give honey to infants during the first 12 months of life.

- Do not limit fat during the first 2 years of life.

2 Years and Older

- Provide a variety of foods, including plenty of fruits, vegetables, and whole grains.

- Use salt (sodium) and sugars in moderation.

- Encourage a diet low in fat, saturated fat, and cholesterol.

- Help your child maintain a healthy weight by providing proper foods and encouraging regular exercise.

Dental/Oral Health

Your child needs regular dental care starting at an early age. Talk with your dentist to schedule the first visit. Good oral health requires good daily care. Follow these guidelines.

For Babies

- If most of your child's nutrition comes from breast feeding, or if you live in an area with too little fluoride in the drinking water (less than .3 ppm for children less than 2 years old, less than .7 ppm for children over 2 years old), your child may need fluoride drops or tablets. Ask your health care provider or local water department about the amount of fluoride in your water.

- Don't use a baby bottle as a pacifier or put your child to sleep with a baby bottle. This can cause tooth decay and ear infections.

- Keep your infant's teeth and gums clean by wiping with a moist cloth after feeding.

- When multiple teeth appear, begin gently brushing your infant's teeth using a soft toothbrush and a very small (pea-sized) amount of toothpaste with fluoride.

For Older Children

- Talk with your dentist about dental sealants. They can help prevent cavities in permanent teeth.

- Use dental floss to help prevent gum disease. Talk with your dentist about when to start.

- Do not permit your child to smoke or chew tobacco. Set a good example: don't use tobacco products yourself.

- If a permanent tooth is knocked out, rinse it gently and put it back into the socket or in a glass of cold milk or water. See a dentist immediately.

Physical Activity

Your child needs regular physical activity through play and sports to stay fit. Good physical activity habits learned early can help your child become an active and healthy adult. Adults who are physically active are less likely to be overweight or to have heart disease, high blood pressure, and other diseases. Adults and children should try to get at least 30 minutes of physical activity most days of the week.

- Encourage your child to participate in physical activities, including sports.

- Encourage involvement in activities that can be enjoyed into adulthood (walking, running, swimming, basketball, tennis, golf, dancing, and bicycle riding).

- Plan physical activities with family or friends; exercise is more fun with others.

- Limit the time your child spends watching TV to less than 2 hours per day. Encourage going out to the playground, park, gym, or swimming pool instead.

- Physical activity should be fun. Don't make winning the only goal.

- Many communities and schools offer exercise or sports programs—find out what is available for your child.

Tobacco Use

Using tobacco in any form is harmful to you and can harm your child's health. Tobacco use—smoking and/or chewing tobacco—causes cancer, heart disease, and other serious illnesses. Children exposed to tobacco smoke are more likely to get infections of the ears, sinuses, and lungs. Smoking in the home may also cause lung cancer in family members who do not smoke.

Discourage your child from using tobacco (in any form). If you smoke, ask your health care provider about getting help quitting.

Safety

More children die from injuries than any other cause. The good news is that most injuries can be prevented by following simple safety guidelines. Talk with your health care provider about ways to protect your child from injuries.

Safety Guidelines Checklist

For All Ages

- Use smoke detectors in your home. Change the batteries every year and check once a month to see that they work.

- If you have a gun in your home, make sure that the gun and ammunition are locked up separately and kept out of children's reach.

- Never drive after drinking alcohol.

- Use car safety belts at all times.

- Teach your child traffic safety. Children under 9 years of age need supervision when crossing streets.

- Teach your children how and when to call 911.

- Learn basic life-saving skills (CPR).

- Keep a bottle of ipecac at home to treat poisoning. Talk with a doctor or the local Poison Control Center before using it. Post the number of the Poison Control Center number near your telephone and write down where you can find it quickly. Also, be sure to check the expiration date on the bottle of ipecac to make sure it is still good.

Infants and Young Children

- Use a car safety seat at all times until your child weighs at least 40 pounds.

- Car seats must be properly secured in the back seat, preferably in the middle.

- Keep medicines, cleaning solutions and other dangerous substances in childproof containers, locked up and out of reach of children.

- Use safety gates across stairways (top and bottom) and guards on windows above the first floor.

- Keep hot water heater temperatures below 120° F.

- Keep unused electrical outlets covered with plastic guards.

- Provide constant supervision for babies using a baby walker. Block the access to stairways and to objects that can fall (such as lamps) or cause burns (such as stoves).

- Keep objects and foods that can cause choking away from your child, such as coins, balloons, small toy parts, hot dogs (unmashed), peanuts and hard candies.

- Use fences that go all the way around pools and keep gates to pools locked.

Older Children

- Use car safety belts at all times.

- Until children are tall enough so that the lap belt stays on their hips and the shoul der belt crosses their shoulder, they should use a car booster seat.

- Make sure your child wears a helmet while riding on a bicycle or motorcycle.

- Make sure your child uses protective equipment for rollerblading and skateboarding (helmet, wrist and knee pads).

- Warn your child of the dangers of using alcohol and drugs. Many driving and sports-related injuries are caused by the use of alcohol and drugs.

A Special Message about SIDS

Sudden Infant Death Syndrome (SIDS) is the leading cause of death for infants. Place sleeping infants on their backs to decrease the risk of SIDS.

Child Abuse

Child abuse is a hidden, serious problem. It can happen in any family. The scars, both physical and emotional, can last for a lifetime. Because children can't protect themselves, we must protect them.

Ways to Prevent Child Abuse

- Teach your child not to let anyone touch his or her private parts.

- Tell your child to say "No" and run away from sexual touches.

- Take any reports by your child of physical or sexual abuse seriously.

- Report any abuse to your local or state child protection agency.

- If you feel angry and out of control, leave the room, take a walk, take deep breaths, or count to 100. Don't drink alcohol or take drugs. These can make your anger harder to control. If you are afraid you might harm your child, get help NOW. Call someone and ask for help. Talk with a friend or relative, other parents, your clergy, or your health care provider. Take time for yourself. Share child care between parents, trade babysitting with friends, or use day care.

Counseling

As your child grows, your health care provider should take time to talk to you (and/or your child) about the following topics:

- Development
- Nutrition
- Physical activity

- Safety

- Unintentional injuries and poisonings

- Violent behaviors and firearms

- Sexually transmitted diseases and HIV

- Family planning

- Tobacco use

- Drug use

Talk to your health care provider about these important issues—even while your child is still young. Start early to teach your child to make responsible choices—irresponsible choices can have a lifelong effect. Your child needs you. Take the time to " be there" for your child—listening, advising, and supporting. The rewards will be well worth the effort.

Chapter 20

Ten Things You Need to Know about Immunizations

1. Why should my child be immunized?

Children need immunizations (shots) to protect them form danger-ous childhood diseases. These diseases have serious complications and can even kill children.

2. What diseases do vaccines prevent?

- Measles
- Mumps
- Polio
- Rubella (German Measles)
- Pertussis
- Diphtheria
- Tetanus
- *Haemophilus influenzae* type b (Hib disease)
- Hepatitis B
- Varicella (chickenpox)

3. How many shots does my child need?

The following vaccinations are recommended by age two and can be given in five visits to a doctor or clinic:

Reprinted from the Centers for Disease Control and Prevention (CDC), un-dated.

- 1 vaccination against measles/mumps/rubella (MMR)
- 4 vaccinations against Hib (a major cause of spinal meningitis)
- 3 vaccinations against polio
- 4 vaccinations against diphtheria, tetanus, and pertussis (DTP)
- 3 vaccinations against hepatitis B
- 1 vaccination against varicella

4. Are the vaccines safe?

Serious reactions to vaccines are extremely rare, but do occur. However, the risks of serious disease from not vaccinating are far greater than the risks of serious reaction to the vaccination.

5. Do the vaccines have any side effects?

Yes, side effects can occur with vaccination, depending on the vaccine: slight fever, rash or soreness at the site of injection. Slight discomfort is normal and should not be a cause for alarm. Your health care provider can assist you with additional information.

6. What do I do if my child has a serious reaction?

If you think your child is experiencing a persistent or severe reaction, call your doctor or get the child to a doctor right away. Write down what happened and the date and time it happened. Ask your doctor, nurse or health department to file a *Vaccine Adverse Event Report* form or call 1-800-338-2382.

7. Why can't I wait until school to have my child immunized?

Immunizations must begin at birth and most vaccinations completed by age 2. By immunizing on time (by age 2), you can protect your child from being infected and prevent the infection of others at school or at day care centers. Children under 5 are especially susceptible to diseases because their immune systems have not built up the necessary defenses to fight infection.

8. Why is a vaccination health record important?

A vaccination and health record helps you and your health care provider keep your child on schedule. A record should be started at birth when your child should receive his/her first vaccination and updated each time your child receives the next scheduled vaccination. This information will help you if you move to a new area or change health care providers, or when your child is enrolled in day care or starts school. Remember to bring this record with you every time your child has a health care visit.

9. Where can I get free vaccines?

The Vaccines for Children Program will provide free vaccines to needy children. Eligible children include those without health insurance coverage, all those who are enrolled in Medicaid, American Indians and Alaskan Natives.

10. Where can I get more information?

You can call the National Immunization Information Hotline for further immunization information at 1-800-232-2552 (English) or at 1-800-232-0233 (Spanish).

Internet address: http://www.cdc.gov/nip

Chapter 21

Vaccine-Preventable Childhood Diseases

Polio

- Serious cases cause paralysis and death
- Mild cases cause fever, sore throat, nausea, headaches, and stomach aches; may also cause neck and back pain or stiffness
- Polio vaccine can prevent this disease

Diphtheria

- Respiratory disease spread by coughing and sneezing
- Gradual onset of sore throat, and low-grade fever
- Heart failure or paralysis can result if disease is not treated
- Diphtheria toxoid (contained in DT, DTaP and Td vaccines) can prevent this disease

Tetanus

- Neurologic disease also known as lockjaw
- Bacteria enters the body through a break in the skin
- Produces a poison (toxin) that attacks the nervous system

Centers for Disease Control and Prevention (CDC), March 1999.

- Early symptoms are headache, irritability, and stiffness in the jaw and neck

- Later, causes severe muscle spasms in the jaw, neck, arms, legs, back and abdomen

- May require intensive care in hospital

- In the U.S., most cases are in adults; 4 out of every 10 tetanus cases aged 20 or older will die from the disease

- In developing countries, tetanus frequently affects newborn babies; more than 500,000 babies died from neonatal tetanus in 1993

- Tetanus toxoid (contained in DTP, DT, DTaP and Td vaccines) can prevent this disease

Pertussis

- Highly contagious respiratory disease also known as whooping cough

- Causes severe spasms of coughing that can interfere with eating, drinking and breathing

- Complications include pneumonia, convulsions and encephalitis

- One out of every 3 cases of pertussis encephalitis will die, another 1 of 3 will have permanent brain damage

- In the U.S., most cases are in children under age 5, and half of those are in infants under 1 year old

- About 5,000 cases are reported in the U.S. each year

- Pertussis vaccine (contained in DTP and DTaP) can prevent this disease

Measles

- Highly contagious respiratory disease

- Causes rash, high fever, cough, runny nose and red, watery eyes, lasting about a week

- Causes ear infections and pneumonia in 1 out of every 12 children who get it

- Causes encephalitis that can lead to convulsions, deafness or mental retardation in 1 to 2 of every 2,000 people who get it

- Of every 1,000 people who get measles, 1 to 2 will die
- Measles vaccine (contained in MMR, MR and measles vaccines) can prevent this disease

Mumps

- Causes fever, headache and swelling of one or both cheeks or sides of the jaw
- Four to six persons out of 100 who get mumps will get meningitis
- Inflammation of the testicles occurs in about 4 of every 10 adult males who get mumps
- May result in hearing loss, which is usually permanent
- Mumps vaccine (contained in MMR) can prevent this disease

Rubella

- Also known as German measles
- Mild disease in children and young adults, causing rash and fever for 2 to 3 days
- Causes devastating birth defects if acquired by a pregnant woman; there is at least 20% chance of damage to the fetus if a woman is infected early in pregnancy
- Rubella vaccine (contained in MMR vaccine) can prevent this disease

Haemophilus influenzae *type b (Hib)*

- Causes meningitis, pneumonia, sepsis, arthritis, and skin and throat infections
- More serious in children under age 1; after age 5, there is little risk of getting the disease
- Before 1992, Hib was the most common cause of bacterial meningitis in the U.S.
- Before the introduction of infant vaccination, 1 child in 200 was affected before age 5
- One out of 20 children who get Hib meningitis will die and 10%–30% of survivors will have permanent brain damage

- Hib vaccine can prevent this disease

Varicella

- Also known as chickenpox
- Varicella-zoster is a virus of the herpes family
- Highly contagious, it causes a skin rash of a few or hundreds of blister-like lesions, usually on the face, scalp, or trunk
- Usually more severe in older children (13 or older) and adults
- Although complications are rare, annually 9,000 hospitalizations for chickenpox occur in the United States, with up to 100 deaths
- Complications include bacterial infection of the skin, swelling of the brain, and pneumonia
- Often leads to quarantine, causing children to miss school and parents to miss work
- Varicella vaccine can prevent this disease

Hepatitis B

- Can destroy the liver (cirrhosis)
- Lead to liver cancer
- Causes pain in muscles, joints or stomach
- Hepatitis B vaccine can prevent this disease

Chapter 22

Six Common Misconceptions about Vaccination

A great deal of information about vaccinations is available to parents. This is good, because parents should have access to any information that will help them make informed decisions about vaccination. However, information is sometimes published that is inaccurate or can be misleading when taken out of context. Following are six misconceptions that appear in literature about vaccination, along with explanations of why they are misconceptions.

1. Diseases had already begun to disappear before vaccines were introduced, because of better hygiene and sanitation

2. The majority of people who get disease have been vaccinated

3. There are "hot lots" of vaccine that have been associated with more adverse events and deaths than others

4. Vaccines cause many harmful side effects, illnesses, and even death

5. Vaccine-preventable diseases have been virtually eliminated from the Unites States

6. Giving a child multiple vaccinations for different diseases at the same time increases the risk of harmful side effects and can overload the immune system.

Reprinted from the Centers for Disease Control and Prevention (CDC), undated.

Introduction

As a practitioner giving vaccinations, you will encounter patients who have reservations about getting vaccinations for themselves or their children. There can be many reasons for fear of or opposition to vaccination. Some people have religious or philosophic objections. Some see mandatory vaccination as interference by the government into what they believe should be a personal choice. Others are concerned about the safety or efficacy of vaccines, or may believe that vaccine-preventable diseases do not pose a serious health risk.

A practitioner has a responsibility to listen to and try to understand a patient's concerns, fears, and beliefs about vaccination and to take them into consideration when offering vaccines. These efforts will not only help to strengthen the bond of trust between you and the patient but will also help you decide which, if any, arguments might be most effective in persuading these patients to accept vaccination.

The purpose of this chapter is to address six common misconceptions about vaccination that are often cited by concerned parents as reasons to question the wisdom of vaccinating their children. If we can respond with accurate rebuttals perhaps we can not only ease their minds on these specific issues but discourage them from accepting other anti-vaccine "facts" at face value. Our goal is not to browbeat parents into vaccinating, but to make sure they have accurate information with which to make an informed decision.

1. Diseases had already begun to disappear before vaccines were introduced, because of better hygiene and sanitation.

Statements like this are very common in anti-vaccine literature, the intent apparently being to suggest that vaccines are not needed. Improved socioeconomic conditions have undoubtedly had an indirect impact on disease. Better nutrition, not to mention the development of antibiotics and other treatments, have increased survival rates among the sick; less crowded living conditions have reduced disease transmission; and lower birth rates have decreased the number of susceptible household contacts. But looking at the actual incidence of disease over the years can leave little doubt of the significant direct impact vaccines have had, even in modern times. A graph showing the reported incidence of measles from 1920 to the present shows periodic peaks and valleys throughout the years, but the real, permanent drop coincided with the licensure and wide use of measles vaccine beginning in 1963. Graphs for other vaccine-preventable diseases show a roughly similar pattern, with all except hepatitis B* showing a significant drop in cases corresponding with the advent of vaccine use. Are we expected to believe that better sanitation caused incidence of each disease to drop, just at the time a vaccine for that disease was introduced?

*The incidence rate of hepatitis B has not dropped so dramatically yet because the infants we began vaccinating in 1991 will not be at high risk for the disease until they are at least teenagers. We therefore expect about a 15 year lag between the start of universal infant vaccination and a significant drop in disease incidence.

Hib vaccine is another good example, because Hib disease was prevalent until just a few years ago, when conjugate vaccines that can be used for infants were finally developed. (The polysaccharide vaccine previously available could not be used for infants, in whom most of cases of the disease were occurring.) Since sanitation is not better now than it was in 1990, it is hard to attribute the virtual disappearance of Hib disease in children in recent years (from an estimated 20,000 cases a year to 1,419 cases in 1993, and dropping) to anything other than the vaccine.

Varicella can also be used to illustrate the point, since modern sanitation has obviously not prevented nearly 4 million cases each year in the United States. If diseases were disappearing, we should expect varicella to be disappearing along with the rest of them. But nearly all children in the United States get the disease today, just as they did 20 years ago or 80 years ago. Based on experience with the varicella vaccine in studies before licensure, we can expect the incidence of varicella to drop significantly now that a vaccine has been licensed for the United States.

Finally, we can look at the experiences of several developed countries after they let their immunization levels drop. Three countries— Great Britain, Sweden, and Japan—cut back the use of pertussis vaccine because of fear about the vaccine. The effect was dramatic and immediate. In Great Britain, a drop in pertussis vaccination in 1974 was followed by an epidemic of more than 100,000 cases of pertussis and 36 deaths by 1978. In Japan, around the same time, a drop in vaccination rates from 70% to 20%-40% led to a jump in pertussis from 393 cases and no deaths in 1974 to 13,000 cases and 41 deaths in 1979. In Sweden, the annual incidence rate of pertussis per 100,000 children 0-6 years of age increased from 700 cases in 1981 to 3,200 in

1985. It seems clear from these experiences that not only would diseases not be disappearing without vaccines, but if we were to stop vaccinating, they would come back.

Of more immediate interest is the major epidemic of diphtheria now occurring in the former Soviet Union, where low primary immunization rates for children and the lack of booster vaccinations for adults have resulted in an increase from 839 cases in 1989 to nearly 50,000 cases and 1,700 deaths in 1994. There have already been at least 20 imported cases in Europe and two cases in U.S. citizens working in the former Soviet Union.

2. The majority of people who get disease have been vaccinated.

This is another argument frequently found in anti-vaccine literature—the implication being that this proves vaccines are not effective. In fact it is true that in an outbreak those who have been vaccinated often outnumber those who have not—even with vaccines such as measles, which we know to be about 98% effective when used as recommended.

This apparent paradox is explained by two factors. First, no vaccine is 100% effective. To make vaccines safer than the disease, the bacteria or virus is killed or weakened (attenuated). For reasons related to the individual, not all vaccinated persons develop immunity. Most routine childhood vaccines are effective for 85% to 95% of recipients. Second, in a country such as the United States the people who have been vaccinated vastly outnumber those who have not. How these two factors work together to result in outbreaks in which the majority of cases have been vaccinated can be more easily understood by looking at a hypothetical example.

In a high school of 1,000 students, none has ever had measles. All but 5 of the students have had two doses of measles vaccine, and so are fully immunized. The entire student body is exposed to measles, and every susceptible student becomes infected. The 5 unvaccinated students will be infected, of course. But of the 995 who have been vaccinated, we would expect several not to respond to the vaccine. The efficacy rate for two doses of measles vaccine can be as high as >99%. In this class, 7 students do not respond, and they, too, become infected. Therefore 7 of 12, or about 58%, of the cases occur in students who have been fully vaccinated.

As you can see, this doesn't prove the vaccine didn't work—only that most of the children in the class had been vaccinated, so those who were vaccinated and did not respond outnumbered those who had not been vaccinated. Looking at it another way, 100% of the children who had not been vaccinated got measles, compared with less than 1% of those who had been vaccinated. Measles vaccine protected most of the class; if nobody in the class had been vaccinated, there would probably have been 1,000 cases of measles.

3. There are "hot lots" of vaccine that have been associated with more adverse events and deaths than others. Parents should find the numbers of these lots and not allow their children to receive vaccines from them.

This misconception got considerable publicity recently when vaccine safety was the subject of a television news program. First of all, the concept of a "hot lot" of vaccine as it is used in this context is wrong. It is based on the presumption that the more reports to VAERS (Vaccine Adverse Event Reporting System) a vaccine lot is associated with, the more dangerous the vaccine in that lot; and that by consulting a list of the number of reports per lot, a parent can identify vaccine lots to avoid.

This is misleading for two reasons:

- VAERS is a system for reporting events that are temporally associated with receipt of vaccine; VAERS reports should not be interpreted to imply causality. In other words, a VAERS report does not mean that the vaccine caused the event. Statistically, a certain number of serious illnesses, even deaths, can be expected to occur by chance alone among children recently vaccinated. Although vaccines are known to cause minor, temporary side effects such as soreness or fever, there is little, if any, evidence linking vaccination with permanent health problems or death. The point is that just because an adverse event has been reported to VAERS does not mean it was caused by a vaccine.

- Vaccine lots are not the same. The sizes of vaccine lots might vary from several hundred thousand doses to several million, and some are in distribution much longer than others. Naturally a larger lot or one that is in distribution longer will be associated with more adverse events, simply by chance. Also, more coincidental deaths are associated with vaccines given in infancy than later in childhood, since the background death rates for children are highest during the first year of life. So knowing that lot A has been associated with x number of adverse events while lot B has been associated with y number would not necessarily say anything about the relative safety of the two lots, even if the vaccine did cause the events.

Reviewing published lists of "hot lots" will not help parents identify the best or worst vaccines for their children. If the number and type of VAERS reports for a particular vaccine lot suggested that it was associated with more serious adverse events or deaths than are expected by chance, the Food and Drug Administration (FDA) has the legal authority to immediately recall that lot. To date, no vaccine lot in the modern era has been found to be unsafe on the basis of VAERS reports.

All vaccine manufacturing facilities and vaccine products are licensed by the FDA. In addition, every vaccine lot is safety-tested by the manufacturer. The results of these tests are reviewed by FDA, who may repeat some of these tests as an additional protective measure. FDA also inspects vaccine-manufacturing facilities regularly to ensure adherence to manufacturing procedures and product-testing regulations, and reviews the weekly VAERS reports for each lot searching for unusual patterns. FDA would recall a lot of vaccine at the first sign of problems. There is no benefit to either the FDA or the manufacturer in allowing unsafe vaccine to remain on the market. The American public would not tolerate vaccines if they did not have to conform to the most rigorous safety standards. The mere fact is that a vaccine lot still in distribution says that the FDA considers it safe.

4. Vaccines cause many harmful side effects, illnesses, and even death—not to mention possible long-term effects we don't even know about.

Vaccines are actually very safe, despite implications to the contrary in many anti-vaccine publications (which sometimes contain the number of reports received by VAERS, and allow the reader to infer that all of them represent genuine vaccine side-effects). Most vaccine adverse events are minor and temporary, such as a sore arm or mild fever. These can often be controlled by taking acetaminophen before or after vaccination. More serious adverse events occur rarely (on the order of one per thousands to one per millions of doses), and some are so rare that risk cannot be accurately assessed. As for vaccines causing death, again so few deaths can plausibly be attributed to vaccines that it is hard to assess the risk statistically. Of all deaths reported to VAERS between 1990 and 1992, only one is believed to be even possibly associated with a vaccine. Each death reported to VAERS is thoroughly examined to ensure that it is not related to a new vaccine-related problem, but little or no evidence suggests that vaccines have contributed to any of the reported deaths. The Institute of Medicine in its 1994 report states that the risk of death from vaccines is "extraordinarily low."

DTP Vaccine and SIDS

One myth that won't seem to go away is that DTP vaccine causes sudden infant death syndrome (SIDS). This belief came about because a moderate proportion of children who die of SIDS have recently been vaccinated with DTP; and on the surface, this seems to point toward a causal connection. But this logic is faulty; you might as well say that eating bread causes car crashes, since most drivers who crash their cars could probably be shown to have eaten bread within the past 24 hours.

If you consider that most SIDS deaths occur during the age range when 3 shots of DTP are given, you would expect DTP shots to precede a fair number of SIDS deaths simply by chance. In fact, when a number of well-controlled studies were conducted during the 1980's, the investigators found, nearly unanimously, that the number of SIDS deaths temporally associated with DTP vaccination was within the range expected to occur by chance. In other words, the SIDS deaths would have occurred even if no vaccinations had been given. In fact, in several of the studies children who had recently gotten a DTP shot were less likely to get SIDS. The Institute of Medicine reported that "all controlled studies that have compared immunized versus nonimmunized children have found either no association . . . or a decreased risk . . . of SIDS among immunized children" and concluded that "the evidence does not indicate a causal relation between [DTP] vaccine and SIDS."

But looking at risk alone is not enough—you must always look at both risks and benefits. Even one serious adverse effect in a million doses of vaccine cannot be justified if there is no benefit from the vaccination. If there were no vaccines, there would be many more cases of disease, and along with them, more serious side effects and more deaths. For example, according to an analysis of the benefit and risk of DTP immunization, if we had no immunization program in the United States, pertussis cases could increase 71-fold and deaths due to pertussis could increase 4-fold. Comparing the risk from disease

191

with the risk from the vaccines can give us an idea of the benefits we get from vaccinating our children.

The fact is that a child is far more likely to be seriously injured by one of these diseases than by any vaccine. While any serious injury or death caused by vaccines is too many, it is also clear that the benefits of vaccination greatly outweigh the slight risk, and that many, many more injuries and deaths would occur without vaccinations. In fact, to have a medical intervention as effective as vaccination in preventing disease and not use it would be unconscionable.

Research is underway by the U.S. Public Health Service to better understand which vaccine adverse events are truly caused by vaccines and how to reduce even further the already low risk of serious vaccine-related injury.

Table 22.1 Risk from Disease vs. Risk from Vaccines

Disease	Vaccines
Measles Pneumonia: 1 in 20 Encephalitis: 1 in 2,000 Death: 1 in 3,000 **Mumps** Encephalitis: 1 in 300 **Rubella** Congenital Rubella Syndrome: 1 in 4 (if woman becomes infected early in pregnancy)	**MMR** Encephalitis or severe allergic reaction: 1 in 1,000,000
Diphtheria Death: 1 in 20 **Tetanus** Death: 3 in 100 **Pertussis** Pneumonia: 1 in 8 Encephalitis: 1 in 20 Death: 1 in 200	**DTP** Continuous crying, then full recovery: 1 in 100 Convulsions or shock, then full recovery: 1 in 1,750 Acute encephalopathy: 0-10.5 in 1,000,000 Death: None proven

5. Vaccine-preventable diseases have been virtually eliminated from the United States, so there is no need for my child to be vaccinated.

It's true that vaccination has enabled us to reduce most vaccine-preventable diseases to very low levels in the United States. However, some of them are still quite prevalent—even epidemic—in other parts of the world. Travelers can unknowingly bring these diseases into the United States, and if we were not protected by vaccinations these diseases could quickly spread throughout the population, causing epidemics here. At the same time, the relatively few cases we currently have in the U.S. could very quickly become tens or hundreds of thousands of cases without the protection we get from vaccines.

We should still be vaccinated, then, for two reasons. The first is to protect ourselves. Even if we think our chances of getting any of these diseases are small, the diseases still exist and can still infect anyone who is not protected. A few years ago in California a child who had just entered school caught diphtheria and died. He was the only unvaccinated pupil in his class.

The second reason to get vaccinated is to protect those around us. There is a small number of people who cannot be vaccinated (because of severe allergies to vaccine components, for example), and a small percentage of people don't respond to vaccines. These people are susceptible to disease, and their only hope of protection is that people around them are immune and cannot pass disease along to them. A successful vaccination program, like a successful society, depends on the cooperation of every individual to ensure the good of all. We would think it irresponsible of a driver to ignore all traffic regulations on the presumption that other drivers will watch out for him or her. In the same way we shouldn't rely on people around us to stop the spread of disease; we, too, must do what we can.

6. Giving a child multiple vaccinations for different diseases at the same time increases the risk of harmful side effects and can overload the immune system.

Children are exposed to many foreign antigens every day. Eating food introduces new bacteria into the body, and numerous bacteria live in the mouth and nose, exposing the immune system to still more antigens. An upper respiratory viral infection exposes a child to 4–10 antigens, and a case of "strep throat" to 25–50. According to *Adverse Events Associated with Childhood Vaccines*, a 1994 report from the

Institute of Medicine, "In the face of these normal events, it seems unlikely that the number of separate antigens contained in childhood vaccines . . . would represent an appreciable added burden on the immune system that would be immunosuppressive." And, indeed, available scientific data show that simultaneous vaccination with multiple vaccines has no adverse effect on the normal childhood immune system.

A number of studies have been conducted to examine the effects of giving various combinations of vaccines simultaneously. In fact, neither the Advisory Committee on Immunization Practices (ACIP) nor the American Academy of Pediatrics (AAP) would recommend the simultaneous administration of any vaccines until such studies showed the combinations to be both safe and effective. These studies have shown that the recommended vaccines are as effective in combination as they are individually, and that such combinations carry no greater risk for adverse side effects. Consequently, both the ACIP and AAP recommend simultaneous administration of all routine childhood vaccines when appropriate. Research is under way to find ways to combine more antigens in a single vaccine injection (for example, MMR and chickenpox). This will provide all the advantages of the individual vaccines, but will require fewer shots.

There are two practical factors in favor of giving a child several vaccinations during the same visit. First, we want to immunize children as early as possible to give them protection during the vulnerable early months of their lives. This generally means giving inactivated vaccines beginning at 2 months and live vaccines at 12 months. The various vaccine doses thus tend to fall due at the same time. Second, giving several vaccinations at the same time will mean fewer office visits for vaccinations, which saves parents both time and money and may be less traumatic for the child.

Chapter 23

Rotavirus and Rotavirus Vaccine

How much of a health problem is rotavirus disease?

Rotavirus is the most common cause of severe diarrhea in children in the United States. Virtually all children have one or more rotavirus infections in the first 5 years of life. Each year in the United States, rotavirus is responsible for approximately 500,000 physician visits and 50,000 hospitalizations (30-50% of all hospitalizations for diarrhea in children under 5 years of age). Children aged 3 to 24 months have the highest rates of severe disease and hospitalization.

What causes rotavirus disease?

The etiologic agents of rotavirus disease are the group A rotaviruses which are wheel-shaped (therefore named rota-) RNA viruses. Human strains are present worldwide; related species of rotaviruses affect other mammalian species.

The clinical manifestations of infection with human rotaviruses range from asymptomatic shedding to life-threatening gastroenteritis with severe vomiting and diarrhea. Although multiple human rotavirus serotypes have been identified, virtually all disease in the United States appears to be caused by four serotypes.

Reprinted from the Centers for Disease Control and Prevention (CDC), revised October 2, 1998.

How is rotavirus transmitted?

Rotavirus is highly infectious; a dose of a very small number (<100) of virus particles is enough to infect a person and lead to disease. Fecal-oral transmission is the likely major mode of transmission; the roles of droplet or direct transmission have not yet been well characterized. Rotavirus is stable in the environment, and contamination of surfaces, such as toys and diaper pail handles, probably contributes to spread of infection.

How can disease from rotavirus be prevented or managed?

Prior to the availability of a vaccine, there were no effective methods for the prevention or control of rotavirus infection. Hygienic measures have not been successful in the United States and other developed countries as documented by the near-universal infection of young children.

Appropriate management of childhood gastroenteritis with rehydration therapy is usually effective in preventing dehydration. Nevertheless, many children in the United States continue to be hospitalized for dehydration despite widespread over-the-counter availability of rehydration solutions.

How is the vaccine produced?

Rotavirus vaccine is a live viral vaccine, licensed by the Food and Drug Administration in August 1998. The vaccine was developed by the National Institutes of Health, and is licensed to Wyeth-Lederle Vaccines and Pediatrics. Wyeth calls the vaccine Rotashield®, and it is generically called RRV-TV.

The vaccine contains four different rotavirus strains, all of which are derived from an attenuated rhesus monkey rotavirus strain (RRV-1). RRV-1 is antigenically similar to one of the major human rotavirus serotypes. Three additional strains of rotavirus have been developed from RRV-1 which contain genes from the other human rotavirus serotypes commonly found in the United States. Given as a single tetravalent vaccine, these four strains produce immunity to the four human rotavirus serotypes which are responsible for almost all of rotavirus disease in the United States.

How effective is this vaccine?

In four placebo-controlled randomized trials, three doses of vaccine gave a vaccine efficacy of about 50% against any diarrhea caused

196

by rotavirus and 70%-95% against severe rotavirus diarrhea. In the one clinical trial large enough to study hospitalizations, the vaccine was 100% effective against hospitalization due to rotavirus diarrhea.

Will the vaccine prevent all diarrhea in small children?

Although rotavirus vaccine is highly effective against severe rotavirus disease, a large number of milder cases of rotavirus diarrhea will still occur and childhood diarrhea from other causes will not be prevented by vaccination. Fifty to seventy percent of hospitalizations for diarrhea are due to non-rotaviral etiologies. Parents will need to be educated that this vaccine does not prevent all childhood diarrhea.

What is the recommended schedule for rotavirus vaccine?

The recommended schedule for routine administration is a series of three oral doses at 2, 4, and 6 months of age. The first dose may be given as early as 6 weeks of age and the minimum interval between doses is 3 weeks. The first dose is not recommended to be given to infants 6 months of age or older due to a preliminary study which found a higher incidence of fever with first doses given to infants over this age. Rotavirus vaccine is not currently recommended for children 12 months of age and older due to a lack of data on use in this age group.

How is the vaccine provided? What are the storage requirements for the vaccine?

The vaccine is supplied in boxes of 12 doses as lyophilized powder in individual-dose bottles and 12 individual droppers with 2.5 cc of citrate-bicarbonate diluent. The vaccine and diluent are approved for storage at room temperature below 25° C (77° F). The vaccine and diluent may also be stored at refrigerator temperature, but must not be frozen.

How many doses of rotavirus vaccine are needed to provide protection?

Available data indicate that three doses reliably provide a high degree of protection from severe rotavirus disease. Earlier studies, in which only one dose was given, did not find a high degree of protection. No studies were conducted using a two-dose schedule, and it is unknown if children who receive two doses of vaccine will be protected.

Are there circumstances where using an accelerated vaccination schedule would be of benefit?

Rotavirus is a seasonal disease in the United States with the vast majority of the disease occurring in the winter months, consistently peaking in early winter (November) in the southwestern states and late winter/spring (April) in the northeastern states. Many of the children born in late summer or in the fall will enter the peak season of rotavirus transmission without having received three doses of rotavirus vaccine if immunized on the standard 2, 4, and 6 month schedule. Most of these children could receive three doses if immunized on an accelerated schedule. The feasibility of setting up programs to administer rotavirus vaccine on such a schedule needs to be considered.

Can the rotavirus vaccine be administered simultaneously with other vaccines?

Data show that immunogenicity against any antigen was unaffected by simultaneous administration with DPT-Hib, OPV, IPV, or Hepatitis B vaccines.

If the infant spits out or vomits the dose of rotavirus vaccine, should the dose be repeated?

There is no information available on the effect of repeating a dose that is spit out or regurgitated. Unlike with oral polio vaccine, the spit out or regurgitated dose should not be repeated. However, if the infant needs subsequent doses in the series, they should be administered on schedule.

What kind of adverse reactions are associated with the vaccine?

In the prelicensure studies, the only adverse reaction was fever. Temperature of 38° C (100.4° F) or higher attributable to the vaccine was observed in 3%-25% of vaccinated children. Most episodes of fever were seen following the first dose of vaccine, mostly on days 3-5 after administration. Temperature of 39° C (102.2° F) was observed in 1%-2% of children, usually after the first dose. Rotavirus vaccine has not been reported to cause diarrhea or vomiting.

Why is vaccination with the first dose not recommended for children 6 months of age or older? Why is vaccination with the second and third doses not recommended for children 12 months of age or older?

Infants 6 months of age or older had a higher rate of high fevers after vaccination with the first dose of rotavirus vaccine in a small trial. This is thought to be due to a loss of maternal antibody in these older infants.

Prelicensure studies included some children up to 8 months of age who received second and third doses. Fever was not a common reaction after second and third doses of vaccine in these studies. Safety and efficacy data are not available for older children.

Should premature infants be vaccinated?

Available data suggest that premature infants are at increased risk for death due to diarrhea, and may be at increased risk for hospitalization due to rotavirus diarrhea.

There are very limited data available on the use of rotavirus vaccine among premature infants. These limited data do not show an increased rate of febrile reactions after vaccination with rotavirus vaccine. However, if the fever observed in children 6 months of age or older after a first dose of vaccine is due to a loss of maternal antibody, premature infants (who have decreased levels of maternal antibody) would theoretically be at increased risk for febrile reactions.

Although some experts believe the benefit from vaccination with rotavirus vaccine is greater than the theoretical risk, available data are insufficient. It is likely that the final recommendations will not recommend routine vaccination of premature infants although not making prematurity an absolute contraindication.

How much does it cost? Is it cost-effective?

The manufacturer's catalog price for rotavirus vaccine is $38 per dose. At this price, the vaccine will not be cost-saving using direct medical costs alone. However, when indirect costs are included, the vaccine will probably be cost-saving. Annual direct medical costs from rotavirus disease are estimated at $270-450 million and annual total societal costs (including lost parental time from work) are estimated at $1 billion.

Has the ACIP issued a recommendation on the use of rotavirus vaccine?

Neither ACIP or AAP has published recommendations on the use of rotavirus vaccine. At an ACIP meeting in June 1998, the ACIP unanimously went on record as being in favor of a recommendation for routine use of rotavirus vaccine among infants. [Note: Recommendations on the use of rotavirus vaccine were published by the Centers for Disease Control and Prevention in March 1999 (See "Rotavirus Vaccine for the Prevention of Rotavirus Gastroenteritis among Children Recommendations of the Advisory Committee on Immunization Practices," *Morbidity and Mortality Weekly Report (MMWR)*, March 19, 1999, 48(RR-2); 1-23 or view online at www.cdc.gov/epo/mmwr/preview/mmwrhtml/00056669.htm). The recommendations were withdrawn, however, in October 1999 based on reports to the Vaccine Adverse Event Reporting System of a type of bowel obstruction, called intussusception, among 15 infants who received rotavirus vaccine (see "Withdrawal of Rotavirus Vaccine Recommendation," *MMWR* November 5, 1999, 48(43);1007 or view on line at www.cdc.gov/epo/mmwr/preview/mmwrhtml/mm 4843a5.htm).]

How will CDC monitor the effectiveness of a rotavirus vaccination program?

Recommendations for a rotavirus disease monitoring system are now being developed. Because testing for rotavirus is not done routinely on cases of childhood diarrhea, it is likely that a form of sentinel surveillance for rotavirus will need to be implemented. In such a program, a limited number of sites such as hospitals or large clinics would perform routine testing for rotavirus on pediatric patients with gastroenteritis.

Chapter 24

The Coming Vaccine against Pneumococcal Disease in Children

An experimental vaccine intended to protect children against pneumococcal disease has been shown in a pivotal study to be highly effective against two invasive forms of the disease—bacterial meningitis and bloodstream infection (bacteremia).

The three-year, Phase III clinical trial involved more than 38,000 children, at 23 Kaiser Permanente sites throughout Northern California. It was ended ahead of schedule because of very favorable results.

Pneumococcal disease, a group of illnesses caused by the pneumococcus bacteria (also known as *Streptococcus pneumoniae*), includes the common childhood ear infection otitis media, pneumonia, and invasive, potentially fatal and crippling infections such as bacterial meningitis (brain or spinal cord infection) and bacteremia. Among children who survive bacterial meningitis, many are left with lifelong disabilities, including blindness, deafness or paralysis.

In the United States, infants and young children are at greatest risk for invasive pneumococcal disease, with more than 10,000 cases reported each year in that age group. Worldwide, more than 1.2 million children under age 5 die each year as a result of pneumococcal disease.

"We are delighted by these findings," said Steven Black, MD, co-director of the Kaiser Permanente Vaccine Study Center, which conducted the clinical trial. "We are entering an era in which effective protection against invasive pneumococcal disease and, potentially, otitis media, should become a reality for children throughout the world."

Vaccine Results

The results of the trial were presented at the 38th Interscience Conference on Antimicrobial Agents and Chemotherapy (ICAAC) in San Diego in 1998.

Data from the study will be further analyzed to determine the vaccine's effectiveness against ear infections and pneumonia, as well as the cost-effectiveness of vaccinating all U.S. children. "We are especially hopeful the vaccine will prevent a significant number of ear infections in children of all ages," said Dr. Black. "Ear infections are responsible for more than 30 million pediatric visits in this country each year."

Currently, no vaccine on the market is approved for prevention of pneumococcal disease in children under age 2, or otitis media in children of any age.

"We've traditionally treated these infections with penicillin and other antibiotics," said Henry Shinefield, MD, co-director of the Vaccine Study Center, "However, the pneumococcus bacteria has become increasingly resistant to those drugs during the past decade, increasing the risk of death or complications from the disease. That's created an urgent need for a vaccine to protect young children."

The vaccine used in this study, a seven-valent pneumococcal conjugate vaccine, is formulated to protect against the seven strains of pneumococci that cause approximately 85 percent of the invasive pneumococcal disease in U.S. children.

In a randomized, double-blind study, half of the infants received the pneumococcal conjugate vaccine and half received a control vaccine. Each child was given doses at two, four and six months, with a booster dose at 12 to 15 months. As of August 1998 and the study's close, 22 cases of invasive pneumococcal disease caused by one of the seven strains represented in the trial vaccine had been identified. All of the cases were in the control group; none were in the vaccine group—an efficacy of 100 percent.

An analysis of safety data from the study is under way. In an earlier study, adverse experiences commonly noted from the pneumococcal vaccine were local reactions at the injection site and mild to moderate fever.

Chapter 25

Hearing Screening

An estimated 1% to 2% of infants and children in the United States suffer from hearing impairment. Approximately half of these cases are congenital or are acquired during infancy. Severe or profound hearing loss affects one of every 750 live births. Approximately 5% of infants in neonatal intensive care units have evidence of significant hearing loss. Some 8 million school-aged children experience temporary hearing loss, which usually occurs as a complication of otitis media with middle ear effusion.

Hearing is necessary for normal development of speech and language and is also important for acquiring psychosocial skills during infancy and childhood. Because most speech and language development occurs between birth and 3 years of age, early detection of hearing impairment in infants and children and initiation of medical and educational interventions are critical.

Recommendations of Major Authorities

Normal-Risk Children

American Academy of Pediatrics and **Bright Futures** endorse the recommendation by the joint Committee on Infant Hearing and also recommend that pure-tone audiometry be performed at 3, 4, 5, 10, 12, 15, and 18 years of age. Subjective assessment of hearing should be performed at other ages.

Excerpted from *Clinician's Handbook of Preventive Services, Second Edition*, U.S. Department of Health and Human Services, Office of Disease Prevention and Health Promotion, 1998.

American Speech-Language-Hearing Association—Annual pure-tone audiometry should be performed for children functioning at a developmental level of age 3 years to grade 3 and for any high-risk children, including those above grade 3.

Canadian Task Force on the Periodic Health Examination—Repeated examination of hearing is recommended for young children, especially during the first year of life. Suggested guidelines for this examination include checking the startle or turning response to a novel noise produced outside the infant's field of vision at birth and 6 months of age and checking for the absence of babbling at 6 months of age. Screening using auditory brainstem responses or evoked otoacoustic emission by 3 months of age is not recommended pending further evaluation. Routine hearing assessment of asymptomatic preschoolers using history-taking, audiometry, tympanometry, or acoustic reflexometry is not recommended.

Joint Committee on Infant Hearing (American Speech-Language-Hearing Association, American Academy of Pediatrics, American Academy of Otolaryngology–Head and Neck Surgery, American Academy of Audiology, and the Directors of Speech and Hearing Programs in State Health and Welfare Agencies) and **Bright Futures** endorse the goal of universal detection of infants with hearing loss as early as possible using auditory brainstem response or otoacoustic emissions. All infants should be screened before 3 months of age.

U.S. Preventive Services Task Force—There is insufficient evidence to recommend for or against routine screening of asymptomatic neonates for congenital hearing loss using evoked otoacoustic emission (EOE) testing or auditory brainstem response (ABR). Routine hearing screening of asymptomatic children beyond age 3 years is not recommended. There is insufficient evidence to recommend for or against routinely screening asymptomatic adolescents for hearing impairment. However, screening of workers for noise-induced hearing loss should be performed in the context of existing worksite programs and occupational medicine guidelines.

High-Risk Children

American Academy of Pediatrics and **American Speech-Language-Hearing Association (ASHA)**—Children with frequently recurring otitis media or middle ear effusion, or both, should have audiology screening and monitoring of communication skills development. ASHA recommends annual pure-tone audiometry testing for all children at high risk for hearing impairment.

Joint Committee on Infant Hearing (American Speech-Language-Hearing Association, American Academy of Pediatrics, American Academy of Otolaryngology–Head and Neck Surgery, American Academy of Audiology, and the Directors of Speech and Hearing Programs in State Health and Welfare Agencies)—Neonates (birth to 28 days of age) with one or more of the neonatal risk criteria should have audiology screening, preferably before hospital discharge but no later than 3 months of age.

Neonatal Risk Criteria: Family history of hereditary sensorineural hearing loss; in utero infection (e.g., cytomegalovirus, rubella, syphilis, herpes, or toxoplasmosis); craniofacial anomalies, including those with morphological abnormalities of the pinna [external ear] and ear canal; birth weight less than 1500 grams (3.3 lbs); hyperbilirubinemia at a serum level requiring exchange transfusion; ototoxic medications, including but not limited to aminoglycosides, used in multiple courses or in combination with loop diuretics; bacterial meningitis; Apgar scores of 0 to 4 at 1 minute or 0 to 6 at 5 minutes; mechanical ventilation lasting 5 days or longer; and stigmata or other findings associated with a syndrome known to include a sensorineural and/or conductive hearing loss.

Infants and children less than 2 years of age with one or more of the following risk criteria should have audiology screening.

Risk Criteria for Ages 29 days to 2 Years: Parent/caregiver concern regarding hearing, speech, language, and/or developmental delay; bacterial meningitis or other infections associated with sensorineural hearing loss; head trauma associated with loss of consciousness or skull fracture; stigmata or other findings associated with a syndrome known to include a sensorineural and/or conductive hearing loss; ototoxic medications, including but not limited to aminoglycosides, used in multiple courses or in combination with loop diuretics; recurrent or persistent otitis media with effusion for at least 3 months associated with hearing loss; anatomic deformities and other disorders that affect eustachian tube function; neurofibromatosis type II and neurodegenerative disorders.

Infants and children with the following risk factors for delayed-onset hearing loss require hearing evaluation every 6 months until 3 years of age.

Risk Factors for Delayed-Onset Hearing Loss: Family history of hereditary childhood hearing loss; in utero infection, such as cytomegalovirus, rubella, syphilis, herpes, or toxoplasmosis; neurofibromatosis type II and neurodegenerative disorders; recurrent or persistent otitis media with effusion, anatomic deformities, and other disorders that affect eustachian tube function; neurodegenerative disorders.

US Preventive Services Task Force—Screening for hearing impairment in high-risk infants can be recommended based on the relatively high prevalence of hearing impairment, parental anxiety, and the potential beneficial effect on language development from early treatment of infants with moderate or severe hearing loss. Refer to neonatal risk criteria listed above under joint Committee on Infant Hearing. Clinicians examining any infant or young child should remain alert for symptoms or signs of hearing impairment, including parent/caregiver concern regarding hearing, speech, language, and/or developmental delay.

Basics of Hearing Screening

1. Assess the family and medical history of every child for risk factors for hearing impairment.

2. Ask parents about the auditory responsiveness and speech and language development of young children. Any parental reports of impairment should be seriously evaluated.

3. In infants, assessment of hearing by observational techniques is very imprecise. Consider referring all infants and young children with suspected hearing difficulties to an audiologist.

4. When performing physical examinations, remain alert for structural defects of the ear, head, and neck. Remain alert for abnormalities of the ear canal (inflammation, cerumen impaction, tumors, or foreign bodies) and the eardrum (perforation, retraction, or evidence of effusion).

5. Children as young as 6 months of age, depending on how cooperative they are, may be screened by pure-tone audiometry.

Two screening methods are suggested as the most appropriate tools for children who are functioning at 6 months to 3 years developmental age: visual reinforcement audiometry (VRA) and conditioned play audiometry (CPA). For children from approximately 6 months through 2 years of age, VRA is the recognized method of choice. As children mature beyond their second birthday, CPA may be attempted. For those children who can be conditioned for VRA, screen using earphones (conventional or insert), with 1000, 2000, and 4000 Hz tones at 30 dB HL. For those children who can be conditioned for play audiometry, screen using earphones (conventional or insert), with 1000, 2000, and 4000 Hz tones at 20 dB HL. Hand-held audiometers are of unproven effectiveness in screening children.

After 6 months of age, any child may be screened for middle ear dysfunction using tympanometry. Perform tympanometry with a low frequency (220, 226 Hz) probe tone and a positive to negative air pressure sweep. Middle ear pressure peaks between – 150 mmhos and + 150 mmhos are considered normal. Patients with pressure peaks outside this range or lack of any identifiable pressure peak should be referred for otologic follow-up.

6. Repeat screening to substantiate audiometric evidence of hearing impairment. Remove and reposition the earphones and carefully repeat the instructions to the child to assure proper understanding and attention to the test. Referral to a qualified specialist (i.e., audiologist, otolaryngologist) is recommended for confirmation and work-up of hearing impairment.

Patient Resources

Is My Baby's Hearing Normal? American Academy of Otolaryngology–Head and Neck Surgery, Order Department, 1 Prince St, Alexandria, VA 22314; (703) 836-4444.

Answers to Questions about Otitis Media, Hearing, and Language Development; How Does Your Child Hear and Talk?; Recognizing Communication Disorders. American Speech-Language-Hearing Association, 10801 Rockville Pike, Rockville, MD 20852. For general information, call: (800) 638-8255. To order, call: (301) 897-5700, ext. 218; Internet address: http://www.asha.org.

Middle Ear Fluid in Young Children: Parent Guide; Ear Infection in Children. The American Academy of Pediatrics, P.O. Box 927, Elk Grove Village, IL 60009-0927; (800) 433-9016. Internet address: http://www.aap.org.

Provider Resources

Bright Futures: Guidelines for Health Supervision of Infants, Children and Adolescents; Bright Futures Pocket Guide; Bright Futures Anticipatory Guidance Cards. Available from the National Center for Education in Maternal and Child Health, 2000 15th Street North, Suite 701, Arlington, VA 22201-2617; (703) 524-7802. Internet address: http://www.brightfutures.org

National Institute on Deafness and Other Communication Disorders. Internet address: http://www.nih.gov/nidcd.

American Speech-Language-Hearing Association. Internet address: http://www.asha.org.

Chapter 26

Vision Screening

Refractive errors are the most common vision disorders in children, occurring in 20% of children by age 16 years. Amblyopia ("lazy eye") develops in 2% to 5% of children, and the risk of developing this disorder is greatest during the first 2 to 3 years of life. The potential for its development exists, however, until visual development is complete at 9 years of age. Untreated amblyopia may result in irreversible visual deficits. Strabismus, one of the primary causes of amblyopia, occurs in 2% of children. Other eye diseases occurring during infancy and childhood include cataracts (1 per 1000 live births), congenital glaucoma (1 per 10,000 live births), and retinoblastoma (1 per 20,000 live births).

Through careful history, examination, vision testing, and appropriate referral, amblyopia and other ophthalmologic disorders can be detected and visual impairment can be lessened or averted. Early detection and prompt intervention are essential.

Recommendations of Major Authorities

Normal-Risk Children

American Academy of Family Physicians—Children should be screened for amblyopia and strabismus at 3 to 4 years of age.

Excerpted from *Clinician's Handbook of Preventive Services, Second Edition*, U.S. Department of Health and Human Services, Office of Disease Prevention and Health Promotion, 1998.

American Academy of Pediatrics and **Bright Futures**—Visual acuity testing should first be performed at 3 years of age. If the child is uncooperative, retesting should occur 6 months later. Subsequent testing should occur at 4, 5, 10, 12, 15, and 18 years of age. Subjective assessment by history should occur at visits at all other ages. All infants should be examined by 6 months of age to evaluate fixation preference, alignment, and presence of any eye disease. Children should again be medically evaluated for these problems by 3 to 4 years of age.

American Academy of Ophthalmology (AAO), American Association for Pediatric Ophthalmology and Strabismus (AAPOS), and **American Optometric Association (AOA)**—Eye and vision screening should be performed at birth and at approximately 6 months, 3 years, and 5 years of age. AAO has published recommendations regarding screening methods and indications for referral to be used by primary care clinicians in screening preschool children. AAO and AAPOS recommend that screening after 5 years of age be carried out at routine school checks or after the appearance of symptoms. AOA recommends optometric examinations every 2 years throughout school years.

Canadian Task Force on the Periodic Health Examination—Repeat examination of the eyes for strabismus is recommended during well-baby visits, especially during the first 6 months of life. There is fair evidence to include testing of visual acuity in the periodic health examination of preschool children.

US Preventive Services Task Force—All children should have testing for amblyopia and strabismus once before entering school, preferably at 3 to 4 years of age. Stereoacuity testing may be more effective than visual acuity testing in detecting these conditions. There is insufficient evidence to recommend for or against routine screening for diminished visual acuity among asymptomatic school children. Recommendations against such screening can be made on other grounds, including the inconvenience and cost of routine screening and the fact that refractive errors can be readily corrected when they produce symptoms. Clinicians should be alert for signs of ocular misalignment when examining all newborns, infants, and children.

High-Risk Children

American Academy of Ophthalmology—Asymptomatic children should have a comprehensive examination by an ophthalmologist if they are at high risk because of health and developmental problems that make screening by the primary care clinician difficult or inaccurate (e.g., retinopathy of prematurity or diagnostic evaluation of a complex disease with ophthalmic manifestations); a family history of conditions that cause or are associated with eye or vision problems (e.g., retinoblastoma, significant hyperopia, strabismus [particularly accommodative esotropia], amblyopia, congenital cataract, or glaucoma); multiple health problems, systemic disease, or use of medications that are known to be associated with eye disease and vision abnormalities (e.g., neurodegenerative disease, juvenile rheumatoid arthritis, systemic steroid therapy, systemic syndromes with ocular manifestations, or developmental delay with visual system manifestations).

American Optometric Association—The primary care clinician should remain alert for visual/ocular abnormalities associated with the following high-risk groups: infants who are premature, with low birth weight, or whose mothers have had rubella, venereal disease, AIDS-related infection, or a history of substance abuse or other medical problems during pregnancy, and children failing to progress educationally or exhibiting reading and/or learning disabilities. The presence of high refractive error or a family history of eye disease, crossed eyes, or congenital eye disorders also places infants and children at risk. Infants at risk should be examined by a doctor of optometry by 6 months of age. Children at risk should be examined at 3 years of age and annually beginning at 6 years of age. All infants and children may be referred to an optometrist for a comprehensive eye and/or vision examination.

Basics of Vision Screening

History

When screening for present or potential visual disorders, consider the following factors:

- Family history of vision or eye problems.

- History of maternal, intrapartum, or neonatal conditions that may place the child at high risk for visual disorders.

- Parental concerns about a child's visual functioning.

- Worsening grades and other school difficulties.

211

Physical Examination

A comprehensive examination of the eye includes the lids, lashes, tear ducts, orbit, conjunctiva, sclera, cornea, iris, pupillary responsiveness, range of motion, anterior chamber, lens, vitreous, retina, and optic nerve and vessels. Gaining the cooperation of a young child with an ophthalmoscopic examination can be difficult. It may be helpful to demonstrate the examination procedure on the parent beforehand and to have the child sit on the parent's lap.

Testing Procedures

Red Reflex: Perform this exam with an ophthalmoscope or other light source. In a darkened room, hold the light source at arm's length from the infant, and draw the infant's attention to look directly at the light. Both retinal reflexes should be red or red-orange and of equal intensity.

Corneal Light Reflex: To detect strabismus, perform this test with an ophthalmoscope or other light source. Corneal light reflections should fall symmetrically on corresponding points of the patient's eyes. Improper alignment will appear as asymmetry of reflections.

Differential Occlusion: Gently cover the infant's eyes, one at a time. Aversion to the occlusion is normal. This test may give a false-positive result and is generally less accurate than the corneal light reflex test for detecting strabismus.

Fixation: Hold a light or a small object in front of the infant. Normal eyes will be aligned in the same direction, without deviation.

Cover/Uncover: Have the child focus on a stationary target. Place a hand or cover in front of one eye, and observe the other eye. Movement of the observed eye is abnormal and demonstrates the presence of strabismus. As the covered eye is uncovered, observe it for movement. Movement is abnormal and indicates the presence of heterophoria.

Stereo testing: To detect stereopsis (binocular depth perception), use a stereo testing technique, such as the Random Dot E stereogram. While wearing polarized glasses, the child views test cards that contain fields of random dots. If stereopsis is present, the child will see a form stand out from the background of the cards.

Visual Acuity: Several eye charts are available to test visual acuity in children. In order of decreasing cognitive difficulty, these are: Snellen Letters, Snellen Numbers, Tumbling E, HOTV, Allen Figures, and LH (Leah Hyvarinen) Test. Use the test with the highest level of difficulty that the child is capable of performing. In general, the Snellen tests are too advanced for preschool-aged children. Test for visual acuity at 10, 15, or 20 feet using the appropriate chart. Using a distance of 10 feet for young children may result in better compliance because of closer interaction with the examiner. To ensure that a young child does not "peek" with the eye not being tested, hold the occluder for the child or use an adhesive occluder. Give a passing score for each line on which the child gives more than 50% correct responses. Recommended criteria for referral to an ophthalmologist or optometrist vary slightly. In general, refer any child with a difference between eye scores of two or more lines; children younger than age 5 years who score 20/40 or worse in either eye; and children aged 5 years or older who score 20/30 or worse in either eye.

Safety Counseling

Counsel parents and children about eye safety and the appropriate use of protective equipment. Children who participate in school shop or science labs or in certain sports (i.e., racquetball, squash) should wear safety lenses and safety frames approved by the American National Standards Institute. Children with good vision in only one eye should wear safety lenses and safety frames to protect the good eye, even if they do not otherwise need to wear glasses.

Patient Resources

Amblyopia: Is it Affecting Your Child's Sight?; Cataracts in Children: Eye Safety and Children; Eyeglasses for Infants and Children; Home Eye Test for Strabismus. American Academy of Ophthalmology, P.O. Box 7424, San Francisco, CA 94120. Send a business-size, self-addressed, stamped envelop with your request.

Your Child's Eyes. American Academy of Pediatrics, 141 Northwest Point Blvd., P.O. Box 927, Elk Grove Village, IL 60009-0927; (800) 433-9016. Internet address: http://www.aap.org.

Answers to Your Questions About: Lazy Eye, Nearsightedness, Astigmatism, Eye Coordination, Color Deficiency, Crossed-Eyes; Signs of a *Child's Vision Problems; Toys, Games and Your Child's Vision; Your Child's Eyes; Your Preschool Child's Eyes; Your School-Aged Child's Eyes*. American Optometric Association, 243 N. Lindbergh Blvd., St. Louis, MO 63141; (314) 991-4100. Internet address: http://www. aoanet.org/aoanet.

Provider Resources

Bright Futures: Guidelines for Health Supervision of Infants, Children and Adolescents; Bright Futures Pocket Guide; Bright Futures Anticipatory Guidance Cards. Available from the National Center for Education in Maternal and Child Health, 2000 15th Street North, Suite 701, Arlington, VA 22201-2617; (703) 524-7802. Internet address: http://www.brightfutures.org.

Policy Statement: Frequency of Ocular Examinations; National Eyecare Project (for those who do not have an eye doctor); Glaucoma 2001 Project (for people at risk for glaucoma). American Academy of Ophthalmology, P.O. Box 7424, San Francisco, CA 94120. Send a business-size, self-addressed, stamped envelope with your request.

Pediatric Eye and Vision Examination, Care of the Patient with Amblyopia, and other clinical practice guidelines. American Optometric Association, 243 N. Lindbergh Blvd., St. Louis, MO 63141; (800) 262-2210. Internet address: http://www.aoanet.org.

Part Four

Tips for Parents

Chapter 27

The Circumcision Decision: Pros and Cons

Description

Circumcision means cutting off the foreskin or ring of tissue that covers the head (glans) of the penis. This surgical procedure is usually performed on newborns on the day of discharge from the hospital.

Fewer children in the U.S. are being circumcised now than several years ago. According to a survey, 60 percent of American newborn males were circumcised in 1986, whereas 90 percent were circumcised in 1979.

The following information should help you decide what is best for your son.

Cultural Aspects

Followers of the Jewish and Moslem faiths perform circumcision for religious reasons. Nonreligious circumcision became popular in English-speaking countries between 1920 and 1950 because it was thought that circumcision might help prevent sexually transmitted diseases. Circumcision never became a common practice in Asia, South America, Central America, or most of Europe.

Over 80 percent of the world's male population is not circumcised. The circumcision rates have fallen to 1 percent of newborn males in Britain, 10 percent in New Zealand, and 40 percent in Canada.

Reprinted with permission of Barton Schmitt from *Clinical Reference Systems*, December 1997, p1286. © 1997 Clinical Reference Systems Ltd.

Purpose of the Foreskin

The presence of the foreskin is not some cosmic error. The foreskin protects the glans against urine, feces, and other types of irritation. Although rare events, infection of the urinary opening (meatitis) and scarring of the opening (meatal stenosis) occur almost exclusively in a circumcised penis. The foreskin may also serve a sexual function, namely protecting the sensitivity of the glans.

Benefits of Circumcision

In 1989, the American Academy of Pediatrics issued a new statement on circumcision, clarifying that the procedure carried small potential risks and benefits that parents needed to consider. According to a recent study by Dr. T.E. Wiswell, circumcision may protect against urinary tract infections during the first year of life. However, there is only a 1-percent chance that an uncircumcised infant will get a urinary tract infection. Should we circumcise all infants to prevent such a small percentage of urinary tract infections (which are treatable)? Probably not.

Removal of the foreskin prevents infections under the foreskin (posthitis) and persistent tight foreskin (phimosis). However, both of these conditions are uncommon and usually due to excessive attempts to retract the foreskin.

In general, circumcision does not prevent sexually transmitted disease later in life. While it does protect against cancer of the penis, good hygiene offers equal protection against this very rare condition.

Another argument for circumcision is "so he will look like other boys in his school," or "like his father." However, the psychological harm of being different from the father has never been documented. In general, boys don't mind looking different from other males in their family. However, they do mind being harassed in the locker room or shower, which may occur if most of their buddies are circumcised. It can be emotionally painful to be a trailblazer about the appearance of one's genitals.

In the final analysis, nonreligious circumcision is mainly cosmetic surgery.

Risks of Circumcision

Like any surgical procedure, circumcision may cause complications (in less than 1 per 100 circumcisions). Complications that might occur are skin infections, bloodstream infections, bleeding, gangrene, scarring, and various surgical accidents. A recent study showed that 1 of every 500 circumcised newborns suffered a serious side effect.

In addition, the procedure itself causes pain. However, this pain can be minimized if physicians use a local anesthetic to block the nerves of the foreskin.

Finally, the cost of circumcision is about $100 per procedure in the U.S. (A total of $200 million is spent on circumcisions each year.) You may have to pay for the procedure yourself because many medical insurance companies do not cover the costs of this procedure.

Recommendations

Circumcision of boys for religious purposes will continue. The need to circumcise other boys is open to question. Just because a father was circumcised doesn't mean that this optional procedure must be performed on the son. Because the foreskin comes as standard equipment, you might consider leaving it intact, unless your son will be attending a school where everyone else is likely to be circumcised. The risks and benefits are both too small to swing the vote either way. This is a parental decision, not a medical decision.

Chapter 28

Caring for a New Baby's Navel

Caring for the umbilical cord is a very simple process—nothing for parents to be squeamish about, says Dr. Herbert Pomerance, a professor of pediatrics at the University of South Florida in Tampa. Keeping the area clean and dry promotes healing, so doctors advise sponge baths for the newborn. Wipe his umbilical stump and the surrounding area of his belly with rubbing alcohol after every diaper change, and fold the diaper away from the cord to prevent it from getting damp or irritated. Parents should consult their pediatrician if they notice a yellowish fluid with an odor where stump meets stomach, or if the navel area or cord looks red or feels warm—all possible signs of infection.

When the cord finally drops off, there may be minimal bleeding; if so, apply steady pressure with a clean, dry cloth. Because the newly exposed navel is tender, gentle treatment is still required, says Dr. Kurt Metzl, a clinical professor of pediatrics at the University of Missouri-Kansas City School of Medicine. Continue to swab the area with alcohol after each diapering until the belly button has healed, typically one or two days later. At this stage, Metzl adds, tub baths are OK. (If an infant's navel hasn't healed within two weeks, a pediatrician can painlessly cauterize the tissue with silver nitrate.)

The belly button can also be affected by an umbilical hernia, an unusual weakness in the abdominal wall that causes the navel to distend—often when the baby cries. "There's only one thing to do about

"Navel Intelligence: Caring for a New Baby's Sensitive Belly Button," by Patty Ames, *Parenting*, undated; reprinted with permission.

that. Leave it alone," says Pomerance, cautioning against the old-fashioned remedy of taping a silver dollar over the belly button. "Putting a coin on it actually prevents healing." In some cases, when the condition doesn't heal by the time a child is five, surgery may be needed.

One question remains: What causes innies and outies? It has to do with the way the cord falls off, says Metzl. Days after it's gone, "you may get an idea of how the navel will eventually look," he adds, "but I wouldn't give written guarantees on it."

Chapter 29

Bathing Your Baby

Bathing can be a fun time for you and your baby. It is a good time to talk to your baby and check him/her for any new marks or rashes. A mild soap bath 3 or 4 times a week will help keep your baby clean and free from skin rashes and chafing. A plain water bath can be given on other days if desired or if your baby is hot and sweaty.

Safety Tips

Here are some safety tips to remember when giving a bath:

- Gather all the things you will need before you start giving the bath.

- Keep the room temperature 75-80 degrees to keep the baby from chilling. Avoid drafts.

- Always keep a firm hold on the baby after lathering. Soapy bodies are slippery.

- Test the bath water before bathing to prevent chilling or burning. Water should feel warm when tested with your elbow.

- Never leave your baby alone during the bath, not even "for a second." Never take your eyes off the baby, not even "for a second"

Children's Hospital Medical Center (Cincinnati), Patient Education Program, July 1987, revised February 1996. Used with permission of Children's Hospital Medical Center—Cincinnati.

You Will Need

- Clean basin or tub
- Bath towels
- Soft washcloth
- Shirt or gown
- Cotton balls
- Mild soap
- Diaper and pins

Bathing Your Baby

Your baby should be bathed on a pad until he is old enough to sit up. Make a bath pad by putting a clean towel on top of a folded blanket.

1. Wash your hands.

2. Fill washbasin with about 3 inches of warm water. Test the temperature.

3. Arrange all items within easy reach.

4. Undress your baby. You may leave baby dressed until after washing his face.

5. Place your baby on a pad near the washbasin.

6. Face: Wash his face with clear water using a soft washcloth.

7. Eyes: Wash his eyes gently with moist cotton ball. Start at the inner corner and wash toward his ears. Use fresh cotton ball for each eye.

8. Ears: Wash the outer ear with moist cotton twists, pat dry. Do not insert any objects into ears to clean them, except cotton twists.

9. Hair and Scalp: You may find that holding your baby while washing his head may be easier. Using the "football hold" may help you. This hold can be done by supporting your baby's head with your hand and his body with your forearm. Rest the baby's buttocks on your hip. Wet the baby's head with clear

water. Apply a small amount of soap to his head, including the soft spot, and rub gently in a circular motion. Rinse his hair with clear water, then towel dry, being sure hair is completely dry.

10. Body: Place the baby back on the pad. Start at the baby's neck and work your way down until you have washed the entire body. It may be easier at first to wash and dry the arms, then move to the stomach and back, and then finishing with the legs. Be sure to clean well between all skin folds. Rinse soap with clear water and dry baby completely with a soft towel.

11. Genital Area: If your baby is uncircumcised, pull the foreskin back and wash gently with soapy water. Rinse and dry. *Then pull the foreskin over the head of the penis.* The penis of a circumcised boy should be gently rinsed and dried. Do not put the baby's buttocks into water until after the circumcision has healed completely. If your baby is a girl, spread the labia (folds of the genitals) apart and wash gently from front to back using soapy water. Rinse with clear water and dry.

After Bathing

Dressing your baby after bathing should be done in the same way you would dress yourself. If it is warm outside, your baby does not need blankets and a sweater. If you are comfortable in lightweight clothing, so is your baby. Remember: dress him as you would yourself.

Clip your baby's nails as needed. Use a manicure scissors to trim fingernails and toenails. If nails are not kept short, your baby could scratch his face. Hint: Clip the baby's nails while the baby is asleep.

Special Scalp Care

If your baby's scalp does not look clean or becomes dry and scaly, wash the scalp well and dry every day. If you do this several times and his scalp does not improve, consult your doctor.

Chapter 30

Tips for Caring for and Preventing Diaper Rash

Diaper Rash—Guidelines for Parents

Diaper rash affects most babies, but it is usually not serious. Below we explain the causes of diaper rash, steps you can take to help prevent it, and how to treat it if it develops.

What is diaper rash?

Diaper rash can be any rash that develops inside the diaper area. In mild cases, the skin might be red. In more severe cases, there may be painful open sores. You will usually see a rash around the abdomen, genitalia, and inside the skin folds of the thighs and buttocks. Mild cases clear up within 3 to 4 days without any treatment. If a rash persists or develops again after treatment, consult your pediatrician.

What causes diaper rash?

Over the years diaper rash has been blamed on various causes, such as teething, diet, and ammonia in the urine. However, medical experts now believe it is caused by any of the following:

- Too much moisture
- Chafing or rubbing
- Prolonged contact of the skin with urine, feces, or both

- Yeast infection
- Bacterial infection
- Allergic reaction to diaper material

When skin stays wet for too long, the layers that protect it start to break down. When wet skin is rubbed, it also damages more easily. Moisture from a soiled diaper can harm your baby's skin and make it more prone to chafing. When this happens, a diaper rash may develop.

Further rubbing between the moist folds of the skin only makes the rash worse. This is why diaper rash often forms in the skin folds of the groin and upper thighs.

More than half of babies between 4 months and 15 months of age develop diaper rash at least once in a 2-month period. Diaper rash occurs more often in the following instances:

- As infants get older—mostly between 8 to 10 months of age
- If babies are not kept clean and dry
- In babies who have frequent stools, especially when the stools stay in their diapers overnight
- When babies begin to eat solid foods
- When babies are taking antibiotics, or in nursing babies whose mothers are taking antibiotics

Infants taking antibiotics are more likely to get diaper rashes caused by yeast infections. Yeast infects the weakened skin and causes a bright red rash with red spots at its edges. You can treat this with over-the-counter antifungal medications. If you see these symptoms, you may wish to consult with your pediatrician.

What can I do to prevent diaper rash?

To help prevent diaper rash from developing, you should:

- Change the diaper promptly after your child wets or has a bowel movement. This limits moisture on the skin.
- Do not put the diaper on airtight, especially overnight. Keep the diaper loose so that the wet and soiled parts do not rub against the skin as much.
- Gently clean the diaper area with water. You do not need to use soap with every diaper change or after every bowel movement.

(Breastfed infants may stool as many as 8 times a day.) Use soap only when the stool does not come off easily.

- Do not use talcum or baby powder because they could cause breathing problems in your infant.

- Avoid over-cleansing with wipes that can dry out the skin. The alcohol or perfume in these products may irritate some babies' skin.

What can I do if my baby gets diaper rash?

If diaper rash develops despite your best efforts to prevent it, try the following:

- Change wet or soiled diapers often.

- Use clear water to cleanse the diaper area with each diaper change.

- Using water in a squirt bottle lets you clean and rinse without rubbing.

- Pat dry; do not rub. Allow the area to air dry fully.

- Apply a thick layer of protective ointment or cream (such as one that contains zinc oxide or petrolatum) to form a protective coating on the skin. These ointments are usually thick and pasty and do not have to be completely removed at the next diaper change.

- Remember, heavy scrubbing or rubbing will only damage the skin more.

- Check with your pediatrician if the rash:
  - Has blisters or pus-filled sores
  - Does not so away within 48 to 72 hours
  - Gets worse

- Use creams with steroids only if your pediatrician recommends them. They are rarely needed and may be harmful.

Which type of diaper should I use?

There are many different brands of diapers. Diapers are made of cloth or disposable materials. After they get soiled, you can wash cloth diapers and use them again and you throw away disposable diapers.

Research suggests that diaper rash is less common with the use of disposable diapers. In child care settings, children who wear super-absorbent disposable diapers tend to have lower rates of diaper rash. Regardless of which type of diaper you use, diaper rash occurs less often and is less severe when you change diapers often.

If you use a cloth diaper, you can use a stay-dry liner inside it to keep your baby drier. If you choose not to wash cloth diapers yourself, you can have a diaper service clean them. If you do your own washing, you will need to presoak heavily soiled diapers. Keep and wash soiled diapers separate from other clothes. Use hot water and double-rinse each wash. Do not use fabric softeners or antistatic products on the diapers because they may cause rashes in young, sensitive skin.

Whether you use cloth diapers, disposables, or both, always change diapers as needed to keep your baby clean, dry, and healthy.

Remember—never leave your baby alone on the changing table or on any other surface above the floor. Even a newborn can make a sudden turn and fall to the floor.

Diaper rash is usually not serious, but it can cause your child discomfort. Follow the steps listed above to help prevent and treat diaper rash. Discuss any questions you have about these steps with your pediatrician.

Chapter 31

A Healthy Mouth for Your Baby

Before Your Baby Is Born

What you eat when you are pregnant is important. Eating right will help you and your growing baby stay healthy. Follow your doctor's advice for eating the right foods and taking vitamins.

It's also time to think about how you'll feed your baby. Remember, breast-feeding is best.

Protect Your Baby's Teeth with Fluoride

Fluoride (said like floor-eyed) protects teeth from tooth decay and helps heal early decay. Fluoride is in the drinking water of some towns and cities. Ask your dentist or doctor if your water has fluoride in it. If it doesn't, talk to your dentist or doctor about giving you a prescription for fluoride drops for your baby.

Check and Clean Your Baby's Teeth

Check Your Baby's Teeth. Healthy teeth should be all one color. If you see spots or stains on the teeth, take your baby to your dentist.

Clean Your Baby's Teeth. Clean your baby's teeth as soon as they come in with a clean, soft cloth or a baby's toothbrush. Clean the teeth

From "A Healthy Mouth for Your Baby," National Institute of Dental and Craniofacial Research (NIDCR), available at www.nidcr.nih.gov. For printed copies, write to: National Institute of Dental and Craniofacial Research, P.O. Box 54793, Washington, DC 20032.

at least once a day. It's best to clean them right before bedtime. At about age 2, most of your child's teeth will be in. Now you can start brushing them with a small drop of fluoride toothpaste. As your child gets older let him use his own toothbrush—but you put the toothpaste on the toothbrush until about age 6. Very young children cannot get their teeth clean by themselves. Until your children are about 7 years old, you should brush their teeth after they do.

Feed Your Baby Healthy Food

Choose foods that do not have a lot of sugar in them. Give your child fruits and vegetables instead of candy and cookies.

Prevent Baby Bottle Tooth Decay

- Do not put your baby to bed with a bottle at night or at nap time. (If you put your baby to bed with a bottle, fill it only with water.)

- Milk, formula, juices, and other sweet drinks such as soda all have sugar in them. Sucking on a bottle filled with liquids that have sugar in them can cause tooth decay. Decayed teeth can cause pain and can cost a lot to fill.

- During the day, do not give your baby a bottle filled with sweet drinks to use like a pacifier.

- If your baby uses a pacifier, do not dip it in anything sweet like sugar or honey.

- Near his first birthday, you should teach your child to drink from a cup instead of a bottle.

Take Your Child to the Dentist

Ask your dentist when to bring your child in for his first visit. Usually, the dentist will want to see a child between ages 1 and 2. At this first visit, your dentist can quickly check your child's teeth.

For More Information

National Institute of Dental and Craniofacial Research
National Institutes of Health
31 Center Drive MSC 2290
Bethesda, MD 20892-2290

Chapter 32

Taking a Temperature

Types and Definition of Temperatures

- Oral—temperature taken by mouth.
- Axillary—temperature taken in the armpit (axilla).
- Rectal—temperature taken by rectum (bottom).

Reading a Thermometer

To read a thermometer: the space between the short marks is 0.2 (two tenths) of a degree. The space between the large marks is 1 (one) degree. 98.6 degrees is the normal reading.

1. Check to make sure the bulb of the thermometer is not broken or cracked.

2. Hold the thermometer at eye level. Turn until you see the scale markings and numbers. Bring it down slightly below eye level and turn it slowly. You will see a shining band.

3. Read the number at the end of the band. This is the temperature.

Children's Hospital Medical Center (Cincinnati), Patient Education Program, September 1990. Used with permission of Children's Hospital Medical Center—Cincinnati.

233

4. If the mercury is above 94 degrees, shake it down by grasping the thermometer firmly and snapping the wrist sharply. Read the thermometer.

5. General rule for age: If the child is newborn to 6 years, take temperature by rectum or axillary. If the child is 6 years and over, take the temperature by mouth if child is cooperative.

6. Deciding which method to use to take temperature:

    Axillary temperatures are always safe to take.

    Oral temperatures are safe to take if the child will hold the thermometer under the tongue with lips closed and will not bite thermometer. (May not be safe to take oral temperature on child under 6 years.)

    Rectal temperatures are used most often in babies unless they are having diarrhea, convulsions (fits), bleeding from rectum, or are extremely restless.

To Take an Oral Temperature (by Mouth)

1. Use a thermometer with a long bulb.

2. Place thermometer under the child's tongue. Tell child to keep lips firmly closed but not to bite it.

3. Leave thermometer in place for 3 minutes. Read it.

To Take a Rectal Temperature (by Rectum)

1. Use a thermometer with stubby bulb.

2. Place infant on stomach. Put Vaseline on bulb of thermometer.

3. Put thermometer 1 inch into rectum. Hold in place for 3 minutes. Remove it and read it.

To Take an Axillary Temperature (at the Armpit)

1. Place bulb of thermometer between body and arm in the armpit.

2. Hold arm tightly against body for 5 minutes. Remove it and read.

Care of the Thermometer

To clean a thermometer, draw it through a soapy cotton ball or tissue. Rinse in cool water. Store it in a safe place, out of the reach of children.

Remember: You are placing a piece of glass into your child's body. Never leave the child alone while taking his temperature.

Chapter 33

Suctioning the Nose with a Bulb Syringe

Taking mucus out of your baby's nose with a bulb syringe makes it easier for him to breathe and eat. Before using the bulb syringe, you should thin the mucus with normal saline (salt water) nose drops.

You Will Need

- 1 8oz. cup warm water
- Kitchen measuring spoon
- Salt
- Clean jar with cover
- Small blanket roll
- Nose droppers
- Tissues
- Bulb syringe

To Make the Saline Nose Drops

1. Fill 1 cup (8 ounces) with warm (not hot) tap water.
2. Add 1/4 level teaspoon of salt.

Children's Hospital Medical Center (Cincinnati), Patient Education Program, July 1990. Used with permission of Children's Hospital Medical Center—Cincinnati.

3. Stir to dissolve the salt.

4. Keep this salt water in a clean, covered jar.

5. Discard this solution after one week.

How to Put Nose Drops into Child's Nose

1. Roll up a small blanket and place under baby's shoulders.

2. Using nose dropper, drop drops of saline into each nostril (check with your pediatrician for a recommended number of drops).

3. Hold your baby in this position for about two minutes. This will give the saline enough time to thin the secretions. Then suction.

To Suction

1. Suction your baby's nose before feeding. (If you suction it after the baby has been fed, the saline and suctioning may cause vomiting.)

2. Squeeze the air out of the bulb (Step 1).

3. Gently place the tip of the bulb into a nostril (Step 2).

4. Let the air come back into the bulb. The suction will pull the mucus out of the nose and into the bulb (Step 3).

5. Squeeze mucus out of bulb into a tissue.

6. Suction the other nostril the same way.

7. Gently wipe off the mucus around the nose with tissues to prevent skin irritation.

After Suctioning

Wash the cup, dropper, and bulb syringe in cool, soapy water. Squeeze the bulb several times to clean out the mucus. Rinse with clear water.

If you have any questions, call your pediatrician.

Chapter 34

Thumbsucking and Pacifiers

Thumbsucking

Before you call in the guards, be assured that thumbsucking is a normal habit in babies and children. Even before birth, some babies can be seen in ultrasound pictures sucking their fingers or thumb in the womb. Sucking is an instinct, and a source of comfort for babies. If your baby finds comfort in sucking her thumb, be happy that she has found a way to calm herself.

More than half of all thumbsucking babies stop the habit on their own around six or seven months of age. But if your child continues to suck her thumb, other adults may suggest that you replace it with a pacifier, saying that a child who sucks her thumb has "a complex," or is insecure. If you do so, your child will simply replace one sucking habit for another, while you add to your burdens the whereabouts of her pacifier. In addition, you will eventually be the one who must physically take away the pacifier when she is "too old." Thumbs have the added advantage of being completely portable and sanitary: they cannot be lost or dropped during the night or on outings, making the trauma of a missing pacifier nonexistent.

If you allow your child the power to comfort herself, but are worried that she will ruin her teeth, remember that children usually stop

---

This chapter combines text from "Thumbsucking," www.kidsdoctor.com, reprinted with permission and "Kicking the Pacifier Habit," by Vicki Lansky, The Parenting Resource Center on the web, www.parentsplace.com, reprinted with permission from the author.

239

sucking their thumbs as soon as peer pressure begins to work. Thumbsucking may then be reserved for private moments or times of particular upset, but even that will gradually disappear. If your child sucks her thumb after age four, you may be legitimately concerned about her developing palate. Talk with your child, and together think of ways that she can try to reduce her sucking. If she still has trouble, your dentist may have suggestions for other approaches, like mouth 'appliances' and bitter thumb coatings, that can be effective in discouraging thumbsucking.

Some parents have found success with putting a band-aid over the thumb, which is unpleasant to suck, but has none of the intrusiveness of an appliance. Try not to push your child too hard on this point, as you may end up giving her a real "complex" after all: a negative focus may bring about guilt or increased insecurity. Scolding or punishing generally does more harm than good, and even a committed thumbsucker will eventually stop on her own.

Kicking the Pacifier Habit

Habits that parents don't like aren't necessarily bad ones; most often they're just annoying. If your child is hooked on a pacifier, and it bothers you, there are some things you can try. Remember that you can't break a child's habit, you can only help your child break it.

- Try putting some pickle juice or something sour or bitter on the pacifier. If it doesn't taste good, it might lose its appeal.

- Lose the pacifier if your child's older than 18 months of age. After that, a child can usually understand the concept of losing things and won't question the fact that it's gone.

- You can also start a little hole in a pacifier and enlarge it a bit every few days until the taste and the shape are no longer appealing.

- Tell the child that when the pacifier is lost or worn out, there will be no more. Advanced notice often makes it easier to accept. Or just explain matter of factly that nobody over two uses a pacifier.

If none of this works for you, and your child refuses to give it up, have patience. You can still limit the places or times when pacifier use is acceptable. Within a month or so, you can always try again. Sooner or later your child will give it up. I guarantee it.

—This section by Vicki Lansky

Chapter 35

The Crying Baby

Crying is a new baby's only means of communicating. At first it isn't always possible to tell why your baby is crying.

Is it because your baby is hungry, thirsty, lonely, tired, too hot or too cold, in pain, or just wants a cuddle?

The "average" healthy baby cries for a total of two hours a day during the first three months, according to findings of the Infant Crying Study conducted by the Thomas Coram Research Unit of London University. There was no evidence that babies of first time mothers cried more than other babies.

The way in which you respond to crying is important. Research has also shown that mothers who respond quickly to their baby's cries have babies who are contented and secure, whereas babies whose cries are ignored tend to cry even more. Perhaps this is why most mothers respond so quickly when their babies cry.

Follow Your Instincts

Always follow your instincts when your baby is crying. In our culture, there is a tendency to equate frequent nursing of babies with "spoiling." But young babies need a lot of loving and physical contact and cannot be "spoilt" in this way. They are likely to be more contented. Don't blame yourself. Other studies have shown that some babies cry more than others, even when their care is identical. Babies whose mothers were given drugs during labor tend to cry more

Reprinted with permission from www.babyworld.com; undated.

and sleep less. Some babies who had a difficult birth also tend to be more irritable.

Calling the Doctor

Consult your doctor without delay if you feel that your baby is crying excessively, or if cries sound unnatural. Because persistent crying may be due to conditions needing urgent attention (including pain and meningitis), early medical investigation is an essential precaution. If, after careful examination, the doctor pronounces your baby fit and well, you will need to look for another explanation.

Causes of Crying

Hunger: This is the most common cause of crying. If you think your baby is hungry, offer a feeding. Most young babies need frequent feedings during the first few weeks. Sometimes your baby may just want a short comfort feeding, or may be thirsty. If you are breast-feeding, offer the breast, as the "foremilk" is a good thirst quencher. If your baby is bottle fed, offer cool boiled water or well diluted fruit juice. However, you will need to remember that babies can vary in their appetite for food at different times. So it is worthwhile offering extra milk or a few extra breast feedings, if your baby seems hungrier than usual. By the age of four months, it may also be time to start introducing small amounts of weaning foods.

Undressing: Most new babies hate being undressed and bathed. So if necessary, keep these activities to a minimum until your baby gets used to being handled.

Temperature: Check that your baby is comfortable. Add or remove a blanket, if necessary. Hands and feet won't give an accurate indication of temperature. The best way to check quickly is to place your hand on your baby's tummy.

Discomfort: Check to see if your baby's diaper needs changing, that clothing is not too tight, and that diaper pins are secure.

Loneliness: Your baby may just need a cuddle or may feel bored if left lying awake for a long period.

Fear: A loud noise or sudden movement may frighten your baby. At about five or six months, babies develop a fear of strangers.

Tiredness: Some babies cry when they feel tired or over-stimulated.

Pain: Some babies cry a lot when ill or teething. If you think that your baby is ill, seek advice.

Colic: ("Three-month colic") is one of the most common causes of crying up to the age of three months. The cause is thought to be pain due to gas bubbles trapped in the baby's intestines. (Don't assume that persistent crying is due to colic. Always consult your doctor.) In a typical colic attack the baby has a shrill, piercing cry which can last for several hours. The problem is more common in the early evening, but it can occur during the day. The baby usually appears tense, with some distension of the abdomen; and the knees may be drawn up, indicating abdominal pain. The baby is unlikely to have diarrhea, vomiting or a rise in temperature, and usually is otherwise healthy. Soothing, rhythmic movement such as rocking, gently bouncing, arm carrying or a car ride may help. Infant "colic drops" can be purchased from pharmacists. Or you may like to try a small amount of camomile tea, or camomile colic drops.

Help List for a Crying Baby

- Check if your baby's diaper needs changing
- Make sure your baby is not hungry or thirsty
- Check that your baby is not too hot or cold
- Check that your baby is not physically ill
- Treat colic or teething problems
- Rock your baby in a rocking chair or swing
- Bounce your baby gently in your arms or in a bouncing cradle
- Talk and sing to your baby
- Carry your baby in a baby sling
- Talk to your health visitor, pediatrician, or a parents' helpline
- Take your baby for a walk, or car ride
- Turn the radio or television on loudly
- Switch on the vacuum cleaner
- Leave your baby in another room for a short period
- Leave your baby with someone else and take a break
- Play soothing music or a 'womb sounds' recording

- Accept that some babies will cry whatever you do
- Remember that this phase will soon pass

Getting Help

Sometimes, no matter what you do, your baby continues to cry. Parents of babies who cry continuously for long periods can become extremely stressed and exhausted. This can place a great strain on their relationship. Sometimes there may even be a risk of harm to the child. The danger of serious brain damage, if a parent shakes a child during a prolonged crying fit, is stressed in a new campaign by the National Society for Prevention of Cruelty to Children (NSPCC).

National Society for Prevention of Cruelty to Children
42 Curtain Road
London EC2 A3H UK

In the United States, contact:

La Leche League International
1400 Meacham
Schaumburg, IL 60173
(847) 519-7730
(800) LA-LECHE

National Maternal and Child Health Clearinghouse
2070 Chain Bridge Rd.
Suite 450
Vienna, VA 22182
(703) 356-1964

Chapter 36

Coping with Colic

Your baby cries every afternoon for hours at a time. The crying has worn you down to the point where you feel like joining in. When a healthy baby cries like this, chances are that he has colic. What exactly is colic? What causes it, and what can you do about it?

Colic is not a physical disorder or disease. Doctors at The Nemours Children's Clinic—Jacksonville define colic as three or more hours a day of continued crying. The crying is not due to hunger, a wet diaper, or other visible causes, and the child cannot be calmed down.

A baby's fussiness may not be colic at all. The first thing to do is look for signs of illness. Colicky babies have a healthy sucking reflex and a good appetite. Sick babies may appear colicky but won't have the same strong sucking reflex, and they'll also drink less milk. Colicky babies like to be cuddled and handled. Sick babies appear "sore," because they don't like to be handled despite their fussiness. Colicky babies may spit up from time to time, but if your baby is actually vomiting, you should call the doctor. True vomiting is not a sign of colic.

Contrary to one popular belief, doctors at Nemours believe that colic is rarely, if ever, caused by a milk allergy. After all, breast-fed babies also get colic. They also believe that colic is not caused by gas. It may be hard to tell which came first, the gas or the colic, but they suggest that more often than not, a colicky baby has developed gas

---

From www.kidshealth.org, "Colic and a Baby's Temperament," © 1999 The Nemours Foundation. Used with permission.

by swallowing too much air during crying spells. They add that prescribing anti-gas drops has not proven to be a very effective way to treat colic.

Many doctors think that colic is due to the baby's own temperament. Some babies just take a little bit longer to get adjusted to the world, or a day and night cycle. This is perfectly normal, and the colic will go away.

There are some things you can do for your colicky baby that may make life easier for both of you during those crying spells. First, make sure your baby is not hungry. If he isn't, don't continue trying to feed him. Instead, try to console him.

- Walk with your baby or rock him.

- Place him across your lap on his belly and rub his back.

- Put him in a swing. The motion may have a soothing effect.

- Take breaks and let another adult care for your baby for a while.

- If all else fails, put him in the car and go for a ride. Somehow the vibration and movement of the car generally calm a baby.

Chapter 37

Sleep Problems in Children

Sleep problems are very common among children during the first few years of life. Problems include reluctance to go to sleep, waking up in the middle of the night, nightmares, and sleepwalking. It is important to remember that children vary in the amount of sleep they need, the amount of time they require to fall asleep, how easily they are awakened, and how easily they can be resettled. The good news is that most sleep problems can be solved and your pediatrician can help. This chapter has been developed to help parents know what to expect, and how to help their children develop consistent sleep patterns.

Night Waking

Infants are born with irregular sleep cycles, which take about 6 months to mature. As children get older, their need for sleep decreases; however, different children have different needs. It's normal for them to wake up briefly during the night but these awakenings should only last a few minutes and children should be expected to go back to sleep easily on their own.

While newborns sleep an average of 16 to 17 hours per day, they may only sleep 1 or 2 hours at a time. Sometimes newborns will get their days and nights "mixed up," and do most of their sleeping during the day. To prevent or break this habit, try to keep your infant awake for longer periods during the day. Also, when feeding or changing your baby during the night, try to keep him as calm and quiet as possible so he can easily fall back to sleep. Remember, if your infant sleeps for large blocks of time during the day, she will be more likely to be awake during the night.

Steps to Take That May Help to Prevent Night Waking

- Don't let your infant sleep as long during the day. For example, if your baby sleeps for 4 hours during the day, try to wake him at 3½ hours, 3 hours, and then 2 hours. To make up for the lost sleep, your baby should sleep longer at night.

- Put your baby into the crib at the first signs of drowsiness. Ideally it is best to let the baby learn to relax himself to sleep. If you hold or rock him until he falls asleep, he may depend on your being there upon awakening. This may interfere with his learning to soothe himself and fall asleep alone. However, many infants are more likely to fall asleep and stay asleep with the security of a favorite blanket or toy.

- Avoid putting your baby to bed with a pacifier; she may wake up without it and begin to cry. Pacifiers should not be used to help a baby sleep, but to satisfy the baby's need to suck. If your baby falls asleep with the pacifier, gently remove it before putting her in bed.

- Begin to delay your reaction to infant fussing at 4 to 6 months of age. Wait 5 minutes before you go in to check him, because he will probably fall back to sleep in a few minutes anyway. If he continues to cry, check on him, but avoid turning on the light, playing, picking up, or rocking him. If crying continues, wait a few more minutes and then recheck the baby. If he still can't settle, be sure he isn't hungry, wet or soiled, feverish, or otherwise acting sick.

If your baby is ill, these suggestions should be relaxed. After your baby feels better, begin to reestablish sleep patterns.

How to Avoid Sleep Problems in Toddlers and Preschoolers

Many parents find their toddler's bedtime one of the hardest parts of the day. It is common for children this age to resist going to sleep, especially if there are older siblings who are still awake. However, children of this age usually need 10 to 12 hours of sleep each night.

To help prepare your child for sleep, make sure there is a quiet period before he goes to bed. Establishing a pleasant routine that includes reading, singing, or a warm bath will help your child understand that it will soon be time to go to sleep. Try to set a consistent schedule for him by making bedtime the same time every night. His sleep patterns will adjust accordingly. If parents work late hours, it may be tempting to play with their child before bedtime; however, active play just before bedtime may leave the child excited and unable to sleep.

Many children have a favorite teddy bear or toy that they take to bed each night; others may have a special blanket. Such comforting "transitional objects" often help children fall asleep—especially if they awaken during the middle of the night. Whatever sort of comfort your child takes to bed, make sure it is safe. A teddy bear may have a ribbon, button, or other part that may pose a choking hazard for your child. Look for sturdy construction at the seams, because stuffing or pellets inside the stuffed animal may also cause suffocation.

Make sure that the temperature in your child's room is comfortable. Clothes should not restrict movement. Some children may like to have a drink of water. Be sure to put the child into bed while he is still awake. A child may want a night-light left on or the door left slightly open. Try to anticipate and handle your child's needs before bedtime so that he doesn't use them to avoid going to bed.

Try not to return to your child's room every time she complains or calls out. A child will quickly learn if you always give in to her demands at bedtime. Also, try to avoid letting your child sleep with you. This will only make it harder for her to learn to fall asleep when she is alone.

Do the following when your child calls out:

- Wait several seconds before answering. Your response time should be longer each time to give your child an opportunity to fall asleep on her own.

- Reassure your child that you are there. If you need to go into her room, don't stay too long.

- Move farther from your child's bed every time you reassure her, until you can do this verbally from the adjoining room.

Nightmares

Nightmares are scary dreams followed by complete awakening. They usually happen during the second half of the night when dreaming is most intense. After the nightmare is over, your child will usually wake up and tell you what occurred. Children may be crying or fearful after a nightmare but will be aware of your presence. They may have trouble falling back to sleep, because they can remember the details of the dream.

Handling nightmares:

- Reach the child as quickly as possible.

- Arouse her and assure her that you are there and won't let anything harm her.

- Allowing the child to have the bedroom light on for a short period may be reassuring.

- If your child is crying or shaking, comfort and calm him.

- Keep in mind that a nightmare is real to a child. Listen to him and encourage him to tell you what happened in the dream.

- Once the child is calm, encourage her to go back to sleep.

Night Terrors

Night terrors are different from nightmares and far less common. Night terrors happen when there is a switch from deep sleep to lighter sleep, usually an hour or so after a child falls asleep. During a night terror, it is almost impossible to wake the child who may be thrashing, screaming, kicking, and/or staring without signs of recognizing his parents. A child may also sweat, shake, breathe heavily, and run around the room.

A child may try to push you away, especially when you try to restrain him or her. The night terror may last for as long as 45 minutes. Usually, children seem to fall right back to sleep after a night terror, but they have not actually been awake. Like nightmares, a night terror may represent the way a child views the events of the day or may relate to aggressive feelings or fears. However, unlike a nightmare, a child does not remember a night terror.

Handling night terrors:

- Remain calm. Night terrors are usually more frightening for the parent than for the child.

- Do not try to wake your child.

- If the child tries to get out of bed, gently restrain him.

- Remember, your child will probably relax and sleep quietly again as suddenly as he "awoke."

- If your child has night terrors, be sure to explain to any babysitters what may occur and what to do.

Keep in mind that night terrors are often more scary for parents than for children and they rarely indicate any serious problems. Night terrors happen most often during early childhood, and usually disappear by the time a child reaches grade school. It is rare for night terrors to happen frequently or for long periods of time. If they do persist, talk to your pediatrician.

Sleepwalking and Sleeptalking

Sleepwalking and sleeptalking commonly happen when a child is awakening from a deep sleep. Sleepwalking children will often return to bed by themselves and don't even remember that they've gotten out of bed. Children are often difficult to awaken during sleepwalking and/or sleeptalking episodes. Sleepwalking tends to run in families. Most children overcome this problem by about 6 years of age.

To make sure your child doesn't get injured during a sleepwalking episode, clear the bedroom area of any toys, furniture, or other potential hazards that your child could trip over or fall on. There is no need to try to wake your child when she is sleepwalking; merely lead her back to bed and she will probably settle down on her own.

Teeth Grinding

This behavior produces an unpleasant sound, but is not harmful to the teeth. It is frequently related to tension and anxiety and usually disappears in a short while; however, it may reappear with the next stressful episode.

Finding the Cause of Sleep Problems

First examine what your child does during the day. There may be a simple explanation for why a child is having trouble sleeping. Does your son or daughter get too much sleep during the day? Is he watching too much TV or playing video games all day?

Family and other stresses that you are experiencing may also affect your child. Even changes that seem minor to you may totally disrupt your child's life. Problems may include: fighting between parents, a recent divorce, a death in the family, illness, fights with siblings, problems at school, moving, a new baby in the house, or even a new teacher.

It may be helpful for you in preparation for discussing a sleep problem with your pediatrician to keep a sleep diary for your child. Chart the following: where the child sleeps, what time she was put to bed, the time it takes the child to fall asleep, the time the child awoke in the morning, the time and length of naps, the time the child awakened during the night, how long it took the child to fall back to sleep, what you did to comfort and console the child, any changes or stresses in the home, and even the time that you went to bed. Keep in mind that every child is different and no two children have the same sleep patterns or problems.

Handling your child's sleep problems may be difficult and it is normal to become upset when a child keeps you awake at night. Just keep in mind that sleep problems are very common and with time and your pediatrician's support, your child will outgrow them.

Try to be understanding. A negative response by a parent can sometimes make a sleep problem worse, especially if it is associated with a stressful situation like divorce, a new sibling, or some other recent change in the family.

If the problem persists, it could mean there is a physical or emotional reason that your child can't sleep. Keep in mind that every child is different and most sleep problems last only a short time. However, if you feel you need additional help, start a sleep diary and discuss this problem with your child's pediatrician.

Chapter 38

Temper Tantrums

Question

My 25 month-old son throws temper tantrums at the worst possible times, like in the grocery store (which happened to me yesterday). What do I do? I'm so embarrassed! *Anonymous*

Answer

You are not alone! Most parents who have had a two-year-old have experienced the same situation and the same feelings. Temper tantrums are very common at this age, and when viewed in context, they can be an extremely constructive part of the development of a healthy child.

Newborns and infants are quite happy as long as their basic physical needs are met. Children in the developmental stage known as the "Terrible Twos," or "First Adolescence," become aware of the choices available to them and as a result become angry or frustrated when they are powerless over those choices. The result is often "Temper Tantrums" or what I like to call "Emotional Storms."

Let's look at the example you mentioned of the grocery store—as an adult, you can choose whether or not you want to go to the grocery store, when to go, what products you are going to buy, and which products you will not purchase. When you are in the middle of shopping

From Dr. Greene's House Calls at http://www.drgreen.com, May 21, 1996. Reprinted with permission of Dr. Alan Greene.

in the grocery store, your child will see things he wants. To make the supermarket situation worse, there are cleverly-designed packages up and down the aisles that scream, "Buy me! Buy me! Buy me!" To a large extent we are able to tune that out (although it affects us much more than we think). For a small child who is just learning to make choices, it's like going to a deafening rock concert. Visually they are overwhelmed by high-decibel choices. They are compelled to start wanting multiple attractive items. When they can't have what they want, they dissolve into tears and worse—deafening screams. Of course, everybody in the store turns and looks at your child, and (shudder) at you!

Surveys have shown that there are two common reactions of parents in this situation. The first is to spank or discipline the child in some way. Our role during this phase is to teach our children to make choices, to teach them to grow up as independent, highly functioning people. If you discipline a child for a temper tantrum in a store, you are teaching a powerful unconscious lesson: down the road, when he or she is in second adolescence, and is confused, hurting, scared, and doesn't know what choices to make—don't talk to Mom or Dad, because they will not understand and it will hurt.

The second major way that people deal with temper tantrums in stores is to give the children whatever they had the temper tantrums to get. Basically, this teaches kids that if they cry hard enough, or act out sufficiently, they will get whatever they want. We don't want to teach our children that either.

So, what does one do about temper tantrums? Try to avoid emotional storms whenever possible. Children are most susceptible to storms when they are tired, hungry, uncomfortable or bored. When possible, plan shopping for times when your child is rested, fed, and healthy. Interact with your son throughout shopping and/or bring along stimulating toys or books.

Remember the situation from your child's perspective: you are going along making choice, after choice, after choice, but when he tries to make a choice, he doesn't get what he wants. You can see how frustrating this would be. It's often helpful to let your child pick out one or two things when at the store. A good way to do this is when a child asks for something, instead of saying, "No," (which will immediately make him or her say, "Yes!") say, "Let's write that down." Then write it down. When your child asks for something else, write that down, too. Then when you are all done, read back a few of the things on the list that you think would be good choices, and let him pick one or two of the things on the list. If children can make some choices, they will both learn more and feel better. Another thing that is really worthwhile is for you to make a list before you go to the store. That way it won't look so arbitrary when you pick what you want off the shelf, and your child doesn't get his choice. As you shop, whenever you put something in your basket, check it off your list (even if it is not on your list, check it off. The list is to teach that each item has a purpose, not that you had thought of it previously).

These strategies can greatly reduce the number of emotional storms, but their appearance is inevitable. What then?

First, take a deep breath. I've been in a grocery store with my children having temper tantrums, as a pediatrician, with my patients in the checkout line. The first thing you feel is, "I just wish I could drop into the floor someplace so nobody would see me." A lot of people won't understand. They will look at you and think your child is spoiled, or you are a bad parent. The truth of the matter is you probably have a normal child and are a good parent.

It is not a defect in parenting that your child is acting this way. People who don't have kids may not understand, yet. That is their problem, though. Try to be patient with them.

When I see a parent whose child is having a tantrum in a store, I am reminded of labor. When I look at a mom in labor, I see something that is heroic, and triumphant, and beautiful. Tears come to my eyes when I am privileged to be a part of a birth. So, the next time this painful situation happens to you, take a deep breath and remember, if Dr. Greene were here, he would see something heroic and beautiful.

Next, while you are taking a deep breath, consciously relax. Kids really play off your emotions. It's so hard to relax in this situation, but just let your muscles go. The more uptight you are, the more energy is available for their tantrums. Kids thrive on attention, even negative attention.

Where you go from here depends on your child. Some children will calm down if you pick them up and hold them. My first son was like that. His storm would dissolve if you just gave him a big hug and told him it would be all right. If you picked up my second son during a storm, he would hit you—there are different ways to get him to calm down. Each child is unique. One thing that often works very well is to try to voice to the child what he is going through. "You must really want to get this, don't you?" Then he may melt and say, "Uh huh." You will have to experiment with your son to see what it is that can help him understand that everything is okay, these bad feelings will pass, and that it's all a normal part of growing up.

Whatever you do, if your child had a temper tantrum to try to get something, don't give it to him, even if you would have ordinarily done so. Giving in to tantrums is what spoils a child. Giving in is the easiest, quickest solution in the short run, but it damages your child, prolongs this phase, and ultimately creates far more discomfort for you. Choosing your son's long-term gain over such dramatic short-term relief is part of what makes properly handling temper tantrums so heroic.

Instead you might say, "Sorry, I would love to give you what you want, but because you had a temper tantrum, I can't right now. Next time, let's do that." Stand by your child during this difficult time for both of you. When you feel yourself getting tense, again say to yourself: temper tantrums are a beautiful, albeit painful, part of growing up, so take a deep breath, relax, and remember, "Dr. Greene thinks you are beautiful, courageous, and worthy of high praise!"

—by Alan Greene, M.D., F.A.A.P.

Chapter 39

Early Child Care

About the Study

The National Institute of Child Health and Human Development
(NICHD) Study of Early Child Care is the most comprehensive child
care study conducted to date to determine how variations in child care
are related to children's development. In 1991, a team of NICHD-
supported researchers enrolled 1,364 children in the study and have
now followed most of them through the first seven years of their lives.
Over the past two years, the research team has presented its findings on the relationship between child care and children's development through the age of three, and will continue to analyze the
information they have gathered from the 10 child care study sites
across the U.S.

Child Care in the United States

Child care is becoming a fact of life for many American families.
As increasing numbers of women enter and remain in the work force
after pregnancy, and more are single parents, more families are rely-
ing on non-maternal care for their infants and children. In 1975, 39%

From "The National Institute of Child Health and Human Development
(NICHD) Study of Early Child Care," prepared by Robin Peth-Pierce, Public
Information and Communications Branch, NICHD, Spring 1998. A complete copy
of this report, including a list of investigators and sites and a bibliography of
publications and presentations, is available on line at http://www.nih.gov/
nichd/html/news/early-child/Early_Child_Care.htm.

of mothers with children under six years of age worked outside the home; today, 62% of mothers do so (Bureau of Labor Statistics). Since most of these mothers return to work in their child's first three to five months of life, their children spend much of their early lives in a variety of child care situations.

In the wake of this increasing use of early child care, parents, psychologists, and policy makers began questioning the relationship between early child care and children's development, asking fundamental questions about the effects of early child care. Some child care experts have argued that child care poses risks for infants because healthy development requires care given by a single person. Yet others have said that children may thrive in child care of high quality. Some contend that child care arrangements do not affect development unless the care is of very poor quality.

These differing views about the relationship between early child care and children's development have been argued for many years, but no one team or investigator had, until now, examined a large diverse group of children prospectively from birth to find out how variations in family characteristics, in child characteristics, and in child care characteristics influence developmental outcomes in the same children over several years.

Aware of the growing use of child care and the increasing public and congressional concern about this issue, the National Institute of Child Health and Human Development (NICHD), National Institutes of Health, U.S. Department of Health and Human Services, set out to develop a comprehensive, longitudinal study about the relationship between the child care experience of children and their development over time. In 1989, the NICHD issued a request for applications (RFA), inviting the scientific community to participate with NICHD in a multi-site cooperative research endeavor, now known as the NICHD Study of Early Child Care. The goal of the study:

To answer the many questions about the relationship between child care experiences and characteristics—and children's developmental outcomes. Child care characteristics include the age of entry into care, quantity of care, stability of care, quality of care, and type of care; other aspects of child care, such as the provider's education and training, the adult to child ratio, group size, safety, and health issues, were also included. After a thorough scientific review of the applications, the NICHD selected a research team located at universities across the U.S. and at the NICHD, together providing multiple perspectives on and interests in child care research. This team of researchers worked cooperatively to design and implement the study, and in 1991, enrolled a very diverse sample of children and their families at 10 locations across the U.S.

The NICHD Study of Early Child Care is the most comprehensive child care study conducted to date in the U.S. and is characterized by a complex and detailed study design which takes into account many variables, including characteristics of the child care and the family environment. Researchers are assessing children's development using multiple methods (trained observers, interviews, questionnaires, and testing) and measuring many facets of children's development (social, emotional, intellectual, language development, behavior problems and adjustment, and physical health). Finally, researchers are following the children, measuring their development at frequent intervals during their first seven years of life.

Currently, the researchers are analyzing the information they have collected to determine the relationship between child care and children's development, taking into account not only the child care environment, but the home and family, as well as individual differences among children.

What Questions Will the NICHD Study of Early Child Care Answer?

A major way this study contributes to our understanding of the relationship between child care and children's development is by moving beyond the global questions about whether child care is good or bad for children. Instead, the study focuses on how the different aspects of care, such as quantity and quality, are related to various aspects of children's development. More specifically, researchers are evaluating the relationship between child care and children's cognitive and language development, children's relationship with their mothers, and their self-control, compliance, and problem behaviors, as well as peer relations and physical health.

The Study Will Answer These Questions

- Which family characteristics influence how early children are placed in care, how many hours they spend in care, how many care arrangements they are experiencing over time, and the quality of care they receive?

- What is the relationship between the aspects of child care that are possible to regulate and the quality of care children receive in child care?

- Is the family influence on children's development diminished when children are in extensive child care as compared to being cared for exclusively by their mothers?

- Is the average number of hours that children spend in child care associated with their psychological development or their physical health?

- Is the quality of the child care experience associated with the psychological or health development of children?

- Are past experiences in child care predictive of later psychological or health outcomes?

- Is the age of entry into care, the number of care arrangements, and type of care associated with children's psychological development or their physical health?

- Is the relationship between child care and children's development different for disadvantaged and/or for minority children?

- Are there certain time periods in children's lives in which child care experiences are more important for their psychological or health development?

The Children and Families Enrolled in the Study: Who are They?

A total of 1,364 children and their families from diverse economic and ethnic backgrounds across the United States were enrolled in the study beginning in 1991. Recruited from 10 locations throughout the country, the families vary in socioeconomic background, race, and family structure. About 76% of the families are white of non-Hispanic origin, nearly 13% of families are black, 6% are of Hispanic origin, 1% are Asian/Pacific Islanders/American Indians, and 4% are other minorities, mirroring the United States population overall. This diversity allows the research team to investigate the possibility that children from different ethnic backgrounds may be affected in different ways by the different characteristics of child care.

In addition to ensuring that the families reflected racial diversity, the research team included mothers and their partners with a wide variety of educational attainment. About 10% of the mothers had less than a 12th grade education, slightly over 20% of the mothers had a high school diploma, one-third had some college, 20% had a college degree, and 15% had a graduate or professional

Table 39.1. Ethnicity of Children Enrolled the NICHD Study of Early Child Care, 1991

Ethnicity	%
White, non-Hispanic	76.4
Black, non-Hispanic	12.7
Hispanic	6.1
Asian-Pacific	1.4
American Indian	0.1
Other	3.3

degree (compared with 24%, 30%, 27%, 12% and 6% respectively, in the U.S. population).

In terms of socioeconomic status, families in the study had a mean income of $37,781, as compared to a mean income of $36,875 for families in the U.S. About 20% of the study participants were receiving public assistance.

What Type of Child Care Was Used by Study Participants?

In the study, parents—rather than the researchers—selected the type and timing of child care that their children received, and, in fact, families were enrolled in the study without regard to their plans for child care. Children were placed in a wide variety of child care settings: care by fathers, other relatives, in-home care givers, child care home providers, and center-based care. These child care situations varied, from a formally trained nanny caring for a single child to a center-based program with a group of children. Close to half of the infants were cared for by a relative when they first entered care, but there was a discernible shift towards reliance on child care centers and family day care homes during the course of, as well as after, the first year of life.

Just as there was no attempt by the study to control or select for type of care, there was no attempt to control or select for quality of care. Quality was measured in several ways and was highly variable, but since there is no study that has assessed quality of child care on a national basis, there is no way to judge precisely how representative the care in this study is of child care nationally.

Table 39.2. Type of Child Care Used

	At 6 Months of Age	At 36 Months of Age
Mother	35%	21%
Child Care Home	22%	20%
Center Care	9%	30%
Father	13%	13%
Grandparent	10%	8%
In-home	10%	7%
Other	1%	1%

What Information about Child Care, the Family, and the Child did Researchers Consider?

The research team collected and studied many different types of information about many characteristics of the children and their environment. The researchers assessed the child care characteristics, such as the adult to child ratio, the group size, and the child care experience of each child, including the quality of care and number of hours spent in care, the age of entry into care, as well as the number of different child care settings a child entered simultaneously and over time. Family characteristics were also assessed, including the family's economic situation, family structure (single parent vs. partnered parent), and maternal vocabulary (a proxy for intelligence). Other family variables included in the analyses were the mother's education, her psychological adjustment (as measured by a questionnaire) and her child rearing attitudes, the quality of mother-child interaction, and the extent to which the home environment contributed to the optimal development of children. Various aspects of individual children, such as their gender and their temperament, were also considered.

In this study, researchers are asking about the unique contribution that child care characteristics and experiences make to children's development above and beyond the contributions made by the family and child characteristics. Previous studies have established that, in general, the quality of care children get in the family environment is very similar to the quality they receive in child care. Therefore, the research team focused on determining the added contribution of child care to children's development.

Because the data were analyzed many different ways to answer the many different research questions about children's development, not every variable was included in each analysis; for each summary of findings reported below, the list of relevant variables used is noted.

What Have We Learned?

Using multiple sources of information (parents, child care providers, trained observers and testers), the research team collected detailed information about the family environment, the child care environment, and children's development, as well as their physical growth and health status over their first seven years.

The research findings can be categorized into four main categories. The first set of descriptive findings paints a picture of the care that children in the NICHD study are receiving. This includes a look at the "regulable" characteristics of care, like the adult to child ratio, the patterns of care used during the first year of life, and child care for children in poverty. Other categories include the role of family for children in child care, child care and its relationship to children's development, and child care and children's relationship with their mothers. Within these categories are findings related to the extent to which child care experiences are associated with different developmental outcomes for low income children, as compared to more affluent children, and for minority children, as compared to white, non-Hispanic children. There are also comparisons of current and past child care experiences as predictors of children's performance or mother-child interaction.

The History of Child Care Experiences across the First Year of Life

The number of hours children spent in care varied.

On average, each child in care received 33 hours of care per week, but his varied with ethnicity of the child and the family. White non-Hispanics averaged the fewest hours of care and black non-Hispanics the most; white Hispanics and others fell in between.

263

In general, most infants experienced more than one type of child care arrangement during the first year.

When they first entered care, close to half of the infants were cared for either by a father/partner or grandparent, just over 20% were placed in a child care home, and only 8% were placed in center care.

Most infants were placed in care prior to 4 months of age.

Overall, the findings indicate a very high reliance on infant care, with very early entry into care.

Most infants spent the first year of their lives not in center care, but in less formal care arrangements.

Does Poverty Predict the Child Care Experience?

Nearly 35 percent of the families and children included in the study were living in poverty or near-poverty.

Poverty was defined using the income-to-needs ratio, a standard measure of a family's economic situation (U.S. Department of Commerce). This is computed by taking the family income, exclusive of federal aid, and dividing this by the federal poverty threshold for that family (the federal poverty line for a family of four in 1991 was $13,924). Of the families in the study, 16.7% had an income-to-needs ratio below 1.0, and 18.4% had an income to needs ration between 1.0 and 1.99.

The research team asked if poverty during the child's first year of life was a predictor of age of entry into care, type of care experienced, and quantity or quality of care used.

Families and children in poverty (income-to-needs ratio 1.0) were compared to those families and children in near-poverty (income-to-needs ration of 1.0-1.99) or more affluent families, to determine if poverty determined the characteristics of the child care used.

With regard to the age of entry into care, families who moved in and out of poverty, known as transitory poverty, were most likely to place their infants in child care very early, before 3 months of age. The research team hypothesized that this early entry into care is due to the fact that extensive maternal employment may be required to pull the family out of poverty. Infants from families who were consistently poor and receiving public assistance over 15 months were less likely to enter care early or to be in any care at 15 months of age.

Families living in poverty were less likely to use any child care than other families, but if they did, they used just as many hours of care as children from other income groups. Children who were not in care had mothers with the lowest level of education and were from the largest families. These families also tended to experience persistent poverty.

In general, children from families in poverty who were cared for in home settings (by a child care home provider or family member) received relatively low-quality care. Children from families living in poverty who attended center care received better quality care—comparable to the center care received by affluent children. Children in near-poverty (income to needs ratio between 1.00–1.99) received lower quality of center care than children in poverty, presumably because those in near-poverty do not qualify for the subsidized care that those in poverty do.

In sum, partly because in the first year of life most infants are not in center care, infants from poor and near-poor families are more likely to receive relatively lower quality care.

Child Care Characteristics that Comprise High Quality of Care

The research team studied the different child care settings to determine those characteristics that contributed to positive care giving, and thus, high quality care.

Positive care giving is measured by observing and documenting the frequency of interaction, and then rating the quality of the interaction.

The child care settings were also measured both in terms of their "regulable" characteristics, or guidelines recommended by governments, such as group size, child-adult ratio, and physical environment; and of the care giver's characteristics, such as formal education, specialized training, child care experience, and beliefs about child rearing.

The research team found that child care situations with safer, cleaner, more stimulating physical environments and smaller group sizes, lower child-adult ratios, and care givers who allowed children to express their feelings and took their views into account, also had care givers who were observed to provide more sensitive, responsive, and cognitively stimulating care—quality of care that was expected to be associated with better developmental outcomes for children.

Demographic and Family Characteristics: Do They Predict the Type of Care Used?

One of the objectives of the study was to determine the extent to which demographic and family variables predict the type of care that is used by each family. The research team examined three sets of variables, including demographic characteristics (ethnicity, maternal education, and family structure), economic characteristics (maternal and non-maternal income) and family quality characteristics (maternal attitudes and beliefs and the quality of the home environment) to determine their relationship to the age of entry, and type, quantity and quality of care.

Family economics accounted primarily for both the amount, the age of entry into care and type and quality of care infants received. Families more dependent on a mother's income placed their infants in child care at an earlier age, and used more hours of care than families less dependent on a mother's income. Employed mothers who earned the highest incomes were most likely to place their infants in early care at 3-5 months, and were most likely to use in-home child care for the first 15 months. Children from families at the lowest and highest income levels received higher quality of care than those in the middle.

Beyond the economic factors (maternal and family income), mothers who believed that their children would do well when they were employed chose to begin child care in infancy and to use more care. Those who thought their employment posed risks to their child, tended to choose informal family-based or in-home care; those mothers who thought employment posed low risks to their child were more likely to use formal care in child care centers or homes.

Family Influences on Children in Extensive Child Care and Children in Nearly Exclusive Care by their Mother

Another objective of the study was to compare the influence of family on children's development for children both in nearly exclusive care by their mother (less than 10 hours of child care per week) and children in extensive child care (more than 30 hours of child care per week).

Family characteristics, including the family income and the mother's education, were strong predictors of children's outcomes—for both those children in nearly exclusive maternal care, and those children in extensive child care. These findings suggest that the influence of families on children's development is not significantly reduced or changed by extensive, nonparental care.

The Relationship between Child Care and Mother-Child Attachment

The research team examined several child care variables, including the amount of care, the age of entry into care, and the type of care, to determine how these factors were related to infants' attachment to their mothers. Attachment is the sense of trust the infant has in his or her mother.

The research team found that child care in and of itself neither adversely affects nor promotes the security of infants' attachment to their mothers at the 15-month-age point. Researchers measured infants' attachment to their mothers using a standard 30-minute procedure of separating and reuniting the mother and child.

Certain child care conditions, in combination with certain home environments, did increase the probability that infants would be insecurely attached to their mothers. Infants who received either poor quality of care, more than 10 hours per week of care, or were in more than one child care setting in the first 15 months of life, were more likely to be insecurely attached, only if their mothers were lower in sensitivity. For example, when both the mothers and the child care providers fell in the bottom 25% of the sample in terms of providing sensitive care to the child, the likelihood that the children would be securely attached was only 45%, in contrast to those with more sensitive mothers and care givers, among whom 62% were securely attached.

Child Care and the Quality of the Mother-Child Interaction

In addition to analyzing children's attachment to their mothers, the research team also studied the relationship between child care and the mother-child interaction, or interchanges between the mother and child. Maternal behaviors that were studied pertained to mothers' sensitivity, positive involvement, and negativity. Children's behaviors were observed to assess their involvement. Researchers analyzed child care quality, quantity, and family characteristics (maternal education and income) to determine their relationship to the mother-child interaction when the children were 6, 15, 24, and 36 months of age.

Mother-child interaction was evaluated by videotaping mother and child together during play and at home and observing the mother's behavior toward the child to see how attentive, responsive, positively affectionate, or restrictive the mother was when faced with multiple competing tasks (i.e., monitoring child, talking with interviewer).

Researchers found that the quality and amount of child care had a small but statistically significant relationship to the quality of the mother-child interaction. An increased amount of child care was modestly associated with less sensitive and less engaged mother-child interactions. Throughout the first three years of the children's lives, spending more hours in nonmaternal care was associated with somewhat less positive behaviors of the mother toward the child. Toddlers in longer hours of child care were slightly less engaged with their mothers.

The association that was found between the full history of the quantity of care and mother-child interaction led the research team to ask if the quantity of care in the earlier time periods was associated with subsequent qualities of mother-child interaction. The researchers found that more hours of care in the first 6 months of life were associated with lower maternal sensitivity and lower child positive engagement at 36 months. However, a combination of family and home characteristics, including income, maternal education, two parent family status, maternal separation anxiety, and maternal depression, predicted the quality of mother-child interaction more than the children's experiences in child care.

Higher quality child care (positive provider-child interaction) modestly predicted greater involvement and sensitivity by the mother (at 15 and 36 months) and greater positive engagement of the child with the mother (at 36 months). Low-income mothers using full-time higher quality care had higher positive involvement at 6 months than low-income mothers not using care or those using lower-quality full-time care.

Child Care and Compliance, Self-Control and Problem Behavior

Child care characteristics (quality, quantity, age of entry into care, type, and stability) and family characteristics were studied to determine how they were related to children's self-control, compliance and problem behavior. Researchers found that characteristics of the family—particularly the sensitivity of the mother—were stronger predictors of children's behavior than their child care experience.

Researchers determined that such child care characteristics were, at best, modest predictors of children's problem behavior compliance and self-control. Child care quality was the most consistent predictor of children's behavior. Children in care receiving more sensitive and responsive attention had fewer caregiver-reported problems at age two and three.

Although more hours in care during the first two years predicted greater caregiver-reported problems at age two, these effects disappeared by age three. Children who spent more time in group arrangements with more than three other children had fewer behavior problems (as reported by the caregiver) and were observed to be more cooperative in child care.

Child Care and Children's Cognitive and Language Development in the First Three Years of Life

Another main goal of the study was to determine if child care characteristics (quality, number of hours in care, type, stability) predict children's cognitive and language development, as well as school readiness.

Children's cognitive development and school readiness were measured using standardized tests; language development was assessed using standardized tests and maternal reports.

Quality child care was defined as positive care giving and language stimulation—how often care givers spoke to children, asked, and responded to children's questions.

The quality of child care over the first three years of life is consistently but modestly associated with children's cognitive and language development.

The higher the quality of child care (more positive language stimulation and interaction between the child and provider), the greater the child's language abilities at 15, 24, and 36 months, the better the child's cognitive development at age two, and the more school readiness the child showed at age three.

However, again, the combination of family income, maternal vocabulary, home environment, and maternal cognitive stimulation were stronger predictors of children's cognitive development at 15, 24, and 36 months of age and of language development at 36 months.

In terms of cognitive and language development, researchers found no benefit for children in exclusive care by their mother. Among children in care for more than 10 hours per week, those in center care, and to a lesser extent, those in child care homes, performed better on cognitive and language measures than children in other types of care, when the quality of the care giver-child interaction was taken into account. Child care experiences did not predict differently the cognitive, language or school readiness level of children from varying income groups or ethnic backgrounds.

Characteristics of Child Care That Can Be Regulated and Child Development

Another objective of the study was to determine the relationship between the "regulable" aspects of child care centers and children's development. The center care regulable aspects included in the analysis were the child-staff ratio, the group size, teacher training, and the teacher education, as recommended by professional organizations of educators, pediatricians and public health professionals.

The research team found that most child care center classes did not meet all four recommended guidelines for child-staff ratios, group sizes, teacher training, and teacher education. Children in centers that met more guidelines had better language comprehension and school readiness. They also had fewer behavior problems at 24 and 36 months. Children in classes that met none of the guidelines fell below average in their performance on these tests.

Summary

The NICHD Study of Early Child Care has enrolled more than 1,300 children and followed most of them through the first seven years of their lives to determine how variations in child care are related to their development. Scientific papers to date focus on the children's first three years of life. The child care settings children were placed in were selected by their families, based on the availability and affordability of child care in their communities; children were not randomly assigned to different types, amounts, or quality of care. The families were representative of the U.S. population as a whole on many demographic features.

In the NICHD study, and in the families across the nation, the quality of the family circumstances and family environment strongly predict care they choose for their children. Therefore, the research team focused on determining the unique contribution of child care to the development of children, over and above the important and well-recognized association between family characteristics and circumstances and children's developmental outcomes.

The findings from this study will provide some answers to the many questions about child care. We now have a picture of what child care looks like for many American families—a snapshot of how often and how early children are placed in care, as well as the type of child care arrangements many families use today. The researchers have also looked at the relationship between family characteristics and children's development for children in extensive child care and those in nearly exclusive maternal care. They have assessed whether family characteristics predict the child care experience their infants and toddlers receive. Finally, the researchers have examined the child care characteristics and their relationship to children's intellectual development, language development, and school readiness, as well as the association between child care characteristics and the mother-child relationship.

The research team looked for the added—or subtracted—value of child care to children's development, above and beyond the contribution made by the family and individual child characteristics. In general, family characteristics and the quality of the mother's relationship with the child were stronger predictors of children's development than child care factors. This held true for families whether their children were in extensive child care or cared for primarily by their mothers.

Researchers found that some child care characteristics or experiences do contribute, though only slightly, to children's development. The observed effects of child care were generally modest in size, but not insignificant.

Higher quality care was found to be related to:

- Better mother-child relationships
- Lower probability of insecure attachment in infants of mothers low in sensitivity
- Fewer reports of children's problem behaviors
- Higher cognitive performance of children in child care
- Higher children's language ability
- Higher level of school readiness

The converse is also true. Lower quality care predicted:

- Less harmonious mother-child relationships
- A higher probability of insecure mother-child attachment of mothers who are already low in sensitivity to their children
- More problem behaviors, lower cognitive and language ability, and lower school readiness scores

Higher quantity of care or a history of more hours in child care was associated with:

- Less harmonious mother-child interaction
- More reported problem behaviors when the children were two years old
- Higher probability of insecure attachment in infants of mothers low in sensitivity

Lower quantity of care is associated with:

• Better outcomes for mother-child interaction

• Lower probability of insecure attachment of infants of mothers low in sensitivity

• Fewer problem behaviors at 24 months

Center care is associated with better cognitive and language outcomes and a higher level of school readiness, as compared to outcomes in other settings with comparable quality of care. Group care is associated with fewer reports of problem behavior at age three.

Instability of care, as measured by the number of entries into new care arrangements, was found to be associated with higher probability of insecure attachment in infancy if mothers were not providing sensitive and responsive care.

Most of the children in the study are now turning seven years old and are in the first grade. Researchers will continue to analyze the data over the next several years, releasing additional research findings at professional meetings and in scientific journals, to answer some of the remaining questions about the relationship between child care and children's development.

Chapter 40

Four Steps to Selecting a Child Care Provider

1. Interview Caregivers

Call First

Ask....

- Is there an opening for my child?
- What hours and days are you open and where are you located?
- How much does care cost? Is financial assistance available?
- How many children are in your care?
- What age groups do you serve?
- Do you provide transportation?
- Do you provide meals (breakfast, lunch, dinner, snacks)?
- Do you have a license, accreditation, or other certification?
- When can I come to visit?

Visit Next (Visit more than once, stay as long as you can!)

Look for....

- Responsive, nurturing, warm interactions between caregiver and children.

U.S. Department of Health and Human Services (DHHS), Administration for Children and Families, May 11, 1998.

- Children who are happily involved in daily activities and comfortable with their caregiver.

- A clean, safe, and healthy indoor and outdoor environment, especially napping, eating and toileting areas.

- A variety of toys and learning materials, such as books, puzzles, blocks, and climbing equipment, that your child will find interesting and which will contribute to their growth and development.

- Children getting individual attention.

Ask....

- Can I visit at any time?

- How do you handle discipline?

- What do you do if a child is sick?

- What would you do in case of an emergency?

- What training have you (and other staff/substitutes) had?

- Are all children and staff required to be immunized?

- May I see a copy of your license or other certification?

- Do you have a substitute or back-up caregiver?

- May I have a list of parents (current and former) who have used your care?

- Where do children nap? Do you know that babies should go to sleep on their backs?

2. Check References

Ask other parents....

- Was the caregiver reliable on a daily basis?

- How did the caregiver discipline your child?

- Did your child enjoy the child care experience?

- How did the caregiver respond to you as a parent?

- Was the caregiver respectful of your values and culture?

- Would you recommend the caregiver without reservation?

- If your child is no longer with the caregiver, why did you leave?

Ask the local child care resource and referral program or licensing office....

- What regulations should child care providers meet in my area?

- Is there a record of complaints about the child care provider I am considering and how do I find out about it?

3. Make the Decision for Quality Care

From what you heard and saw, ask yourself....

- Which child care should I choose so that my child will be happy and grow?

- Which caregiver can meet the special needs of my child?

- Are the caregiver's values compatible with my family's values?

- Is the child care available and affordable according to my family's needs and resources?

- Do I feel good about my decision?

4. Stay Involved

Ask yourself....

- How can I arrange my schedule so that I can....
  - Talk to my caregiver every day?
  - Talk to my child every day about how the day went?
  - Visit and observe my child in care at different times of the day?
  - Be involved in my child's activities?

- How can I work with my caregiver to resolve issues and concerns that may arise?

- How do I keep informed about my child's growth and development while in care?

- How can I promote good working conditions for my child care provider?

- How can I network with other parents?

These steps are only the beginning. Gather as much information as possible to help you find the best care for your child. To find the

Child Care Resource and Referral Program nearest you, call Child Care Aware: (800) 424-2246. For more complete guidelines on health and safety in child care, call the National Resource Center for Health and Safety in Child Care: (800) 598-KIDS (5437).

Chapter 41

If You Are Considering the Adoption of an Infant Prenatally Exposed to Alcohol or Other Drugs

Child Assessment

"Children born to mothers suspected of using drugs or alcohol during pregnancy need accurate assessments and diagnoses." Melina 1997.

Accurate assessment and diagnosis of health and developmental problems associated with prenatal alcohol and drug exposure are critical. However, accurate assessment/ diagnosis may be impeded by:

- Difficulties in differentiating among the specific effects of various substances in the case of polydrug abuse.

- Difficulties in determining the timing and frequency of substance use.

- Individual differences among pregnant women, including the ways in which substances are metabolized, nutritional status, prenatal health care, and exposure to communicable diseases.

- Lack of correlation between newborn behaviors related to prenatal exposure and long-term effects (at one end of the spectrum, there are infants who are seemingly symptom free at birth but for whom health and developmental effects become apparent later—including learning problems; at the other end of the spectrum, there are infants who are clearly experiencing withdrawal symptoms at birth but who normally develop).

- Insufficient sensitivity of current standardized measure for evaluating infant and toddler development.

Assessment Options

Infants and Young Children: Some standardized tests are available (such as the Bayley Scales of Infant Development, the Gesell Development Schedules, and the Denver Developmental Screening Test) to evaluate infants' and young children's skills in: personal/social, language, adoptive/cognitive, and motor areas.

- Benefits: Information about current strengths and problems areas and may suggest future problems with moderate to severe mental retardation.

- Limitations: Not sufficiently sensitive to identify a particular child who may subsequently exhibit short attention span, learning disabilities, hyperactivity, or other developmental problems over time.

Children Age 3 through Preschool: Tests are available to measure IQ (Weschler and McCarthy scales to measure cognitive abilities) and social and behavioral problems (such as the Achenbach Child Behavioral Checklist).

- Benefits: Help to identify warning signs (delayed language development, poor fine motor coordination, hyperactivity, short attention span) for future learning difficulties.

- Limitations: Indicate risk status only and cannot be used to predict specific learning problems.

Ten Tips for Families Considering Adopting a Child Who Has Been Prenatally Exposed to Alcohol or Other Drugs

1. Work with informed professionals in adoption agencies that the community regards as offering quality adoption services.

2. Take the time to explore your own feelings about substance abuse in general and your experiences with substance

abuse—in your own personal background, with family and friends, and in the work place.

3. Take the time to explore your own feelings about birth families who abuse alcohol and other drugs, and particularly about women who abuse alcohol or drugs during pregnancy.

4. Spend time with your social worker discussing the child's background with respect to the birth parents' alcohol or other drug abuse and their related life style so that you have a realistic picture.

5. Ask for written summaries of the child's diagnoses and any medical complications, the treatment services that have been and are being provided, and the follow up care that the child will need.

6. Ask for information on the services and resources in the community that will be available to help meet the child's ongoing needs. Explore the child's eligibility for adoption subsidies and/or health coverage under Medicaid.

7. Obtain as much information as possible on how to reduce the impact of the child's biological risks through promoting a nurturing, responsive, and healthy caregiving environment.

8. Recognize that you must be prepared for and able to tolerate the uncertainties and ambiguities that are part of adopting a child who is prenatally exposed to drugs and alcohol.

9. Resist portrayals of children prenatally exposed to drugs or alcohol as "walking time bombs" or "oblivious to affection." Such labels overlook the individuality of each child and overemphasize problems as stemming from a single source—prenatal substance exposure—when other factors (culture, environment, supports, caregiving) need to be recognized.

10. Recognize the importance of timely identification of problems and the helpfulness of early interventions and services.

Adapted from: Susan Edelstein, *Children with Prenatal Alcohol and / or Other Drug Exposure: Weighing the Risks of Adoption*. Washington, DC: CWLA Press, 1995.

Part Five

Common Medical Concerns during Early Childhood

Chapter 42

Allergies and Asthma

Nearly everyone knows someone who suffers from asthma or allergies. Asthma, hay fever, hives and eczema are familiar words to most of us. In fact, in the United States more than 35 million adults and children have allergies.

Allergy symptoms can be as minor as sneezing and itching; or more serious, such as difficulty in breathing. Whether minor or serious, allergies can be controlled. Common forms of allergic reactions include:

- Asthma is a swelling of the airways and narrowing of the air passages in the lungs, often caused by an allergic reaction.

- Hay fever is an allergic reaction mainly in the nasal passages. It can occur seasonally or all year long.

- Eczema and hives are allergic reactions of the skin.

- Contact dermatitis is a skin rash caused by touching, rubbing or coming into contact with a substance like poison ivy, chemicals or detergents.

Kosair Children's Hospital, undated; reprinted with permission from Norton Healthcare. Kosair Children's Hospital is Kentucky's only free-standing, full-service hospital dedicated exclusively to caring for children, adolescents and young adults. We have a strong commitment to the health and safety of all children. For more information on allergies and asthma or to inquire about free fact sheets on a variety of health and safety subjects, call (502) 629-KIDS or (800) 852-1770 or visit our website at www.kosairchildrens.com.

What Causes Allergies?

Allergies are found in individuals who for some reason develop an reaction to substances that cause no problems in non-allergic people. When the human body's natural defense system wrongly identifies an otherwise harmless substance (like pollen) as harmful, it then overreacts in an attempt to protect the body. The result is called an allergy.

Some people have more active natural defense systems that make them very allergic. This is often passed on in families. For example, if a parent has hay fever, there is a 50 percent chance that his/her child will also be allergic to pollen; this increases to 70 percent if both parents are allergic.

Allergens are the substances that cause the body to overreact when defending itself. Allergens may be inhaled, eaten, or come in contact with the skin. Some of the more common allergens are:

- pollens
- molds
- house dust
- mites
- animal dander and saliva
- chemicals used in industry or cleaning
- cosmetics
- plants such as poison ivy or poison oak
- some foods—such as eggs, peanuts, milk, nuts, soy, fish, wheat, and shellfish
- venom from insect stings
- medicines—such as aspirin or penicillin

Grass pollen is a significant cause of allergy symptoms in this region of the country. Common grasses that can cause allergic symptoms are Kentucky bluegrass, fescue, rye, timothy, orchard, redtop, Johnson, sweet vernal and Bermuda.

Allergies can appear at any time. Some children show signs of allergic reactions to certain foods—such as cow's milk—during infancy. Other children experience their first problems during adolescence. However, most children show the first signs of asthma or hay fever while in elementary school. Some children who have severe eczema or dermatitis during infancy will develop hay fever and asthma later in life. For many children, the problems do not continue into adulthood.

Allergy Treatment

Avoidance is the best treatment for allergy symptoms, especially when such allergies trigger an asthma attack. People with allergies and asthma can help minimize the symptoms by keeping windows closed, staying indoors on windy days and wearing a mask when doing yard work.

Treatments for allergies include antihistamines, with or without decongestants, to help decrease the allergic reaction and dry up drainage. Antihistamines and decongestants may cause side effects. Antihistamines may cause drowsiness and some are not recommended for children. Decongestants may make children "fussy" or hyper.

Before using any medication, talk to your child's doctor and carefully read warnings on the label. Over-the-counter cough preparations are usually not very effective for the hacking, dry cough associated with allergies. Allergy shots may be recommended for patients who have asthma or significant allergies that cannot be controlled by medication.

What Is Asthma?

Asthma is a chronic lung disease that involves inflammation of the lining of the bronchial tubes. Asthma is the most common disease of the human respiratory tract and the most common absence from school. Allergies can often trigger asthma attacks.

Asthma can be difficult to diagnose—so parents shouldn't even attempt to diagnose their children. But if a child has any of the following symptoms, see your child's doctor because asthma could be the cause:

- a chronic cough or cold that doesn't go away within a week
- repeated episodes of brochiolitis
- allergies
- shortness of breath after exercise
- wheezing or difficulty breathing
- chest tightness
- a dry, hacking cough, especially at night or early in the morning

Severe asthma that is not adequately treated can lead to chronic lung disease, irreversible lung damage, or even death. Asthma cannot be prevented or cured, but it can be controlled. The first step is education: Find our what triggers the attacks and learn how to avoid or reduce those triggers.

Your child's doctor will also develop an individual treatment plan to control your child's asthma. Children with severe or persistent asthma should take their medications daily as instructed, even if they're free of symptoms and continue follow-up visits with their physician.

Allergy Prevention Tips

While allergies can't really be prevented, triggers to allergic reactions can be minimized. Follow these suggestions:

- If possible, keep windows closed during the pollen season, especially on windy days when dust and pollen blows around and in the morning when pollen counts are the highest.

- Keep the house clean and dry to reduce mold and dust mites.

- Keep the house free of pets and indoor plants.

- Avoid foods or other substances known to cause an allergic reaction.

- Avoid being around cigarette, cigar and pipe smoke.

Chapter 43

Autism

Isolated in worlds of their own, people with autism appear indifferent and remote and are unable to form emotional bonds with others. Although people with this baffling brain disorder can display a wide range of symptoms and disability, many are incapable of understanding other people's thoughts, feelings, and needs. Often, language and intelligence fail to develop fully, making communication and social relationships difficult. Many people with autism engage in repetitive activities, like rocking or banging their heads, or rigidly following familiar patterns in their everyday routines. Some are painfully sensitive to sound, touch, sight, or smell.

Children with autism do not follow the typical patterns of child development. In some children, hints of future problems may be apparent from birth. In most cases, the problems become more noticeable as the child slips farther behind other children the same age. Other children start off well enough. But between 18 and 36 months old, they suddenly reject people, act strangely, and lose language and social skills they had already acquired.

As a parent, teacher, or caregiver you may know the frustration of trying to communicate and connect with children or adults who have autism. You may feel ignored as they engage in endlessly repetitive behaviors. You may despair at the bizarre ways they express their inner needs. And you may feel sorrow that your hopes and dreams for them may never materialize.

Excerpted from "Autism," National Institute of Mental Health (NIMH), NIH Pub. No, 97-4023, 1997.

But there is help—and hope. Gone are the days when people with autism were isolated, typically sent away to institutions. Today, many youngsters can be helped to attend school with other children. Methods are available to help improve their social, language, and academic skills. Even though more than 60 percent of adults with autism continue to need care throughout their lives, some programs are beginning to demonstrate that with appropriate support, many people with autism can be trained to do meaningful work and participate in the life of the community.

Autism is found in every country and region of the world, and in families of all racial, ethnic, religious, and economic backgrounds. Emerging in childhood, it affects about 1 or 2 people in every thousand and is three to four times more common in boys than girls. Girls with the disorder, however, tend to have more severe symptoms and lower intelligence. In addition to loss of personal potential, the cost of health and educational services to those affected exceeds $3 billion each year. So, at some level, autism affects us all.

Understanding the Problem

What Is Autism?

Autism is a brain disorder that typically affects a person's ability to communicate, form relationships with others, and respond appropriately to the environment. Some people with autism are relatively high-functioning, with speech and intelligence intact. Others are mentally retarded, mute, or have serious language delays. For some, autism makes them seem closed off and shut down; others seem locked into repetitive behaviors and rigid patterns of thinking.

Although people with autism do not have exactly the same symptoms and deficits, they tend to share certain social, communication, motor, and sensory problems that affect their behavior in predictable ways.

Social Symptoms

From the start, most infants are social beings. Early in life, they gaze at people, turn toward voices, endearingly grasp a finger, and even smile.

In contrast, most children with autism seem to have tremendous difficulty learning to engage in the give-and-take of everyday human interaction. Even in the first few months of life, many do not interact and they avoid eye contact. They seem to prefer being alone. They may

Table 43.1. Difference in the Behaviors of Infants With and Without Autism

Infants with Autism	Normal Infants
Communication	
• Avoid eye contact	• Study mother's face
• Seem deaf	• Easily stimulated by sounds
• Start developing language, then abruptly stop talking altogether	• Keep adding to vocabulary and expanding grammatical usage
Social relationships	
• Act as if unaware of the coming and going of others	• Cry when mother leaves the room and are anxious with strangers
• Physically attack and injure others without provocation	• Get upset when hungry or frustrated
• Inaccessible, as if in a shell	• Recognize familiar faces and smile
Exploration of environment	
• Remain fixated on a single item or activity	• Move from one engrossing object or activity to another
• Practice strange actions like rocking or hand-flapping	• Use body purposefully to reach or acquire objects
• Sniff or lick toys	• Explore and play with toys
• Show no sensitivity to burns or bruises, and engage in self-mutilation, such as eye gouging	• Seek pleasure and avoid pain

NOTE: This list is not intended to be used to assess whether a particular child has autism. Diagnosis should only be done by a specialist using highly detailed background information and behavioral observations.

resist attention and affection or passively accept hugs and cuddling. Later, they seldom seek comfort or respond to anger or affection. Unlike other children, they rarely become upset when the parent leaves or show pleasure when the parent returns. Parents who looked forward to the joys of cuddling, teaching, and playing with their child may feel crushed by this lack of response.

Children with autism also take longer to learn to interpret what others are thinking and feeling. Subtle social cues—whether a smile, a wink, or a grimace—may have little meaning. To a child who misses these cues, "Come here," always means the same thing, whether the speaker is smiling and extending her arms for a hug or squinting and planting her fists on her hips. Without the ability to interpret gestures and facial expressions, the social world may seem bewildering.

To compound the problem, people with autism have problems seeing things from another person's perspective. Most 5-year-olds understand that other people have different information, feelings, and goals than they have. A person with autism may lack such understanding. This inability leaves them unable to predict or understand other people's actions.

Some people with autism also tend to be physically aggressive at times, making social relationships still more difficult. Some lose control, particularly when they're in a strange or overwhelming environment, or when angry and frustrated. They are capable at times of breaking things, attacking others, or harming themselves. Others are self-destructive, banging their heads, pulling their hair, or biting their arms.

Language Difficulties

By age 3, most children have passed several predictable milestones on the path to learning language. One of the earliest is babbling. By the first birthday, a typical toddler says words, turns when he hears his name, points when he wants a toy, and when offered something distasteful, makes it very clear that his answer is no. By age 2, most children begin to put together sentences like "See doggie," or "More cookie," and can follow simple directions.

Research shows that about half of the children diagnosed with autism remain mute throughout their lives. Some infants who later show signs of autism do coo and babble during the first 6 months of life. But they soon stop. Although they may learn to communicate using sign language or special electronic equipment, they may never speak. Others may be delayed, developing language as late as age 5 to 8.

Those who do speak often use language in unusual ways. Some seem unable to combine words into meaningful sentences. Some speak only single words. Others repeat the same phrase no matter what the situation.

Some children with autism are only able to parrot what they hear, a condition called echolalia. Without persistent training, echoing other people's phrases may be the only language that people with autism ever acquire. What they repeat might be a question they were just asked, or an advertisement on television. Or out of the blue, a child may shout, "Stay on your own side of the road!"—something he heard his father say weeks before. Although children without autism go through a stage where they repeat what they hear, it normally passes by the time they are 3.

People with autism also tend to confuse pronouns. They fail to grasp that words like "my," "I," and "you," change meaning depending on who is speaking.

Some children say the same phrase in a variety of different situations. One child, for example, says "Get in the car," at random times throughout the day. While on the surface, her statement seems bizarre, there may be a meaningful pattern in what the child says. The child may be saying, "Get in the car," whenever she wants to go outdoors. In her own mind, she's associated "Get in the car," with leaving the house. Another child, who says "Milk and cookies" whenever he is pleased, may be associating his good feelings around this treat with other things that give him pleasure.

It can be equally difficult to understand the body language of a person with autism. Most of us smile when we talk about things we enjoy, or shrug when we can't answer a question. But for children with autism, facial expressions, movements, and gestures rarely match what they are saying. Their tone of voice also fails to reflect their feelings. A high-pitched, sing-song, or flat, robot-like voice is common.

Without meaningful gestures or the language to ask for things, people with autism are at a loss to let others know what they need. As a result, children with autism may simply scream or grab what they want. Until they are taught better means of expressing their needs, people with autism do whatever they can to get through to others.

Repetitive Behaviors and Obsessions

Although children with autism usually appear physically normal and have good muscle control, odd repetitive motions may set them off from other children. A child might spend hours repeatedly flicking or flapping her fingers or rocking back and forth. Many flail their arms or walk on their toes. Some suddenly freeze in position. Experts call such behaviors stereotypies or self-stimulation.

Some people with autism also tend to repeat certain actions over and over. A child might spend hours lining up pretzel sticks.

Some children with autism develop troublesome fixations with specific objects, which can lead to unhealthy or dangerous behaviors. For example, one child insists on carrying feces from the bathroom into her classroom. Other behaviors are simply startling, humorous, or embarrassing to those around them. One girl, obsessed with digital watches, grabs the arms of strangers to look at their wrists.

For unexplained reasons, people with autism demand consistency in their environment. Many insist on eating the same foods, at the same time, sitting at precisely the same place at the table every day. They may get furious if a picture is tilted on the wall, or wildly upset if their toothbrush has been moved even slightly. A minor change in their routine, like taking a different route to school, may be tremendously upsetting.

Scientists are exploring several possible explanations for such repetitive, obsessive behavior. Perhaps the order and sameness lends some stability in a world of sensory confusion. Perhaps focused behaviors help them to block out painful stimuli. Yet another theory is that these behaviors are linked to the senses that work well or poorly. A child who sniffs everything in sight may be using a stable sense of smell to explore his environment. Or perhaps the reverse is true: he may be trying to stimulate a sense that is dim.

Imaginative play, too, is limited by these repetitive behaviors and obsessions. Most children, as early as age 2, use their imagination to pretend. They create new uses for an object, perhaps using a bowl for a hat. Or they pretend to be someone else, like a mother cooking dinner for her "family" of dolls. In contrast, children with autism rarely pretend. Rather than rocking a doll or rolling a toy car, they may simply hold it, smell it, or spin it for hours on end.

Sensory Symptoms

When children's perceptions are accurate, they can learn from what they see, feel, or hear. On the other hand, if sensory information is faulty or if the input from the various senses fails to merge into a coherent picture, the child's experiences of the world can be confusing. People with autism seem to have one or both of these problems. There may be problems in the sensory signals that reach the brain or in the integration of the sensory signals—and quite possibly, both.

Apparently, as a result of a brain malfunction, many children with autism are highly attuned or even painfully sensitive to certain sounds, textures, tastes, and smells. Some children find the feel of clothes touching their skin so disturbing that they can't focus on anything else. For others, a gentle hug may be overwhelming. Some children cover their ears and scream at the sound of a vacuum cleaner, a distant airplane, a telephone ring, or even the wind.

In autism, the brain also seems unable to balance the senses appropriately. Some children with autism seem oblivious to extreme cold or pain, but react hysterically to things that wouldn't bother other children. A child with autism may break her arm in a fall and never cry. Another child might bash his head on the wall without a wince. On the other hand, a light touch may make the child scream with alarm.

In some people, the senses are even scrambled. One child gags when she feels a certain texture. A man with autism hears a sound when someone touches a point on his chin. Another experiences certain sounds as colors.

Unusual Abilities

Some people with autism display remarkable abilities. A few demonstrate skills far out of the ordinary. At a young age, when other children are drawing straight lines and scribbling, some children with autism are able to draw detailed, realistic pictures in three-dimensional perspective. Some toddlers who are autistic are so visually skilled that they can put complex jigsaw puzzles together. Many begin to read exceptionally early—sometimes even before they begin to speak. Some who have a keenly developed sense of hearing can play musical instruments they have never been taught, play a song accurately after hearing it once, or name any note they hear. Like the person played by Dustin Hoffman in the movie *Rain Man*, some people with autism can memorize entire television shows, pages of the phone book, or the scores of every major league baseball game for the past 20 years. However, such skills, known as islets of intelligence or savant skills, are rare.

How Is Autism Diagnosed?

Parents are usually the first to notice unusual behaviors in their child. In many cases, their baby seemed "different" from birth—being unresponsive to people and toys, or focusing intently on one item for long periods of time. The first signs of autism may also appear in children who had been developing normally. When an affectionate, babbling toddler suddenly becomes silent, withdrawn, violent, or self-abusive, something is wrong.

Even so, years may go by before the family seeks a diagnosis. Well-meaning friends and relatives sometimes help parents ignore the problems with reassurances that "Every child is different," or "Janie can talk—she just doesn't want to!" Unfortunately, this only delays getting appropriate assessment and treatment for the child.

Diagnostic Procedures

To date, there are no medical tests like x-rays or blood tests that detect autism. And no two children with the disorder behave the same way. In addition, several conditions can cause symptoms that resemble those of autism. So parents and the child's pediatrician need to rule out other disorders, including hearing loss, speech problems, mental retardation, and neurological problems. But once these possibilities have been eliminated, a visit to a professional who specializes in autism is necessary. Such specialists include people with the professional titles of child psychiatrist, child psychologist, developmental pediatrician, or pediatric neurologist.

Autism specialists use a variety of methods to identify the disorder. Using a standardized rating scale, the specialist closely observes and evaluates the child's language and social behavior. A structured interview is also used to elicit information from parents about the child's behavior and early development. Reviewing family videotapes, photos, and baby albums may help parents recall when each behavior first occurred and when the child reached certain developmental milestones. The specialists may also test for certain genetic and neurological problems.

Specialists may also consider other conditions that produce many of the same behaviors and symptoms as autism, such as Rett's Disorder or Asperger's Disorder. Rett's Disorder is a progressive brain disease that only affects girls but, like autism, produces repetitive hand movements and leads to loss of language and social skills. Children with Asperger's Disorder are very like high-functioning children with autism. Although they have repetitive behaviors, severe social problems, and clumsy movements, their language and intelligence are usually intact. Unlike autism, the symptoms of Asperger's Disorder typically appear later in childhood.

Diagnostic Criteria

After assessing observations and test results, the specialist makes a diagnosis of autism only if there is clear evidence of:

- poor or limited social relationships
- underdeveloped communication skills
- repetitive behaviors, interests, and activities.

People with autism generally have some impairment within each category, although the severity of each symptom may vary. The diagnostic criteria also require that these symptoms appear by age 3.

However, some specialists are reluctant to give a diagnosis of autism. They fear that it will cause parents to lose hope. As a result, they may apply a more general term that simply describes the child's behaviors or sensory deficits. "Severe communication disorder with autism-like behaviors," "multi-sensory system disorder," and "sensory integration dysfunction" are some of the terms that are used. Children with milder or fewer symptoms are often diagnosed as having Pervasive Developmental Disorder (PDD).

Although terms like Asperger's Disorder and PDD do not significantly change treatment options, they may keep the child from receiving the full range of specialized educational services available to children diagnosed with autism. They may also give parents false hope that their child's problems are only temporary.

Are There Accompanying Disorders?

Several disorders commonly accompany autism. To some extent, these may be caused by a common underlying problem in brain functioning.

Mental Retardation

Of the problems that can occur with autism, mental retardation is the most widespread. Seventy-five to 80 percent of people with autism are mentally retarded to some extent. Fifteen to 20 percent are considered severely retarded, with IQs below 35. (A score of 100 represents average intelligence.) But autism does not necessarily correspond with mental impairment. More than 10 percent of people with autism have an average or above average IQ. A few show exceptional intelligence.

Interpreting IQ scores is difficult, however, because most intelligence tests are not designed for people with autism. People with autism do not perceive or relate to their environment in typical ways. When tested, some areas of ability are normal or even above average, and some areas may be especially weak. For example, a child with autism may do extremely well on the parts of the test that measure visual skills but earn low scores on the language subtests.

Seizures

About one-third of the children with autism develop seizures, starting either in early childhood or adolescence. Researchers are trying to learn if there is any significance to the time of onset, since the seizures often first appear when certain neurotransmitters become active.

Since seizures range from brief blackouts to full-blown body convulsions, an electroencephalogram (EEG) can help confirm their presence. Fortunately, in most cases, seizures can be controlled with medication.

Fragile X

One disorder, Fragile X syndrome, has been found in about 10 percent of people with autism, mostly males. This inherited disorder is named for a defective piece of the X-chromosome that appears pinched and fragile when seen under a microscope.

People who inherit this faulty bit of genetic code are more likely to have mental retardation and many of the same symptoms as autism along with unusual physical features that are not typical of autism.

Tuberous Sclerosis

There is also some relationship between autism and Tuberous Sclerosis, a genetic condition that causes abnormal tissue growth in the brain and problems in other organs. Although Tuberous Sclerosis is a rare disorder, occurring less than once in 10,000 births, about a fourth of those affected are also autistic.

Scientists are exploring genetic conditions such as Fragile X and Tuberous Sclerosis to see why they so often coincide with autism. Understanding exactly how these conditions disrupt normal brain development may provide insights to the biological and genetic mechanisms of autism.

Is There Reason for Hope?

When parents learn that their child is autistic, most wish they could magically make the problem go away. They looked forward to having a baby and watching their child learn and grow. Instead, they must face the fact that they have a child who may not live up to their dreams and will daily challenge their patience. Some families deny the problem or fantasize about an instant cure. They may take the child from one specialist to another, hoping for a different diagnosis. It is important for the family to eventually overcome their pain and deal with the problem, while still cherishing hopes for their child's future. Most families realize that their lives can move on.

Today, more than ever before, people with autism can be helped. A combination of early intervention, special education, family support, and in some cases, medication, is helping increasing numbers of children with autism to live more normal lives. Special interventions and education programs can expand their capacity to learn, communicate, and relate to others, while reducing the severity and frequency of disruptive behaviors. Medications can be used to help alleviate certain symptoms. So, while no cure is in sight, it is possible to greatly improve the day-to-day life of children and adults with autism.

Today, a child who receives effective therapy and education has every hope of using his or her unique capacity to learn. Even some who are seriously mentally retarded can often master many self-help skills like cooking, dressing, doing laundry, and handling money. For such children, greater independence and self-care may be the primary training goals. Other youngsters may go on to learn basic academic skills, like reading, writing, and simple math. Many complete high school. Some may even earn college degrees. Like anyone else, their personal interests provide strong incentives to learn. Clearly, an important factor in developing a child's long-term potential for independence and success is early intervention. The sooner a child begins to receive help, the more opportunity for learning. Furthermore, because a young child's brain is still forming, scientists believe that early intervention gives children the best chance of developing their full potential. Even so, no matter when the child is diagnosed, it's never too late to begin treatment.

Can Social Skills and Behavior Be Improved?

A number of treatment approaches have evolved in the decades since autism was first identified. Some therapeutic programs focus on developing skills and replacing dysfunctional behaviors with more appropriate ones. Others focus on creating a stimulating learning environment tailored to the unique needs of children with autism.

Researchers have begun to identify factors that make certain treatment programs more effective in reducing—or reversing—the limitations imposed by autism. Treatment programs that build on the child's interests, offer a predictable schedule, teach tasks as a series of simple steps, actively engage the child's attention in highly structured activities, and provide regular reinforcement of behavior, seem to produce the greatest gains.

Parent involvement has also emerged as a major factor in treatment success. Parents work with teachers and therapists to identify the behaviors to be changed and the skills to be taught. Recognizing that parents are the child's earliest teachers, more programs are beginning to train parents to continue the therapy at home. Research is beginning to suggest that mothers and fathers who are trained to work with their child can be as effective as professional teachers and therapists.

Developmental Approaches

Professionals have found that many children with autism learn best in an environment that builds on their skills and interests while accommodating their special needs. Programs employing a developmental approach provide consistency and structure along with appropriate levels of stimulation. For example, a predictable schedule of activities each day helps children with autism plan and organize their experiences. Using a certain area of the classroom for each activity helps students know what they are expected to do. For those with sensory problems, activities that sensitize or desensitize the child to certain kinds of stimulation may be especially helpful.

In one developmental preschool classroom, a typical session starts with a physical activity to help develop balance, coordination, and body awareness. Children string beads, piece puzzles together, paint and participate in other structured activities. At snack time, the teacher encourages social interaction and models how to use language to ask for more juice. Later, the teacher stimulates creative play by prompting the children to pretend being a train. As in any classroom, the children learn by doing.

Although higher-functioning children may be able to handle academic work, they too need help to organize the task and avoid distractions. A student with autism might be assigned the same addition problems as her classmates. But instead of assigning several pages in the textbook, the teacher might give her one page at a time or make a list of specific tasks to be checked off as each is done.

Behaviorist Approaches

When people are rewarded for a certain behavior, they are more likely to repeat or continue that behavior. Behaviorist training approaches are based on this principle. When children with autism are rewarded each time they attempt or perform a new skill, they are likely to perform it more often. With enough practice, they eventually acquire the skill. For example, a child who is rewarded whenever she looks at the therapist may gradually learn to make eye contact on her own.

Dr. O. Ivar Lovaas pioneered the use of behaviorist methods for children with autism more than 25 years ago. His methods involve time-intensive, highly structured, repetitive sequences in which a child is given a command and rewarded each time he responds correctly. For example, in teaching a young boy to sit still, a therapist might place him in front of a chair and tell him to sit. If the child doesn't respond, the therapist nudges him into the chair. Once seated, the child is immediately rewarded in some way. A reward might be a bit of chocolate, a sip of juice, a hug, or applause—whatever the child enjoys. The process is repeated many times over a period of up to two hours. Eventually, the child begins to respond without being nudged and sits for longer periods of time. Learning to sit still and follow directions then provides a foundation for learning more complex behaviors. Using this approach for up to 40 hours a week, some children may be brought to the point of near-normal behavior. Others are much less responsive to the treatment.

However, some researchers and therapists believe that less intensive treatments, particularly those begun early in a child's life, may be more efficient and just as effective. So, over the years, researchers sponsored by NIMH and other agencies have continued to study and modify the behaviorist approach. Today, some of these behaviorist treatment programs are more individualized and built around the child's own interests and capabilities. Many programs also involve parents or other non-autistic children in teaching the child. Instruction is no longer limited to a controlled environment, but takes place in natural, everyday settings. Thus, a trip to the supermarket may be an opportunity to practice using words for size and shape. Although rewarding desired behavior is still a key element, the rewards are varied and appropriate to the situation. A child who makes eye contact may be rewarded with a smile, rather than candy. NIMH is funding several types of behaviorist treatment approaches to help determine the best time for treatment to start, the optimum treatment intensity and duration, and the most effective methods to reach both high- and low-functioning children.

Nonstandard Approaches

In trying to do everything possible to help their children, many parents are quick to try new treatments. Some treatments are developed by reputable therapists or by parents of a child with autism, yet when tested scientifically, cannot be proven to help. Before spending time and money and possibly slowing their child's progress, the family should talk with experts and evaluate the findings of objective reviewers. Following are some of the approaches that have not been shown to be effective in treating the majority of children with autism:

- *Facilitated Communication*, which assumes that by supporting a nonverbal child's arms and fingers so that he can type on a keyboard, the child will be able to type out his inner thoughts. Several scientific studies have shown that the typed messages actually reflect the thoughts of the person providing the support.

- *Holding Therapy*, in which the parent hugs the child for long periods of time, even if the child resists. Those who use this technique contend that it forges a bond between the parent and child. Some claim that it helps stimulate parts of the brain as the child senses the boundaries of her own body. There is no scientific evidence, however, to support these claims.

- *Auditory Integration Training*, in which the child listens to a variety of sounds with the goal of improving language comprehension. Advocates of this method suggest that it helps people with autism receive more balanced sensory input from their environment. When tested using scientific procedures, the method was shown to be no more effective than listening to music.

- *Dolman/Delcato Method*, in which people are made to crawl and move as they did at each stage of early development, in an attempt to learn missing skills. Again, no scientific studies support the effectiveness of the method.

It is critical that parents obtain reliable, objective information before enrolling their child in any treatment program. Programs that are not based on sound principles and tested through solid research can do more harm than good. They may frustrate the child and cause the family to lose money, time, and hope.

Selecting a Treatment Program

Parents are often disappointed to learn that there is no single best treatment for all children with autism; possibly not even for a specific child.

Even after a child has been thoroughly tested and formally diagnosed, there is no clear "right" course of action. The diagnostic team may suggest treatment methods and service providers, but ultimately it is up to the parents to consider their child's unique needs, research the various options, and decide.

Above all, parents should consider their own sense of what will work for their child. Keeping in mind that autism takes many forms, parents need to consider whether a specific program has helped children like their own.

Exploring Treatment Options

Parents may find these questions helpful as they consider various treatment programs:

- How successful has the program been for other children?
- How many children have gone on to placement in a regular school and how have they performed?
- Do staff members have training and experience in working with children and adolescents with autism?
- How are activities planned and organized?
- Are there predictable daily schedules and routines?
- How much individual attention will my child receive?
- How is progress measured? Will my child's behavior be closely observed and recorded?
- Will my child be given tasks and rewards that are personally motivating?
- Is the environment designed to minimize distractions?
- Will the program prepare me to continue the therapy at home?
- What is the cost, time commitment, and location of the program?

What Medications Are Available?

No medication can correct the brain structures or impaired nerve connections that seem to underlie autism. Scientists have found, however, that drugs developed to treat other disorders with similar symptoms are sometimes effective in treating the symptoms and behaviors that make it hard for people with autism to function at home, school, or work. It is important to note that none of the medications described in this section has been approved for autism by the Food and Drug Administration (FDA). The FDA is the Federal agency that authorizes the use of drugs for specific disorders.

Medications used to treat anxiety and depression are being explored as a way to relieve certain symptoms of autism. These drugs include fluoxetine (Prozac™), fluvoxamine (Luvox™), sertraline (Zoloft™), and clomipramine (Anafranil™). Some scientists believe that autism and these disorders may share a problem in the functioning of the neurotransmitter serotonin, which these medications apparently help.

One study found that about 60 percent of patients with autism who used fluoxetine became less distraught and aggressive. They became calmer and better able to handle changes in their routine or environment. However, fenfluramine, another medication that affects serotonin levels, has not proven to be helpful.

People with an anxiety disorder called obsessive-compulsive disorder (OCD), like people with autism, are plagued by repetitive actions they can't control. Based on the premise that the two disorders may be related, one NIMH research study found that clomipramine, a medication used to treat OCD, does appear to be effective in reducing obsessive, repetitive behavior in some people with autism. Children with autism who were given the medication also seemed less withdrawn, angry, and anxious. But more research needs to be done to see if the findings of this study can be repeated.

Some children with autism experience hyperactivity, the frenzied activity that is seen in people with attention deficit hyperactivity disorder (ADHD). Since stimulant drugs like Ritalin™ are helpful in treating many people with ADHD, doctors have tried them to reduce the hyperactivity sometimes seen in autism. The drugs seem to be most effective when given to higher-functioning children with autism who do not have seizures or other neurological problems.

Because many children with autism have sensory disturbances and often seem impervious to pain, scientists are also looking for medications that increase or decrease the transmission of physical sensations.

Endorphins are natural painkillers produced by the body. But in certain people with autism, the endorphins seem to go too far in suppressing feeling. Scientists are exploring substances that block the effects of endorphins, to see if they can bring the sense of touch to a more normal range. Such drugs may be helpful to children who experience too little sensation. And once they can sense pain, such children could be less likely to bite themselves, bang their heads, or hurt themselves in other ways.

Chlorpromazine, theoridazine, and haloperidol have also been used. Although these powerful drugs are typically used to treat adults with severe psychiatric disorders, they are sometimes given to people with autism to temporarily reduce agitation, aggression, and repetitive behaviors. However, since major tranquilizers are powerful medications that can produce serious and sometimes permanent side effects, they should be prescribed and used with extreme caution.

Vitamin B_6, taken with magnesium, is also being explored as a way to stimulate brain activity. Because vitamin B_6 plays an important role in creating enzymes needed by the brain, some experts predict that large doses might foster greater brain activity in people with autism. However, clinical studies of the vitamin have been inconclusive and further study is needed.

Like drugs, vitamins change the balance of chemicals in the body and may cause unwanted side effects. For this reason, large doses of vitamins should only be given under the supervision of a doctor. This is true of all vitamins and medications.

Can Autism Be Outgrown?

At present, there is no cure for autism. Nor do children outgrow it. But the capacity to learn and develop new skills is within every child.

With time, children with autism mature and new strengths emerge. Many children with autism seem to go through developmental spurts between ages 5 and 13. Some spontaneously begin to talk—even if repetitively—around age 5 or later. Over time, and with help, children may learn to play with toys appropriately, function socially, and tolerate mild changes in routine. Some children in treatment programs lose enough of their most disabling symptoms to function reasonably well in a regular classroom. Some children with autism make truly dramatic strides. Of course, those with normal or near-normal intelligence and those who develop language tend to have the best outcomes. But even children who start off poorly may make impressive progress. For example, one boy, after 9 years in a program that involved parents as co-therapists, advanced from an IQ of 70 to an IQ of 100 and began to get average grades at a regular school.

While it is natural for parents to hope that their child will "become normal," they should take pride in whatever strides their child does make. Many parents, looking back over the years, find their child has progressed far beyond their initial expectations.

How Do Families Learn to Cope?

The task of rearing a child with autism is among the most demanding and stressful that a family faces. The child's screaming fits and tantrums can put everyone on edge. Because the child needs almost constant attention, brothers and sisters often feel ignored or jealous. Younger children may need to be reassured that they will not catch autism or grow to become like their sibling. Older children may be concerned about the prospect of having a child with autism themselves. The tensions can strain a marriage.

While friends and family may try to be supportive, they can't understand the difficulties in raising a child with autism. They may criticize the parents for letting their child "get away" with certain behaviors and announce how they would handle the child. Some parents of children with autism feel envious of their friends' children. This may cause them to grow distant from people who once gave them support.

Families may also be uncomfortable taking their child to public places. Children who throw tantrums, walk on their toes, flail their arms, or climb under restaurant tables to play with strangers' socks, can be very embarrassing.

Many parents feel deeply disappointed that their child may never engage in normal activities or attain some of life's milestones. Parents may mourn that their child may never learn to play baseball, drive, get a diploma, marry, or have children. However, most parents come to accept these feelings and focus on helping their children achieve what they can. Parents begin to find joy and pleasure in their child despite the limitations.

Support Groups

Many parents find that others who face the same concerns are their strongest allies. Parents of children with autism tend to form communities of mutual caring and support. Parents gain not only encouragement and inspiration from other families' stories, but also practical advice, information on the latest research, and referrals to community services and qualified professionals. By talking with other people who have similar experiences, families dealing with autism learn they are not alone.

The Autism Society of America, listed at the end of this chapter, has spawned parent support groups in communities across the country. In such groups, parents share emotional support, affirmation, and suggestions for solving problems. Its newsletter, *The Advocate*, is filled with up-to-date medical and practical information.

Coping Strategies

The following suggestions are based on the experiences of families in dealing with autism, and on NIMH-sponsored studies of effective strategies for dealing with stress.

- *Work as a family.* In times of stress, family members tend to take their frustrations out on each other when they most need mutual support. Despite the difficulties in finding child care, couples find that taking breaks without their children helps renew their bonds. The other children also need attention, and need to have a voice in expressing and solving problems.

- *Keep a sense of humor.* Parents find that the ability to laugh and say, "You won't believe what our child has done now!" helps them maintain a healthy sense of perspective.

- *Notice progress.* When it seems that all the help, love, and support is going nowhere, it's important to remember that over time, real progress is being made. Families are better able to maintain their hope if they celebrate the small signs of growth and change they see.

- *Take action.* Many parents gain strength working with others on behalf of all children with autism. Working to win additional resources, community programs, or school services helps parents see themselves as important contributors to the well-being of others as well as their own child.

- *Plan ahead.* Naturally, most parents want to know that when they die, their offspring will be safe and cared for. Having a plan in place helps relieve some of the worry. Some parents form a contract with a professional guardian, who agrees to look after the interests of the person with autism, such as observing birthdays and arranging for care.

What Are Sources of Information and Support?

Parents often find that books and movies about autism that have happy endings cheer them, but raise false hopes. In such stories, a parent's novel approach suddenly works or the child simply outgrows the autistic behaviors. But there really are no cures for autism and growth takes time and patience. Parents should seek practical, realistic sources of information, particularly those based on careful research.

Similarly, certain sources of information are more reliable than others. Some popular magazines and newspapers are quick to report new "miracle cures" before they have been thoroughly researched. Scientific and professional materials, such as those published by the Autism Society of America and other organizations that take the time to thoroughly evaluate such claims, provide current information based on well-documented data and carefully controlled clinical research.

The following resources provide a good starting point for gaining insight, practical information, and support. Further information on autism can be found at libraries, book stores, and local chapters of the Autism Society of America.

Books for Parents

Baron-Cohen, S., and Bolton, B. *Autism: The Facts*. New York: Oxford University Press, 1993.

Harris, S., and Handelman, J. eds. *Preschool Programs for Children with Autism*. Austin, TX: PRO-ED, 1993.

Hart, C. *A Parent's Guide to Autism*, New York: Simon & Schuster, Pocket Books, 1993.

Lovaas, O. *Teaching Developmentally Disabled Children: The ME Book*. Austin, TX: PRO-ED, 1981.

May, J. *Circles of Care and Understanding: Support Groups for Fathers of Children with Special Needs*. Bethesda, MD: Association for the Care of Children's Health, 1993.

Powers, M. *Children with Autism: A Parents' Guide*. Rockville, MD: Woodbine House, 1989.

Sacks, O. *An Anthropologist on Mars*. New York: Knopf, 1995.

Advocacy Manual: A Parent's How-to Guide for Special Education Services. Pittsburgh: Learning Disabilities Association of America, 1992.

Directory for Exceptional Children: A Listing of Educational and Training Facilities. Boston: Porter Sargent Publications, 1994.

Pocket Guide to Federal Help for Individuals with Disabilities. Pueblo, CO: U. S. Government Printing Office, Consumer Information Center.

Books for Children

Amenta, C. *Russell Is Extra Special.* New York: Magination Press, 1992.

Gold, P. *Please Don't Say Hello.* New York: Human Sciences Press/ Plenum Publications, 1986.

Katz, I., and Ritvo, E. *Joey and Sam.* Northridge, CA: Real Life Storybooks, 1993.

Agencies and Associations

American Association of University Affiliated Programs for Persons with Developmental Disabilities (AAUAP)
8630 Fenton Street, Suite 410
Silver Spring, MD 20910
(301) 588-8252

Prepares professionals for careers in the field of developmental disabilities. Also provides technical assistance and training, and disseminates information to service providers to support the independence, productivity, integration, and inclusion into the community of persons with developmental disabilities and their families.

American Speech-Language-Hearing Association
10801 Rockville Pike
Rockville, MD 20852
(800) 638-8255

Provides information on speech, language, and hearing disorders, as well as referrals to certified speech-language pathologists and audiologists.

The Association of Persons with Severe Handicaps (TASH)
29 West Susquehanna Avenue, Suite 210
Baltimore, MD 21204
(410) 828-8274

An advocacy group that works toward school and community inclusion of children and adults with disabilities. Provides information and referrals to services. Publishes a newsletter and journal.

The Autism National Committee
635 Ardmore Avenue
Ardmore, PA 19003
(610) 649-9139

Publishes *The Communicator*; provides referrals, and sponsors an annual conference.

Autism Research Institute
4182 Adams Ave.
San Diego, CA 92116
(619) 281-7165

Publishes the quarterly journal, *Autism Research Review International*. Provides up to date information on current research.

Autism Society of America, Inc.
7910 Woodmont Avenue
Suite 650
Bethesda, MD 20814
(301) 657-0881 or (800)-3-AUTISM

Provides a wide range of services and information to families and educators. Organizes a national conference. Publishes *The Advocate*, with articles by parents and autism experts. Local chapters make referrals to regional programs and services, and sponsor parent support groups. Offers information on educating children with autism, including a bibliography of instructional materials for and about children with special needs.

The Beach Center on Families and Disability
3111 Haworth Hall
University of Kansas
Lawrence, KA 66045
(913) 864-7600

Provides professional and emotional support, as well as education and training materials to families with members who have disabilities. Collaborates with professionals and policy makers to influence national policy toward people with developmental disabilities.

Council for Exceptional Children
11920 Association Drive
Reston, VA 20191-1589
(703) 620-3660 or (800) 641-7824

Provides publications for educators. Can also provide referral to ERIC Clearinghouse for Handicapped and Gifted Children.

Cure Autism Now (CAN)
5225 Wilshire Boulevard
Suite 503
Los Angeles, CA 90036
(213) 549-0500

Serves as an information exchange for families affected by autism. Founded by parents dedicated to finding effective biological treatments for autism. Sponsors talks, conferences, and research.

Department of Education
Office of Special Education Programs
330 C Street, SW
Mail Stop 2651
Washington, DC 20202
(202) 205-9058, (202) 205-8824

Federal agency providing information on educational rights under the law, as well as referrals to the Parent Training Information Center and Protection and Advocacy Agency in each state.

Division TEACCH
Campus Box 7180
University of North Carolina
Chapel Hill, NC 27599-7180
(919) 966-2173

Publishes the *Journal of Autism and Developmental Disorders*. Also offers workshops for parents and professionals.

Federation of Families for Children's Mental Health
1021 Prince Street
Alexandria, VA 22314
(703) 684-7710

Provides information, support, and referrals through local chapters throughout the country. This national parent-run organization focuses on the needs of families of children and youth with emotional, behavioral, or mental disorders.

Indiana Resource Center on Autism
Institute for the Study of Developmental Disabilities
Indiana University
2853 East Tenth Street
Bloomington, IN 47408-2601
(812) 855-6508

Offers publications, films and videocassettes on a range of topics related to autism.

National Alliance for Autism Research
414 Wall Street, Research Park
Princeton, NJ 08540
(888) 777-NAAR; (609) 430-9160

Dedicated to advancing biomedical research into the causes, prevention, and treatment of the autism spectrum disorders. Sponsors research and conferences.

National Information Center for Children and Youth with Disabilities (NICHCY)
P.O. Box 1492
Washington, DC 20013-1492
(800) 695-0285

Publishes information for the public and professionals in helping youth become participating members of the home and the community.

University of California at Los Angeles (UCLA)
Department of Psychology
1282-A Franz Hall
P.O. Box 951563
Los Angeles, CA 90095-1563
(310) 825-2319

Provides information on Lovaas treatment methods and behavior modification approaches.

Other National Institutes of Health Agencies that Sponsor Research on Autism and Related Disorders

National Institute of Child Health and Human Development
Bldg. 31, Room 2A32, MSC 2425
31 Center Drive
Bethesda, MD 20892-2425
(301) 496-5133

National Institute on Deafness and Other Communication Disorders
31 Center Drive
MSC 2320; Room 3C35
Bethesda, MD 20892
(800) 241-1044, (301) 496-7243

National Institute of Neurological Disorders and Stroke
P.O. Box 5801
Bethesda, MD 20824
(800) 352-9424, (301) 496-5751

Chapter 44

Bronchiolitis

Signs and Symptoms

Bronchiolitis involves inflammation of the lower airway, with the result that a child has difficulty breathing in and out. The first symptoms are the same as those of a common cold: stuffiness, runny nose, mild cough. These symptoms last a day or two and are followed by gradually increasing breathing difficulty characterized by wheezing; rapid, shallow breathing (60 to 80 times a minute); rapid heartbeat; retractions (the drawing in of neck and chest with each breath); and cough. The child may have a fever. There usually is no vomiting or diarrhea. In mild cases, symptoms last one to three days. In severe cases, symptoms may progress more rapidly. A child with severe bronchiolitis may tire out from the work of breathing and, due to the clogging and collapse of the small airways, have poor air movement in and out of the lungs—despite the effort. In addition, the infant can become dehydrated due to the increased work of breathing and decreased fluid intake.

Description

Bronchiolis is a common infection of the lower respiratory tract. It's usually caused by a viral infection, the most common (over 50% of cases) being respiratory syncytial virus (RSV). This virus is most common in the winter and early spring. Other infectious agents that are associated with bronchiolitis include parainfluenza virus, influenza virus, mycoplasma, and some adenoviruses. Bronchiolitis occurs during the first two years of life, peaking at about six months of age. The very tiny airways in the lung, called bronchioles, become inflamed and swell—and mucous collects in the airways. These small airways become blocked, making it difficult for the child to breathe in and out.

Prevention

Currently there are no specific preventive measures for bronchiolitis. Bronchiolitis occurs more commonly in males between three and six months of age who have not been breast-fed and who live in crowded conditions. Infants who are exposed to cigarette smoke are more likely to develop bronchiolitis and other respiratory illnesses. Try to avoid contact with others who are in the early stages of respiratory infections.

Incubation

The incubation period is several days to one week, depending on the underlying infection.

Duration

Most cases of bronchiolitis last about seven days, but children with severe cases can cough for weeks. Children who have two or more episodes of wheezy breathing may be more likely to develop asthma.

Contagiousness

Bronchiolitis (or more accurately, the viral infection which triggers bronchiolitis) is contagious, and winter epidemics tend to occur every two or three years. The viruses responsible may be transmitted by airborne droplets. Infants in day care centers are at greater risk.

Home Treatment

Infants with breathing difficulties should always be evaluated by a physician. The illness peaks at about the second to third day after the onset of cough and difficulty breathing. Fortunately, most infants have relatively mild cases that do not require hospitalization. For these relatively mild cases, the only treatment is "time" and oral fluids.

With mild bronchiolitis, many parents use a cool-mist vaporizer during the dry winter months to keep the humidity in the child's room at a reasonable level. The intention is to keep dry winter air from drying out the child's airway and making the mucous stickier. Hot-water or steam humidifiers can be hazardous and cause scalding. If a cool-mist humidifier is used, be sure to clean it out with household bleach on a daily basis—otherwise mold may grow. Sometimes, tilting the baby's mattress up slightly may help decrease the work of breathing. As a practical matter this may be difficult since you don't want the baby rolling sideways. Make sure the infant drinks enough fluids. The child should drink clear fluids frequently: water, juice or gelatin-water. This can be a difficult task for parents, since infants with bronchiolitis may not feel like drinking.

Professional Treatment

Bronchiolitis usually is a mild, limited illness that requires no specific professional treatment. Infants who are severely ill may need hospital admission for fluids, humidified oxygen, and close observation. Antibiotics have no value unless there is an additional (secondary) bacterial infection—a circumstance which is not common. Other drugs may be used to reduce inflammation and open the airways.

When to Call Your Pediatrician

If an infant (or anybody, for that matter) has respiratory distress or appears significantly ill, you need to see your doctor as soon as possible. If you have any questions or doubt as to whether that is necessary, you need to call. If your child is excessively drowsy, has rapid breathing, or is wheezing, seek medical attention immediately.

Chapter 45

Colds

Sneezing, scratchy throat, runny nose—everyone knows the first signs of a cold, probably the most common illness known. Although the common cold is usually mild, with symptoms lasting a week or less, it is a leading cause of doctor visits and of school and job absenteeism.

The Problem

In the course of a year, individuals in the United States suffer 1 billion colds, according to some estimates.

Colds are most prevalent among children, and seem to be related to youngsters' relative lack of resistance to infection and to contacts with other children in day-care centers and schools. Children have about six to ten colds a year. In families with children in school, the number of colds per child can be as high as 12 a year. Adults average about two to four colds a year, although the range varies widely. Women, especially those aged 20 to 30 years, have more colds than men, possibly because of their closer contact with children. On average, individuals older than 60 have fewer than one cold a year.

The economic impact of the common cold is enormous. The National Center for Health Statistics (NCHS) estimates that, in 1994, 66 million cases of the common cold in the United States required medical attention or resulted in restricted activity. In 1994, colds caused 24

"The Common Cold," National Institute of Allergy and Infectious Diseases (NIAID), May 1998, and "Is It a Cold or the Flu?" NIAID, undated.

million days of restricted activity and 20 million days lost from school, according to NCHS.

The Causes

The Viruses

More than 200 different viruses are known to cause the symptoms of the common cold. Some, such as the rhinoviruses, seldom produce serious illnesses. Others, such as parainfluenza and respiratory syncytial virus, produce mild infections in adults but can precipitate severe lower respiratory infections in young children.

Rhinoviruses (from the Greek *rhin*, meaning "nose") cause an estimated 30 to 35 percent of all adult colds, and are most active in early fall, spring, and summer. More than 110 distinct rhinovirus types have been identified. These agents grow best at temperatures of 33 degrees Celsius [about 91 degrees Fahrenheit (F)], the temperature of the human nasal mucosa.

Coronaviruses are believed to cause a large percentage of all adult colds. They induce colds primarily in the winter and early spring. Of the more than 30 isolated strains, three or four infect humans. The importance of coronaviruses as causative agents is hard to assess because, unlike rhinoviruses, they are difficult to grow in the laboratory.

Approximately 10 to 15 percent of adult colds are caused by viruses also responsible for other, more severe illnesses: adenoviruses, coxsackieviruses, echoviruses, orthomyxoviruses (including influenza A and B viruses), paramyxoviruses (including several parainfluenza viruses), respiratory syncytial virus, and enteroviruses.

The causes of 30 to 50 percent of adult colds, presumed to be viral, remain unidentified. The same viruses that produce colds in adults appear to cause colds in children. The relative importance of various viruses in pediatric colds, however, is unclear because of the difficulty in isolating the precise cause of symptoms in studies of children with colds.

Does Cold Weather Cause a Cold?

Although many people are convinced that a cold results from exposure to cold weather, or from getting chilled or overheated, NIAID grantees have found that these conditions have little or no effect on the development or severity of a cold. Nor is susceptibility apparently related to factors such as exercise, diet, or enlarged tonsils or adenoids. On the other hand, research suggests that psychological stress, allergic disorders affecting the nasal passages or pharynx (throat), and menstrual cycles may have an impact on a person's susceptibility to colds.

The Cold Season

In the United States, most colds occur during the fall and winter. Beginning in late August or early September, the incidence of colds increases slowly for a few weeks and remains high until March or April, when it declines. The seasonal variation may relate to the opening of schools and to cold weather, which prompt people to spend more time indoors and increase the chances that viruses will spread from person to person.

Seasonal changes in relative humidity also may affect the prevalence of colds. The most common cold-causing viruses survive better when humidity is low—the colder months of the year. Cold weather also may make the nasal passages' lining drier and more vulnerable to viral infection.

Cold Symptoms

Symptoms of the common cold usually begin two to three days after infection and often include nasal discharge, obstruction of nasal breathing, swelling of the sinus membranes, sneezing, sore throat, cough, and headache. Fever is usually slight but can climb to 102° F in infants and young children. Cold symptoms can last from two to 14 days, but two-thirds of people recover in a week. If symptoms occur often or last much longer than two weeks, they may be the result of an allergy rather than a cold.

Colds occasionally can lead to secondary bacterial infections of the middle ear or sinuses, requiring treatment with antibiotics. High fever, significantly swollen glands, severe facial pain in the sinuses, and a cough that produces mucus, may indicate a complication or more serious illness requiring a doctor's attention.

How Cold Viruses Cause Disease

Viruses cause infection by overcoming the body's complex defense system. The body's first line of defense is mucus, produced by the membranes in the nose and throat. Mucus traps the material we inhale:

pollen, dust, bacteria and viruses. When a virus penetrates the mucus and enters a cell, it commandeers the protein-making machinery to manufacture new viruses which, in turn, attack surrounding cells.

Cold Symptoms: The Body Fights Back

Cold symptoms are probably the result of the body's immune response to the viral invasion. Virus-infected cells in the nose send out signals that recruit specialized white blood cells to the site of the infection. In turn, these cells emit a range of immune system chemicals such as kinins. These chemicals probably lead to the symptoms of the common cold by causing swelling and inflammation of the nasal membranes, leakage of proteins and fluid from capillaries and lymph vessels, and the increased production of mucus.

Kinins and other chemicals released by immune system cells in the nasal membranes are the subject of intensive research. Researchers are examining whether drugs to block them, or the receptors on cells to which they bind, might benefit people with colds.

How Colds Are Spread

Depending on the virus type, any or all of the following routes of transmission may be common:

- Touching infectious respiratory secretions on skin and on environmental surfaces and then touching the eyes or nose.

- Inhaling relatively large particles of respiratory secretions transported briefly in the air.

- Inhaling droplet nuclei: smaller infectious particles suspended in the air for long periods of time.

Research on Rhinovirus Transmission

Much of the research on the transmission of the common cold has been done with rhinoviruses, which are shed in the highest concentration in nasal secretions. Studies suggest a person is most likely to transmit rhinoviruses in the second to fourth day of infection, when the amount of virus in nasal secretions is highest. Researchers also have shown that using aspirin to treat colds increases the amount of virus shed in nasal secretions, possibly making the cold sufferer more of a hazard to others.

Prevention

Handwashing is the simplest and most effective way to keep from getting rhinovirus colds. Not touching the nose or eyes is another. Individuals with colds should always sneeze or cough into a facial tissue, and promptly throw it away. If possible, one should avoid close, prolonged exposure to persons who have colds.

Because rhinoviruses can survive up to three hours outside the nasal passages on inanimate objects and skin, cleaning environmental surfaces with a virus-killing disinfectant might help prevent spread of infection.

A Cold Vaccine?

The development of a vaccine that could prevent the common cold has reached an impasse because of the discovery of many different

Table 45.1. Is It a Cold or the Flu?

Symptoms	Cold	Flu
Fever	Rare	Characteristic, high (102-104° F); lasts 3-4 days
Headache	Rare	Prominent
General Aches, Pains	Slight	Usual; often severe
Fatigue, Weakness	Quite mild	Can last up to 2-3 weeks
Extreme Exhaustion	Never	Early and prominent
Stuffy Nose	Common	Sometimes
Sneezing	Usual	Sometimes
Sore Throat	Common	Sometimes
Chest Discomfort, Cough	Mild to moderate; hacking cough	Common; can become severe
Complications	Sinus congestion or earache	Bronchitis, pneumonia; can be life-threatening
Prevention	None	Annual vaccination; amantadine or rimantadine (antiviral drugs)
Treatment	Only temporary relief of symptoms	Amantadine or rimantadine within 24-28 hours after onset of symptoms

cold viruses. Each virus carries its own specific antigens, substances that induce the formation of specific protective proteins (antibodies) produced by the body. Until ways are found to combine many viral antigens in one vaccine, or take advantage of the antigenic cross-relationships that exist, prospects for a vaccine are dim. Evidence that changes occur in common-cold virus antigens further complicate development of a vaccine. Such changes occur in some influenza virus antigens and make it necessary to alter the influenza vaccine each year.

Treatment

Only symptomatic treatment is available for uncomplicated cases of the common cold: bed rest, plenty of fluids, gargling with warm salt water, petroleum jelly for a raw nose, and aspirin or acetaminophen to relieve headache or fever.

A word of caution: Several studies have linked the use of aspirin to the development of Reye's syndrome in children recovering from influenza or chickenpox. Reye's syndrome is a rare but serious illness that usually occurs in children between the ages of three and 12 years. It can affect all organs of the body, but most often injures the brain and liver. While most children who survive an episode of Reye's syndrome do not suffer any lasting consequences, the illness can lead to permanent brain damage or death. The American Academy of Pediatrics recommends children and teenagers not be given aspirin or any medications containing aspirin when they have any viral illness, particularly chickenpox or influenza. Many doctors recommend these medications be used for colds in adults only when headache or fever is present. Researchers, however, have found that aspirin and acetaminophen can suppress certain immune responses and increase nasal stuffiness in adults.

Nonprescription cold remedies, including decongestants and cough suppressants, may relieve some cold symptoms but will not prevent, cure, or even shorten the duration of illness. Moreover, most have some side effects, such as drowsiness, dizziness, insomnia, or upset stomach, and should be taken with care.

Nonprescription antihistamines may have some effect in relieving inflammatory responses such as runny nose and watery eyes that are commonly associated with colds.

Antibiotics do not kill viruses. These prescription drugs should be used only for rare bacterial complications, such as sinusitis or ear infections, that can develop as secondary infections. The use of anti-biotics "just in case" will not prevent secondary bacterial infections.

Does Vitamin C Have a Role?

Many people are convinced that taking large quantities of vitamin C will prevent colds or relieve symptoms. To test this theory, several large-scale, controlled studies involving children and adults have been conducted. To date, no conclusive data has shown that large doses of vitamin C prevent colds. The vitamin may reduce the severity or duration of symptoms, but there is no definitive evidence.

Taking vitamin C over long periods of time in large amounts may be harmful. Too much vitamin C can cause severe diarrhea, a particular danger for elderly people and small children. In addition, too much vitamin C distorts results of tests commonly used to measure the amount of glucose in urine and blood. Combining oral anticoagulant drugs and excessive amounts of vitamin C can produce abnormal results in blood-clotting tests.

Other Treatments

Inhaling steam also has been proposed as a treatment of colds on the assumption that increasing the temperature inside the nose inhibits rhinovirus replication. Recent studies found that this approach had no effect on the symptoms or amount of viral shedding in individuals with rhinovirus colds. But steam may temporarily relieve symptoms of congestion associated with colds.

Interferon-alpha has been studied extensively for the treatment of the common cold. Investigators have shown interferon, given in daily doses by nasal spray, can prevent infection and illness. Interferon, however, causes unacceptable side effects such as nosebleeds and does not appear useful in treating established colds. Most cold researchers are concentrating on other approaches to combating cold viruses.

The Outlook

Thanks to basic research, scientists know more about the rhinovirus than almost any other virus, and have powerful new tools for developing antiviral drugs. Although the common cold may never be uncommon, further investigations offer the hope of reducing the huge burden of this universal problem.

Chapter 46

Constipation

What is chronic constipation?

Children with chronic constipation (constipation that goes on for some time) resist the urge to have a bowel movement. They do this by tightening their anal muscles, squeezing their buttocks together and standing up straight or lying down flat. After a while, the urge to have a bowel movement goes away.

As they continue to do this, stool builds up in the lower bowel. The stool becomes harder and larger, and passage of stool causes great pain. The pain increases the child's desire not to have bowel movements.

If the child doesn't pass the huge stool after some time, the rectal and anal muscles may get tired and partly relax. Soft or liquid stool may leak out around the hard stool that has collected in the lower bowel. It is often foul smelling and may stain the child's clothing. This is called stool soiling. The child cannot prevent it.

How did my child develop chronic constipation?

This question isn't always easy to answer. Chronic constipation may start as simple constipation caused by not eating enough fiber or drinking enough fluids. One large stool can cause a crack in the anus that makes having a bowel movement painful, so the child resists the urge. Sometimes, a tendency toward constipation runs in families.

An illness that leads to poor food intake, physical inactivity or fever can also result in constipation that lasts after the illness goes away. A few children withhold stools because of emotional problems. In many children, no cause can be found. Whatever the cause of stool withholding, once it begins, the large, hard stools that result make the pattern continue.

What are the signs of constipation in children?

- Small, very hard, dry, rock-like stools (even if your child has a bowel movement daily)
- Firm stools that are passed with difficulty, pain or crying
- Blood-streaked stools
- Stool soiling
- Long straining during a bowel movement
- Abdominal pain and bloating
- Crankiness and/or listlessness
- Loss of appetite
- Fear of using the toilet
- Screaming that occurs when your child has the urge to have a bowel movement or during a bowel movement

How should I manage my child's constipation?

The first step in treatment involves removing the stool that has gathered in the lower bowel. This must be done before your child can begin to learn or relearn normal bowel habits. Your doctor will probably do this in the office. He or she may use an enema, a suppository or high doses of laxatives to remove the stool.

After the stool is removed, it is important to be sure that your child can have bowel movements easily in order to prevent another large collection of stool. During this part of retraining, your child's bowel should be kept empty so it can regain tone and function. The treatment includes changing your child's diet and giving daily laxatives to help soften the stools.

What changes must be made in my child's diet?

Your child should drink more fluids and eat more fiber. Recommended amounts of fluid each day are:

- 2 cups for a 7-lb child
- 3 1/3 cups for a 12-lb child

- 5 cups for a 21-lb child
- 7 cups for a 35-lb child
- 9 cups for a 60-lb child

Only foods from plants contain fiber. These foods include fruits, vegetables, whole-grain cereals and breads, nuts, seeds and beans.

What about laxatives?

Your family doctor can tell you which laxatives to use and how much to give your child. The laxative must be taken every day to get your child's body into rhythm.

Laxatives may be given for three months or longer. The laxative your doctor prescribes will be safe for young children, even if it is used for a long time. If your child's stools are too loose, you can reduce the amount of laxative, but keep giving your child a laxative every day. Some laxatives taste better if they are mixed into orange juice, chocolate milk or other drinks.

If your doctor thinks emotional problems are part of the cause of stool withholding and constipation, your child should have help to deal with these problems during this part of the treatment. Your doctor can suggest a child counselor.

Your child may try to withhold stools at first in spite of the loose bowel movements produced by diet changes and laxatives. He or she may still be afraid of painful bowel movements. The stool withholding will stop after a while.

Should I try to toilet train my child now?

No. The first goal in treating a child with constipation is regular, painless, easy-to-pass bowel movements. Wait until about a month after starting treatment to begin toilet training if your child is old enough.

Encourage the child to sit on the toilet with proper support for the feet. Have your child sit on the toilet at least three times every day for 5 minutes to try to have a bowel movement. After meals is a good time for this. Give rewards and praise for sitting on the toilet and, later, for having bowel movements into the toilet.

How do I know if the treatment is working?

Every day, keep a written record of bowel movements and the use of medicines. This record will help you and your doctor figure out if the treatment is working. Your child should have daily bowel movements while taking laxatives. Large, hard bowel movements, soiling, or abdominal bloating and pain usually mean that your child needs to take a larger amount of laxative.

What's the final step of treatment?

After the retraining phase, you can slowly reduce the laxative your child is taking, cutting the dose down a little every week. For many children, constipation returns if the laxative is stopped all at once. If your child's constipation comes back after he or she has stopped taking the laxative, you should begin giving the laxative again at a dose that prevents the constipation problem.

Chronic constipation requires patience and effort on your part. Talk with your doctor regularly so he or she can follow the treatment's progress and help you make needed changes in the treatment plan.

This information provides a general overview on managing constipation in children and may not apply to everyone. Talk to your family doctor to find out if this information applies to you and to get more information on this subject.

Chapter 47

Cradle Cap
(Seborrheic Dermatitis)

Seborrheic dermatitis is a common skin disorder that can be easily treated.

What Is Seborrheic Dermatitis?

This condition is a red, scaly, itchy rash in areas various locations on the body. The scalp, sides of the nose, eyebrows, eyelids, and the skin behind the ears and middle of the chest are the most common sites. Other areas, such as the navel (belly button) and skin folds under the arms, breasts, groin and buttocks, may also be involved. These areas have the highest concentration of sebaceous glands.

Are Dandruff, Seborrhea and Seborrheic Dermatitis the Same?

Dandruff appears as scaling on the scalp without redness. Seborrhea is oiliness of the skin, especially of the scalp and face, without redness or scaling. Patients with seborrhea may later get seborrheic dermatitis. Seborrheic dermatitis has both redness and scaling.

Who Gets Seborrheic Dermatitis?

This condition is most common in three age groups—infancy when it's called "cradle cap," middle age, and the elderly. Cradle cap usually clears without treatment by age 8 to 12 months. This may be due to the gradual disappearance of hormones passed from the mother to the child before birth. In some infants, seborrheic dermatitis may develop only in the diaper area where it could be confused with other forms of diaper rash. When seborrheic dermatitis develops at other ages it can come and go.

Seborrheic dermatitis is also common in people with oily skin or hair. It may also be seen in people with acne or psoriasis.

A yeast-like organism may be important in causing seborrheic dermatitis.

Is this Condition Associated with Other Diseases?

Seborrheic dermatitis may occur in patients with other illnesses. There does appear to be more seborrheic dermatitis in adults with disease of the nervous system, such as Parkinson's disease. Patients recovering from stressful medical conditions, such as a heart attack, may also develop this problem. People in hospitals or nursing homes and those with immune system disorders appear to be more prone to this disorder. People with seborrheic dermatitis have no increased risk of other skin diseases. This condition does not progress to or cause skin cancer, no matter how long it remains untreated.

How Long Does this Disease Last?

Seborrheic dermatitis may get better on its own, but it usually improves with treatment. However, it may recur.

Can It Be Prevented?

There is no way to prevent or cure seborrheic dermatitis. However, it can be effectively treated.

Are Laboratory Tests Useful in Diagnosing this Disease?

For most patients, there is no need to perform blood, urine or allergy tests. In rare cases of chronic seborrheic dermatitis that do not respond to treatment, a skin biopsy or other laboratory testing may be done to eliminate the possibility of another disease.

How Is this Condition Treated?

This skin disorder is treatable but may recur. Gentle shampooing with a mild shampoo is helpful for infants with cradle cap. A low strength corticosteroid cream or lotion may also be applied to the affected areas of skin. Adult patients may need to use a medicated shampoo and a stronger corticosteroid preparation. Nonprescription shampoos containing tar, zinc pyrithione, selenium sulfide, sulfur and/or salicylic acid may be recommended by a dermatologist or a prescription shampoo may be given. However, patients should follow their dermatologist's advice, excessive use of stronger preparations can cause side effects.

Chapter 48

Croup

Signs and Symptoms

Croup is characterized by a loud cough that resembles the barking of a seal, difficulty breathing, and a grunting noise or wheezing on breathing. At first a child may have an upper respiratory infection for several days before the onset of cough. As the upper airway (vocal cords and the areas just below them) become progressively inflamed and swollen, the child may become hoarse, with a harsh, barking cough. If the upper airway becomes more obstructed, the labor of breathing becomes intense. With severe croup there may be a high-pitched noise ("stridor") when breathing in.

Children with viral croup may have a fever. Symptoms often worsen at night and with crying. In addition to the effects on the upper airway, the infections that cause croup can result in inflammation further down the airway, including the bronchi (breathing tubes) and the lungs. Possible airway obstruction is a major concern.

Description

The term "croup" does not refer to a single illness, but rather a group of conditions involving inflammation of the upper airway, that lead to the characteristic "croupy" sound, particularly when the child is crying. Most croup is caused by viruses and occasionally by bacteria.

The viruses most commonly involved are parainfluenza virus (accounting for about 75% of cases), adenovirus, respiratory syncytial virus, influenza, and measles.

Most children with viral croup are between the ages of three months and five years. Symptoms are most severe in children under three years of age. The incidence of croup is more common among males and during the cold season of the year. Most croup due to viruses is mild and "self-limiting," though rarely viral croup can be severe and even life-threatening.

The term "spasmodic croup" refers to a condition similar to viral croup, except that there are no symptoms of an infection. This frequently begins at night with a sudden onset. The child usually has no fever with spasmodic croup.

Prevention

At this time, there are no specific ways to prevent viral croup.

Duration

Croup resulting from viral infection usually lasts five to six days, though this varies. Complications of croup, such as ear infection and pneumonia, can occur as the respiratory symptoms are fading.

Contagiousness

Croup tends to occur in outbreaks in late fall and winter when the viruses that usually cause it peak. Most children who come in contact with the viruses that cause croup will not get croup.

Home Treatment

Most (though not all) cases of viral croup are mild. Inhalation of warm, moist air seems to relieve some of the symptoms. One way to humidify the air is to use a cool-mist humidifier filled with warm water. Don't use a hot vaporizer; this can be hazardous. Having the child breathe in the humid mist through an open mouth may work.

Another thing to try is to mist up the bathroom with hot shower steam, and have the child sit in the bathroom for 10 minutes. You can cuddle your child and read a bedtime story to help calm her or him.

Though no one knows exactly why it works, sometimes taking the child into the outside air for a few minutes seems to break the episode of spasmodic croup.

After you break the croupy attack, you should consider sleeping in the same room as your child to be able to provide close observation. There should not be any smoking in the household, since this can make croup worse.

Professional Treatment

Most mild croup doesn't require professional intervention. Medical professionals will need to evaluate a child if there is any suspicion of airway blockage or bacterial infection.

When to Call Your Pediatrician

Immediately call your physician if your child has ANY of the following:

- difficulty breathing
- continuous stridor
- drooling or difficulty swallowing
- difficulty bending the neck
- decreased consciousness
- high fever
- very sick appearance
- or other worrisome sign or seems particularly ill.

Chapter 49

Dehydration in Children

Petite even for a 3-year-old, Tiffany Pressnell weighed 27 pounds in February 1995 when a stomach virus swept her town of Oak Ridge, Tenn.

When Tiffany caught the bug, she had vomiting and diarrhea so severe that she lost 3 pounds in two days.

"Her eyes were sunken. Her lips were dry," remembers her mother, Tammy. "Her mouth didn't have any wetness in it. Her skin was white—when we pinched it, it stayed pinched."

Tiffany was severely dehydrated. Admitted to the local hospital by her pediatrician, she was given intravenous fluids to restore the water and minerals she had lost. Her weight slipped another 2 pounds, however, before the virus subsided and she was well enough to go home.

"Now if she has any diarrhea at all, we give her Pedialyte," says Tammy Pressnell. "We keep it on the shelf, and I keep the travel pack in a diaper bag. You just never know."

Pedialyte is a brand name for a fluid known as oral rehydration therapy (ORT). Along with other brands like Infalyte, Naturalyte and Rehydralyte, it is a simple mixture of water, salts and carbohydrates to prevent dehydration in children with bouts of diarrhea and vomiting.

ORT, regulated by the Food and Drug Administration as a medical food, is perhaps one of the greatest advances in life-saving treatments

FDA Consumer, July-August 1996

of the 20th century, especially in developing countries where diarrhea-producing diseases like cholera, combined with unsanitary water and food, kill 4 million children annually.

Here in the United States, an estimated 500 American children die annually from diarrhea, and the illness is not seen as a major threat. As a result, doctors often do not recommend ORT for their young patients.

The deaths that do occur happen mostly in the winter months while the flu season is in full swing. Nearly all of them are preventable, researchers say, because dehydration can be avoided with proper medical attention and oral rehydration fluid.

Treating Diarrhea

Oral rehydration therapy was developed in the 1950s for developing countries, where diarrhea is common. American children average only one or two bouts with diarrhea yearly. But those illnesses can still be dangerous. The best way for parents to keep their children from getting dehydrated is by stocking the medicine chest with at least one bottle of oral rehydration fluid.

"I think it's very reasonable for every family to have it at home," says John Snyder, M.D., a researcher in the field of ORT and professor of pediatrics at the University of California Medical School in San Francisco. "Diarrhea frequently starts at night, and a small child can get dehydrated very quickly."

Yet many physicians do not recommend ORT for children suffering from diarrhea. According to a 1991 study published in the medical journal, *Pediatrics*, most pediatricians don't follow the guidelines for treating diarrhea set by the American Academy of Pediatrics in 1985.

More commonly, doctors frequently tell parents to withhold food from a child and give clear liquids such as fruit juice, chicken broth, and sports drinks. Neither of these practices is recommended by the academy.

Common clear liquids don't contain the proper balance of sodium, chloride and potassium salts that the body needs. These and other minerals change in the body into electrically charged particles called ions. If electrolytes are not perfectly balanced in the body, many organs, including the heart, cannot function properly. Children under 5 are especially vulnerable to diarrhea because their bodies are small. It doesn't take much fluid loss to get their electrolytes out of balance.

Only a physician can diagnose dehydration, but parents can watch for some obvious signs: a dry mouth, no tears, sunken eyes, a reduction in urination, and skin that stays compressed when pinched.

The AAP guidelines are:

- For diarrhea with no dehydration, feed the child normally and give supplemental commercial rehydration fluids within four to six hours after a diarrheal episode. If the diarrhea persists, call the child's doctor.

- For diarrhea with mild dehydration, take the child to a physician. The child should be given oral rehydration fluids in the doctor's office, with food and rehydration fluid continued at home.

- For moderate or severe dehydration, the child should be treated in a health-care facility. Moderate dehydration may be treated orally, but severe dehydration requires intravenous fluids.

The old advice to let the intestine "rest" after a bout with diarrhea is now not recommended by AAP.

"Early feeding isn't just a good idea, it helps to make the diarrhea better," says Snyder.

Food can help the intestine absorb more water, which helps slow down the diarrhea. A child should eat as soon as possible after a bout of diarrhea, and at least within six hours. A balanced diet rich in calories is recommended. Foods such as rice, wheat, potatoes, sorghum, corn, and chicken have all been proven helpful in slowing diarrhea. Just about anything the child tolerates is ok, except for foods high in sugar or salt.

Milk products, because they can be difficult to digest, can be withheld for 24 to 48 hours during significant bouts of diarrhea. Infants who are bottle-fed, however, should continue drinking formula diluted to half strength. Breast-fed infants should continue nursing.

The once favored "BRAT" diet—an acronym for bananas, rice, applesauce, and toast—is no longer recommended for children. Instead, parents should offer a more balanced diet that is higher in calories.

Giving anti-diarrhea medicine to children is not the best treatment, according to John Udall, M.D., Ph.D., chairman of pediatric nutrition and gastroenterology at the Children's Hospital in New Orleans.

"Diarrhea is really a purging of the intestine," he says. "Giving medicines to slow down the intestine actually gives the bacteria more time to grow, which prolongs the illness."

Allowing the illness to run its course, while preventing dehydration with fluids, is usually the quickest way toward health.

Dosage information for ORT depends on weight and is listed on the label. Side effects with ORT are rare, but parents should watch for signs of too much sodium in the body: dizziness, a fast heartbeat, irritability, muscle twitching, restlessness, swelling of the feet or lower legs, weakness, and convulsions.

Rehydration fluids have a brief shelf life. Once a bottle has been opened or a mix prepared, it must be used or thrown out within 24 hours because bacteria rapidly grow in the solution. A child could easily drink three or four bottles of the fluid during an illness.

ORT is effective to a lesser degree when the child is vomiting. If the child can keep the liquid down, it will be absorbed. But if the child vomits it back up, intravenous rehydration may be necessary.

ORT is effective for all ages, although the brands available at most grocery stores and drugstores are usually formulated just for children. Adults are usually able to tolerate a bout with diarrhea better than small children because they have more fluid reserves in their bodies. But older adults and those weakened by diseases like cancer and AIDS are at a greater risk for complications from diarrhea. These patients should call their doctors if diarrhea and vomiting persist.

Parents should also remember that ORT will not stop the diarrheal illness. In fact, the child may have even more episodes of vomiting and diarrhea until the illness runs its course. As long as the child is keeping some rehydration fluid down, however, the chances of dehydration are greatly reduced.

If a child under 5 has diarrhea and vomiting for longer than an hour or so, it's always a good idea to call a physician.

According to Snyder, "Parents should have a low threshold of concern to [prompt them to] phone the pediatrician."

Parents don't have to wait for a prescription to use oral rehydration fluids, however. The products are available at grocery stores and drugstores in premixed bottles. National brands can cost as much as $6 per liter, but less expensive generic brands are available as well for as little as $2.

According to a 1991 study in the *Journal of the American Medical Association*, cost is one reason why more parents do not use ORT for their children suffering from diarrhea. Deaths from diarrhea are most common in the South and in low-income, African-American families headed by young single mothers.

To help with that expense, the federally funded and state-administered WIC (Women, Infants and Children) Program pays for ORT along with certain foods for pregnant women, new mothers, and children under 5. In most states, Medicaid also covers ORT if a doctor prescribes it.

As the use of ORT increases, the number of deaths from diarrhea is slowly declining in the United States. This simple solution of water, minerals and carbohydrates will not eliminate the problem of stomach viruses and flu, but perhaps it will make diarrhea less of a life-threatening risk to America's children.

by Rebecca D. Williams

Rebecca D. Williams is a writer in Oak Ridge, Tenn.

Chapter 50

Ear Infections (Acute Otitis Media)

Signs and Symptoms

Acute otitis media is an inflammation of the area behind the eardrum (tympanic membrane). This area is called the middle ear. Deep within the outer ear canal is the eardrum. The eardrum is a thin, transparent membrane that vibrates in response to sound waves. The middle ear is a small cavity that contains air and sits behind the eardrum. When the eardrum vibrates, tiny bones within the middle ear transmit the sound signals to the inner ear. In the inner ear, nerves are stimulated to relay the sound signals to the brain. The eustachian tube, which connects the middle ear to the nose, normally ventilates and equalizes pressure to the middle ear. When your child's ears "pop" when yawning or swallowing, the eustachian tube is adjusting the air pressure in the middle ear.

Acute otitis media is an infection that produces pus within the middle ear. Older children will often complain about ear pain, ear fullness, or hearing loss. Younger children may demonstrate irritability, fussiness, or difficulty in sleeping, feeding, or hearing. Fever may be present in a child of any age.

These symptoms are frequently associated with signs of upper respiratory infection, such as a runny or stuffy nose or a cough. Severe ear infections may cause the eardrum to rupture. The pus will then

From www.kidshealth.org © 1999 The Nemours Foundation. Used with permission.

start to drain out of the middle ear and into the ear canal. The hole in the eardrum from the rupture will usually heal with medical treatment.

The period of incubation is variable, but usually otitis media is preceded by 4 to 7 days of upper respiratory tract infection.

Description

In children, the eustachian tube is shorter than in adults and allows bacteria and viruses to find their way into the middle ear more easily. This results in acute otitis media, with a buildup of pus within the middle ear. The pressure and inflammation result in pain and the inability of the eardrum to vibrate. During the infection there will usually be some temporary hearing loss.

With proper medical treatment, the bacteria will be killed. As fluid and pus disappear from the middle ear, hearing will improve.

Acute otitis media is a common childhood ailment. Two out of three children under the age of 3 experience at least one episode of acute otitis media.

Acute otitis media frequently occurs with respiratory infections as the nasal membranes and eustachian tube become swollen and congested. Bacteria are responsible for 80% to 85% of cases of acute otitis media. *Streptococcus pneumoniae, Hemophilus influenza, Moraxella catarhalis* are the common bacterial offenders. Viruses can be found in about 15% of the cases. Sometimes a mixture of microorganisms may be found. Infants under 6 weeks of age may show a different group of bacteria in the middle ear.

Standard therapy for acute otitis media is antibiotics. Despite the start of treatment, 10% of children do not respond within the first 48 hours of treatment. Even after effective antibiotic treatment, 40% of children may retain noninfected residual fluid in the middle ear that can cause some temporary hearing loss. This may last for 3 to 6 weeks after the initial antibiotic therapy.

There are other types of otitis media. Otitis media with effusion is the presence of middle ear fluid for 6 weeks or longer from the initial acute otitis media. This occurs when the eustachian tube is not functioning to ventilate the ear and middle ear fluid develops without a prior ear infection.

Chronic otitis media may develop when infection persists for more than 2 weeks. The middle ear and eardrum may start to sustain ongoing damage occasionally resulting in drainage through a nonhealing hole in the eardrum.

The treatment of these conditions may require the care of an ear, nose, and throat (ENT) specialist.

An upper respiratory infection often precedes acute otitis media. Even with the elimination of infection, the middle ear fluid may persist for weeks or months. During this time a hearing loss may persist. In the majority of children, this fluid will eventually clear spontaneously.

Duration

The duration of acute otitis media is variable. There may be improvement within 48 hours even without treatment. Treatment with antibiotics for a week to 10 days is usually effective. Even after antibiotic treatment, fluid may persist in the middle ear for 2 weeks to 2 months. In most children, acute otitis media clears spontaneously after antibiotic treatment. Hearing may be reduced during this period.

Contagiousness

Acute otitis media is not contagious, though the upper respiratory tract infection that may precede it could be.

Prevention

In infants, breastfeeding helps to pass along immunities that prevent acute otitis media. Also, the position of the child when breastfeeding is better than the bottle-feeding position for eustachian tube function. If a child needs to be bottle-fed, holding the infant rather than allowing the child to lie down with the bottle is best. A child should not take the bottle to bed. In addition to increasing the chance for acute otitis media, falling asleep with milk in the mouth increases the incidence of tooth decay.

Multiple upper respiratory infections may lead to frequent acute otitis media. For this reason, exposure to large groups of children, such as in child care centers, results in more frequent colds and therefore more earaches. Environmental irritants, such as secondhand tobacco smoke, should also be avoided.

Some medical conditions are associated with frequent otitis media, specifically Down syndrome, cleft palate, and allergies. Certain groups of people are also more frequent sufferers of ear infections, particularly Native Americans. Males are also more commonly affected than females. Children who have acute otitis media when younger than 6 months may be more prone to frequent bouts of ear infection.

Children who are prone to recurring bouts of otitis media or who have deficiencies in their immune system may be prescribed antibiotics or a tympanostomy tube by their doctor to prevent future infections. A tympanostomy tube is inserted into the ear during surgery to permit fluid to drain from the middle ear. Antibiotics are not an effective treatment for otitis media with effusion.

When to Call Your Child's Doctor

Unresolved otitis media can lead to complications, so children with earache or a sense of fullness in the ear, especially when combined with fever or a prior upper respiratory tract infection, should always be evaluated by a doctor. There are also other conditions that can result in earaches: dental ailments (teething), a foreign object in the ear, ear canal injury (as from cotton swabs), or hard ear wax. Your child's doctor can diagnose the exact cause of the discomfort by careful examination of the eardrum and offer specific therapy.

Professional Treatment

Antibiotics may be prescribed by your child's doctor. There are broad spectrum medications or drugs directed at specific bacteria usually implicated in otitis media. In infants younger than 6 weeks, intravenous antibiotics and tympanocentesis (surgical drainage of the infection to get a sample of pus for the laboratory to use in identifying the germ) may rarely be necessary. If there is drainage from the ear, antibiotic ear drops also may be prescribed.

If your child has a bulging eardrum and is experiencing severe pain, a myringotomy (surgical incision of the eardrum to release the pus) may be necessary. The eardrum usually heals within a week.

Children with recurring otitis media infections may be given a low dose antibiotic treatment that will last for a few months.

Many parents are concerned about permanent hearing loss. If medications are taken as directed, the chances of permanent hearing loss are minimal.

Home Treatment

The purpose of home treatment, after the initial doctor's evaluation, is to make the child comfortable. Medications to relieve pain and fever may be necessary so the child can sleep. The child can continue to go outside.

What little medical literature there is suggests that a child with otitis media can travel by airplane. If the eustachian tube is not functioning well, however, changes in outside pressure (such as that occurring in a plane or underwater) can cause discomfort. It is generally recommended that children with draining ears should not swim or travel by airplane.

Chapter 51

Eczema

Help for Eczema

Question

My 5-month-old has always had facial eczema which her pediatrician refers to as a "mild" condition. We have been using an over-the-counter hydrocortisone cream every day. This is not much help. I am really reluctant to use any prescription cortisone creams since her face may get addicted to it. Even though it may be considered "mild," her face hasn't improved. Some days she scratches all over her face and the condition gets worse. The eczema is also on her legs. The eczema doesn't seem to be improving. What can I do?

Answer

Eczema on your baby's face is frustrating. It is, of course, far worse on the days she is scheduled to have her pictures taken or to see a distant relative. In fact, it is so bad that you wonder if it is all people see when they look at your darling little girl. You hope she'll grow out of it, but what if she doesn't?

Eczema is one of the most common skin problems for children. It is a condition of dry, extra-sensitive skin. Most infants will outgrow it by the time they are 2 to 3 years old. Children who still have it will usually outgrow it by the time they become teenagers, just in time

From Dr. Greene's House Calls at http://www.drgreen.com, March 1, 1996. Reprinted with permission of Dr. Alan Greene.

for acne (sometimes life doesn't seem fair). If eczema runs in the family, it is more likely to be a lifelong condition. Even so, it is often worse in the first years of life.

Eczema is a vicious cycle! Something irritates your daughter's skin, which then becomes red and inflamed. It itches. She rubs it. The skin becomes more inflamed. The outer, protective layer of the skin is lost. The affected area is extra-extra-sensitive to irritants, and dries out easily. She continues to be exposed to whatever it was that triggered the episode in the first place. Even more rash develops. The cycle perpetuates itself.

Many different things can be the irritating agent or trigger. Here is a list of common triggers to watch for:

- rubbing the skin
- moisture, such as saliva or milk
- overheating
- common housedust
- wool or other scratchy fabric
- dog or cat dander
- cigarette smoke
- clothes washed in irritating detergent
- body soap
- water

Occasionally the eczema is caused by an allergic reaction to food or foods in the baby's diet. In general breast milk is tremendous for controlling eczema (in fact, 6 months of nursing can actually prevent eczema in some children). In some cases, if the nursing mom is consuming dairy products, nuts, eggs, seafood, or possibly other foods (which vary from individual to individual) the baby will be negatively affected. Known foods children directly consume that can make eczema worse include cows' milk, egg whites, citrus (such as tomatoes, strawberries, oranges, and lemons), chocolate, and nuts. If you are using a cows'-milk-based formula you may want to try using a soy formula or another hypo-allergenic formula.

The first step in treating eczema is to identify the precipitating event or trigger and avoid it if possible! You may not see an immediate improvement, but if you are going to successfully treat eczema it is important to break the cycle! Here are some tips that will help:

- avoid situations that will make your baby sweat—don't pile on blankets or put her in a blanket sleeper

- cut cows' milk, eggs, citrus fruits, and peanut products from her diet

- wash her clothes in a laundry detergent made for sensitive skin, such as Dreft Laundry Detergent

- avoid dressing your daughter (or yourself for that matter) in wool or any other harsh material (cotton is excellent)

To keep the skin healthy it is generally better to wash less frequently. Bathing removes the moisture-retaining layer of sensitive skin. Cut baths down to once or twice a week, in lukewarm water, and use a small amount of very mild soap such as Dove or Neutrogena, or better yet, don't use any soap. Some children with eczema can't tolerate baths at all and need to be cleansed with Cetaphil, a water-free cleanser for people with sensitive skin. Apply a moisturizing lotion to the affected areas as least twice a day. If it is a day that you are going to bathe your daughter, apply the moisturizer immediately following her bath, while she is still damp. Use a product like Eucerin, Lubriderm, Alpha Keri, Moisturel, or Aquaphor. This will keep the skin moist and help protect the skin from other irritants.

In the midst of an inflamed cycle, cortisone cream can be very helpful. It is not recommended for everyday use. Use the mildest form of cortisone that will break the cycle. On her face, an over-the-counter strength cortisone cream, such as Cortaid or Hydrocortisone, will usually be sufficient. Do not use anything stronger than the over-the-counter cortisone, unless prescribed for her by her pediatrician. Once the cycle is broken, gradually reduce, then stop, the cortisone over one week to prevent rebound.

You can help to minimize inflamed patches of eczema, but her skin will remain sensitive until she outgrows the condition. A rash on your baby's face invites you to look beyond the shallow covering of the outer layer of skin to see her true beauty that lies beneath.

—Alan Greene, M.D., F.A.A.P.

Chapter 52

Febrile Seizures

What are febrile seizures?

Febrile seizures are convulsions brought on by a fever in infants or small children. During a febrile seizure, a child often loses consciousness and shakes, moving limbs on both sides of the body. Less commonly, the child becomes rigid or has twitches in only a portion of the body, such as an arm or a leg, or on the right or the left side only. Most febrile seizures last a minute or two, although some can be as brief as a few seconds while others last for more than 15 minutes.

The majority of children with febrile seizures have rectal temperatures greater than 102 degrees F. Most febrile seizures occur during the first day of a child's fever.

Children prone to febrile seizures are not considered to have epilepsy, since epilepsy is characterized by recurrent seizures that are not triggered by fever.

How common are febrile seizures?

Approximately one in every 25 children will have at least one febrile seizure, and more than one-third of these children will have additional febrile seizures before they outgrow the tendency to have them. Febrile seizures usually occur in children between the ages of

National Institute of Neurological Disorders and Stroke (NINDS), November 1999.

353

6 months and 5 years and are particularly common in toddlers. Children rarely develop their first febrile seizure before the age of 6 months or after 3 years of age. The older a child is when the first febrile seizure occurs, the less likely that child is to have more.

What makes a child prone to recurrent febrile seizures?

A few factors appear to boost a child's risk of having recurrent febrile seizures, including young age (less than 15 months) during the first seizure, frequent fevers, and having immediate family members with a history of febrile seizures. If the seizure occurs soon after a fever has begun or when the temperature is relatively low, the risk of recurrence is higher. A long initial febrile seizure does not substantially boost the risk of recurrent febrile seizures, either brief or long.

Are febrile seizures harmful?

Although they can be frightening to parents, the vast majority of febrile seizures are harmless. During a seizure, there is a small chance that the child may be injured by falling or may choke from food or saliva in the mouth. Using proper first aid for seizures can help avoid these hazards (see section entitled "What should be done for a child having a febrile seizure?").

There is no evidence that febrile seizures cause brain damage. Large studies have found that children with febrile seizures have normal school achievement and perform as well on intellectual tests as their siblings who don't have seizures. Even in the rare instances of very prolonged seizures (more than 1 hour), most children recover completely.

Between 95 and 98 percent of children who have experienced febrile seizures do not go on to develop epilepsy. However, although the absolute risk remains very small, certain children who have febrile seizures face an increased risk of developing epilepsy. These children include those who have febrile seizures that are lengthy, that affect only part of the body, or that recur within 24 hours, and children with cerebral palsy, delayed development, or other neurological abnormalities. Among children who don't have any of these risk factors, only one in 100 develops epilepsy after a febrile seizure.

What should be done for a child having a febrile seizure?

Parents should stay calm and carefully observe the child. To prevent accidental injury, the child should be placed on a protected surface such as the floor or ground. The child should not be held or restrained during a convulsion. To prevent choking, the child should be placed on his or her side or stomach. When possible, the parent should gently remove all objects in the child's mouth. The parent should never place anything in the child's mouth during a convulsion. Objects placed in the mouth can be broken and obstruct the child's airway. If the seizure lasts longer than 10 minutes, the child should be taken immediately to the nearest medical facility for further treatment. Once the seizure has ended, the child should be taken to his or her doctor to check for the source of the fever. This is especially urgent if the child shows symptoms of stiff neck, extreme lethargy, or abundant vomiting.

How are febrile seizures diagnosed and treated?

Before diagnosing febrile seizures in infants and children, doctors sometimes perform tests to be sure that seizures are not caused by something other than simply the fever itself. For example, if a doctor suspects the child has meningitis (an infection of the membranes surrounding the brain), a spinal tap may be needed to check for signs of the infection in the cerebrospinal fluid (fluid that bathes the brain and spinal cord). If there has been severe diarrhea or vomiting, dehydration could be responsible for seizures. Also, doctors often perform other tests such as examining the blood and urine to pinpoint the cause of the child's fever.

A child who has a febrile seizure usually doesn't need to be hospitalized. If the seizure is prolonged or is accompanied by a serious infection, or if the source of the infection cannot be determined, a doctor may recommend that the child be hospitalized for observation.

How are febrile seizures prevented?

If a child has a fever most parents will use fever-lowering drugs such as acetaminophen or ibuprofen to make the child more comfortable, although there are no studies that prove that this will reduce the risk of a seizure. One preventive measure would be to try to reduce the number of febrile illnesses, although this is often not a practical possibility.

Prolonged daily use of oral anticonvulsants, such as phenobarbital or valproate, to prevent febrile seizures is usually not recommended because of their potential for side effects and questionable effectiveness for preventing such seizures.

Children especially prone to febrile seizures may be treated with the drug diazepam orally or rectally, whenever they have a fever. The majority of children with febrile seizures do not need to be treated with medication, but in some cases a doctor may decide that medicine given only while the child has a fever may be the best alternative. This medication may lower the risk of having another febrile seizure. It is usually well tolerated, although it occasionally can cause drowsiness, a lack of coordination, or hyperactivity. Children vary widely in their susceptibility to such side effects.

What research is being done on febrile seizures?

The National Institute of Neurological Disorders and Stroke (NINDS), a part of the National Institutes of Health (NIH), sponsors research on febrile seizures in medical centers throughout the country. NINDS-supported scientists are exploring what environmental and genetic risk factors make children susceptible to febrile seizures. Some studies suggest that women who smoke or drink alcohol during their pregnancies are more likely to have children with febrile seizures, but more research needs to be done before this link can be clearly established. Scientists are also working to pinpoint factors that can help predict which children are likely to have recurrent or long-lasting febrile seizures.

Investigators continue to monitor the long-term impact that febrile seizures might have on intelligence, behavior, school achievement, and the development of epilepsy. For example, scientists conducting studies in animals are assessing the effects of seizures and anticonvulsant drugs on brain development.

Investigators also continue to explore which drugs can effectively treat or prevent febrile seizures and to check for side effects of these medicines.

Additional Information

Additional information for patients, families, and physicians is available from:

Epilepsy Foundation
4351 Garden City Drive
Landover, Maryland 20785
(301) 459-3700
(800) EFA-1000 (332-1000)

For more information on research on febrile seizures, you may wish to contact:

Office of Communications and Public Liaison
National Institute of Neurological Disorders and Stroke
National Institutes of Health
Bethesda, Maryland 20892-2540

Chapter 53

Fever: What to Do

Most parents are confused as to what temperature is actually considered fever. A temperature of 97 is not fever but is a lower than normal temperature. This is usually seen if a person is exposed to the cold for too long a period of time, but is more commonly seen with oral temperatures, where the person is mouth breathing while the temperature is being taken. It can also be seen on a rectal temperature if the thermometer has been left in for too short a period of time or is not properly placed in the rectum. Even though 98.6 is supposed to be average some people run either a little higher or lower. If you have symptoms of an illness, any temperature 99.8-100. may be considered a low grade fever. Any temperature 101-102 is mild fever, 102-103 is moderate fever and anything close to 104 is high fever. Please remember to shake down your thermometer before taking you child's temperature. Many a false alarm has occurred when a parent forgets to do this and starts with a thermometer reading of 101 or higher.

When your child has fever his/her body is telling you that there is an infection or inflammatory process going on. Having fever does not tell you what is causing it. One could have a viral infection or a severe bacterial infection and not know the difference.

Most parents are overly concerned with how high the fever is or how high the fever is going to go. Unfortunately the height of the fever is not a good indication of how mild or severe the infection your child has. You could have walking pneumonia with no temperature

From DRS 4 Kids at www.drs4kids.com; reprinted with permission. **Note:** Temperatures in this chapter are given in degrees Fahrenheit (°F).

at all and meningitis with 101. You could have the flu and have 104 or just a cold and have 102. This is not to say that the temperatures could be the other way around but just the fact that it could go either way tells you how unpredictable an indicator it is.

The other reason most parents are afraid of high fevers is that they are worried that their child might convulse if the temperature gets too high. Most people don't realize that it is not how high the fever is but how rapidly the temperature goes up that causes a febrile convulsion. Of course if there is a family predilection to febrile convulsions your child will be at somewhat greater risk (about 4 %) over the general population to have them.

If your child appears to have a fever it is best to take his/her temperature with a rectal thermometer (if an infant or young child) or an oral thermometer (if an older child or teenager). The new ear thermometers are extremely good for a child one year or older (if the ear canal is too small you cannot get a proper reading from the ear). Taking a temperature reading directly off the skin is unreliable, especially if the skin is warm for other reasons (e.g., sunburn). The temperature reading should give you a good idea about the fever but it is not really necessary to know if the fever is exactly 101.8 or 102.2.

Once you have decided that your child does have fever you can give Acetaminophen (Tylenol™, Tempra™, Feverall™) or Ibuprofen (Advil™ or Motrin™) or both. Acetaminophen is given in a dose of about 120 mg for every 20 pounds every 4 hours (e.g., a 20 pound infant would take 120 mg or approx. 1.2 ml of the drops or 3/4 tsp. of the liquid). If Ibuprofen is taken it is given in a dose of 1 tsp. for every 22 pounds every 6 hours. A 44 pound child could take 1 tablet if you crush it up or if he/she could swallow it. If the temperature is under 102.6 then you should start by giving the acetaminophen alone every 4 hours. If the fever is greater than 102.6 then you can give both the Acetaminophen and the Ibuprofen at the same time but afterward at the required time intervals. The Acetaminophen should always be given first and then the Ibuprofen added to the regimen if the fever is not going down. Not to confuse the issue but some parents feel that they would rather start with the Ibuprofen because they feel it works better and that is all right too. If your child is vomiting there are Acetaminophen suppositories in strengths of 120 mg and 325 mg and these can be cut in half to the approximate dose. If your child hates the taste of the oral medicine, Feverall™ is tasteless and colorless and can be mixed in anything.

If you find that the fever is still not budging you can give your child a tepid bath (water that is neither too cool or too warm to the touch) for about 10 to 15 minutes. There is also a product called "cool skin" which is a gel-like sheet that is placed over the child's naked body. It works by extracting the heat from the body and cooling down the skin. Alcohol rub downs are no longer being done, at least in the younger children, since the alcohol vapors can cause a lowering of the blood sugar.

If all of these attempts at lowering the temperature fail then please give your doctor a call so that he/she can further guide you. Remember that the doctor should be contacted if any fever persists for more than 2 days.

Chapter 54

Gastroesophageal Reflux

Gastroesophageal Reflux in Infants

Most infants occasionally "spit up" or "throw up" after they eat. Some infants spit up or throw up so frequently that they are said to have gastroesophageal reflux. This term describes splashing or pushing of stomach contents backwards up into the esophagus, and sometimes, out the mouth. All of us have some reflux every day. Most of the time, reflux causes no problems or discomfort, and often, we are not even aware when it happens.

When a baby throws up after nearly every feeding and numerous times between feedings, parents often become concerned and they seek medical advice. They may be worried that there is something seriously wrong with their baby's stomach or intestinal tract. They may be concerned that:

- there is an area of blockage or narrowing in their baby's intestinal tract
- the baby is not keeping enough food down to grow
- the baby has an ulcer
- the baby is allergic to milk

Fortunately, in the vast majority of cases, none of these are true. Most of the time, reflux in infants and children is due to incoordination

of the upper intestinal tract rather than to any distinct anatomic abnormality and as a result, *almost all babies with gastroesophageal
reflux will ultimately outgrow this problem!*

Most children suffering from gastroesophageal reflux are otherwise
normal and healthy. However, children who have developmental or
neurological disabilities are more likely to suffer from gastroesophageal reflux than are children who are neurologically normal, and the
symptoms of reflux in children with developmental disabilities are
often more severe and/or more persistent. Often, parents of children
with disabilities become worried that the frequent vomiting associated with GER may limit their child's growth and development, or
cause the child to aspirate and develop pneumonia or other respiratory symptoms.

How Can We Treat Gastroesophageal Reflux?

The most important thing to remember when treating gastroesophageal reflux is that in almost all cases, the problem will get better on
its own! With that in mind, most of our treatments are geared towards
lessening the symptoms of the reflux, not fixing it. Given enough time,
the baby will fix the problem on his or her own.

If you think of gastroesophageal reflux as incoordination of the
baby's upper intestinal tract, then, as the baby's overall coordination
improves, the reflux will improve too. Most of the time, when the child
is able to sit-up well without any assistance, the reflux starts to get
better. This is usually around six months of age. Most of the time,
when the baby is able to walk proficiently, the reflux tends to disappear. This is usually around twelve months of age.

Treatments for reflux can best by summarized in several broad
categories:

- positioning
- dietary treatments
- changing feeding schedules
- medications
- surgery

Positioning

Theoretically, the best position to but a baby with reflux in after
meals is lying on their stomach with their head propped up about 30
degrees. Lying in this position causes the stomach to fall forward, clos-
ing the connection between the stomach and the esophagus. Remember,

this is only theoretical! Some infants will not lie in this position without crying, and if the baby cries all the time, they fill up their stomach with air, grunt, and strain, which tends to make their reflux worse.

Perhaps more important than using the "best" position, is avoiding "bad" positions. In young infants who don't have much control of their abdominal or chest muscles, when they are placed in an infant seat or swing, they tend to slump down. This increases the pressure in the their stomachs which tends to worsen their reflux. It is much better to lie them down or place them in a seat that reclines a bit than to have them slumped down.

Dietary Treatments

While many parents and families attribute gastroesophageal reflux to sensitivities or allergies to milk or formula, there is no convincing evidence to support this. While many infants will have less vomiting when they are switched from one type of milk to another, in most cases, this improvement only lasts two or three days. While there are certainly some infants who do better on one type of formula than another, most infants continue to vomit no matter what type of milk they are fed with (including breast milk).

Many parents are instructed to thicken their infants feedings with cereal as a way of lessening reflux. By thickening the feedings with cereal, the milk is physically heavier, and thus less likely to come back up. There are however, some problems with thickening feedings with cereal. It is not possible to thicken feedings if the baby is largely breast fed. Also, many infants with reflux are very vigorous or voracious feeders. When the milk is thickened with cereal, the baby has to suck harder to get the milk through the nipple. This may cause the baby to fill their stomach with air, which can actually worsen the symptoms of reflux.

Many parents find that their babies keep solid foods down more effectively than liquids. This may simply be because solid foods are heavier and thus less likely to come back up, but also, solid foods are emptied out of the stomach differently than liquids are. In any case, there is no evidence to suggest that feeding young infants solid foods with a spoon or from an infant feeder is harmful. In many cultures around the world, infants have been fed solid foods in the first month of life for centuries without any problems. There is no evidence to suggest that early introduction of solid foods predisposes to allergies later in life.

Changing Feeding Schedules

Parents are sometimes instructed to feed their babies smaller amounts more often with the idea that over-feeding tends to make reflux worse. Unfortunately, many babies with reflux are not satisfied with only one and a half or two ounces of milk, and they will cry for more. Again, when babies cry for extended periods, they fill their stomachs with air, they grunt, and they strain, all of which tend to make reflux worse.

Medications

While many different medications may be used to try and treat reflux, most of the medications fall into three groups:

- medications that break down or lessen intestinal gas
- medications that decrease or neutralize stomach acid
- medications that improve intestinal coordination

Medications that break down or lessen intestinal gas

- Mylicon®
- Gaviscon®

Medications that decrease or neutralize stomach acid—antacids

- Mylanta®
- Maalox®
- Carafate® (sucralfate)

Medicines that inhibit stomach acid secretion or production

- Tagamet® (cimetidine)
- Zantac® (ranitidine)
- Pepcid® (famotidine)
- Axid® (nizatidine)
- Prilosec® (omeprazole)
- Prevacid® (lansoprazole)

It is assumed that decreasing the amount of stomach acid will lessen the symptoms of reflux. While this has clearly been shown in adults, very few studies have been published examining the effectiveness of these medicines in young children. In theory, these types of medications should be helpful to those babies who are having "heartburn" and nearly three fourths of parents report that their babies spit up or throw up less and seem to have less "heartburn" when they take Gaviscon®.

For the most part, medicines that decrease intestinal gas or neutralize stomach acid (antacids) are very safe. At high doses, Mylicon®, Gaviscon®, Maalox®, and Mylanta® may function as laxatives and cause some diarrhea. Chronic use of very high doses of Maalox® or Mylanta® may be associated with an increased risk of rickets (thinning of the bones).

Side effects from medications that inhibit the production of stomach acid are quite uncommon. A small number of children may develop some sleepiness when they take Zantac®, Pepcid®, Axid®, or Tagamet®. Tagamet® can increase blood levels of certain other medicines including the blood thinner Coumadin® and the anti-seizure medicine Dilantin®.

Medications that improve intestinal coordination

- Reglan® (metoclopramide)
- Propulcid® (cisapride)

While Reglan® increases the pressure of the lower esophageal sphincter (LES) and helps that stomach to empty more quickly, in most infants, this medicine does not improve the symptoms of reflux. Rarely, Reglan® can cause frightening side effects. Young infants may develop dystonia (tenseness or stiffness of the muscles) and children with epilepsy appear to be at increased risk of having seizures when taking Reglan®.

Like Reglan®, Propulcid® increases the pressure of the lower esophageal sphincter (LES). Propulcid® increases emptying of the stomach as well as the rate which food moves through the lower intestines. Nearly three fourths of parents report that their babies spit up or throw up less and seem to have less "heartburn" when they take Propulcid®. Serious side effects from Propulcid® are uncommon. Some children will experience some cramping or diarrhea, particularly at higher doses. There have been some reports of children taking Propulcid® developing abnormal heart rhythms. This side-effect seems to be more likely if the Propulcid® is taken with certain other medicines including the antibiotics erythromycin and clarithromycin and the anti-fungal medicines Nizoral® (ketoconazole) and Diflucan® (fluconazole).

Surgery

Fortunately, it is extremely rare for children suffering from gastroesophageal reflux to require surgery. In those very few children who do require surgery, the most commonly performed operation is called Nissen fundoplication. With this operation, the top part of the stomach (the fundus) is wrapped around the bottom of the esophagus to create a collar. After the operation, every time the stomach contracts, the collar around the esophagus contracts preventing reflux.

This operation is very effective at eliminating gastroesophageal reflux with long-term success rates approaching 90%, however, some children may develop very disturbing and debilitating symptoms following fundoplication. The risks and benefits of surgery must therefore be weighed very carefully.

What Are Some of the Symptoms of Gastroesophageal Reflux?

Remember, we all have some gastroesophageal reflux. We only consider reflux abnormal when there is too much of it or there are unusual symptoms associated with it. Most of the time, we don't feel much when we reflux, however sometimes when adults have gastroesophageal reflux, they complain of:

- heartburn
- indigestion
- a feeling of food getting stuck in their throat (the medical term for this is dysphagia)
- recurrent or persistent hiccoughs

While we assume that young infants may have the same symptoms, we don't know for sure. The most common symptoms that young infants seem to experience with gastroesophageal reflux are:

- frequent or recurrent vomiting
- heartburn, gas, or abdominal pain

Many other symptoms are sometimes blamed on gastroesophageal reflux, but much of the time, we really aren't sure whether reflux actually causes them. Some less common problems seen in young infants that are blamed on gastroesophageal reflux include:

- colic or recurrent abdominal pain

- recurrent episodes of choking or gagging
- feeding problems
- poor growth
- unusual posturing such as wry-neck (torticollis) or arching (opisthotonus)
- apnea
- recurrent episodes of wheezing or pneumonia

Colic, Abdominal Pain, and Feeding Difficulties and Gastroesophageal Reflux

Older children and adults with chronic reflux sometimes complain of frequent heartburn, chest pain, or indigestion. Some adults experience frequent or recurrent hiccups or complain that food "gets stuck" in their throat (dysphagia). Most of these symptoms are thought to develop when the esophageal lining becomes inflamed or irritated by chronic or repeated exposure to gastric acid and gastric digestive juices (esophagitis).

While we often assume young infants experience similar symptoms with reflux, it is very difficult to know whether a baby's irritability, difficulty sleeping, or feeding problems are caused by reflux. Thirty-six percent of infants experience daily episodes of hiccups, 17% cry for at least an hour each day, and 10% have at least one episode of arching each day so these behaviors are by no means specific for reflux. Nevertheless, there are reports of infants with feeding failure or feeding refusal, repeated arching (opisthotonus), or other unusual forms of posturing whose symptoms improve or resolve with treatment for reflux.

Very rarely, infants with chronic and/or severe reflux may develop erosive or bleeding esophagitis. This can result in blood being visible when the child vomits or spits up. If the esophagitis is extremely severe or it persists for a prolonged period of time, it is possible for esophageal scarring to develop. This is termed an esophageal stricture. It is very difficult to determine how many children with chronic reflux develop esophageal strictures, but they are clearly very rare. Among adults with chronic esophagitis, only three in 1000 will develop esophageal strictures over many years of follow-up.

Poor Growth and Gastroesophageal Reflux

It is extremely unusual for gastroesophageal reflux to impair or limit a child's growth as long as an adequate number of calories are

369

being provided. In most cases, poor growth in a child with gastroesophageal reflux occurs when a family unintentionally limits their child's intake of calories. To try and lessen the vomiting, they dilute the formula with water or limit milk/formula intake and substitute water or Pedialyte®.

Respiratory Symptoms and Gastroesophageal Reflux

There is a long list of respiratory symptoms that may be associated with gastroesophageal reflux, however, it is often difficult to know whether the reflux causes the lung problems or the other way around. Since the windpipe (trachea) and the esophagus are very close together, many people have assumed that aspiration of refluxed stomach contents leads to respiratory symptoms.

Reflux of stomach contents up into the upper esophagus has been demonstrated in some patients with recurrent respiratory symptoms, however this appears to be very uncommon and is probably extremely rare among children who are neurologically normal.

While children with neurological abnormalities may aspirate refluxed stomach contents, more often, these children aspirate while they are eating. This is called laryngeal penetration and it occurs when swallow-breathe patterns are not well coordinated. Normally, with the initiation of a swallow, there is a pause in breathing and the larynx closes to protect the airway. In children who show no swallowing difficulties, it is reasonable to assume that these protective reflexes will function during an episode of gastroesophageal reflux.

There are reports describing children who suffer from chronic congestion and chronic hoarseness having gastroesophageal reflux. It is thought that aspiration of refluxed stomach contents causes inflammation and swelling of the upper airways and results in noisy breathing (stridor) or spasms of the vocal cords (laryngospasm). If evaluation of the upper airway demonstrates chronic inflammation, it is reasonable to consider GER as a potential source of the symptoms.

The role of GER in apnea (stopping breathing) and bradycardia (slowing of the heart rate) has been of great interest because of the potentially life-threatening nature of these symptoms. Although many studies have demonstrated that infants with apnea may have gastroesophageal reflux, there is usually little or no correlation between apneic episodes and reflux episodes. Instances in which apnea and GER have been directly associated in a cause-and-effect manner are extremely uncommon.

Both children and adults with chronic asthma have an increased incidence of gastroesophageal reflux. However, it is extremely difficult to know whether reflux causes asthma or asthma causes reflux. Chronic asthma may precipitate reflux since chronic coughing and increased respiratory efforts increase abdominal pressure, which tends to force stomach contents upwards. Among children with chronic asthma, the overall incidence of gastroesophageal reflux has been reported to range between 46 and 75%. In one study, 82% of adult asthmatics had evidence of reflux. Relatively few children with chronic asthma experience significant improvement in their asthma when they are treated for reflux so while reflux should be considered as a possible cause of uncontrolled chronic respiratory symptoms in children, it is important to remember that many of the trigger factors for wheezing also trigger gastroesophageal reflux.

How Do Doctors Diagnose Gastroesophageal Reflux?

Most of the time, just hearing the parents' story and seeing the child is enough to make the diagnosis, but sometimes testing may be recommended. The tests that are most commonly used to diagnose gastroesophageal reflux include:

- barium swallow or upper GI series
- technetium gastric emptying study
- pH probe
- endoscopy with biopsies
- summary

Barium Swallow or Upper GI Series

This is a special x-ray that allows doctors to follow food down the baby's esophagus, through the stomach and into the first part of the small intestine. The baby is fed a chalky-white liquid called barium. A video x-ray machine follows the barium through the upper intestinal tract and lets doctors see if there are any abnormal twists, kinks or narrowings of the upper intestinal tract. This x-ray test does not, however, give doctors much information on how the intestine works when food is in it and therefore it is not a very reliable way of diagnosing gastroesophageal reflux.

Many children with severe symptoms of gastroesophageal reflux will not demonstrate reflux on a barium swallow (poor sensitivity) and conversely, children who demonstrate reflux on a barium swallow have no symptoms of gastroesophageal reflux (poor specificity). Perhaps more important, the severity of reflux observed on a barium swallow does not help to predict the severity of symptoms of reflux nor does it help to predict the ultimate outcome. Less than 30% of adults with symptoms of chronic gastroesophageal reflux demonstrate reflux on a barium swallow and less than 30% of adults with esophagitis as a result of chronic gastroesophageal reflux will demonstrate reflux on a barium swallow.

Technetium Reflux Scan

With this test, the infant drinks milk mixed with technetium, a very weak radioactive chemical, and then the technetium is followed through the intestinal tract using a particular type of camera. This test is helpful in determining whether some of the milk/technetium ends up in the lungs (aspiration). It may also be helpful in determining how long milk sits in an infants stomach.

pH Probe

With this test, a small wire with an acid sensor is placed through the infants nose down to the bottom of the esophagus. The sensor can detect when acid from the stomach is "refluxed" into the esophagus. This information is generally recorded on a computer. Usually, the sensor is left in place between 12 and 24 hours. At the conclusion of the test, you are able to determine how often the infant "refluxes" acid into his or her esophagus and whether he or she has any symptoms when that occurs.

The biggest problem with this test is that the severity of the reflux as measured by pH probe often doesn't correlate with the severity of symptoms . . . that is, some infants with very frequent vomiting will have normal pH probe studies. Perhaps more important, the severity of reflux measured by a pH probe does not help to predict the ultimate outcome. While pH probe analysis is abnormal in nearly 80% of infants with mild symptoms of reflux (i.e. occasional spitting and vomiting), one third of the infants with severe symptoms have a normal pH probe study. Moreover, less than 40% of infants with severe esophagitis due to chronic gastroesophageal reflux will demonstrate abnormal pH probe studies.

Perhaps the greatest potential value of pH probe analysis is in trying to correlate gastroesophageal reflux with unusual or persistent symptoms such as apnea, stridor, coughing or wheezing, choking, gagging, or unexplained irritability. If these symptoms occur frequently enough, a pH probe analysis can be performed to determine if these symptoms occur at the same time as episodes of acid reflux into the esophagus.

Endoscopy with Biopsies

This is the most invasive of all of our tests. With this procedure, a flexible endoscope with lights and lenses is passed down through the infant's mouth into the esophagus, stomach, and duodenum. This allows the doctor to get a direct look at the esophagus, stomach, and duodenum and see if there is any irritation or inflammation present. In some children with gastroesophageal reflux, repeated exposure of the esophagus to stomach acid causes some inflammation (esophagitis). The greatest problem with this test is that most infants with symptoms of gastroesophageal reflux do not develop esophagitis (less than half of infants with severe symptoms of gastroesophageal reflux demonstrate esophagitis at endoscopy) and so a normal test does not necessarily mean the child does not have reflux.

As you can see, none of these tests is perfect . . . they all have strengths and weaknesses and they each provide a different type of information. In most cases, the diagnosis of gastroesophageal reflux can be made clinically based on a careful history and physical examination. In children whose development is delayed or disordered, it is appropriate to consider gastroesophageal reflux when the child suffers from recurrent pneumonia or aspiration, is chronically irritable without any apparent explanation, or does not grow well despite receiving adequate numbers of calories. Diagnostic tests are primarily useful when trying to associate these types of unusual or severe symptoms with gastroesophageal reflux, but offer little information about the ultimate outcome or appropriate treatment strategies.

Why Do Some Babies Have Gastroesophageal Reflux?

In almost all cases, gastroesophageal reflux is caused by incoordination or immaturity of the upper part of the intestinal tract. Before we can understand why reflux occurs, we need to understand how the upper part of the intestinal tract works.

There are three main parts of the upper intestinal tract:

- esophagus
- stomach
- duodenum

The esophagus is a long muscular tube connecting your mouth and your stomach. There are muscles at the top and bottom of the esophagus that control things coming and going, much like control valves. These muscles are called the upper and lower esophageal sphincters (pronounced sfink-ters).

The stomach is hollow and surrounded by two very thick layers of muscle. The stomach functions as a reservoir or holding tank for the food we eat. In children, when the stomach is empty, it is about the size of a fist, but it can get much bigger as you put things into it.

The duodenum is the uppermost part of the small intestine. The small intestine is a very long tube where food gets broken into very tiny "microscopic" particles and then absorbed into the blood.

How Things Work Normally

When things are working normally, after chewing your food, you swallow. When you swallow, you are pushing the food into the back of your throat and then down your esophagus. At the bottom of the esophagus is the lower esophageal sphincter. This muscle works to keep food in the stomach when the stomach is contracting or squeezing. When you swallow food, it doesn't just fall down the esophagus, it is pushed down the esophagus towards the stomach. The esophagus squeezes in a coordinated fashion with the squeeze moving from the top of the esophagus downwards towards the stomach (this coordinated type of squeezing is called peristalsis). As the food gets down to the bottom of the esophagus, the lower esophageal sphincter opens to let the food pass into the stomach and then the sphincter muscle closes again. Every time we swallow food or saliva, our esophagus squeezes in this coordinated fashion and the lower esophageal sphincter temporarily opens.

Once food gets into the stomach, it is mixed with stomach acid and other digestive juices. The stomach works like a blender. It mixes food with acid and digestive juices and mashes the food into very tiny pieces. Once the food is completely mashed, the muscle at the bottom of the stomach called the pylorus opens and closes to very slowly dribble the food into the first part of the small intestine called the duodenum.

In the small intestine, the mashed food is broken into very tiny microscopic pieces by other digestive juices and then the "digested" food is absorbed . . . passed across the lining of the intestine and into the blood.

What Happens with Gastroesophageal Reflux

As you can see, this is a very complicated process. In children with gastroesophageal reflux, there is some incoordination of the upper intestinal tract that accounts for their problems. Most children with reflux are good eaters . . . in fact, many times they are guzzlers . . . when they are hungry, they cannot be put off. They often become quite frantic, screaming and clawing at their faces. Once they are fed, they tend to gulp down their milk or formula very quickly. They usually don't choke or gag during feedings. This suggests they have no difficulty getting the food from their mouth to their esophagus.

Once the food is in their stomach, the stomach begins contracting— mashing the food and mixing it with acid and digestive juices. In children with reflux, out of the blue, the lower-esophageal sphincter opens so that as the stomach squeezes, there is nothing to keep the food in the stomach and so it comes back up the esophagus. This is gastroesophageal reflux! Sometimes, the food and acid come all the way up the esophagus and out the mouth and the child "spits up" or "vomits". Other times, the food or acid may only come part way up. In you and I, this is what we call heartburn or indigestion.

Anything that increases the pressure in the stomach has a tendency to make reflux worse. This is why many infants with reflux will spit up when they are straining to pass a bowel movement or when they cough, sneeze, or laugh.

Since reflux usually takes place when the stomach is contracting normally, most of the time, when an infant "throws-up" or "spits-up" with reflux, they don't have much pain or discomfort. In fact, many infants with reflux are not bothered at all by their reflux. They will be perfectly content immediately before they throw-up, and seem fine immediately afterwards too. Much of the time, it seems as if the baby isn't aware of any problem before they throw-up. This is very different than when we vomit because we have an intestinal flu-virus or an intestinal blockage. With that type of vomiting, we feel sick beforehand. We become very nauseous, we start sweating, salivating, and swallowing. We do all sorts of things to prepare ourselves for the vomiting including running to the bathroom.

References

1. Allen, M.L., Castell, J.A., DiMarino, A.J. Mechanisms of gastroesophageal acid reflux and esophageal acid clearance in heartburn patients. *Am J Gastro*. 1996; 91:1739-1744.

2. Barone, J.A., Jessen, L.M., Colaizzi, J.L., Bierman, R.H. Cisapride: a gastrointestinal prokinetic drug. *Ann Pharacother*. 1994; 28:488-500.

3. Borowitz, S.M., Borowitz, K.C. Gastroesophageal reflux in babies: impact on growth and development. *Infants and Young Children*, 10: 14-26, 1997.

4. Borowitz SM, Borowitz KC: Oral dysfunction following Nissen fundoplication. *Dysphagia*, 7: 234-237, 1992.

5. Borowitz, S.M., Sutphen, J.L., Hutcheson, R.L. Percutaneous endoscopic gastrostomy without an antireflux procedure in neurologically disabled children. *Clin Pediatr*. 1997; 36:25-29.

6. Burton, D.M., Pransky, S.M. Pediatric airway manifestations of gastroesophageal reflux. *Ann Oto Rhin Laryng*. 1992; 101:742-749.

7. Colletti, R.B., Christie, D.L., Orenstein, S.R. Indications for pediatric esophageal pH monitoring. *J Ped Gastro Nutr*. 1995; 21:253-262.

8. Dellert, S.F., Hyams, J.S., Treem, W.R., Geertsma, M.A. Feeding resistance and gastroesophageal reflux in infancy. *J Ped Gastro Nutr*. 1993; 17:66-71.

9. Ekstrom, T., Tibbling, L. Gastro-oesophageal reflux and triggering of bronchial asthma: a negative report. *Eur J Respir Dis*. 1987; 71:177-180.

10. Euler, A.R., Ament, M. Value of esophageal manometric studies in the gastroesophageal reflux of infancy. *Pediatr*. 1977; 59:58-62.

11. Ferreira, C., Lohouses, M.J., Bensoussan, A., Yazbeck, S., Brouchu, P., Roy, C.C. Prohlonged pH monitoring is of limited usefulness for gastroesophageal reflux. *Am J Dis Child*. 1991; 147:662-664.

12. Greally, P., Hampton, F.J., MacFayden, U.M., Simpson, H. Gaviscon and Carobel compared with cisapride in gastro-oesophageal reflux. *Arch Dis Child*. 1992; 67:618-621.

13. Heine, R.G., Jaquiery, A., Lubitz, L., Cameron, D.J., Catto-smith, A.G. Role of gastro-oesophageal reflux in infant irritability. *Arch Dis Child*. 1995; 73:121-125.

14. Hervada, A.R, Newman, D.R. Weaning: historical perspectives, practical recommendations, and current controversies. *Curr Prob Pediatr*. 1992; 22:223-40.

15. Hillmeier, A.C., Gastroesophageal reflux; diagnostic and therapeutic approaches. *Pediatr Clin N Amer.* 1996; 43:197-212.

16. Isolauri, J. and Laippala, P. Prevalence of symptoms suggestive of gastro-oesophageal reflux disease in an adult population. *Ann Med.* 1995; 27:67-70.

17. Kahn, A., Rebuffat, E., Sottiaux, M., Dufour, D., Cadranel, S., Reiterer, F. Lack of temporal relation between acid reflux in the proximal oesophagus and cardiorespiratory events in sleeping infants. *Eur J Pediatr.* 1992; 151:208-212.

18. Kibel, M.A., in Gellis S.S. (Ed): *Gastroesophageal reflux, report of the seventy-sixth Ross Conference on Pediatric Research.* Columbus, Ohio, Ross Laboratories, 1979, 39-42.

19. Mandel, H., Tirosh, E., Berant, M. Sandifer syndrome reconsidered. *Acta Paediatr Scand.* 1989; 78:797-799.

20. McCauley, R.G., Darling, D.B., Leonidas, J.C., Schwartz, A.M. Gastroesophageal reflux in infants and children: a useful classification and reliable physiologic technique for its demonstration. *AJR.* 1978; 130:47-50.

21. McLain, B.I., Cameron, D.J., Barnes, G.L. Is cow's milk protein intolerance a cause of gastro-oesophageal reflux in infancy. *J Paediatr Child Health.* 1994; 30:316-318.

22. McVeagh, P., Howman-Giles, R., Kemp, A. Pulmonary aspiration studied by radionuclide milk scanning and barium swallow roentgenography. *Am J Dis Child.* 1987; 141:917-921.

23. Narcy, P. Gastropharyngeal reflux in infants and children. *Arch Oto Head Neck Surg.* 1992; 118:1028-1030.

24. Nelson, S.H. Gastroesophageal reflux and pulmonary disease. *J Allergy Clin Immunol.* 1984; 73:547-556.

25. Orenstein, S.A., Magill, H.L., Brooks, P. Thickening of infant feedings for therapy of GER. *J Pediatr.* 1987; 110:181-186.

26. Orenstein, S.R., Dent, J., Deneault, L.G., Lutz, J.W., Wessel, H.B., Kelsey, S.F., Shalaby, T.M. Regurgitant reflux versus non-regurgitant reflux is preceded by rectus abdominus contractions in infants. *Neurogastro Motil.* 1994; 6:271-277.

27. Orenstein, S.R., Shalaby, T.M., Cohn, J.F. Reflux symptoms in 100 normal infants: diagnostic validity of the infant gastroesophageal reflux questionnaire. *Clin Pediatr.* 1996; 35:607-614.

28. Orenstein, S.R., Shalaby, T.M., Putnam, P.E. Thickened feedings as a cause of increased coughing when used as therapy for gastroesophageal reflux in infants. *J Pediatr.* 1992; 121:913-915.

29. Orenstein, S.R., Whitington, P.E. Positioning for prevention of infant gastroesophageal reflux. *J Pediatr.* 1983; 103:534-537.

30. Ott, D.J., Gelfand, D.W., Wu, W.C. Reflux esophagitis: radiographic and endoscopic correlation. *Radiol.* 1979; 130:583-8.

31. Paton, J.Y., Cosgriff, P.S., Nanayakkara, C.S. The analytical sensitivity of Tc-99m radionuclide milk scanning in the detection of gastroesophageal reflux in infants. *Pediatr Radiol.* 1985; 15:381-383.

32. Paton, J.Y., Macfadyen, U., Williams, A., Simpson, H. Gastro-oesophageal reflux and apnoeic pauses during sleep in infancy—no direct relation. *Eur J Pediatr.* 1990; 149:680-688.

33. Penagini, R., Schoeman, M.N., Dent, J., Tippett, M.D., Holloway, R.H. Motor events underlying gastro-oesophageal reflux in ambulant patients with reflux oesophagitis. *Neurogastro Motil.* 1996; 8:131-141.

34. Rejeb, M.B., Bouche, O., Zeitoun, P. Study of 47 consecutive patients with peptic esophageal stricture compared with 3880 cases of reflux esophagitis. *Dig Dis Sci.* 1992; 37:733-736.

35. Schoeman, M.N., Tippett, M.D., Akkermans, L.M., Dent, J., Holloway, R.H. Mechanisms of gastroesophageal reflux in ambulant human subjects. *Gastro.* 1995; 108:83-91.

36. Shapiro, G.G., Christie, D.L. Gastroesophageal reflux in steroid-dependent asthmatic youths. *Pediatr.* 1979; 63:207-212.

37. Shepherd, R.W., Wren, J., Evans, S., Lander, M., Ong, T.H. Gastroesophgeal reflux in children. Clinical profile, course and outcome, with active therapy in 126 cases. *Clin Pediatr.* 1987; 26:55-60.

38. Sontag, S.J., O'Connell, S., Khandelwal, S., Miller, T., Nemchausky, B., Schnell, T.G. Serlovsky, R. Most asthmatics have gastroesophageal reflux with or without bronchodilator therapy. *Gastro.* 1990; 99:613-620.

39. Sutphen, J.L. Pediatric gastroesophageal reflux disease. *Gastro Clin N Amer*. 1990; 19:617-629.

40. Thompson, J.K., Koehler, R.E., Richter, J.E. Detection of gastroesophageal reflux: value of barium studies compared with 24-hr pH monitoring. *AJR*. 1994; 162:621-626.

41. Tolia, V., Kuhns, L., Kauffman, R.E. Comparison of simultaneous esophgaeal pH monitoring and scintigraphy in infants with gastroesophageal reflux. *Amer J Gastro*. 1993; 88:661-664.

42. Tucci, F., Resti, M., Fontana, R., Novembre, E., Lami, C.A., Vierucci, A. Gastroesophageal reflux and bronchial asthma: prevalence and effect of cisapride therapy. *J Ped Gastro Nutr* 1993; 17:265-270.

43. Vandenplas, Y. Asthma and gastroesophageal reflux. *J Ped Gastro Nutr*. 1997; 24:89-90.

44. Werlin, S.L., Dodds, W.J., Hogan, W.J., Arndorfer, R.C. Mechanisms of gastroesophageal reflux in children. *J Pediatr*. 1980; 97:244-9.

Chapter 55

Giardiasis

Signs and Symptoms

Giardiasis is an intestinal illness caused by a microscopic parasite called *Giardia lamblia*. In some parts of the world, especially in developing countries, giardiasis is an endemic disease (a disease that is generally found in people who live in a particular area). In these cases, over two-thirds of infected persons may have no signs or symptoms of illness, even though the parasite is living in their intestines.

When the parasite does cause symptoms, the illness usually begins with severe bouts of watery diarrhea, without blood or mucus. Because giardiasis affects the body's ability to absorb fats from the diet, the diarrhea seen in giardiasis contains unabsorbed fats—so it floats and is very foul-smelling and shiny. Other symptoms include: abdominal cramps, especially in the area above the navel; a distended abdomen (abnormally large belly); large amounts of intestinal gas; loss of appetite; nausea and vomiting; and sometimes a low-grade fever. These symptoms may last for 5-7 days, or longer. If symptoms last longer, a child may lose a significant amount of weight and begin to show signs of poor nutrition.

Sometimes, after acute symptoms of giardiasis pass, the disease begins a chronic phase. Symptoms of chronic giardiasis include: bouts of intestinal gas; abdominal pain in the area above the navel; and poorly formed, "mushy" bowel movements.

From www.kidshealth.org © 1999 The Nemours Foundation. Used with permission.

Description

Giardiasis is an intestinal infection caused by a microscopic parasite called *Giardia lamblia*. The parasite attaches itself to the lining of the small intestines in humans, where it sabotages the body's absorption of fats and carbohydrates from digested foods.

In the United States, *Giardia* is the most common cause of diarrhea due to contaminated water. It can survive routine concentrations of chlorine used to purify community water supplies, and it can live for more than two months in cold water. It takes as few as 10 of the microscopic parasites in a glass of water to begin a severe case of giardiasis in a human being.

It is estimated that between 1% and 20% of the U.S. population has giardiasis, but in developing countries this figure may be 20% or higher. Young children are three times more likely to have giardiasis than adults; this statistic leads some experts to believe that our bodies gradually develop some form of immunity to the parasite as we grow older. It is not unusual, however, for an entire family to have giardiasis, with some of the family having diarrhea, some just crampy abdominal pains, and some with few or no symptoms.

Prevention

You can prevent giardiasis by drinking only from water supplies that have been approved by local health authorities. When you go camping or hiking, bring your own water instead of drinking from sources like mountain streams. Wash raw fruits and vegetables well before you eat them. Wash your own hands well before you cook food for yourself or for your family. Encourage your children to wash their hands after every trip to the bathroom, and especially before they eat.

If someone in your family has giardiasis, wash your hands often as you care for him or her.

It is questionable (at least, to our way of thinking) whether infants and toddlers still in diapers should be sharing public pools. Certainly they should not if they are having loose stools.

Incubation

The incubation period for giardiasis is 1-3 weeks after exposure to the parasite.

Duration

Most children recover spontaneously within one month, but treatment with antiparasitic medication will help them recover even faster. Medication also shortens the time that children are contagious.

Contagiousness

People and animals (mainly dogs and beavers) who have giardiasis can pass the parasite in their stool. The stool can then contaminate public water supplies, community swimming pools, and "natural" water sources like mountain streams. Uncooked foods that have been rinsed in contaminated water may also spread the infection. In daycare centers and care facilities for the mentally handicapped, giardiasis can easily pass from person to person. At home, an infected family dog with diarrhea may pass the parasite to human family members who take care of the sick animal.

Home Treatment

If your child has giardiasis and your doctor has prescribed medication, be sure to give all doses on schedule for as long as your doctor directs. This will help your child recover faster and will kill parasites that might infect others in your family. Encourage all family members to wash their hands frequently, especially after using the bathroom and before eating.

A child who has diarrhea from giardiasis may lose too much fluid in the stool and suffer from dehydration. Make sure the child drinks plenty of fluids—but no caffeinated beverages, because they make the body lose water faster.

Ask your doctor before you give your child any non-prescription drugs for cramps or diarrhea, since these medicines may mask your child's symptoms and interfere with treatment.

Professional Treatment

Doctors confirm the diagnosis of giardiasis by finding *Giardia* parasites in samples of an infected person's stool. Stool samples are sent to the laboratory for examination. Several samples may be needed before the parasites are found. A new rapid test on stool (ELISA) can facilitate the diagnosis and is very accurate. Less often, doctors make the diagnosis by looking at the lining of the small intestine with an instrument called an endoscope and taking samples from inside the intestine to be sent to a laboratory.

Giardiasis is treated with prescription medicines that kill the parasites. Treatment typically takes 7-10 days, and the medicine is usually given as a liquid suspension that your child can drink. Some of these medicines may have side effects, so your doctor will tell you what to watch for.

When to Call Your Pediatrician

Call your doctor whenever your child has large amounts of diarrhea, especially if the child also has a fever and/or abdominal pain. Also call your doctor if your child has occasional small bouts of diarrhea that continue for several days, especially if appetite is poor, and the child is either gradually losing weight or not gaining as much as expected.

Chapter 56

Hepatitis

Signs and Symptoms

Hepatitis is an inflammatory process involving the liver. Hepatitis, in its early stages, may cause flu-like symptoms. These symptoms may include malaise (a general ill feeling), fever, muscle aches, loss of appetite, nausea, vomiting, diarrhea, and jaundice.

If hepatitis progresses, its symptoms begin to point to the liver as the source of illness. Chemicals normally secreted by the liver begin to build up in the blood. This causes jaundice (a yellowing of the skin and whites of the eyes), foul breath, and a bitter taste in the mouth. Urine turns dark or "tea-colored," and stools become white, light, or "clay-colored." There also can be abdominal pain, which may be centered below the right ribs (over a tender, swollen liver) or below the left ribs (over a tender spleen).

Description

The word hepatitis simply means an inflammation of the liver, without pinpointing a specific cause. Someone with hepatitis may be suffering from one of several disorders, including a viral infection of the liver; liver injury caused by a toxin (poison); liver damage caused by interruption of the organ's normal blood supply; or trauma.

From www.kidshealth.org © 1999 The Nemours Foundation. Used with permission.

Most commonly, hepatitis is caused by one of three viruses: the hepatitis A virus; the hepatitis B virus; or the hepatitis C virus (also called non-A, non-B hepatitis). In some cases, mononucleosis can also result in hepatitis.

In children, the most common form of hepatitis is hepatitis A, also called "infectious hepatitis." This form is caused by the hepatitis A virus (HAV), which lives in the stools of infected individuals. When someone touches or eats anything that is contaminated with HAV-infected stool, the virus can pass into the body through the mouth. This makes it easy for HAV to spread in overcrowded, unsanitary living conditions. HAV also spreads in contaminated water, milk, and foods, especially in shellfish. Because hepatitis A can be a mild infection, particularly in children, it is possible for some people to be unaware that they have had the illness. In fact, although medical tests show that about 40% of urban Americans have had hepatitis A, only about 5% recall being sick.

Hepatitis B, also called "serum hepatitis," is caused by the hepatitis B virus (HBV). HBV spreads through infected body fluids, such as blood, saliva, semen, vaginal fluids, tears, breast milk, and urine. Infections may occur through a contaminated blood transfusion (uncommon in the United States), shared contaminated needles or syringes for injecting drugs, or sexual activity with an HBV-infected person. HBV-infected mothers can also pass the virus to their newborn babies.

Hepatitis C (also called "non-A, non-B hepatitis") may be spread through sexual contact, but it usually develops after a contaminated blood transfusion. Hepatitis C is also a common threat in kidney dialysis centers.

All of these viral hepatitis conditions can be diagnosed and followed through the use of readily available blood tests.

Incubation

The incubation period for viral hepatitis varies depending on which hepatitis virus causes the disease. For hepatitis A, the incubation period is 2 to 6 weeks. For hepatitis B, the incubation period is between 1 and 5 months. For hepatitis C, the incubation period is 2 to 26 weeks after a contaminated blood transfusion.

Duration

Children with hepatitis A usually have mild symptoms or are without symptoms. They may be more fatigued than normal, but they are rarely jaundiced. Almost all previously healthy persons who develop hepatitis A will completely recover from their illness in a few weeks or months without long-term complications.

With hepatitis B, 90% to 95% of patients recover from their illness completely within 6 months, without long-term complications. In some cases, however, persons with either hepatitis B or C can go on to develop chronic hepatitis and cirrhosis (chronic degeneration) of the liver. Some persons with hepatitis B or C may also become lifelong carriers of these viruses and can spread them to other people.

Contagiousness

Hepatitis A is contagious, and its virus can be spread in contaminated food or water, as well as in unsanitary conditions in child care facilities or schools. Toilets and sinks used by an infected person should be cleaned with antiseptic cleansers. All persons who live with or care for someone with hepatitis should wash their hands after contact with the infected person. In addition, when traveling to countries where hepatitis A is prevalent, your child should be vaccinated with at least two doses of the hepatitis A vaccine.

Hepatitis B is contagious, and its virus can be found in virtually all body fluids. Its main routes of infection, however, are through sexual contact, contaminated blood transfusions, and shared needles for drug injections. Use of the hepatitis B vaccine should greatly decrease the incidence of this infection. Ask your child's doctor about this vaccine.

Like hepatitis B, hepatitis C is contagious and can be spread through sexual contact, contaminated blood products, or shared drug paraphernalia. Hepatitis C can be spread from mother to fetus during pregnancy, however, the risk of passing hepatitis C to the fetus is about 5%. If you are pregnant, contact your doctor if you contract hepatitis C.

Household contact with adults with hepatitis B or C can put people at risk for contracting hepatitis. Frequent handwashing and good hygiene practices can reduce the risk of hepatitis B or C infection.

Over the past several years, improved medical technology has almost eliminated the risk of catching hepatitis from contaminated blood products and blood transfusions. But, as tattoos and acupuncture have become more popular, the risk of developing hepatitis from improperly sterilized equipment used in these procedures has increased.

Prevention

In general, to prevent viral hepatitis you should follow good hygiene and avoid crowded, unhealthy living conditions. If you travel to areas of the world where sanitation is poor and water quality is uncertain, extra care is necessary, particularly when drinking and swimming. Never eat shellfish from waters contaminated by sewage. You should also remind children to wash their hands thoroughly after using the toilet and before eating. If someone in the family develops hepatitis, antiseptic cleansers should be used to clean any toilet, sink, potty-chair, or bedpan used by that person.

Since contaminated needles and syringes are a major source of hepatitis infection, you should encourage drug awareness programs in your community and schools. At home, speak to your children frankly and frequently about the dangers of drug use. Also encourage abstinence and safe sex for teens, in order to eliminate their risk of hepatitis infection through sexual contact.

A hepatitis A vaccine is available, and is especially recommended for travelers, sexually active individuals, and people in high-risk occupations, such as health care and child care personnel. The vaccine is especially useful for staff of child care facilities or schools, family members of infected persons, or sexual partners of someone with hepatitis A.

There is also a hepatitis B vaccine, which should be given to both children and adults as part of routine immunization. Talk to your child's doctor about vaccinations for hepatitis.

When to Call Your Child's Doctor

Call your child's doctor if your child has symptoms of hepatitis, attends a school or child care facility where someone has hepatitis, or has been exposed to a friend or relative with the illness.

If older children volunteer at a first-aid station, hospital, or nursing home, be sure that they are aware of proper safety procedures for preventing contact with blood or body fluids. Such employment may warrant an immunization against HBV. Call your doctor if you believe that your child may have been exposed to a patient with hepatitis.

If you already know that your child has hepatitis, call your child's doctor if you notice any of the following symptoms: confusion or extreme drowsiness, skin rash, or itching. Monitor your child's appetite and digestive functions, and call your child's doctor if appetite decreases, or if nausea, vomiting, diarrhea, or jaundice increase.

Professional Treatment

When symptoms are severe or laboratory tests show liver damage, hospital treatment of hepatitis is sometimes necessary.

Home Treatment

Children with mild hepatitis may be treated at home. Except for using the bathroom, they should rest in bed until fever and jaundice are gone and appetite is normal. Children with a lack of appetite should try smaller, more frequent meals and fluids that are high in calories (like milk shakes). They should eat healthy foods rich in protein and carbohydrates and drink plenty of water.

Chapter 57

Hypospadias and Undescended Testicles

Hypospadias

Some boys are born with their urinary opening abnormally located somewhere along the underneath portion of the penis shaft. This is known as hypospadias. There is a 6% chance of this abnormality showing up again in the family.

The most common abnormal location of the opening is just below the penis tip (the glans), and with increasing rarity, farther down the shaft and, very rarely, at the penis base. Most of the time, there is a non-functioning but normal-looking opening in the tip of the penis. In the mildest cases, the opening can be in an off-center position on the glans, and won't need repair.

10% of boys with hypospadias also have undescended testicles. Groin hernias are found more often in these boys. Infants having hypospadias plus undescended testicles, should have genetic studies done to definitely establish true gender. Chordee of the penis (penis curved downwards) accompanies hypospadias in some cases. In most hypospadias, the foreskin is only partial, and is found on the upper portion of the penis tip. This should NOT be removed (circumcised) because it is used in making the surgical repair.

Surgical correction of hypospadias in the milder forms (the opening close to the glans) is said to be cosmetic (unless you count wetting

---

This chapter includes text from "Hypospadias," www.kidsdoctor.com, reprinted with permission; and "Undescended Testicles," www.babycenter.com, reprinted with permission.

the floor and shoes as being a drawback...but a boy can learn to position his penis properly to avoid this). When the defect is farther down the shaft, surgical correction is essential for a well-directed stream and for reproductive effectiveness.

Undescended Testicles

My newborn has an undescended testicle. What is it, and how common is this condition?

It's not unusual for a baby boy, especially one who arrives early, to enter the world with one or both testicles undescended into the scrotum. That's why your healthcare provider will thoroughly examine your baby's genitals during the initial exam to confirm that both have dropped into the scrotum or at least into the canal just above it. If they haven't, the condition will usually correct itself within the first year.

What causes it?

No one knows for sure, but it's believed to occur around the seventh month in utero since that's when a fetus' testicles normally begin their descent from the abdomen into the scrotal sac. The American Academy of Pediatrics' book, *Caring for Your Baby and Young Child* cites the following possible reasons for this condition:

- Insufficient hormones from the mother or developing testicles to stimulate normal development
- Testes themselves may be abnormal in response to the hormones
- A physical blockage has prevented normal descent
- Hormones taken during pregnancy may affect a male fetus' testes

Can it be corrected?

Luckily, in 2/3 of all cases, the condition corrects itself. If it hasn't by a boy's first birthday, treatment may be necessary. Two treatments are used for undescended testicles:

- Hormone therapy, which stimulates the testes to increase the testosterone level: This is usually done by administering twice-weekly injections of human chorionic gonadotropin, a hormone that stimulates the maturation of the testicles and jump-starts their downward migration over the course of several weeks. This treatment is effective in about 20 percent of all cases; and the lower the undescended testis is, the better the chances of the treatment is of succeeding. In the event that it's unsuccessful, doctors will resort to surgery.

- Surgery, which is used if a basic abnormality is the cause of the problem: For example, if a band of fibrous tissue blocks the testicles' descent into the scrotum, the tissue must be removed surgically. If the ligament that supports the testicles is too short then it can be lengthened.

- Surgery is also used if the condition is accompanied by an inguinal hernia, a common complication in which a loop of the child's intestine pushes its way into the canal or even down into the scrotum. Both procedures involve minor outpatient surgery.

What happens if it's left untreated?

Testicles don't seem to mature normally when they aren't in the scrotum, so the risk of testicular cancer and infertility is greatly increased if undescended testicles aren't cared for. In very rare cases, an undescended testicle can become twisted, cutting off the blood supply and causing pain in the groin or scrotal area.

In any case, as long as your son's testicles are corrected (either on their own or with some intervention), there's nothing to worry about. An undescended testicle in infancy has absolutely no bearing on the later appearance of his genitals or his fertility.

Chapter 58

Impetigo

Signs and Symptoms

Impetigo is a skin infection caused by bacteria. It may affect skin anywhere on the body but usually attacks the area around the nose and mouth. Impetigo is characterized by blisters that may burst, ooze fluid, and develop a honey-colored crust.

Impetigo may itch, and it can be spread by scratching. The infection usually spreads along the edges of an affected area, but may also spread to other areas of the body.

Description

Impetigo is a skin infection that is generally caused by one of two bacteria: Group A streptococcus or *Staphylococcus aureus*. Impetigo usually affects preschool- and school-age children, especially in the summer months. Impetigo has a special preference for skin that has already been injured by other skin problems, such as eczema, poison ivy, or skin allergy to soap or makeup.

When impetigo is caused by Group A streptococcus, it begins as tiny blisters. These blisters eventually burst to reveal small wet patches of red skin that may weep fluid. Gradually, a tan or yellowish-brown crust covers the affected area, making it look like it's been coated with honey or brown sugar.

From www.kidshealth.org © 1999 The Nemours Foundation. Used with permission.

Impetigo that is not caused by Group A streptococcus may be caused by staphylococcus. This type of impetigo may cause larger blisters containing fluid that is first clear, then cloudy. These blisters are more likely to stay intact longer on the skin without bursting.

Duration

With antibiotic treatment, healing should begin within 3 days. A child with impetigo may return to school when the infection is not contagious. This usually is about 48 hours after treatment is started.

Contagiousness

Impetigo is a bacterial infection, and it is contagious. Children can spread impetigo from one area of the body to another when they touch themselves with fingers that have been in contact with scratched, infected skin. When someone has impetigo, the infection can spread to other household members on clothing, towels, and bed linens that have touched the person's infected skin. It can also be spread among playmates or classmates who come in contact with infected skin.

Prevention

You can help prevent impetigo by following good hygiene practices in caring for your child's skin. This includes giving your child a daily bath or shower with soap and water. Pay special attention to areas of the skin that have been injured, such as cuts, scrapes, areas of eczema, and rashes caused by allergic reactions or poison ivy. Keep these areas clean and covered.

If someone in your family already has impetigo, make sure that fingernails are cut short and that the impetigo sores are covered with gauze and tape. Prevent impetigo infection from spreading to other family members by using antibacterial soap and making sure that each family member uses a separate towel. If necessary, substitute paper towels for cloth ones until the impetigo is gone. Separate the child's bed linens, towels, and clothing from those of other family members, and wash these items in very hot water.

When to Call Your Child's Doctor

Call your child's doctor if your child has signs of impetigo, especially if the child has been exposed to a family member or classmate with the infection. If your child is already being treated for impetigo, call the doctor if the child's skin doesn't begin to heal after 3 days of treatment, or if a fever develops. If the affected area becomes red, warm, or tender to the touch, notify your child's doctor.

Professional Treatment

Impetigo usually is treated with antibiotics, which may be given orally or by injection. In very mild cases, a topical (on the skin) antibiotic creme may be used.

Home Treatment

If your doctor has prescribed antibiotics, make sure that your child takes them on schedule for the full number of days prescribed. If your doctor has ordered an antibiotic ointment, apply it as directed.

Wash areas of infected skin gently with a piece of clean gauze twice a day using antiseptic soap. If an area of skin is crusted, soak it first in warm soapy water to remove any layers of crust. It is not necessary to completely remove all of the crust but it is important to keep the area clean.

To keep your child from spreading impetigo to other parts of the body, cover infected areas of skin, if possible, with gauze and tape or a loose plastic bandage as instructed by your child's doctor or nurse. Keep your child's fingernails short.

Chapter 59

Kawasaki Syndrome

What is Kawasaki Syndrome?

Kawasaki syndrome (mucocutaneous lymph node syndrome) is a serious rash illness of children. It is a relatively rare disease; fewer than 200 cases are reported each year in New York State.

Who gets Kawasaki Syndrome?

Most cases occur in infants and children under age five.

How is Kawasaki Syndrome spread?

Little is known about the way a person gets this syndrome or how it spreads. It does not appear to be transmitted from person to person. Since outbreaks occur, it may be caused by an infectious agent.

What are the symptoms of Kawasaki Syndrome?

Most cases have a high spiking fever that does not respond to antibiotics. The fever lasts more than five days and is associated with irritability, swollen lymph nodes, red eyes, lips, throat and tongue. The rash may cover the entire body and is sometimes followed by a peeling of the skin on the hands and fingers.

New York State Department of Health, February 1999.

Does past infection make a person immune?

Recurrences have been reported but they are extremely rare.

What is the treatment for Kawasaki Syndrome?

Most patients are treated in the hospital where they can be closely watched. Aspirin and immunoglobulins are often prescribed.

What are the complications associated with Kawasaki Syndrome?

The most frequent complication is coronary artery aneurysms (ballooning out of vessels in the heart). Other organs may be involved as well. Approximately 1-2 percent of cases die of the disease and its complications.

How can Kawasaki Syndrome be prevented?

At the present time, preventive measures are unknown.

Chapter 60

Meningitis

Signs and Symptoms

The signs and symptoms of meningitis are variable and, to a great extent, depend on the age of the child with the infection and which bacteria or virus is causing it. The first signs may be those common to a number of illnesses, such as fever, lethargy, vomiting, and irritability. Older children may complain of a headache. A stiff neck may be found on examination by a doctor. Seizures occur in about a third of patients with bacterial meningitis and sometimes are the only symptoms. As the disease develops, other symptoms set in: increased irritability with a high-pitched cry and difficulty breathing.

Newborns with meningitis may lack the classical signs described above and simply be extremely irritable or lethargic (have decreased consciousness). Under usual circumstances, when an infant isn't feeling well, she is comforted when her mother picks her up. With meningitis, we might see something called "paradoxical irritability," when picking up and rocking a child may make her more distressed. This can be a sign of an irritated meninges (the covering of the central nervous system).

Other signs that can be seen in an infant with meningitis include jaundice (a yellowish tint to the skin) and a stiffness of the body and of the neck ("neck rigidity"). There may be bulging fontanelles (the "soft spot" at the top/front of the baby's skull where the bones of the skull join and are still open at that age).

Meningococcal meningitis may be accompanied by a purplish rash (purpura) in approximately half of cases. Other types of bacterial meningitis, such as those caused by *Streptococcus pneumoniae* and *Haemophilus influenzae*, may also have a similar rash, though less commonly.

Invasive meningococcal infections also may be complicated by arthritis, myocarditis (inflammation of the heart muscle), pericarditis (the "pouch" around the heart), or pneumonia.

Description

Meningitis is a general name for inflammation of the meninges (sheaths that cover the brain and spinal cord) and the cerebrospinal fluid (the fluid that circulates in the spaces in and around the brain and spinal cord.) Meningitis can be caused by infectious or noninfectious agents. Infectious agents include bacteria, viruses, fungi, and other organisms such as protozoa and rickettsia.

The most frequent cause of meningitis is the entry of microorganisms from an infection elsewhere in the body through the blood into the cerebrospinal fluid. *Streptococcus pneumoniae* and *Neisseria meningitides* (meningococcus) are the common organisms that cause meningitis in children. *Escherichia coli* may cause meningitis in newborns.

The infection most frequently begins in the respiratory system. Rare sources of meningitis include infection of heart valves, bones, and other parts of the body as well as invasion by bacteria located near the central nervous system from infected ears, nose, or teeth. Of course, infections of these areas rarely lead to meningitis.

Seventy percent of all cases of meningitis occur in the first five years of life, with the peak incidence between six and 12 months of age. There are no specific signs and symptoms that can definitively distinguish bacterial meningitis from meningitis resulting from other causes.

Prevention

In certain cases of meningitis it may be wise to administer antibiotics to close contacts of the case in order to help prevent further cases from occurring. Physicians in charge will decide who should receive the preventive antibiotics. The use of immunization against *Haemophilus influenzae* Type B (HIB) has dramatically decreased meningitis due to this organism. All children should receive the vaccination. In addition, certain high-risk children should also be immunized against *Streptococcus pneumoniae*.

Incubation

This varies with the organism and the underlying cause of the meningitis, but once the organisms have entered the cerebrospinal fluid, the body defenses cannot control their rapid growth as well as they could when the organisms were only in the bloodstream. Once the bacteria, for example, have entered the spinal fluid, the child usually shows symptoms fairly rapidly.

Duration

This is variable, as bacterial meningitis can present acutely (symptoms rapidly evolve over one to 24 hours), subacutely (over one to seven days) or chronically (over a week). Once established—and even with proper treatment—meningitis takes many days (and sometimes weeks) to resolve.

Contagiousness

Meningitis is usually infectious in origin, and patients may be contagious until antibiotic therapy has been initiated for about 24 hours. This can vary.

Home Treatment

Meningitis is treated by professionals in a health care facility.

Professional Treatment

All children with possible meningitis require aggressive efforts at diagnosis and treatment. This almost always means a lumbar puncture (spinal tap) in order to obtain spinal fluid for examination and culture. Diagnosis cannot be made through imaging tests, such as x-rays.

Once the diagnosis of meningitis is made (or sufficiently suspected), intravenous antibiotics are given as soon as possible, often before the exact organism causing the infection is identified. The antibiotics can be changed, if necessary, once the microorganism is identified through laboratory tests. A combination of antibiotics may be required. Corticosteroids may be necessary to combat the inflammatory response.

The first three or four days of treatment of bacterial meningitis are particularly critical. Vital signs such as pulse and respiration will be monitored frequently until the patient is stable. If there are complications, they will be treated as appropriate.

Follow-up measures may also be necessary. Since impairment of hearing may result from this illness, children should be tested for hearing about a month after recovery from the disease.

The long-term outlook for children with meningitis is quite variable, and depends on the child's age, the organism involved, the presence of any other complications, and the appropriateness of the treatment.

When to Call Your Pediatrician

Seek medical attention immediately if you suspect meningitis or if your child exhibits symptoms such as vomiting, headache, lethargy or confusion, neck stiffness, rash, and fever. In infants, fever, irritability, poor feeding, and lethargy may be significant.

If your child has had contact with patients with meningitis (for example, in a day-care center or college dorm), consult your doctor to check if preventive measures are called for.

Chapter 61

Orthopedic Conditions

Bowlegs, flatfeet, knock-knees, pigeon toes, toe-walking. Lots of children have these common orthopedic conditions, but do they represent medical problems that can and should be corrected? Here's the reassuring word on some common orthopedic conditions.

Flatfeet

In decades past, men with flatfeet were not allowed to serve in the U.S. Army. Because about 20% of people with flatfeet experience some foot pain, it was thought that they would not make good foot soldiers. Having flatfeet is no longer a disqualifying factor for service. Physicians today recognize that this condition usually represents no hindrance to the many people it affects.

"Babies tend to have a flat arch, which often corrects itself as the child grows," says Robert Stanton, M.D., a pediatric orthopedic surgeon at the Alfred I. duPont Hospital for Children. In children with flatfeet, the arch never fully develops. Parents often first notice their child has what they describe as "weak ankles." The ankles appear to turn inward because of the way the feet are planted. "What parents are seeing is so common that it is considered to be a normal variation of human anatomy," explains Dr. Stanton.

"Flatfeet usually do not represent an impairment of any kind for the child," Dr. Stanton adds. He does not recommend any special footwear, such as shoes with ankle or arch supports, because these "treatments" do not affect arch development. He says parents with flat-footed children occasionally say their child is clumsier than other children. However, Dr. Stanton reassures them that flatfeet in an otherwise normal child is not a cause for concern. "A child with flatfeet has just as much athletic potential as any other child," he says. Physicians consider treatment only if the condition becomes painful to the child.

Toe-Walking

Toe-walking, according to Dr. Stanton, is common among toddlers first learning to walk, especially during the second 12 months of life. Generally, the tendency is gone by age 2 although in some children, it persists. "Intermittent toe-walking is nothing to worry about," comments Dr. Stanton. "The only time it's a problem is when it is associated with other problems." Children who walk on their toes almost exclusively and continue to do so after age 2 are medically evaluated to rule out conditions such as mild cerebral palsy.

Dr. Stanton says persistent toe-walking, with no other symptoms, occasionally requires treatment. This involves casting the foot and ankle for about 6 weeks, which generally corrects the problem.

Pigeon Toes

Pigeon toes, or inwardly turned toes, is another normal variation in the way the legs and feet line up. Dr. Stanton describes a natural turning in of the legs at about 8 to 15 months of age, when babies begin standing. Special shoes and braces (commonly used in the past to "treat" this problem) have never been shown to speed up the natural slow improvement in this condition. Dr. Stanton emphasizes that pigeon toes, like flatfeet, are no barrier to athletic participation.

Bowlegs

Dr. Stanton describes bowlegs in young infants as "an inherited tendency that often gets better with time." He notes, however, that pronounced bowlegs past the age of 2 years should be evaluated since it can be an indicator of disease, including rickets and Blount's disease.

Rickets is a bone growth problem, usually caused by lack of vitamin D in the diet, and evidenced by severe bowing of the legs. Rickets is much less common today than it used to be. Fortunately, nutritional rickets and the resulting bowlegs are almost always corrected by adding vitamin D to the diet.

Severe bowlegs can also occur as a result of Blount's disease, a condition that affects the tibia bone of the leg. Bowing from Blount's disease is seen at about 2 years. To correct the problem, the child may require bracing or surgery between 3 and 4 years of age. You should also take your child to the doctor if the bowlegs occur only on one side or get progressively worse.

Knock-knees

Many children show a moderate tendency toward knock-knees between the ages of 4 and 6. "The body goes through a natural shifting of alignment during the first 6 years of life, then tends to straighten up," explains Dr. Stanton. Only when an inward turning of the knees is severe and associated with other problems is further evaluation or treatment necessary.

Dr. Stanton says that most pediatricians and family doctors can recognize when involvement is severe enough to warrant specialty care. However, parents may want to seek a specialist's opinion for peace of mind if they think their child's feet or legs are not developing normally. Dr. Stanton reminds us that, "Just as dimples or cleft chins are normal facial variations, bowlegs, flatfeet, knock-knees, pigeon toes, and toe-walking are examples of normal variations of the human anatomy and rarely require treatment."

Chapter 62

Respiratory Syncytial Virus

Signs and Symptoms

Respiratory syncytial virus (RSV) is a major cause of respiratory illness in young children. RSV infection produces a variety of signs and symptoms involving different areas of the respiratory tract, from the nose to the lungs.

In adults and children above age three, RSV usually causes symptoms of a simple upper respiratory tract illness or "common cold." These symptoms include a stuffy or runny nose, sore throat, mild headache, mild cough, low-grade fever, and a general feeling of being "ill."

In children younger than age three, RSV most often causes a lower respiratory tract illness like bronchiolitis or pneumonia and may lead to respiratory failure. In this case, symptoms may include high fever, severe cough, wheezing, abnormally rapid breathing, difficulty breathing, and a bluish color of the lips or fingernails. In infants with severe RSV infection, there may be abnormal retractions of the muscles between the ribs, as the child struggles to draw breath into infected breathing passages.

Description

RSV is a virus that causes infection of the lungs and breathing passages. It can infect the same person several times during a lifetime,

From www.kidshealth.org © 1999 The Nemours Foundation. Used with permission.

causing more severe illnesses (like pneumonia) in infancy, but only a "common cold" in adulthood. After each RSV infection, the body forms some immunity to the virus, but that immunity is never complete. Re-infections occur, but they usually are less severe than earlier RSV attacks. RSV passes from person to person through infected nasal and oral fluids. It can enter the body when eyes or nose are touched.

RSV infections occur all over the world, most often in epidemics that can last up to five months, from late fall through early spring. Since 1990, epidemics have typically begun sometime between late October and mid-December, and peaked during January and February. Each year during these epidemic periods, about 90,000 infants and young children are hospitalized with RSV infections—and about 4,500 die.

The highest rates of RSV illness occur in infants two to six months old, with a peak at age two to three months. RSV infection is often carried home by a school-aged child and passed onto a younger one, especially an infant. When RSV infects a day-care center, it is not unusual to see 100% of the children come down with an RSV infection. RSV commonly spreads through hospitals, too, infecting both patients and staff.

Prevention

RespiGam is an intravenous vaccine that doctors use to protect infants who are considered to be at-risk for RSV. This new preventive treatment takes several hours to administer.

Since RSV spreads in fluids from the nose and throat of an infected person, it is best to wash your hands after touching anyone who has either a "cold" or a known RSV infection. Also, it is wise not to touch your nose or eyes after contact with someone with RSV since the virus could enter your body through either of these two areas. And whenever a school-aged child comes down with a "cold," keep the child away from an infant brother or sister until the symptoms pass.

Incubation

Incubation period is four to six days.

Duration

RSV infection usually lasts seven to 14 days, but some cases may last up to three weeks. Children who are hospitalized with lower respiratory tract illness usually spend five to seven days in the hospital.

Contagiousness

RSV is contagious and can attack up to 50% of infants during an RSV epidemic. Yearly epidemics occur in the late fall, winter, and early spring—almost never in the summer. Children in day-care centers are at greater risk. Infants are at special risk if they have an older brother or sister in school.

Someone who has an RSV infection, even if it's "just a cold," can pass infectious RSV particles through oral and nasal fluids. Contagiousness is highest during the first two to four days of the illness, but RSV particles may continue to be spread for up to two weeks after the stuffy nose begins.

Home Treatment

In treating RSV infection, the goal is to make children more comfortable while their own bodies fight the virus.

Using a cool-mist vaporizer to humidify the air may help soothe irritated breathing passages and relieve coughing. Give plenty of fluids such as water, fruit juice, and weak tea—these help keep nasal secretions watery and easy to clear.

If necessary to loosen mucus in the nose, you can use salt water (saline) nose drops. If the nostrils are irritated, rub a little petroleum jelly under them.

Treat fever using a nonaspirin fever medicine like acetaminophen. **Aspirin should NOT be used in children with viral illnesses since the use of aspirin in such cases has been associated with the development of Reye's syndrome.**

In children who are too young to blow their own noses, use a nasal aspirator to remove sticky nasal fluids if the child is uncomfortable. Call your doctor if nasal discharge turns from clear to yellow, green, or gray.

Professional Treatment

RSV infection is not treated with antibiotics, since these drugs do not work against viruses. An antiviral medicine called ribavirin may sometimes be given to very ill children who are hospitalized for severe pneumonia caused by RSV.

Younger children, especially infants, who have severe RSV pneumonia or bronchiolitis may need to be treated in a hospital. There they can receive specialized respiratory therapy, including humidified oxygen and medicines to open up their breathing passages.

When to Call Your Pediatrician

Call your doctor if your child has any of the following: fever over 101 degrees F (38.3 degrees C); thick nasal discharge that is yellow, green, or gray; cough that lasts more than four days; cough that produces yellow, green, or gray mucus; chest pain; difficulty breathing; very rapid breathing; bluish or gray color of the lips, skin or fingernails; or is less alert than usual. Of course, call if you have any questions or concerns.

In infants, in addition to symptoms already mentioned, call your doctor if your child is unusually irritable or inactive, or if he refuses to breast-feed or bottle-feed.

Also, ask your child's doctor if your child would benefit from the RSV vaccine, RespiGam.

Chapter 63

Roseola

Signs and Symptoms

Roseola infantum is a viral illness (Human Herpesvirus 6) whose main symptoms are a high fever and few specific localizing symptoms. A pink, raised rash appears as the fever ends. Roseola usually affects children between ages six months and three years, causing high fevers in the range of 102° F to 105° F. Fever may last for 2-5 days, with three days being the average. During this time, the child may appear fussy or irritable, and there may be a sore throat with swollen glands in the neck. In many cases of roseola, the child appears well.

Generally, on the third or fourth day of fever, the temperature rapidly returns to normal (98.6° F or 37° C) just as the roseola rash appears. The rash looks like pink or red spots that blanch (turn white) when you touch them. Individual spots may have a lighter "halo" around them. The rash begins on the trunk and neck, and may spread to the arms, legs, and face. It may fade within hours or last for 1-2 days.

The high fevers of roseola may trigger febrile seizures (convulsions caused by high fevers) in about 10% of young children with their first HHV-6 infection. Signs of a febrile seizure include: unconsciousness; 2-3 minutes of jerking or twitching movements in the arms, legs or face; loss of control of the bladder or bowels (an unconscious, toilet-trained child wets or soils his pants); irritability. The child may sleep when regaining consciousness.

Description

Roseola infantum, also called Exanthem Subitum, is a viral illness caused by Human Herpesvirus 6. This is a different type of herpes virus than those that cause cold sores or genital herpes infections. Roseola infantum usually affects children aged six months to three years. By the age of 4 years, almost all children are immune to HHV-6, since they will have been exposed to it by then.

Prevention

The fact that roseola usually affects young children, but rarely adults, may mean that an attack of roseola in childhood provides some lasting immunity to the illness. Repeat attacks may occur, but not commonly.

Incubation

Incubation period is about 5-15 days after exposure.

Duration

Most children recover spontaneously from roseola within one week.

Contagiousness

Roseola is a contagious viral disease that seems to spread especially well among crowds.

Home Treatment

Take your child's temperature at least once each morning and each evening and keep a record. If fever goes above 103° F (39.4° C), bring it down using nonaspirin fever medications such as acetaminophen. Unless instructed by your child's doctor, avoid giving aspirin to a child who has a viral illness since the use of aspirin in such cases has been associated with the development of Reye's syndrome.

Keep your child cool using a sponge or towel soaked in lukewarm water. Avoid using ice, cold water, alcohol rubs, fans or cold baths.

Encourage your child to drink clear fluids: water, fruit juice, weak tea, and lemonade. Fluids will help replace body water lost in the heat and sweat of fever episodes. Let your child rest in bed until the fever disappears.

Professional Treatment

Antibiotics are not effective in treating viral illnesses like roseola infantum, and most treatment of roseola is aimed at reducing high fevers.

Since the diagnosis of roseola is often unclear until the fever drops and the rash appears, your doctor may order tests to make sure that the fever is not being caused by another type of infection.

When to Call Your Pediatrician

Call your pediatrician if you have any questions about roseola.

Chapter 64

Scarlet Fever

Signs and Symptoms

In scarlet fever, a skin rash appears in a child who has an infection caused by Group A streptococci bacteria. This strep infection is usually seen as a sore throat, but it can also rarely be a skin infection (impetigo).

The rash of scarlet fever usually begins like a bad sunburn with tiny bumps (papules), and it may itch. The rash usually appears first on the neck and face, often leaving a clear unaffected area around the mouth. It spreads to the chest and back, then to the rest of the body. In body creases, especially around the underarms and elbows, the rash forms classic red streaks called Pastia's lines. Areas of rash usually blanch (turn white) when you press on them. By the sixth day of a strep infection the rash usually fades, but the affected skin may begin to peel.

Rash is the most striking symptom of scarlet fever, but there are usually other symptoms that help to confirm the diagnosis. Scarlet fever often begins with a reddened sore throat, a fever above 101F (38.3C), and swollen glands in the neck. The tonsils and back of the throat may be covered with a whitish coating, or appear red, swollen, and dotted with whitish or yellowish specks of pus. Early in the infection, the tongue may have a whitish or yellowish coating (a "furred" tongue), but later in the infection it may turn red, and its surface may begin to peel.

Children with strep throat infections also commonly have: chills, body aches, loss of appetite, nausea and vomiting.

When, rarely, scarlet fever occurs as a result of impetigo there are areas of infected skin along with the rash, rather than a sore throat.

Description

Scarlet fever is caused by an infection with Group A streptococcal bacteria, which produce a poison (toxin) that causes a rash in sensitive persons. Not all streptococci produce this toxin and not all persons are sensitive to it. Two children in the same family may both have strep infections, but one (who is sensitive to the toxin) may have the rash of scarlet fever and the other may not.

Prevention

In everyday life, there is no perfect way to avoid the strep infections that cause scarlet fever. At home, when someone is sick with a strep throat, it's always safest to keep drinking glasses and eating utensils separate from those of other family members, and to wash these items thoroughly in very hot soapy water. Use antibacterial soap if possible. Wash your own hands frequently as you care for a child with a strep infection.

Incubation

The rash of scarlet fever usually appears on the second day of a Group A streptococcal throat infection, and the incubation period for Group A strep throat is usually 2-7 days after exposure.

Duration

When scarlet fever occurs because of a Group A throat infection, the fever typically stops within 3-5 days, and the sore throat passes soon afterward. The scarlet fever rash usually fades on the sixth day after sore throat symptoms began, but skin that was covered by rash may begin to peel. This peeling may last ten days. With antibiotic treatment, the infection itself is usually cured within 10-12 days, but it may take several weeks for tonsils and swollen glands to return to normal.

Contagiousness

Group A streptococcal infections that cause scarlet fever are contagious. Strep bacteria can be passed through contact with the nasal or throat fluids of someone with a strep throat infection. They can also be passed by touching the infected skin of someone who has strep impetigo, or by sharing towels, clothing or bed linen.

Estimates are that in a home where someone already has a strep throat infection, about one out of every four family members will get it too. There are also cases where persons, especially children, can be carriers of strep bacteria without having any symptoms. Among school-aged children, 15-20 percent may be asymptomatic carriers of strep bacteria.

Home Treatment

When a child is sick with scarlet fever due to a strep throat infection, it is wise to isolate him or her from other family members, especially infants and very young brothers and sisters. Keep drinking glass and eating utensils separate, and wash these items thoroughly in very hot water using strong or antibacterial soap. Wash your own hands frequently as you care for the child.

A child with severe strep throat may find that eating is painful, so provide soft foods or a liquid diet if necessary. Include soothing teas and warm nutritious soups, or cool soft drinks, milk shakes and ice cream. Make sure that the child drinks plenty of fluids.

Children who are old enough to gargle can try gargling with either double-strength tea or warm salty water. Be sure that they spit out the salty water after they've finished.

Use a cool-mist humidifier to add moisture to the air, since this will help soothe the child's throat. A moist warm towel may also help to soothe swollen glands around the child's neck.

Make sure that your child takes all prescribed antibiotics on schedule and for as many days as your doctor has directed. This will help prevent complications such as rheumatic fever or an abscess around the tonsils. Antibiotics may also help decrease the severity of your child's symptoms.

If your child's rash itches, make sure that the fingernails are trimmed short to prevent them from damaging the skin. Follow your doctor's directions about skin care when your child's skin is either covered with scarlet fever rash or is peeling after the rash has faded.

Professional Treatment

If your doctor suspects that your child has scarlet fever due to a strep throat infection, he or she will usually take a throat culture (a painless swab of throat secretions) to see if Group A streptococcal bacteria grow in the laboratory. If they do grow, this will confirm that a Group A strep throat infection is the cause of your child's scarlet fever rash. It will also be the basis for your doctor's ordering a full course of antibiotic treatment. In addition to the throat culture, some doctors also use an "instant" strep test that can confirm a strep infection within 10 to 30 minutes during your office visit. This test is also taken from a painless throat swab.

Once a strep infection is confirmed, it is treated with penicillin or another antibiotic that may either be injected or taken by mouth. Since the risk of allergic reactions may be lower when oral medication is given, many doctors prefer to give an antibiotic prescription to be taken at home. They depend on the patient's parents and caregivers to make sure that the full course of antibiotics is taken—and this usually means up to 10 days of medicine at home.

Your doctor may also prescribe medicines to care for the scarlet fever rash itself, or suggest over-the-counter brands that you can purchase in your drugstore or supermarket.

When To Call Your Pediatrician

Call your pediatrician whenever your child suddenly develops a rash, especially if the child also has a fever, sore throat or swollen glands. Call your doctor if your child has any of the symptoms of strep throat, especially if someone in your family or in your child's school has recently had a strep infection.

Chapter 65

Strep Throat

Signs and Symptoms

Approximately 10% of children who have a sore throat and fever are infected by Group A streptococci. When Group A streptococci infect the throat, they cause pharyngitis, which is a painful inflammation of the throat (pharynx). Swallowing may become so painful that the child has difficulty eating.

A child with strep pharyngitis often has a fever above 101°F (38.3°C), with chills, body aches and loss of appetite. There also may be abdominal symptoms, like nausea, vomiting, and abdominal pain. The tonsils and the back of the throat may look red, swollen, and dotted with whitish or yellowish specks of pus. There may be swollen glands in the neck and at the angles of the jaw. Strangely, in spite of all the throat pain, hoarseness and loss of voice are not common.

Some rare cases of strep infection may result in the production of a toxin that causes a bright red skin rash. This is the rash of "scarlet fever," and it usually lasts from the second to the sixth day of the strep throat infection.

In infants, strep throat infections—although rare—tend to cause symptoms that seem less limited to the throat. Infants may have a runny nose, crusting and sores around the nostrils and a low fever. They may also begin to feed poorly.

From www.kidshealth.org © 1999 The Nemours Foundation. Used with permission.

421

Strep throat infections that are either untreated or incompletely treated can in rare cases lead to rheumatic fever, an illness that can result in heart disease and arthritis. Another rare complication of a group A strep infection is acute glomerulonephritis, a kidney problem that begins two to three weeks after the initial infection.

Group A streptococci may also cause sinusitis, ear infections, pneumonia and skin infections.

Description

Group A streptococci are bacteria. They cause throat infections (pharyngitis), especially during cold winter months when people are crowded together indoors. Strep A bacteria spread from person to person through fluid droplets from the nose or throat of someone with a strep infection. Of all age groups, children ages five to 15 are the most affected.

Group A streptococci also cause many different kinds of skin infections, most commonly impetigo. In very rare cases, strep A may also cause pneumonia, most often after a previous viral infection like the flu, measles, chickenpox or whooping cough.

Prevention

In normal everyday life, there is no perfect way to avoid strep throat infections. At home, when someone is sick with strep throat, it's always safest to wash drinking glasses and eating utensils with hot soapy water, and to wash your hands often as you care for the affected person.

Care of a patient with strep-caused rheumatic fever usually requires medical specialists who may recommend ways to avoid future strep infections.

Incubation

The incubation period for Group A strep throat is usually two to seven days after exposure.

Duration

In Group A strep throat infections, fever typically stops within three to five days, and the sore throat passes soon afterward. Antibiotic therapy is usually completed in 10 days. If symptoms have improved, and the patient is without fever, she or he may return to school after 24 hours of antibiotic treatment. It is important, however, that they continue to take the full course of prescribed antibiotics even after they are back in class.

Contagiousness

Strep throat is contagious, and strep bacteria can be passed through contact with the nasal or throat fluids of someone who is infected. Estimates are that in a home where someone already has strep, about one out of every four family members will get it, too. There are also cases where persons, especially children, can be carriers of strep bacteria without having any symptoms (asymptomatic carriers). This means that the bacteria are present, but not causing any apparent problem or disease. Among school-age children, 5-15 percent may be asymptomatic carriers of strep bacteria.

Home Treatment

A child with a severe strep throat may find that eating is painful, so provide soft foods or a liquid diet, if necessary. Include soothing teas and warm nutritious soups, or cool soft drinks, milk shakes, and ice cream. Make sure that plenty of fluids are available, and take the temperature at least once each morning and each evening. Let the child rest in bed and play quietly.

Children who are old enough to gargle can try gargling with either double-strength tea or warm salty water. Be sure that they spit out the salty water after they've finished.

Use a cool-mist humidifier to add moisture to the air, since this will help soothe the child's throat. A moist warm towel may also help soothe swollen glands around the child's neck.

Make sure that the child takes all prescribed antibiotics on schedule and for as many days as your doctor has directed. This will help prevent complications like rheumatic fever or an abscess around the tonsils.

Professional Treatment

A doctor who suspects that your child has a strep throat will take a throat culture (a painless swab of throat secretions) to see if strep A bacteria grow in the laboratory. If they do grow, this will confirm a Group A Strep infection and be the basis for your doctor's ordering antibiotic treatment. Some doctors also use an "instant" strep test that can confirm a strep infection within 10 to 30 minutes while you remain at the office.

Once a strep A infection is confirmed, it is treated with penicillin or another antibiotic that may either be injected or given by mouth. Since the risk of allergic reactions may be lower when oral medication is given, many doctors prefer to give an antibiotic prescription to be taken at home. They depend on the patient or the patient's parents to make sure that the full course of antibiotics is taken. This means up to 10 days of medicine at home.

When to Call Your Pediatrician

Call your doctor if your child has symptoms of strep throat, especially if someone in your family or in your child's school has recently had a strep infection.

If your child is already being treated for strep throat, call your doctor for any of the following symptoms: fever that returns after several days of normal temperature; skin rash; earache; nasal discharge with discolored or bloody mucus; cough, especially if it produces mucus; chest pain, shortness of breath or extreme tiredness; convulsions; painful, red, swollen joints; nausea or vomiting.

Chapter 66

Thrush

Thrush, a yeast infection in a baby's mouth, is usually first noticed by Mom. Her baby will yawn and she will see something that looks like milk curds stuck to his tongue or on the lining of his mouth. Often Mom, while trying to wipe it off with a washcloth, will be surprised to discover a beefy-red looking sore under the "milk curd." Sometimes thrush can be quite painful and the baby will be reluctant to eat or drink.

Many pregnant women have vaginal yeast infections in their last few months of pregnancy, which accounts for most newborn cases of thrush. The yeast organism, picked up by the baby during birth, infects his mouth but may take several weeks to show up as thrush.

As with any fungal organism, the spores of yeast are in the air and everywhere, just waiting to pounce onto or into a warm, moist area and cause problems. Because pacifiers are constantly moist with slobber, it's quite easy for yeast to grow there invisibly and eventually thrive in your baby's mouth.

Thrush is usually treated with an oral mycostatin preparation which is given four times a day after feedings. Frequently, the mycostatin fails to clear thrush and it has to be repeated several times before it is effective, if ever.

There is a natural alternative to mycostatin that often clears thrush faster and more completely; however, it sometimes only acts as a suppressant, keeping the thrush to a minimum until immunity develops. Even so, it seems better than giving the prescribed mycostatin over and over again.

This alternate treatment involves the use of crystallized lactobacillus derived from yogurt. It is a totally natural bacterium that makes life uncomfortable for yeast organisms and so they depart. Babies with a known milk allergy are liable to have a reaction to the lactobacillus and should not be given this treatment.

Crystallized lactobacillus can be bought at a health food store as Megadophilus crystals. Dissolve 1/8 teaspoonful of the crystals in 1-2 tsps. of warm water and give it to your baby four times a day after each feeding. Since it is a natural substance, you can continue using the crystals as long as necessary to either clear the thrush or keep it at bay. In order to minimize reinfection, pacifiers, bottle nipples, and teething rings should be sterilized once daily by boiling them in water for five minutes.

A nursing mother can easily contract a yeast infection on her nipples from her infant during breast feeding. Mothers who don't allow their nipples to air dry after nursing, or who don't change breast pads frequently are also prime candidates for a nipple yeast infection. This is especially true during hot, humid weather.

A nipple yeast infection can cause nipples to crack and become quite sore unless it is treated promptly. Applying the oral mycostatin preparation or an antifungal cream can be helpful. A more natural treatment is to wash the affected nipples after each nursing with a solution of 1 tablespoonful of white vinegar added to 1 cup of water.

Chapter 67

Urinary Tract Infections

Signs and Symptoms

Signs and symptoms of urinary tract infections vary, depending on the age of the child and on which part of the urinary tract is infected. In younger children, especially those too young to tell you how they feel, the symptoms may be very general. The child may seem irritable, begin to feed poorly, or vomit. Sometimes the only symptom is a fever that seems to appear for no reason and doesn't go away.

In older children and adults, signs and symptoms can reveal which part of the urinary tract is infected. In a lower tract infection, also called a bladder infection (cystitis), the child may have a fever and may describe a burning or stinging sensation when she urinates. She may feel an increased urge to urinate, may urinate more often, or (rarely) may lose control and wet her pants. The child may wake up several times at night to go to the bathroom but produce a very small amount of urine. Sometimes she may also have low back pain or abdominal pain in the area of the bladder (generally below the navel and above the crotch). The urine may smell bad or be tinged with blood.

Many of these symptoms may also be seen in an upper tract infection, also called a kidney infection (pyelonephritis), but there may also be fever with shaking chills, a pain or ache in the flank area, or severe fatigue.

From www.kidshealth.org © 1999 The Nemours Foundation. Used with permission.

Description

Urinary tract infections occur in about one percent of boys and three percent of girls and are usually not associated with abnormalities of the urinary tract.

Some risk factors may increase a child's chance of developing a urinary tract infection. The most common risk factor is an abnormality in the structure or function of the urinary tract (for example, a blockage somewhere along the tract of normal urine flow, or an abnormal back flow of urine from the bladder toward the kidneys). Other risk factors include poor hygiene and the use of soaps or bubble baths that irritate the urethra (the opening where urine comes out). Some experts also believe that not being circumcised will increase a boy's chances of developing a urinary tract infection.

Urinary tract infections may be caused by many different types of bacteria. In children, the intestinal bacteria *Escherichia coli* is most common. Other bacteria, such as *Klebsiella*, *Enterobacter*, and *Proteus*, tend to cause infections when the child has a history of many urinary tract infections, or when the child has a urinary tract abnormality that blocks urine flow.

Prevention

There are some simple ways to decrease the risk of urinary tract infections, including: frequent washing (showers may be better than baths), drinking enough fluids, and avoiding caffeine, which is reported to irritate the bladder. Also, after every bowel movement, girls should remember to wipe toilet tissue from front to rear—not rear to front—to prevent intestinal bacteria from spreading to the urethra (opening for urine) and vagina.

Duration

Most urinary tract infections are cured within two weeks with proper medical treatment. Recurrences are common.

Contagiousness

Urinary tract infections are not contagious.

Home Treatment

Give any prescribed antibiotics on schedule for as many days as your physician directs. Keep track of your child's trips to the bathroom, and ask your child about symptoms like pain or burning on urination; these symptoms should improve within two to three days after antibiotics are started. Take your child's temperature once each morning and each evening, and call your doctor if it rises above 101° F (38.3° C). Encourage your child to drink plenty of fluids, but avoid beverages containing caffeine.

Professional Treatment

Urinary tract infections are treated with antibiotics. The type of antibiotic used will depend on the type of bacteria that is causing the infection. A physician may order a urinalysis and a urine culture to check for and identify bacteria causing the infection. After several days of treatment with antibiotics, a physician may repeat these tests to confirm that the infection is gone.

A child with a simple bladder infection usually is treated with antibiotics as an outpatient. However, a child may need to be treated in a hospital, especially in the following situations: the child is less than six months old; there are signs of a kidney infection; bacteria from the infected urinary tract have spread to the blood; the child is dehydrated (has low levels of body fluids), is vomiting, or cannot take any fluids by mouth; intravenous medication is needed.

If a physician suspects that a child has a urinary tract abnormality, he or she may order tests that check for problems in the structure or function of a child's urinary tract. The child may also be referred to a urologist, a physician who specializes in diseases of the urinary tract.

When to Call Your Pediatrician

Call your pediatrician immediately if your child has an unexplained fever with shaking chills, especially if accompanied by back pain and/or any type of discomfort during urination. Also call your doctor if your child has any of the following: unusually frequent urination; frequent urination during the night; bad-smelling urine; bloody or discolored urine; low back pain; abdominal pain, especially below the navel; nausea or vomiting.

In infants, call your doctor if your child has a fever, feeds poorly, vomits repeatedly, or seems unusually irritable.

Chapter 68

Vascular Birthmarks

What Is a "Vascular Birthmark?"

Many babies have what are called "birthmarks" when they're born. In some cases they may appear within the first few weeks of life. They can be brown, tan, blue, pink, or red. More than 10 in 100 babies have vascular birthmarks. These are made up of blood vessels bunched together in the skin. They can be flat or raised, pink, red, or bluish discolorations.

What Causes Birthmarks?

Why do vascular birthmarks occur? The exact causes are unknown. Most vascular birthmarks are not inherited, nor are they caused by anything that happens to the mother during pregnancy.

What Are the Different Types of Vascular Birthmarks?

There are different kinds of vascular birthmarks. Sometimes, the birthmark must be watched for several weeks or months before the specific type can be identified. The most common types of vascular birthmarks are macular stains, hemangiomas, and port wine stains. There are also many rare types of vascular birthmarks.

"Vascular Birthmarks," © American Academy of Dermatology, 1987, 1999. Reprinted with permission from the American Academy of Dermatology. All rights reserved.

Macular Stains

Your physician will call faint, mild red marks macular stains. They are the most common type of vascular birthmarks. They are also called "angel's kisses," when they are located on the forehead or eyelids. When they're found on the back of the neck, they're called "stork bites." They may also occur on the tip of the nose, upper lip or any other body location. They are pink and flat. Angel's kisses almost always go away by age two, but stork bites usually last into adulthood. These birthmarks are harmless and require no treatment.

Hemangiomas

The term "hemangioma" is used to describe many different kinds of blood vessel growths. Most dermatologists prefer to use hemangioma to refer to a common type of vascular birthmark. These marks do not usually appear immediately after birth, but become visible within the first few weeks of life. Hemangiomas are usually divided into two types: strawberry hemangiomas and cavernous hemangiomas.

A strawberry hemangioma is slightly raised, and bright red because the abnormal blood vessels are very close to the surface of the skin.

Cavernous hemangiomas have a blue color because the abnormal vessels are deeper under the skin. Hemangiomas are more common in females and in premature babies. They can be anywhere on the face or body.

Usually, a child will have only one hemangioma, but sometimes there will be two or three. In rare cases, an infant may have many, or even some internally. Unlike other vascular birthmarks, hemangiomas can grow very rapidly. Growth generally begins during the first six weeks of life and continues for about one year. Most never get bigger than two or three inches in diameter, but some may be larger. After the first year, most hemangiomas will stop growing. They then begin to turn white and slowly shrink. Half of all hemangiomas are flat by age five; nine out of ten are flat by age nine. Many will completely go away, but often, a faint mark is left. It's impossible to know how big any hemangioma will grow, or if it will completely disappear.

Complications of Hemangiomas

Occasionally, a hemangioma that's growing or shrinking rapidly can form an open sore or ulcer. These sores can be painful, and can become infected. It's very important to see your dermatologist and keep this sore clean and covered with antibiotic ointment and/or a dressing.

A hemangioma located over the female genitals or rectum, or near an eye, the nose or mouth, can cause special problems. These hemangiomas should be watched closely by your dermatologist who will decide if further treatment is necessary.

Parents are often concerned that a hemangioma will bleed. These birthmarks do look as if they could bleed easily. However, this usually isn't a problem. Bleeding usually occurs only after injury. If the hemangioma starts to bleed, it should be treated like any other injury—clean the area with soap and water or hydrogen peroxide and apply a gauze bandage. Apply firm, but not tight, pressure on the area for five to ten minutes. If the bleeding has not stopped, call your doctor.

A hemangioma will rarely grow suddenly over one or two days. If this occurs, it's important to call your dermatologist. Also, if a bruise begins to develop, your dermatologist should be notified.

Treatment of Hemangiomas

It's very important that a baby with a vascular birthmark be examined by a dermatologist as early as possible, so that a correct diagnosis can be made and the need for treatment discussed.

It's not always easy for parents to watch a hemangioma grow, or wait for it to disappear, without doing anything. However, most hemangiomas do not require treatment. They eventually shrink by themselves, leaving very few signs.

There are several different types of treatments for hemangiomas that need care. No treatment is absolutely safe and effective. The potential benefits must be weighed against the possible risks.

The most widely used treatment for rapidly growing hemangiomas is corticosteroid medication. This is either injected or given by mouth. Long-term or repeated treatment may be necessary. Some of the risks of therapy include poor growth, elevated blood sugar and blood pressure, cataracts and an increased chance of infection.

Lasers can be used to both prevent growth of hemangiomas and remove hemangiomas. Hemangiomas with sores that will not heal can also be treated with lasers. New lasers are being developed and studied by dermatologists to treat this condition.

Port-Wine Stains

The port-wine stain is another type of vascular birthmark that occurs in 3 in 1,000 infants. It is sometimes called a nevus flammeus, or capillary hemangioma, but it should not be confused with a hemangioma.

Port-wine stains appear at birth. They are flat, pink, red or purplish discolorations, found most often on the face, neck, arms or legs. They can be any size. Unlike hemangiomas, port-wine stains grow only as the child grows. Over time, port-wine stains may become thick and develop small bumps or ridges. Port-wine stains do not go away by themselves. They last a lifetime.

Complications of Port-Wine Stains

Port-wine stains, especially those on the face, can have emotional, social, and economic complications. Port-wine stains on the forehead, eyelids or both sides of the face, can be associated with glaucoma as increased pressure within the eye that, left untreated, can cause blindness. These complications occur in less than one-fourth of those with port-wine stains of the forehead and eyelids. All infants with a port-wine stain in those areas should have a thorough eye and brain examination.

Occasionally, there may be very gradual enlargement of tissues surrounding a port-wine stain. All children with large port-wine stains involving an arm or leg should be followed for any growth problems.

With time, port-wine stains can develop small blood vessel growths, called pyogenic granulomas. These can bleed easily, and should be removed.

Treatment of Port-Wine Stains

The use of cover-up makeup has been a common treatment for port-wine stains. Your doctor can provide you with more information about products that are made to cover up birthmarks.

Various methods have been tried in the past to remove port-wine stains, but none have worked well. New types of lasers have shown the best results with the least amount of risk and side effects. Laser treatment of port-wine stains is FDA-approved, and available at many centers around the country. For best results, treatment should begin as early as possible, even in infancy. Laser surgery is performed on an outpatient basis. Several treatments are usually required, given at two month intervals. Younger patients often require fewer treatments than adults. In about one-fourth of the patients, lasers can totally clear up the port-wine stain. Seventy percent will look much better. For reasons that are not understood, a small number of patients will not respond well to laser therapy.

There are several risks of laser therapy. An increase or decrease in skin color can occur, leaving patchy tanning or whitening of the skin. In most cases this is not permanent. Swelling, crusting, or minor bleeding can occur. This is unusual and can be treated easily. Permanent scarring has happened, but is extremely rare. Laser therapy is uncomfortable, but not extremely painful. Anesthesia is not required for most adults. However, anesthesia is often important for toddlers and young children. If putting the child to sleep is required, there are some risks and higher costs.

Summary

Most vascular birthmarks disappear without treatment or can be treated effectively. Through research, dermatologists are learning more about the causes and treatments of all types of vascular birthmarks.

Part Six

Safety and First Aid

Chapter 69

Keeping Kids Safe

Kids are naturally curious and adventuresome. They see something that sparks their interest and they're off! Unfortunately, the same sense of curiosity and adventure that helps children develop mentally and physically also puts them at greater risk of injury. According to C. Everett Koop, M.D., Chairman of the National Safe Kids Campaign and former U.S. Surgeon General, "Unintentional injury takes the lives of more children than all childhood diseases combined." The good news is that most childhood injuries are preventable with proper precautions.

Common Safety Hazards

According to the National Safety Council, motor vehicle injuries, drownings, fires and burns are leading causes of unintentional injury deaths for children and youths aged one to 24 years old. The Coalition for Consumer Health and Safety reports that some of the most *avoidable* safety hazards are:

- Crash injuries from not fastening safety lap belts in vehicles.
- Falls from playground equipment.
- Infant drownings in five-gallon buckets.
- Head injuries from not wearing bicycle helmets.

From www.noah.cuny.edu © 1995 U.S. Healthcare®; reprinted with permission.

- Falls and burns caused by baby walkers. (Approximately 29,000 infants are treated in hospital emergency rooms for walker-related injuries each year.)

Car Safety

From the day you bring your child home from the hospital, he or she must always be properly secured as a passenger in a motor vehicle. Set a good example for your children by buckling up yourself! Guidelines for using infant and child car seats include the following:

- Infants from birth to 20 pounds should be secured in a rear-facing infant car seat or a rear-facing convertible car seat. Never use an infant seat in a forward-facing position. If your car has a passenger side air bag, put the car seat in the back seat. An inflating air bag could cause serious injury to an infant. The back seat is the preferred location for all car seats.

- Use a forward-facing convertible car seat from 20 pounds to about 40 pounds, or as long as the child fits in the seat and as close to 4 years old as possible.

- For children who weigh between 40 and 65 pounds or no longer fit in a convertible car seat, use a booster seat. The booster seat positions the child so that lap and lap/shoulder belts fit properly. There are two types available: a belt-positioning booster seat for use in vehicles with lap/shoulder belts, and a shield booster seat for vehicles with lap-only belts.

- In many states, child safety restraints are required by law through age 4 or 5, regardless of weight. Once your child has met the age requirement for your state and can be properly secured with a lap/shoulder belt or lap-only belt, you may discontinue using a booster seat.

- Car seats and safety belts can only provide protection if they are used correctly. According to Safety Belt Safe, a national nonprofit agency for child passenger safety, there is approximately 90 percent misuse associated with child safety seats and safety belts. Specific requirements vary according to the brand of car seat you are using, so be sure to follow the manufacturer's instructions. It's also a good idea to save the manufacturer's instructions and keep them in a handy location for quick reference. To receive additional information regarding the law, correct usage and car seat recalls, call Safety Belt Safe at (800) 745-SAFE.

Children can also be injured as pedestrians by motor vehicles. To reduce the likelihood that one of your children will be struck by a car, take the following precautions:

- Teach your children to play away from the street.

- Instruct your children to look both ways before crossing the street. Don't let them cross the street by themselves until you feel confident they will remember to look both ways.

- Teach your children the meaning of traffic signs and signals.

- Don't allow your children to play in or around a parked car.

- Make sure your children are not in the driveway when a car is pulling in or out. Always check behind and beneath the car when you are backing out of the driveway or garage.

- Keep young children off the street after dark.

Fire Prevention

Install smoke detectors on every level of your home and in the hallway outside bedrooms. Additional smoke detectors should be placed inside bedrooms, especially in children's rooms. Check the batteries monthly, and replace them yearly. Make sure your kids know what the sound of a smoke detector means and how they should respond in the event of a fire. Practice at least two escape routes during family fire drills. Review the following basic fire safety guidelines with your children:

- Get out of the house as quickly as possible.

- Crawl low in situations where there is heavy smoke. The clearest air is the lowest.

- Stay away from the fire once you've reached safety.

- If clothing catches fire:
  1. Stop. Running will make the fire burn faster.
  2. Shout for help.
  3. Drop to the floor and cover your face.
  4. Roll back and forth to put out the flames.

- Make sure your children's pajamas are labeled "flame resistant."

- Keep a fire extinguisher in your home.

- Position space heaters away from curtains and flammable materials. Let the space heater cool completely before adding fuel. Never use gasoline with a kerosene heater. Use the type of fuel recommended by the manufacturer.

- Properly extinguish all smoking materials. Never smoke in bed.

- Store matches and lighters out of reach of young children. Explain the dangers of playing with matches to your children.

- Don't leave food cooking on the stove unattended.

- Use protective screens over fireplaces. Have the chimney inspected annually.

Burn Prevention

- Lower the temperature of the water heater in your home to 120 degrees Fahrenheit. Consider installing an anti-scald device available in hardware stores on tub faucets and shower heads.

- Whenever possible, cook on rear stove burners and turn pan handles inward on the stove. Be sure to keep hot foods and liquids out of reach and away from the edge of the table and counter.

- Make sure children are well away from the kitchen area when you are moving hot foods or liquids.

- Test the temperature of heated foods and liquids before feeding a child.

- Unplug electrical appliances and store them out of reach when not in use.

Water Safety

A few inches of water is all it takes for a drowning incident to occur. Swimming pools are the most common site of childhood drownings, but smaller bodies of water such as bathtubs, buckets, basins and toilets also present a safety hazard. According to the U.S. Consumer Product Safety Commission, an estimated 50 deaths and 130 emergency-room visits are related to bucket drownings each year. To help prevent a drowning incident, take the following precautions:

- Provide constant adult supervision for children playing in or near water. Flotation devices such as inner tubes or rafts should not be used as a substitute for adult supervision.

- Do not leave objects floating in a pool that would be a temptation for a child to retrieve.

- Remove steps to an above-ground pool when it is not in use.

- Keep a cover on the pool when it's not being used. Teach children never to crawl or walk on a pool cover.

- Never leave babies or young children unattended around buckets, basins or tubs filled with water. Drain these items immediately after use.

- Erect barriers such as locked doors and fences around a backyard pool. Gates should be self-closing and self-latching.

- Teach children to never swim alone and always test the depth of the water before diving. If they see someone in distress in the water, they should throw a rope or any available flotation device and then call for help. They should not attempt to physically rescue anyone unless they are trained in water rescue techniques.

- Parents, caretakers and children should learn how to swim. The minimum recommended age for organized swimming instruction is age three. Regardless of a child's ability to swim, the Council for National Cooperation in Aquatics recommends that no young child ever be considered "water-safe."

- Adults should learn how to perform cardiopulmonary resuscitation (CPR). Prompt and effective CPR can dramatically improve the outcome of a drowning incident. Contact your local chapter of the American Heart Association or the American Red Cross for information on CPR instruction.

Poison Prevention

Based on a ten-year study conducted by the American Association of Poison Control Centers, cleaning products are the leading cause of poisoning nationwide. Other common substances involved in poisonings are pain pills, cosmetics, house and yard plants, and cough and cold remedies. To reduce the potential for poisoning in your home, take the following precautions:

- Post the number of your local Poison Control Center near the telephone. If you think your child has ingested a poisonous substance, call the Poison Control Center immediately. If your child is unconscious or having convulsions, call 911 or your local emergency number.

- Keep Syrup of Ipecac (an over-the-counter medicine that induces vomiting) in your home, but do not give it to your child unless you are advised to do so by a physician or a Poison Control Center.

- Research shows that childhood poisonings most often occur in the kitchen and bathroom areas. Store all medicines, cleaning substances and other poisons well out of children's reach or in a locked cabinet. Consider using safety latches on all drawers and cabinets that contain these items.

- Make sure paints, solvents, lawn chemicals and other poisonous substances commonly stored in basements and garages are tightly sealed and stored on high shelves or in locked cabinets.

- Do not keep vitamins or other medicines on the kitchen table. Choose a vitamin without iron for your child unless your physician specifically recommends a vitamin with iron. When taken in large quantities, iron-enriched vitamins are toxic to young children.

- Buy products with child-resistant caps whenever possible.

- Avoid taking medication in front of children. Never refer to medicine as candy or as tasting like candy.

- Many common house and garden plants are toxic if chewed or ingested. Teach children not to put leaves, berries, flowers, seeds or mushrooms in their mouths. Philodendron and diefenbachia are two common house plants that are highly toxic. Don't keep these plants if you have preschoolers or toddlers in your home. Other toxic plants include: azaleas, buttercups, calla lily, cherry (wild and cultivated), crocus, daffodil, delphinium, four o'clock, foxglove, holly berries, hyacinth, hydrangea, iris, ivy, lily of the valley, morning glory, rhododendron, tobacco and tulips. This is not a complete list of poisonous plants. If your child has ingested any plant, call the Poison Control Center immediately.

- Consider using noncommercial cleaning preparations as an alternative to hazardous commercial products: Baking soda, for example, can be used to clean and deodorize carpets, and bathroom and kitchen surfaces. A combination of baking soda and vinegar is an effective toilet bowl and tub and tile cleaner. It's important to note that "safer alternatives" are not completely harmless. Any product used in a manner that is not intended is potentially harmful.

- The U.S. Centers for Disease Control and Prevention has identified lead poisoning as a major public health problem in the United States, particularly for children. If you live in a home built before 1980, it is possible that your home contains lead paint. Lead is very harmful to the developing brain and nervous system of fetuses and young children. Chronic exposure can cause learning and behavior disorders and stunted growth. Exposure to lead occurs when a child eats chips of lead-based paint or ingests dust and soil contaminated with lead-based paint. If you live in an older home, ask your local or state health department to recommend a lead paint testing company.

Bicycle Safety

- A bicycle helmet should be worn every time a child rides a bike, or rides as a passenger on an adult bike. Experts say that wearing a bicycle helmet can reduce the risk of head injury by 85 percent because it protects the head in the event of a fall or collision by absorbing the shock of the crash and shielding the head from sharp objects. Children's neck muscles are strong enough to support a helmet from the age of 8 months. When purchasing a helmet, make certain the helmet has met the nationally recognized scientific safety standards developed by the American National Standards Institute (ANSI), the Snell Memorial Foundation (SMF), and/or the American Society for Testing and Materials (ASTM).

Roller blading, also referred to as in-line skating, is another sport that requires the use of a helmet. For protection against injury, the Consumer Product Safety Commission recommends that roller bladers wear a helmet, knee pads, elbow pads and wrist guards.

- Only children who are able to sit well unsupported and whose necks are strong enough to support a lightweight helmet should be carried in a rear-mounted seat. Generally, this means a child of at least nine months of age. The seat should have a high back and a sturdy harness and be securely attached over the rear wheel of the bicycle. Use spoke guards to prevent feet and hands from being caught in the wheels.

- Make sure your child's bike is neither too big nor too small.

- Review the following bicycle safety tips with your children:

  1. Ride on the sidewalk or use bike paths whenever possible.
  2. Ride in single file when riding with others.
  3. Stay to the right and ride with the traffic.
  4. Stop at stop signs.
  5. Check for traffic and use hand signals when making a turn.
  6. Walk a bike across busy intersections.
  7. Stay off roads where cars are known to travel at high speed.
  8. Roads are slippery when they are wet. Use extra caution when applying the brakes and making turns.
  9. Wear fluorescent or reflective clothing when cycling at night.
  10. Bikes should be equipped with night reflectors, a rearview mirror and a light.
  11. Don't wear headphones while bike riding.

Playground Safety

According to the American Academy of Pediatrics, approximately 200,000 children are injured on playgrounds in the United States each year. Nearly 75 percent of these injuries are a result of falls from playground equipment. To help prevent playground injuries, take the following precautions:

- Provide adult supervision for children playing on playground equipment.

- Make sure the playground equipment your child plays on is on a soft surface such as sand, mulch, wood chips or rubber matting.

- Make sure the equipment is in good condition and that there are no loose screws or sharp edges that could injure, pinch or entrap your child.

- The American Academy of Pediatrics recommends that play equipment be installed at least six feet from any barrier.

- The U.S. Public Interest Research Group and the Consumer Federation of America recommend that the top rung or platform of playground equipment be no higher than six feet for pre-school children and no higher than seven feet for school-aged children.

- Before putting your child on a metal slide, make sure it is cool to the touch. Plastic slides do not get as hot as metal slides.

- Teach your children to use all equipment as the manufacturer intended.

- Make sure the child is physically capable of the activity he or she is attempting.

Firearms

If you keep firearms in your home, lock guns and ammunition away in separate locations. Carefully maintain all firearms and make sure you are familiar with the procedures for safely loading and unloading weapons. Explain the potential for danger with firearms to your children.

Be Wary of Strangers

A national study by the U.S. Department of Justice on Missing, Abducted, Runaway and Thrownaway Children indicates that hundreds of thousands of children each year are at risk of abduction and exploitation. Young children are particularly vulnerable because they can be easily overtaken physically and easily swayed with offers of gifts, candy or a fun activity. Parents can take the following precautions to help prevent child abduction:

- Teach your children who a stranger is. A stranger is someone the child and parents don't know, even if the person seems friendly, smiles, says hello or calls the child by name. Relatives, friends, neighbors and teachers are not strangers, but the person who might smile in the store or say hello from a car is.

- Children should be taught to never accept offers from a stranger or go anywhere, under any circumstances, with a stranger. Teach children that it is good to refuse the offers of strangers, to ignore strangers, to say no, and run and yell for help or put up a struggle if a stranger is bothering them.

- Never leave an infant or child alone, even for a second, in a car, in a store, or unattended in a shopping cart.

- Teach your child his or her name, full address, and telephone number with the area code. Also teach them how to use the telephone.

For more information about preventing child abduction, call the National Center for Missing and Exploited Children at (800) 843-5678.

Saying NO to Drugs and Alcohol

Most adolescents will eventually be faced with the temptation to experiment with drugs or alcohol. Statistics on drug and alcohol usage among America's youths are listed below:

- According to the National Council On Alcoholism and Drug Dependency (NCADD), first use of alcohol typically begins around age 13.

- A *Weekly Reader National Survey on Drugs and Alcohol* published in 1990 indicates that 35 percent of children in the fourth grade report having been pressured by their classmates to drink alcohol. By the sixth grade, this figure rises to 49 percent.

- The American Heart Association reports that an estimated 2.1 million American children age 12 to 17 smoke cigarettes. Nine million children under five live with a smoker, which puts them at risk for developing asthma and respiratory infections.

- In 1993, the NCADD released survey results indicating that 87 percent of high school seniors have used alcohol; 63 percent have smoked cigarettes; 32 percent have used marijuana and 6 percent have used cocaine.

Help your child avoid the temptation to use drugs and alcohol with the following guidelines:

- Set a good example yourself. Parents who abuse drugs or alcohol put their children at risk for abusing drugs and alcohol.

- Explain the dangers of drug and alcohol use and cigarette smoking to your children.

- Teens often turn to drugs or alcohol to cope with the difficulties of adolescence. Help your children through this difficult time by listening to their concerns, offering advice, and taking an interest in their activities and friendships.

- Help your children feel good about themselves. Kids with a healthy level of self esteem are less likely to succumb to peer pressure to do drugs.

If you suspect your child is using drugs or alcohol, discuss your concerns with your child's physician or contact your Employee Assistance Program (EAP) at work.

Safety Tips Specific to Infants and Toddlers

Children from birth to age three make up the highest risk group for injuries in the home. In addition to the precautions already listed, the following safety tips can help you protect infants and toddlers from injury:

- Crib slats should be no more than 2 3/8 inches apart to prevent the baby's head from getting caught between the bars. Carefully check cribs manufactured before 1974.

- The crib mattress should fit snugly in the crib with no gaps. Make sure the mattress is flame retardant.

- Make sure the crib has no corner posts. Posts can catch clothing and cause strangulation.

- If you are using an older crib, make sure it hasn't been finished with lead paint. In 1978, the Consumer Product Safety Commission banned the manufacture and use of lead paint on residential surfaces, toys and furniture.

- Make sure the crib is not within reach of cords or strings for window treatments.

- Use bumper pads for the first five months. Remove them by the time the baby can pull up to stand.

- Remove mobiles, crib gyms and any hanging toys from the crib by the time the baby can get up on his hands and knees (generally around four months old).

- Use the safety strap on high chairs, strollers and changing tables. Never leave a baby unattended on a changing table. Store toiletry items well out of baby's reach.

- Protect your children from falls by making sure all windows have screens securely in place. Consider using window guards to limit the amount of open space. Don't position cribs or play-pens near a window. Don't leave babies alone on furniture. If you use an infant seat, stay within arms' reach of the baby and never position the seat close to the edge of a table. Use safety gates at the top and bottom of stairs.

- Make sure large pieces of furniture and all heavy items on stands, such as televisions, lamps and books, are secure and can't be tipped over if pushed or held on to.

- Do not put your baby in a baby walker unless you can provide constant supervision. The American Academy of Pediatrics reports that baby walkers are one of the leading causes of head injury and skull fracture in babies six to ten months old.

- Use age-appropriate toys. Toys made for older children are not appropriate for babies. Battery-operated and electrical toys, for example, are not appropriate for infants and toddlers. When choosing toys, check for the following:

  1. Quality construction. Make sure there are no sharp edges that could cut or injure the baby. Also check for small parts that could break off and pose a choking hazard to a baby.

  2. Make sure the product is nontoxic and that any fabric or stuffing is flame retardant.

  3. Round and hard foods present a choking hazard to young children. Foods to avoid include grapes, hot dogs, nuts, popcorn, hard candies and raw carrots. Carefully cut your children's food into bite-size pieces. Keep small round objects like buttons and coins out of baby's reach. Ask your child's physician about the correct procedures for clearing an obstructed airway in children and infants.

  4. Place outlet covers on electrical outlets that are not in use. Do not use electrical extension cords unless absolutely necessary. Children may play with the extra length of cord or even bite it.

  5. Plastic bags, dry-cleaning bags, and plastic packaging for toys and other products are a suffocation hazard to children.

Keep these and similar materials away from children. Teach them not to play with these items.

6. Do not leave your infant or child unattended in the bath or sink. It only takes a second for a baby's head to become submerged in water.

In the Event of an Emergency

Every second counts in an emergency situation. Prepare yourself in advance by posting local emergency numbers and the number of a nearby friend or relative near the telephone. Show your children and baby-sitter(s) the location of these numbers. When calling for help, provide your name, the phone number you are calling from, the exact location of the injured person, and the nature of the injury or accident. Stay on the line until all necessary information has been provided. Ask what you should do until help arrives.

For Kids' Sake

Every child deserves the chance to grow up safely. Although keeping kids safe from injury is not an easy task, safety experts agree that with diligence and patience most childhood injuries are preventable. These safety guidelines are intended to help you help your children avoid serious injury, and enjoy a safe and healthy childhood.

Chapter 70

Tips For Your Baby's Safety

Nursery Equipment Safety Checklist

From the beginning of a child's life, products, such as cribs, high chairs and other equipment intended for a child must be selected with safety in mind. Parents and caretakers of babies and young children need to be aware of the many potential hazards in their environment—hazards occurring through misuse of products or those involved with products that have not been well designed for use by children.

This checklist is a safety guide to help you when buying new or secondhand nursery equipment. It also can be used when checking over nursery equipment now in use in your home or in other facilities that care for infants and young children.

Ask yourself: does the equipment have the safety features in this checklist? If not, can missing or unsafe parts be easily replaced with the proper parts? Can breaks or cracks be repaired to give more safety? Can I fix the older equipment without creating a "new" hazard?

If most of your answers are "No," the equipment is beyond help and should be discarded. If the equipment can be repaired, do the repairs before you allow any child to use it.

The Consumer Product Safety Commission's concern is that the children in your care have a safe environment in which to grow.

Consumer Product Safety Commission (CPSC), Document 4200, undated.

Back Carriers: Yes or No?

1. Carrier has restraining strap to secure child.

2. Leg openings are small enough to prevent child from slipping out.

3. Leg openings are large enough to prevent chafing.

4. Frames have no pinch points in the folding mechanism.

5. Carrier has padded covering over metal frame near baby's face.

The commission recommends: Do not use until baby is 4 or 5 months old. By then baby's neck is able to withstand jolts and not sustain an injury.

Bassinets and Cradles: Yes or No?

1. Bassinet/Cradle has a sturdy bottom and a wide base for stability.

2. Bassinet/Cradle has smooth surfaces—no protruding staples or other hardware that could injure the baby.

3. Legs have strong, effective locks to prevent folding while in use.

4. Mattress is firm and fits snugly.

The commission recommends: Follow manufacturer's guidelines on weight and size of baby who can safely use these products.

Baby Bath Rings or Seats: Yes or No?

1. Suction cups securely fastened to product.

2. Suction cups securely attached to smooth surface of tub.

3. Tub filled only with enough water to cover baby's legs.

4. Baby never left alone or with a sibling while in bath ring, even for a moment!

The commission recommends: Never leave a baby unattended or with a sibling in a tub of water. Do not rely on a bath ring to keep your baby safe.

Carrier Seats: Yes or No?

1. Carrier seat has a wide sturdy base for stability.

2. Carrier has non-skid feet to prevent slipping.

3. Supporting devices lock securely.

4. Carrier seat has crotch and waist strap.

5. Buckle or strap is easy to use.

The commission recommends: Never use the carrier as a car seat.

Changing Tables: Yes or No?

1. Table has safety straps to prevent falls.

2. Table has drawer or shelves that are easily accessible without leaving the baby unattended.

The commission recommends: Do not leave baby on the table unattended. Always use the straps to prevent the baby from falling.

Cribs: Yes or No?

1. Slats are spaced no more than 2 3/8 inches (60 mm) apart.

2. No slats are missing or cracked.

3. Mattress fits snugly—less than two finger width between edge or mattress and crib side.

4. Mattress support is securely attached to the head and footboards.

5. Corner posts are no higher than 1/16 inch (1.5 mm) to prevent entanglement of clothing or other objects worn by child.

6. No cutouts in the head and footboards which allow head entrapment.

7. Drop-side latches cannot be easily released by baby.

8. Drop-side latches securely hold sides in raised position.

9. All screws or bolts which secure components of crib are present and tight.

The commission recommends: Do not place crib near draperies or blinds where child could become entangled and strangle on the cords. When the child reaches 35 inches in height or can climb and/or fall over the sides, the crib should be replaced with a bed.

Crib Toys: Yes or No?

1. No strings with loops or openings having perimeters greater than 14 inches (356 mm).

2. No strings or cords longer than 7 inches (178 mm) should dangle into the crib.

3. Crib gym has label warning to remove from crib when child can push up on hands and knees or reaches 5 months of age, whichever comes first.

4. Components of toys are not small enough to be a choking hazard.

The commission recommends: Avoid hanging toys across the crib or on crib corner posts with strings long enough to result in strangulation. Remove crib gyms when child is able to pull or push up on hands and knees.

Gates and Enclosures: Yes or No?

1. Openings in gate are too small to entrap a child's head.

2. Gate has a pressure bar or other fastener that will resist forces exerted by a child.

The commission recommends: To avoid head entrapment, do not use accordion-style gates or expandable enclosures with large v-shaped openings along the top edge, or diamond-shaped openings within.

High Chairs: Yes or No?

1. High chair has waist and crotch restraining straps that are independent of the tray.

2. Tray locks securely.

3. Buckle on waist strap is easy to use.

4. High chair has a wide stable base.

5. Caps or plugs on tubing are firmly attached and cannot be pulled off and choke a child.

6. If it is a folding high chair, it has an effective locking device to keep the chair from collapsing.

The commission recommends: Always use restraining straps; otherwise child can slide under the tray and strangle.

Hook-On Chairs: Yes or No?

1. Chair has a restraining strap to secure the child.

2. Chair has a clamp that locks onto the table for added security.

3. Caps or plugs on tubing are firmly attached and cannot be pulled off and choke a child.

4. Hook-on chair has a warning never to place the chair where the child can push off with feet.

The commission recommends: Don't leave a child unattended in a hook-on chair.

Pacifiers: Yes or No?

1. No ribbon, string, cord or yarn attached to pacifier.

2. Shield is large enough and firm enough to not fit in child's mouth.

3. Guard or shield has ventilation holes so the baby can breath if the shield does get into the mouth.

4. Pacifier nipple has no holes or tears that might cause it to break off in baby's mouth.

The commission recommends: To prevent strangulation, never hang pacifier or other items on a string around a baby's neck.

Playpens: Yes or No?

1. Drop-side mesh playpen or crib has label warning never to leave side in the down position.

2. Mesh has small weave (less than 1/4 inch openings).

3. Mesh has no tears, holes or loose threads.

4. Mesh is securely attached to top rail and floorplate.

5. Top rail cover has no tears or holes.

6. Wooden playpen has slats spaced no more than 2 inches (60 mm) apart.

7. If staples are used in construction, they are firmly installed and none are missing or loose.

The commission recommends: Never leave an infant in a mesh playpen or crib with the drop-side down. Even a very young infant can roll into the space between the mattress and loose mesh side and suffocate.

Rattles, Squeeze Toys, Teethers: Yes or No?

1. Rattles, squeeze toys and teethers are too large to lodge in a baby's throat.

2. Rattles are of sturdy construction that will not break apart in use.

3. Squeeze toys do not contain a squeaker that could detach and choke a baby.

The commission recommends: Take rattles, squeeze toys, teethers and other toys out of the crib or playpen when the baby sleeps to prevent suffocation.

Strollers & Carriages: Yes or No?

1. Wide base to prevent tipping.

2. Seat belt and crotch strap securely attached to frame.

3. Seat belt buckle is easy to use.

4. Brakes securely lock the wheel(s).

5. Shopping basket is low on the back and directly over or in front of rear wheels for stability.

6. When used in carriage position, leg hold openings can be closed.

The commission recommends: Always secure the seat belts. Never leave a child unattended in a stroller. Keep children's hands away from pinching areas when stroller is being folded or unfolded or the seat back is being reclined.

Toy Chests: Yes or No?

1. No lid latch which could entrap child within the chest.

2. Hinged lid has a spring-loaded lid support that will support the lid in any position and will not require periodic adjustment.

3. Chest has ventilation holes or spaces in front or sides, or under the lid should a child get inside.

The commission recommends: If you already own a toy chest or trunk with a freely falling lid, remove the lid to avoid a head injury to a small child, or install a spring-loaded lid support.

Walkers: Yes or No?

1. Wide wheel base for stability.

2. Covers over coil springs to avoid finger pinching.

3. Seat is securely attached to frame or walker.

4. No x-frames that could pinch or amputate fingers.

The commission recommends: Place gates or guards at top of all stairways, or keep stairway doors closed to prevent falls. Do not use walkers as baby sitters.

For More Information

For more nursery equipment information write for a free copy of The Safe Nursery, A Buyer's Guide, Office of Information and Public Affairs, Washington, D.C., 20207 or look for publications on children's safety on line at http://www.cpsc.gov/cpscpub/pubs.

Chapter 71

Airway Obstruction: Choking, Suffocation, and Strangulation

Airway Obstruction Injury

Airway obstruction injury (suffocation, choking, strangulation) is the leading cause of unintentional injury-related death among children under age 1. The airway obstruction injury death rate among this age group has remained approximately the same since 1987. These injuries occur when children are unable to breathe normally because food or objects block their internal airways (choking); materials block or cover their external airways (suffocation); or items become wrapped around their necks and interfere with breathing (strangulation). Children, especially those under age 3, are particularly vulnerable to airway obstruction death and injury due to the small size of their upper airways, their relative inexperience with chewing, and their natural tendency to put objects in their mouths. Additionally, infants' inability to lift their heads or extricate themselves from tight places puts them at greater risk.

Airway Obstruction Deaths and Injuries

* In 1996, nearly 670 children ages 14 and under died from airway obstruction injuries. Of these children, 80 percent were ages 4 and under.

* In 1996, more than 450 children ages 14 and under died from suffocation, strangulation, and entrapment in household appliances

and toy chests. Of these children, nearly two-thirds were under age 1 and more than 80 percent were ages 4 and under.

- In 1996, 211 children ages 14 and under died from choking (food and nonfood). Of these children, nearly 80 percent were ages 4 and under.

- In 1996, 10 children ages 11 and under died from choking on a toy or toy part, most often a balloon. In addition, one child died from toy-related strangulation. These deaths account for 85 percent of all toy-related fatalities.

- Approximately 5,000 children ages 14 and under are treated in hospital emergency rooms for aspirating and ingesting toys and toy parts each year. More than 75 percent of these children are ages 4 and under.

When and Where Airway Obstruction Deaths and Injuries Occur

- The majority of childhood suffocations, strangulations and chokings occur in the home.

- Children are more likely to suffocate during the summer months and choke during the winter months.

Suffocation

- Infants can suffocate when their faces become wedged against or buried in a mattress, pillow, infant cushion or other soft bedding; someone in the same bed rolls over on them; or their mouths and noses are covered by or pressed against a plastic bag.

- Children can suffocate when they become trapped in household appliances, such as refrigerators or dryers, and toy chests.

- Each year, cribs are involved in more than two-thirds of all nursery product-related deaths among infants. Cribs are responsible for about 45 strangulation and suffocation deaths each year (primarily older, used cribs).

- It is estimated that as many as 30 percent of the infants whose deaths are attributed to Sudden Infant Death Syndrome (SIDS) each year are found in potentially suffocating environments, frequently on their stomachs with their noses and mouths covered by soft bedding.

Choking

- The majority of childhood choking injuries and deaths are associated with food items.

- Children are at risk from choking on small, round foods such as hot dogs, candies, nuts, grapes, carrots and popcorn. Nonfood items tend to be round or conforming objects, including coins, small balls and balloons.

- Balloons are the most common cause of toy-related choking death among children. Unlike other causes of choking death, balloon-related deaths are as common among children ages 3 and older as among younger children.

- Peanuts are the most common item that results in childhood choking injuries.

- Coins, especially pennies, are the most common non-food item that results in childhood choking injuries.

Strangulation

- Strangulation occurs among children when consumer products become wrapped around their necks. Common items include clothing drawstrings, ribbons or other decorations, necklaces, pacifier strings, and window blind and drapery cords.

- Since 1981, more than 350 children have strangled on window covering cords. The majority of deaths occurred when the cord was hanging near the floor or crib, or when furniture was placed near the cord. Nearly 95 percent of these children were ages 3 and under.

- Since 1985, 21 children have died and at least 42 were injured from entangled children's clothing drawstrings, most often the hood/neck drawstrings. In addition, more than half of drawstring entanglement incidents involved playground slides.

- Children strangle in openings that permit the passage of their bodies, yet are too small for, and entrap, their heads. These include spaces in bunk beds, cribs, playground equipment, baby strollers, carriages and high chairs. Since 1990, at least 54 children have died due to entrapment in bunk beds alone.

Who Is at Risk

- Children ages 4 and under, especially under age 1, are at greatest risk for all forms of airway obstruction injury.

- Male, low-income and non-white children are at increased risk from suffocation, choking and strangulation.

- Black infants are more likely than white infants to be placed to sleep on their stomachs and on softer bedding.

Airway Obstruction Prevention Laws and Regulations

- The Child Safety Protection Act requires choking hazard warning labels on packaging for small balls, balloons, marbles, and certain toys and games having small parts that are intended for use by children ages 3 to 6. This Act also bans any toy intended for use by children under age 3 that may pose a choking, aspiration or ingestion hazard.

- The U.S. Consumer Product Safety Commission (CPSC) has issued voluntary guidelines for drawstrings on children's clothing to prevent children from strangling or getting entangled in the neck and waist drawstrings of upper outerwear garments, such as jackets and sweatshirts.

- The CPSC has combined voluntary standards development with mandatory regulations to prevent an estimated 200 crib-related deaths among young children each year.

Health Care Costs and Savings

- The total annual cost of airway obstruction injury among children ages 14 and under exceeds $1.5 billion. Children ages 4 and under account for more than 60 percent of these costs.

Prevention Tips

- Place infants to sleep on their backs on a firm, flat crib mattress in a crib that meets national safety standards—look for a Juvenile Products Manufacturers Association certification label.

Remove pillows, comforters, toys and other soft products from the crib.

- Always supervise young children while they are eating and playing. Do not allow children under age 6 to eat round or hard foods like peanuts and other nuts, raw carrots, popcorn, seeds, or hard candy. Children under age 6 should not eat hot dogs or grapes unless the skin is removed and the food is chopped into small, non-round pieces. Keep small items such as coins, safety pins, jewelry and buttons out of children's reach. Learn First Aid and CPR.

- Consider purchasing a small parts tester to determine whether or not small toys and objects in your home may present a choking hazard to young children.

- Ensure that children play with age-appropriate toys according to safety labels. Inspect old and new toys regularly for damage. Make any necessary repairs or discard damaged toys.

- Remove hood and neck drawstrings from all children's outerwear. To prevent strangulation, never allow children to wear necklaces, purses, scarves or clothing with drawstrings while on playgrounds.

- Tie up all window blind and drapery cords or cut the ends and retrofit with safety tassels. Never hang anything on or above a crib with string or ribbon longer than seven inches.

- Do not allow children under age 6 to sleep on the top bunk of a bunk bed. Ensure that all spaces between the guardrail and bed frame and all spaces in the head and foot boards are less than 3.5 inches.

Chapter 72

Burn Injuries

Thousands of children suffer burn-related injuries each year. Children ages 4 and under are at the greatest risk with an injury rate more than four times that of children ages 5 to 14. Burns have long been recognized as among the most painful and devastating injuries a person can sustain and survive. Burns often require long periods of rehabilitation, multiple skin grafts, and painful physical therapy, leaving victims with lifelong physical and psychological trauma.

Scald burn injury (caused by hot liquids or steam) is the most common type of burn-related injury among young children while flame burns (caused by direct contact with fire) are more prevalent among older children. All children also are at risk for contact, electrical and chemical burns. Because young children have thinner skin than that of older children and adults, their skin burns at lower temperatures and more deeply. A child exposed to hot tap water at 140 degrees F for three seconds will sustain a third degree burn, an injury requiring hospitalization and skin grafts. Children, especially ages 4 and under, may not perceive danger, have less control of their environment, may lack the ability to escape a life-threatening burn situation, and may not be able to tolerate the physical stress of a post-burn injury.

Deaths and Injuries

- In 1996, nearly 800 children ages 14 and under died due to fire and burn-related injury. It is estimated that flames and burns are responsible for one-fourth of all fire-related deaths.

- In 1997, an estimated 83,000 children ages 14 and under were treated in hospital emergency rooms for burn-related injuries. Of these, 59,000 were thermal burns and the remaining 24,000 were scald burns.

- An average of 16 children ages 14 and under die from scald burn-related injuries each year. Children ages 4 and under account for nearly all of these deaths.

- Among children ages 4 and under hospitalized for burn-related injuries, it is estimated that 65 percent are treated for scald burns and 20 percent for contact burns.

- In 1996, nearly 3,000 children ages 14 and under were treated in hospital emergency rooms for fireworks-related injuries.

How and where Burn Deaths and Injuries Occur

- Child-play fires are the leading cause of residential fire-related death and injury among children ages 9 and under.

- Among children ages 14 and under, hair curlers and curling irons, room heaters, ovens and ranges, irons, gasoline and fireworks are the most common causes of product-related thermal burn injuries.

- The majority of scald burns to children, especially among those ages 6 months to 2 years, are from hot foods and liquids spilled in the kitchen or other places where food is prepared and served.

- Hot tap water accounts for nearly one-fourth of all scald burns among children and is associated with more deaths and hospitalizations than other hot liquid burns. Tap water burns most often occur in the bathroom, and tend to be more severe and cover a larger portion of the body than other scald burns.

- Burns account for approximately 60 percent of all fireworks-related injuries, and primarily occur to the hands, head and eyes. Fireworks-related injuries peak during the month surrounding July 4 when 75 percent of them occur.

- Nearly two-thirds of electrical burn injuries among children ages 12 and under are associated with household electrical cords and extension cords. Wall outlets are associated with an additional 14 percent of these injuries.

- The vast majority (95 percent) of microwave burns among children are scald burns. Microwave burns are typically caused by the spilling of hot liquids or food, and injuries are primarily associated with the trunk or the face.

Who Is at Risk

- Children ages 4 and under and children with disabilities are at the greatest risk of burn-related death and injury. These children are especially at risk from scald and contact burns.

- Male children are at higher risk of burn-related death and injury than female children.

- Children in homes without smoke alarms are at greater risk of fires and fire-related death and injury.

- Males, especially those ages 10 to 14, are at the highest risk of fireworks-related injuries. However, children ages 4 and under are at the highest risk for sparkler-related injuries.

Burn Prevention Effectiveness

- During the past two decades, significant declines in the incidence of burn injury have been made. This progress coincides with increased national attention to burn prevention, establishment of burn treatment centers, widespread use of smoke alarms, burn prevention education, and regulation of consumer product safety.

- Smoke alarms are extremely effective at preventing fire-related death and injury. The chances of dying in a residential fire are cut in half when a smoke alarm is present. Smoke alarms and sprinkler systems combined could reduce fire-related deaths by 82 percent and injuries by 46 percent.

- More than 75 percent of all scald burn-related injuries among children ages 2 and under could be prevented through behavioral and environmental modifications. Hot tap water scalds can be prevented by lowering the setting on water heater thermostats to 120 degrees F or below, and by installing anti-scald devices in water faucets and shower heads.

Burn Protection Laws

- Currently, 32 states and the District of Columbia have laws that require smoke alarms to be used in both new and existing dwellings. Seven states have no comprehensive smoke alarm laws. The remaining 11 states have a variety of laws covering specific situations such as new dwellings or multi-occupancy dwellings only.

- In 1994, the U.S. Consumer Product Safety Commission issued a mandatory safety standard requiring disposable and novelty cigarette lighters to be child-resistant. Since this standard has been in effect, the number of child-playing fires has declined 14 percent and the number of deaths and injuries associated with these fires has declined 27 percent and 13 percent, respectively.

- Many communities have established local ordinances or building codes for any new construction, which require the installation of plumbing devices that keep water temperatures at or below 120 degrees F, and prevent sudden changes in water temperature. Such legislation has been effective at reducing the number of scald burn deaths and injuries associated with hot tap water.

Health Care Costs and Savings

- The total annual cost of scald burn-related deaths and injuries among children ages 14 and under is approximately $2.3 billion. Children ages 4 and under account for $2 billion, or 87 percent, of these costs.

- Total charges for pediatric admissions to burn centers average $22,700 per case.

Prevention Tips

- Never leave a child alone, especially in the bathroom or kitchen. If you must leave the room, take the child with you.

- Install smoke alarms in your home on every level and in every sleeping area. Test them once a month, replace the batteries at least once a year (unless the batteries are designed for longer life), and replace the alarms every ten years. Ten-year lithium alarms also are available and do not require an annual battery change.

- Set your water heater thermostat to 120 degrees F or below. The lower the temperature, the lower the risk of sustaining scald burn-related injuries. Consider installing water faucets and shower heads containing anti-scald technology.

- Keep matches, gasoline, lighters and all other flammable materials locked away and out of reach of children.

- Use back burners and turn pot handles to the back of the stove when cooking. Keep appliance cords out of children's reach, especially if the appliances contain hot foods or liquids. Cover unused electrical outlets with safety devices.

- Keep hot foods and liquids away from table and counter edges. Never carry or hold children and hot foods and/or liquids at the same time.

- Never allow children to handle fireworks.

Chapter 73

A Safer Car for Child Passengers

This text was designed to help you make an informed decision when purchasing a vehicle for your family. It includes information on safety features and designs specific to child passengers. It also includes safety tips, information from the federal government and a "Family Car Checklist" to use when you shop for your next vehicle.

Narrowing Your Choices

Here are some important questions to consider before you begin shopping for your next vehicle:

How many children will you be transporting?

A safety belt for each passenger is essential. Remember, all children 12 years and under are safest when properly restrained in the back seat of the vehicle. It is estimated that children are 26 percent less likely to be fatally injured if seated in the rear seat of a passenger vehicle.

What are the ages and sizes of the children?

This information will help determine the type of restraint systems you will need.

Excerpted from *Buying a Safer Car for Child Passengers*, National Highway Traffic Safety Administration (NHTSA), 1999.

Will you be installing child safety seats? Where will you place them?

All children are safest properly restrained in the back seat. NEVER use a rear-facing safety seat in the front seat of a vehicle with a front passenger air bag unless the air bag has been turned off. If your child weighs less than 20 pounds, use a rear-facing infant-only or convertible child seat in the back seat of the vehicle.

If your child weighs more than 20 pounds and is not yet 1 year old, use a rear-facing convertible seat approved for larger infants.

Children more than 1 year old and at least 20 pounds may ride facing forward. When children reach the weight and height limit of the forward-facing seat (about 40 pounds and 40 inches), they should be moved to a belt-positioning booster seat to help the lap and shoulder belt fit correctly.

Check the child seat manufacturer's instructions for further information.

Will the vehicle safety belt system meet the needs of your children?

Correct safety belt use for all vehicle occupants should be the rule in your vehicle.

Children who have outgrown child and booster seats must be able to fit the adult belt system correctly. The lap belt should fit low over the child's upper thighs when he or she is sitting straight against the vehicle seat back. The child's knees should bend comfortably over the edge of the seat. The shoulder belt should stay on the shoulder and be close to the child's chest.

A lap-only belt (without a shoulder strap) should be used to restrain a child only if no other safety belt system is available. Review the vehicle owner's manual to be sure you understand proper belt usage.

What about side air bags?

Automakers using front and rear side air bags are addressing the out-of-position risk to children differently. Read the vehicle owner's manual or check with the dealer for information about children and side air bags.

Safety Features for Child Passengers

Safety is one of the most important considerations when buying a family vehicle. Knowing that, manufacturers have introduced a number of safety features you should look for. Charts list vehicles that include one or more of the following features.

Manual Air Bag On-Off Switch

Some vehicles are equipped with a special switch that lets the driver control the passenger air bag. The switch has a warning light that must be visible to all front-seat passengers to inform them the air bag has been turned off.

A rear-facing infant seat should NEVER be placed in the front seat of a vehicle equipped with an active passenger air bag. Infants and children can be injured—or even killed—if the air bag inflates. Refer to the vehicle owner's manual for information on the proper use of the air bag on-off switch.

Please note: Children are safest when properly restrained in the back seat, whether the vehicle has an air bag or not.

The on-off switch can deactivate driver or passenger air bags. For new vehicles, federal requirements allow the switch only for vehicles with no rear seat or those with rear seats too small to safely accommodate a rear-facing infant seat.

You can get authorization from NHTSA to have an on-off switch installed in your existing vehicle by a dealer or repair shop if you:

- Cannot avoid placing a rear-facing infant seat in the front passenger seat.

- Have been advised by a physician that you have a medical condition that places you at specific risk.

- Cannot adjust the driver's position to keep your breastbone approximately 10 inches from the steering wheel.

- Cannot avoid situations, such as a car pool, that require a child 12 or under to ride in the front seat.

Brochures about on-off switches and installation request forms are available from local vehicle dealerships, AAA offices, state motor vehicle offices, and NHTSA. Since switches are not available for all vehicles, verify availability for your vehicle before you request authorization for its installation.

Some manufacturers offer vehicles with a system that deactivates the passenger air bag when a special child restraint, sold by these manufacturers, is properly installed. At the time of publication, two vehicle manufacturers offer these systems: Mercedes-Benz and Porsche.

Built-In Child Seats

These permanent seats are designed to restrain children at least 1 year old and more than 20 pounds in a forward-facing position. Because they are built into the vehicle, these seats are an effective restraint system for children. They have an advantage over add-on child safety seats because they do not have compatibility problems with vehicle seat designs or safety belt systems.

Rear Center Seat Lap/Shoulder Belt

All rear center seats must be equipped with a lap belt or lap and shoulder belt. All rear outboard seating positions must include lap and shoulder belts. As an added feature, some manufacturers include lap and shoulder belts in rear center seats. This benefits children in booster seats and older children, because the seat provides the same level of protection as rear outboard seating positions.

Adjustable Rear Shoulder Belts

Because seat belts must fit people of all sizes, including children, some manufacturers offer adjustable anchors that allow you to change the height of the shoulder strap. Check the manufacturer's instructions to adjust seat belts in your vehicle properly.

Child Safety Seat Compatibility

Not all safety seats can be installed in all types of vehicles or seating positions. With numerous models of child safety seats, more than 300 models of passenger vehicles and the wide range of belt systems available today, correctly installing a child safety seat can be challenging. The best way to be sure your safety seat is compatible with the vehicle you are considering is to test it—before you purchase or lease the vehicle.

Safety First

To correctly install a child safety seat, place your knee into the seat and lean forward while tightening the belt.

Be sure to read the child safety seat's instruction manual and review all information in the vehicle owner's manual concerning correct installation.

476

Once the safety seat is installed, check it by firmly pulling the base of the seat from side to side and forward. The seat should not move more than one inch in any direction.

Other Factors to Consider

- *Two-door vehicles:* It can be difficult to install child safety seats correctly because you must get into the back seat yourself. It also can be difficult to get your child in and out of the safety seat.

- *Small back seats:* The back seats of small cars and many pickup trucks are too small to properly accommodate some safety seats, especially those in the rear-facing reclined position. In addition, some rear center safety belts in small cars are too close together to fit safety seats with wide bases. Wide bases may block access to buckles for outboard lap and shoulder belts. In this case, try a safety seat with a narrow base.

- *Deep bucket seats:* Many safety seats will not fit in vehicle seats with deep buckets. Try a safety seat with a narrow base or top tether strap.

- *Tether anchorage:* This is a metal plate bolted into the vehicle to attach a top-tether strap that comes with some child safety seats. Tethers may improve protection by attaching the top of the safety seat more securely to the vehicle. Virtually all passenger cars made since January 1989 have pre-drilled holes that can be used for top-tether anchorage.

- *Slope of back seat:* Rear-facing infant and convertible seats should be reclined at a 45 degree angle. The slope of the seat may cause the safety seat to tilt too far forward, putting the infant in an upright rather than reclined position. To remedy this situation, try placing a tightly rolled towel under the base of the safety seat. Always check the safety seat instructions and owner's manual for correct installation.

- *Contour of back seat:* While the rear center seat may seem the safest place to put a child, many back seats have a hump in the center, making it difficult to install a child safety seat correctly. The safest position is where the safety seat fits securely.

- *Split bench seats:* Splits in wide bench seats can make it difficult to install a safety seat correctly.

477

- *Forward-anchored belts:* If the safety belt extends from the seat forward of where the back and seat cushions meet, the safety seat may be too loose. Move it to a different seating position, or try a different style safety seat, perhaps one that can accommodate a top-tether strap.

- *Pickup truck jumpseats / extended cabs:* Child safety seats will not fit properly in many pickup truck rear seats. There is not enough space between the rear of the front seat and the child to allow forward motion in the event of a crash or even a sudden stop. Side-facing jumpseats are not safe for a child safety seat under any circumstances.

Vehicles Manufactured before September 1, 1995

Some vehicles may have safety belt systems—such as automatic safety belts—that require additional hardware to install child safety seats correctly. Be sure to read both the vehicle and safety seat manuals and labels on safety belts.

Vehicles Manufactured after September 1, 1995

Vehicles now are equipped with safety belt locking features—such as locking or switchable retractors—that make installation of child safety seats easier. To be sure, read the vehicle owner's manual and safety belt labels.

Beware: Danger Areas for Children

Kids Are Not Cargo! Never let children ride or play in the cargo area, trunk or bed of any vehicle—even if the area is covered. They can be thrown from the vehicle in the event of a crash, sudden stop, or even rough road.

Trunks. Make sure children do not have access to your vehicle's trunk. Once inside, they may not be able to escape, even if they entered through the interior, since many rear seats only release to the trunk from inside the passenger compartment. Children trapped in trunks can die of suffocation or heat stroke.

Unattended Children. Never allow children unmonitored access to vehicles or leave them unattended in a vehicle. When left in a vehicle, children can quickly become ill or die from heat build-up inside of the vehicle. In addition, never allow children access to car keys or remote locking/unlocking devices. A child could put the vehicle in gear or neutral so it rolls away. Keep children safe by keeping them out of your vehicle unless you are there!

Family Car Checklist

Safety Belt System

- Are there enough safety belts for everyone?

- Can the vehicle's lap/shoulder belt system accommodate children who have outgrown safety seats and booster seats?

- Is there enough room—preferably in the back seat—to install a child safety seat correctly?

- Will the vehicle's seat design interfere with safety seat installation? (Check slope, humps, contours, splits and safety belt anchorages.)

- Do safety belts have locking features (locking or switchable retractor) for safety seats?

- Are tether anchorages available? (Some vehicle manufacturers can provide retrofit anchorage kits.)

- Are adjustable upper belts available?

- Are built-in child restraint systems available?

Other Important Safety Features

- Head restraint protection for rear seats.

- Safety door locks so children cannot open doors from inside vehicle.

- Override window controls.

To Learn More

Available from NHTSA *Buying a Safer Car* and *New Car Safety Features* contain a full range of safety-feature information and crash-test results on cars, light trucks, sport utility vehicles and vans. Safety features include air bags (front and side), advanced safety belts, anti-lock brakes, traction control, rear-seat head restraints and adjustable upper belts. Crash-test ratings from the U.S. Department of Transportation's New Car Assessment Program are included.

To order a copy, stop by your local AAA office or write to:

National Highway Traffic Safety Administration (NHTSA)
400 Seventh Street, SW
NTS-21
Washington, DC 20590
Fax: (202) 439-2062

Or call:

NHTSA Auto Safety Hotline
1-888-DASH-2-DOT
(1-888-327-4236)

Other resources for vehicle safety information that can be obtained from NHTSA include:

• Are You Using It Right? (brochure)

• Protecting Your Newborn (video)

• Child Transportation Safety Tips (guide)

A chart of vehicle safety features, including manual air bag on-off switches, rear center seat lap and shoulder belts, built-in child safety seats, and adjustable upper rear belts can be found on NHTSA's web site at www.nhtsa.dot.gov.

Chapter 74

Preventing Childhood Poisoning

Most people regard their home as a safe haven, a calming oasis in an often stormy world.

But home can be a dangerous place when it comes to accidental poisoning, especially accidental poisoning of children. One tablet of some medicines can wreak havoc in or kill a child.

Childhood poisonings caused by accidental overdoses of iron-containing supplements are the biggest concern of poison control experts, consumer protection groups, and health-care providers. Iron-containing supplements are the leading cause of pediatric poisoning deaths for children under 6 in the United States. According to the American Association of Poison Control Centers, from 1986 to 1994, 38 children between the ages of 9 months and 3 years died from accidentally swallowing iron-containing products. The number of pills consumed by these children varied from as few as five to as many as 98.

In the Jan. 15, 1997, *Federal Register*, FDA published final regulations that will make it harder for small children to gain access to high-potency iron products (30 milligrams of iron or more per tablet). FDA has also taken steps to ensure that health-care providers and consumers are alerted to the dangers associated with accidental overdoses of iron-containing products, including pediatric multivitamin supplements that contain iron.

FDA Consumer, March 1996 with revisions made in June 1997, NIH Pub. No. (FDA) 97-1233

Although iron poisoning is the biggest concern when it comes to childhood poisoning, there is also concern about other drugs.

"Over-the-counter diet pills have the potential to be lethal to children, as do OTC stimulants used to keep you awake and decongestant tablets," says George C. Rodgers, M.D., Ph.D., medical director of the Kentucky Regional Poisoning Center. "Tofranil [imipramine], an antidepressant drug also used for childhood bedwetting, and Catapres [clonidine], a high blood pressure medicine, can be very hazardous because it takes very little to produce life-threatening problems in children. One tablet may do it.

"Antidepressant drugs have a high degree of toxicity," he continues. "They are cardiac and central nervous system toxins, and it doesn't take much of them to do harm, particularly in children. They are prescribed fairly ubiquitously. One of the things we look at when we get kids' poisonings is who had the medicine, and why."

Rodgers also urges extra caution when antidepressant drugs are prescribed for teenage patients who may have behavioral or emotional problems.

"Antidepressant drugs are commonly given to adolescents with behavioral problems, and often a month or two-month supply is prescribed. Teens should not be given more than a week's supply to begin with, and parents need to monitor their usage," he says.

The marketing of pediatric vitamins is also a cause of concern for Rodgers.

"Because they're marketed to look like candy or cartoon characters, it looks like candy and doesn't seem like medicine," he explains.

In addition, children frequently mimic the behavior of their parents. Children who watch their parents take pills may want to do it, too—with potentially fatal results.

Poison-Proofing Your Home

Poison-proofing your home is the key to preventing childhood poisonings. In the case of iron-containing pills or any medicine:

- Always close the container as soon as you've finished using it. Properly secure the child-resistant packaging, and put it away immediately in a place where children can't reach it.

- Keep pills in their original container.

- Keep iron-containing tablets, and all medicines, out of reach— and out of sight—of children.

- Never keep medicines on a countertop or bedside table.

- Follow medicine label directions carefully to avoid accidental overdoses or misdoses that could result in accidental poisoning.

For other substances, buy the least hazardous products that will serve your purposes. When buying art supplies, for example, look for products that are safe for children. For hazardous products such as gasoline, kerosene, and paint thinners that are often kept on hand indefinitely, buy only as much as you need and safely get rid of what you don't use. Never transfer these substances to other containers. People often use cups, soft-drink bottles, or milk cartons to store left-over paint thinner or turpentine. This is a bad idea because children associate cups and bottles with food and drink.

The kitchen and bathroom are the most likely unsafe areas. (Medicines should never be stored in the bathroom for another reason: a bathroom's warm, moist environment tends to cause changes or disintegration of the product in these rooms.) Any cabinet containing a potentially poisonous item should be locked.

"Bathrooms with medicines, kitchens with cleaning products, even cigarette butts left out, can be toxic to kids," Rodgers explains. "And remember that child-resistant caps are child-resistant, not childproof. The legal definition is that it takes greater than five minutes for 80 percent of 5-year-olds to get into it: that means 20 percent can get in in less time! Kids are inventive, and can often figure it out. And left-over liquor in glasses on the counter after parties? Don't do it!"

Alcohol can cause drunkenness as well as serious poisoning leading to seizures, coma, and even death in young children. Children are more sensitive to the toxic effects of alcohol than are adults, and it doesn't take much alcohol to produce such effects. Alcohol-laced products, such as some mouthwashes, aftershaves or colognes, can cause the same problems.

Garages and utility rooms should also be checked for potential poison hazards. Antifreeze, windshield washing fluid, and other products should be stored out of children's reach in a locked cabinet. Childproof safety latches can be purchased at your local hardware store.

In the living room or family room, know your plants' names and their poison potential. Although most houseplants are not poisonous, some are. To be on the safe side, keep houseplants out of the reach of young children. Although much has been made of problems with poinsettias (blamed for a death as early as 1919), recent studies indicate

483

it is not as highly toxic as was once believed. Although ingesting it may cause some stomach irritation and burning in the mouth, it's unlikely to be fatal.

"Plants are mostly a problem for children, since it's a natural response for children to taste things. Few adults eat houseplants," Rodgers points out. "Plants have a high capacity for making you sick, but they are usually low-risk for producing life-threatening symptoms." After poison-proofing your home, prepare for emergencies. Post the numbers of your regional poison control center (which can be found on the inside cover of the Yellow Pages or in the white pages of your phone directory) and your doctor by the phone. Keep syrup of ipecac on hand—safely locked away, of course. (See "Antidotes" below.) Never administer any antidote without first checking with your doctor or poison control center.

Lead Poisoning

Although lead levels in food and drink are the lowest in history, concern remains about lead leaching into food from ceramic ware. Improperly fired or formulated glazes on ceramic ware can allow lead to leach into food or drink.

Long recognized as a toxic substance, adverse health effects can result from exposure to lead over months or years.

After a California family suffered acute lead poisoning in 1969 from drinking orange juice stored in a pitcher bought in Mexico, FDA established "action levels" for lead in ceramic ware used to serve food. Over the years, these original action levels have been revised as research has shown that exposure to even small amounts of lead can be hazardous. The last revision for ceramic foodware was in 1991. On Jan. 12, 1994, FDA published a regulation for decorative ceramic ware not intended for food use, requiring a permanently affixed label on high-lead-leaching products.

"Most lead toxicity comes from multiple exposure and is a slow accumulation over time," says Robert Mueller, a nurse and poison information specialist at the Virginia Poison Center, headquartered at The Medical College of Virginia Hospitals in Richmond. "Refusing to eat, vomiting, convulsions, and malaise can all be symptoms of lead poisoning." Because lead poisoning occurs over time, such symptoms may not show up right away. A blood test is the surest way to determine that your child has not been exposed to significant amounts of lead.

"In general, if a consumer purchases ceramic ware in the U.S. marketplace today, it meets the new action levels," says Julia Hewgley, public affairs specialist with FDA's Center for Food Safety and Applied Nutrition. "But if you travel abroad and buy ceramic ware, be aware that each country has its own safety regulations. Safety can be terribly variable depending on the type of quality control and whether the piece is made by a hobbyist." To guard against poisonings, Hewgley advises that ceramic ware not be used to store foods. Acidic foods—such as orange, tomato and other fruit juices, tomato sauces, vinegar, and wine—stored in improperly glazed containers are potentially the most dangerous. Frequently used products, like cups or pitchers, are also potentially dangerous, especially when used to hold hot, acidic foods.

"Stop using any item if the glaze shows a dusty or chalky gray residue after washing. Limit your use of antique or collectible housewares for food and beverages," she says.

"Buy one of the quick lead tests available at hardware stores and do a screening on inherited pieces."

Iron Poisoning

Iron-containing products remain the biggest problem by far when it comes to childhood poisoning. Between June 1992 and January 1993, five toddlers died after eating iron supplement tablets, according to the national Centers for Disease Control and Prevention's *Morbidity and Mortality Weekly Report* of Feb. 19, 1993. The incidents occurred in a variety of ways: Children ate tablets from uncapped or loosely capped bottles, swallowed tablets found spilled on the floor, and, in one case, a 2-year-old fed an 11-month-old sibling tablets from a box found on the floor.

Iron is always included in prenatal vitamins prescribed for pregnant women, and is often included in multivitamin formulas and children's supplements. Usually available without prescription, iron supplements can be found in grocery stores, drugstores, and health food stores in a wide variety of potencies, ranging from 18 milligrams (mg) to 150 mg per pill. For a small child, as little as 600 mg of iron can be fatal.

Because iron supplements are typically brightly colored, some people are concerned they may look like candy, and, therefore, are particularly attractive to children. In 1993, the Nonprescription Drug Manufacturers Association (NDMA), which manufactures about 95 percent of nonprescription OTC medicines available to Americans today, adopted formulation provisions for iron products containing 30 mg or more of elemental iron per solid dosage form. These provisions also stipulated that such products would not be made with sweet coatings. That same year, NDMA manufacturers also independently agreed to develop new voluntary warning labels for these products. The voluntary labels read: "Warning: Close tightly and keep out of reach of children. Contains iron, which can be harmful or fatal to children in large doses. In case of accidental overdose, seek professional assistance or contact a poison control center immediately."

FDA's new rules, effective July 15, 1997, require unit-dose packaging for iron-containing products with 30 milligrams or more of iron per dosage unit. Because of the time and effort needed to open unit-dose products, FDA believes unit-dose packaging will discourage a youngster, or at least limit the number of tablets a child would swallow, reducing the potential for serious illness or death. This requirement is in addition to existing U.S. Consumer Product Safety Commission regulations, which require child-resistant packaging for most iron-containing products.

The new rules also now require that labels for all iron-containing products taken in solid oral dosage forms contain the following: "Warning: Accidental overdose of iron-containing products is a leading cause of fatal poisoning in children under 6. Keep this product out of reach of children. In case of accidental overdose, call a doctor or poison control center immediately." Iron is an essential nutrient sometimes lacking in people's diets, which is why iron is often recommended for people with conditions such as iron-deficiency anemia. Taken as indicated, iron is safe. But when tablets are taken beyond the proper dose in a short period, especially by toddlers or infants, serious injury or death may result.

Children poisoned with iron face immediate and long-term problems. Within minutes or hours of swallowing iron tablets, nausea, vomiting, diarrhea, and gastrointestinal bleeding can occur. These problems can progress to shock, coma, seizures, and death. Even if a child appears to have no symptoms after accidentally swallowing iron, or appears to be recovering, medical evaluation should still be sought since successful treatment is difficult once iron is absorbed from the small intestine into the bloodstream. And children who survive iron poisoning can experience other problems, such as gastrointestinal obstruction and liver damage, up to four weeks after the ingested poisoning.

FDA regulates iron-containing products as either drugs or foods, depending on the product formulation and on intended use, as defined by labeling and other information sources.

Some iron-containing products have been regulated as prescription drugs because they included pharmacologic doses of folic acid and usually were prescribed to meet high nutritional requirements during pregnancy.

Signs of Poisoning

How can you tell if your child has ingested something poisonous? "Most poisons, with the exception of lead, work fairly quickly. A key is when the child was otherwise well and in a space of hours develops unusual symptoms: They can't follow you with their eyes, they're sleepy before it's their nap time, their eyes go around in circles. Any unusual or new symptoms should make you think of poisoning as a possibility," Rodgers advises. "Poisonings typically affect the stomach and central nervous system. If a child suddenly throws up, that can be more difficult to diagnose."

Other signs of poison ingestion can be burns around the lips or mouth, stains of the substance around the child's mouth, or the smell of a child's breath. Suspect a possible poisoning if you find an opened or spilled bottle of pills.

If you suspect poisoning, remain calm. For medicines, call the nearest poison control center or your physician. For household chemical ingestion, follow first-aid instructions on the label, and then call the poison control center or your doctor. When you call, tell them your child's age, height and weight, existing health conditions, as much as you know about the substance involved, the exposure route (swallowed? inhaled? splashed in the eyes?), and if your child has vomited. If you know what substance the child has ingested, take the remaining solution or bottle with you to the phone when you call. Follow the instructions of the poison control center precisely.

Progress Against Poisonings

The nation's first poison control center opened in Chicago in 1953, after a study of accidental deaths in childhood reported a large number were due to poisoning. Since that time, a combination of public education, the use of child-resistant caps, help through poison control centers, and increased sophistication in medical care have lowered overall death rates.

Often, calling a poison center simply reassures parents that the product ingested is not poisonous. In other cases, following phone instructions prevents an emergency room trip.

Children are not the only victims of accidental poisonings: Older people in particular are at risk because they generally take more medicines, may have problems reading labels correctly, or may take a friend's or spouse's medicine.

In June 1995, the U.S. Consumer Product Safety Commission voted unanimously to require that child-resistant caps be made so adults—especially senior citizens—will have a less frustrating time getting them off. Because many adults who had trouble with child-resistant caps left them off, or transferred their contents to less secure packaging that endangers children, officials say the new caps will be safer for children.

"Childhood poisoning will always be a focus, because children are so vulnerable, especially children under age 5," says Ken Giles, public affairs spokesman for the Consumer Product Safety Commission. "The first two or three years of a child's life are the highest-risk time for all kinds of injuries, so there is a special need to educate new parents. It's essential we keep raising these safety messages that medicines and chemicals can be poisonous."

Protect Yourself Against Tampering

With FDA's new proposed regulations regarding packaging of high-dose, iron-containing pills in mind, it's important to remember that no packaging or warnings can protect without your involvement. Non-prescription OTC drugs sold in the United States are among the most safely packaged consumer products in the world, but "child-resistant" and "tamper-resistant" do not mean "childproof" and "tamperproof."

FDA adopted "tamper-resistant" packaging requirements after seven people in the Chicago area died from taking cyanide-laced Extra-Strength Tylenol capsules in 1982. Although the product met all FDA requirements at the time, it wasn't designed so tampering would leave visible evidence. FDA swiftly enacted new regulations requiring most OTC drug products to be packaged in "tamper-resistant" packaging, defined as "packaging having an indicator or barrier to entry that could reasonably be expected to provide visible evidence that tampering had occurred," and required OTC product labeling to alert consumers to tamper-resistant packaging. In 1989, FDA regulations were amended to require two-piece hard gelatin capsules to be packaged using at least two tamper-resistant features unless sealed with a tamper-resistant technology.

"Consumer vigilance is part of the equation," says Lana Ragazinsky, consumer safety officer with FDA's Center for Drug Evaluation and

Research, division of drug quality evaluation, office of compliance. "The consumer is being led into a false sense of security because they see 'tamper-resistant'... 'tamper evident' means you, the consumer, need to look for evidence of tampering."

FDA has proposed changing the term "tamper-resistant" to "tamper-evident" to underscore the fact that no package design is tamperproof. The most important tool to detect tampering is you! Here are a few tips to help protect against tampering:

- Read the label. OTC medicines with tamper-evident packages tell you what seals and features to look for.

- Inspect the outer packaging before you buy.

- Inspect the medicine when you open the package, and look again before you take it. If it looks suspicious: be suspicious.

- Look for capsules or tablets different in any way from others in the package.

- Don't use any medicine from a package with cuts, tears, slices, or other imperfections.

- Never take medicine in the dark. Read the label and look at the medicine every time you take a dose.

Antidotes

If you suspect childhood poisoning, call the nearest poison control center or your physician first, and follow their instructions precisely.

To induce vomiting in case of accidental poisoning, experts recommend keeping on hand syrup of ipecac—safely stored away from children, of course! Syrup of ipecac induces vomiting, thus ridding the body of the swallowed poison. It usually works within a half-hour of ingestion.

Some medical experts also recommend that parents keep activated charcoal on hand as well: You may have to ask your druggist for it, because it may not be on store shelves. Although some poison control experts recommend having activated charcoal on hand, there is a difference of opinion on its use by consumers. The U.S. Consumer Product Safety Commission, for example, does not recommend that consumers use activated charcoal because it is less palatable to young children.

Activated charcoal (or charcoal treated with substances that increase its absorption abilities) absorbs poison, preventing it from spreading throughout the body. One advantage of activated charcoal is that it can be effective for a considerable time after the poison is swallowed. But activated charcoal should never be used at the same time you administer syrup of ipecac: The charcoal will absorb the ipecac.

For children ages 1 to 12, give one tablespoon of syrup of ipecac followed by one or two glasses of water. Children ages 12 and over should get two tablespoons, followed by one or two glasses of water.

Activated charcoal is usually found in drugstores in liquid form in 30-gram doses. For children under 5, give one gram per every two pounds of body weight. Older children and adults may require much higher doses.

Both antidotes should only be used on conscious poison victims; an unconscious victim should always be treated by professionals.

"Remember to call your local poison control center first before giving your child any at-home antidote," says Robert Mueller, poison information specialist at the Virginia Poison Center in Richmond, Va.

— by Audrey T. Hingley

Audrey T. Hingley is a writer in Mechanicsville, Va.

Chapter 75

Preventing Iron Poisoning in Children

Efforts to protect children from accidental iron poisoning are getting a boost from new FDA regulations published in the Jan. 15, 1997, *Federal Register*. Accidental overdose of iron pills is a leading cause of poisoning deaths among young children.

The regulations, which took effect July 15, 1997, require all iron-containing drugs and dietary supplements to carry a warning about the risk of acute iron poisoning in children under 6 and the need to keep the products out of reach of children.

In addition, most products containing 30 milligrams (mg) or more of iron per dosage unit—such as iron pills for pregnant women—will have to be packaged as individual doses (for example, in blister packages). This is to limit the number of pills or capsules a small child could accidentally consume once the package is opened.

FDA's regulations add to measures already in place, including a U.S. Consumer Product Safety Commission regulation that, since 1987, has required child-resistant packaging for most drugs and food supplements with more than 250 mg of iron per container. Also under way is an FDA education campaign to warn adults to protect children from accidental iron overdose.

Iron Poisoning

Since 1986, poison control centers in the United States have received reports of more than 110,000 incidents of children under 6 accidentally

FDA Backgrounder, January 15, 1997.

491

swallowing iron tablets. Some of the children were hospitalized; more than 35 died.

Accidental iron overdose is a leading cause of poisoning deaths in children under 6 in the United States. Almost 17 percent of children's deaths reported to poison control centers between 1988 and 1992 were due to iron poisoning, compared with 12 percent between 1984 and 1987.

The iron products involved in the poisonings ranged from nonprescription daily multivitamin/mineral supplements for children to high-potency prescription iron supplements for pregnant women. In some cases, the iron products were left within the child's reach in uncapped or loosely capped containers. In others, the child managed to open the container, even though in some cases it appeared to be in child-resistant packaging. In some cases, a sibling opened the container.

The children were poisoned after consuming as few as five to as many as 98 iron-containing tablets. Death occurred from ingesting as little as 200 mg to as much as 5,850 mg of iron.

Iron Needs

Iron is an essential nutrient that is lacking in some people's diets. These often include women of childbearing age, including those who are pregnant, all of whom have high iron needs. The National Academy of Sciences' Recommended Dietary Allowance for iron for females between ages 11 and 50 is 15 mg a day and for pregnant women, 30 mg. For adult men and women over 50, the RDA for iron is 10 mg.

Iron deficiency also can affect children, particularly during the rapid growth period from 6 months to 4 years. The RDA for iron for children in this age group is 10 mg.

To prevent iron-deficiency anemia in these populations, doctors often recommend iron supplements. Some iron products are available without a prescription, either as single-ingredient iron pills, which may contain 30 mg or more of iron per dose, or in combination with vitamins or other minerals—for example, pediatric vitamins with iron—which often have less than 30 mg of iron per dose.

Some iron products are available as prescription drugs, such as combination iron and folic acid pills for pregnant women. These usually contain 30 mg or more of iron per dose.

Taken as indicated on the label or as advised by a doctor, these iron products are safe. But when tablets are taken beyond the proper dose in a short period, especially by infants or toddlers, serious injury or death may result.

This raises a public health concern: how to prevent iron poisoning in children while ensuring the availability of iron supplements for those who need them.

FDA Action

In October 1994, FDA proposed regulations to address that issue. The proposal came in recognition of a recent upsurge in iron poisoning cases among children and in response to three citizen petitions submitted to FDA by the American Association of Poison Control Centers, the attorneys general of 34 states, and the Nonprescription Drug Manufacturers Association.

In March 1995, during the proposal's comment period, FDA conducted eight focus group studies in four U.S. cities. The majority of the participants were women between 18 and 35 with children living at home. The studies' objectives were to identify participants' current perceptions and behavior concerning iron-containing products, to test their understanding of several label warning statements, to evaluate which format they felt was best for conveying the warning on the package label, and to evaluate their likely reaction to such a message.

The studies showed that most participants:

- were not aware of the potential for iron-containing products to cause iron poisoning in young children

- kept iron-containing products at home out of reach of children mainly because they regarded them as pill-type products

- overlooked voluntary warnings on iron-containing products because they were not aware of the degree of the health hazard

- differed in their opinions as to what the warning statements should say

- agreed that the warning should be placed on the back of the package with a box around it to make it stand out

- would continue to buy iron-containing products and would handle them properly, now that they knew about their potential danger.

Final Regulations

The final regulations incorporate the studies' findings and numerous comments received by FDA from public health organizations, physicians, manufacturers, and trade organizations.

Under these regulations, packages of all preparations that contain iron for use as dietary supplements or for therapeutic purposes will have to display prominently and conspicuously this boxed warning:

"WARNING: Accidental overdose of iron-containing products is a leading cause of fatal poisoning in children under six. Keep this product out of reach of children. In case of accidental overdose, call a doctor or poison control center immediately."

The regulation's requirement for unit-dose packaging applies to most of the more potent iron-containing products. Exempt from the unit-dose requirement for one year, however, are products made with carbonyl iron. FDA is allowing this exemption so that manufacturers can collect additional evidence to support their claim that carbonyl iron is less toxic than other common forms of iron, such as ferrous sulfate and ferrous gluconate. FDA believes that because unit-dose packaging will require more time and effort for the child to open, it will reduce the likelihood of the child swallowing a large number of pills.

Education Campaign

In addition to the regulations, FDA is conducting a nationwide public education campaign to protect children from accidental iron overdose. This campaign augments a similar campaign started in 1993 by the Consumer Product Safety Commission and the Nonprescription Drug Manufacturers Association. FDA has produced materials, including a brochure, poster and newspaper columns, informing consumers that:

- iron-containing products can seriously injure and kill young children who accidentally swallow them
- child-resistant packaging of any iron-containing product should be completely reclosed every time it is opened
- iron-containing products should always be kept out of reach of children.

Advice to Adults

Here are other important points FDA wants consumers to know about accidental iron poisoning in children:

- Children who are poisoned with iron face both immediate and long-term problems. Within minutes or hours of swallowing iron tablets, they may suffer nausea, vomiting, diarrhea, and gastrointestinal bleeding, which can progress to shock, coma and death. Even if the child appears to recover from these initial problems, severe gastrointestinal bleeding, lethargy, liver damage, heart failure, and coma can occur from 12 hours to two days later. If the victims survive, they can develop other problems, such as gastrointestinal obstruction and more extensive liver damage, three to six weeks after the poisoning.

- Even if there are no immediate symptoms, parents should contact a doctor or local poison control center immediately if their child has accidentally swallowed a product that contains iron. Sometimes, serious symptoms do not develop right away, and delayed treatment may not be effective. The telephone number for the closest poison control center is listed with other emergency numbers in the front of phone books.

Chapter 76

Dangers of Lead Still Linger

The hazardous substance lead was banned from house paint in 1978. U.S. food canners quit using lead solder in 1991. And a 25-year phaseout of lead in gasoline reached its goal in 1995.

As a result of such efforts, the number of young children with potentially harmful blood lead levels has dropped 85 percent in the last 20 years, as shown in National Health and Nutrition Examination Surveys conducted by the National Center for Health Statistics. Interested in measuring the impact of lead solder's removal from food cans, the Food and Drug Administration funded collection of the data during the 1976-1980 period and has continued to support the survey efforts.

Similarly, FDA's 1994-1996 Total Diet Studies showed that, since 1982-1984, daily intakes of lead from food dropped 96 percent in 2- to 5-year-olds (from 30 micrograms a day to 1.3) and nearly 93 percent in adults (from 38 micrograms a day to 2.5).

Yet in 1997, FDA approved a new, portable blood lead screening test kit for health professionals to use. In the face of so much success, why is another screening tool even necessary?

The answer: Lead is still around.

Lead paint abounds in older housing. The deteriorating paint exposes youngsters indoors to lead-laden dust and paint chips and outdoors to exterior paint lead residues in nearby soil—residues that remain unless removed. Lead particles emitted by the past use of

FDA Consumer, January-February 1998.

leaded gasoline are also in the soil, especially near major highways. Lead persists at some work sites and, occasionally, in drinking water, ceramicware, and a number of other products.

"The risk of lead exposure remains disproportionately high for some groups, including children who are poor, non-Hispanic black, Mexican American, living in large metropolitan areas, or living in older housing," the national Centers for Disease Control and Prevention noted in its Feb. 21, 1997, *Morbidity and Mortality Weekly Report*. Indeed, CDC reports that nearly a million children under 6 still have blood lead levels high enough to damage their health. While CDC considers the blood lead level of concern in adults to be 25 micrograms per deciliter (mcg/dL) of blood, this level in young children is only 10 mcg/dL.

Based on CDC's levels, FDA's "tolerable" daily diet lead intakes are 6 mcg for children under age 6, 25 mcg for pregnant women, and 75 mcg for other adults. However, some risk exists with any level of lead exposure, says toxicologist Michael Bolger, Ph.D., chief of FDA's contaminants branch in the Office of Plant and Dairy Foods and Beverages.

And harmful levels need never occur, according to Sheryl Rosenthal, M.S.P.H., R.D., a lead educator at FDA's Center for Food Safety and Applied Nutrition. "Lead poisoning is preventable and just should not happen today," she says.

Lead Absorption

While adults absorb about 11 percent of lead reaching the digestive tract, children may absorb 30 to 75 percent. When lead is inhaled, up to 50 percent is absorbed, but less than 1 percent of lead is absorbed when it comes in contact with the skin. The body stores lead mainly in bone, where it can accumulate for decades.

"Anyone in poor nutritional status absorbs lead more easily," adds Cecilia Davoli, M.D., a pediatrician with Kennedy Krieger Institute's Lead Poisoning Prevention Program, in Baltimore. Calcium deficiency especially increases lead absorption, as does iron deficiency, which can also increase lead damage to blood cells. A high-fat diet increases lead absorption, and so does an empty stomach.

The Risks of Lead

Lead disrupts the functioning of almost every brain neurotransmitter, says David Bellinger, Ph.D., a psychologist and epidemiologist at Children's Hospital in Boston. Neurotransmitters are chemical messengers between the body's nerve cells. The messenger calcium, for example, is essential to nerve impulse transmission, heart activity, and blood clotting, but if it doesn't work right, affected systems may also be askew.

"Lead fits into binding sites that calcium should," Bellinger says, "so it can disturb cellular processes that depend on calcium. But there's no unifying theory that explains in detail what lead does to the central nervous system, which is where lead typically affects children."

Bellinger estimates that each 10 mcg/dL increase in blood lead lowers a child's IQ about 1 to 3 points.

"Evidence is less clear," he says, "on whether mild blood lead elevations in pregnancy cause permanent effects on the fetus. Studies have tended not to find that early developmental delays related to minor fetal exposure carry through to school age, when IQ is measured." Studying middle- and upper-middle-class children exposed before birth to mild lead levels, Bellinger and colleagues found delays in early sensory-motor development, such as grasping objects, but did not find such effects by school age.

However, he adds, "When lead exposure in the uterus is quite high, the impact can be devastating on the fetus, causing serious neurological problems."

High lead exposures can cause a baby to have low birth weight or be born prematurely, or can result in miscarriage or stillbirth.

"Symptoms of lead poisoning can be highly variable depending, in part, on the age of the child, the amount of lead to which the child is exposed, and how long the exposure goes on," says pediatrician Randolph Wykoff, M.D., FDA associate commissioner for operations. Children exposed to lead may have no symptoms, he says, or may report sometimes vague symptoms, including headache, irritability or abdominal pain.

While a child's chronic exposure to relatively low lead levels may result in learning or behavioral problems, Wykoff says that "higher levels of exposure can be associated with anemia and changes in kidney function, as well as significant changes in the nervous system that may, at extreme exposures, include seizures, coma and death."

In adults, lead poisoning can contr ibute to high blood pressure and damage to the reproductive organs. Severe lead poisoning can cause subtle loss of recently acquired skills, listlessness, bizarre behavior, incoordination, vomiting, altered consciousness, and—as with children—seizures, coma and death. Poisoning without severe brain effects can cause lethargy, appetite loss, sporadic vomiting, abdominal pain, and constipation.

By the time symptoms appear, damage is often already irreversible.

"The most important thing for families to do," says Baltimore's Davoli, "is to learn what steps they can take to prevent lead poisoning. We don't want to get to treatment. And they should take their children to the doctor regularly for checkups and, if the children are at risk, get blood lead tests done."

Critical to prevention is focusing on the important lead sources. FDA's Rosenthal says, "Dealing with sources of lead means recognizing them in your family's environment, knowing which ones contribute significant exposures, and eliminating or avoiding those exposures."

Top Contaminator: Lead Paint

America's No. 1 source of lead exposure in children is deteriorating lead paint in older housing. Because young children frequently put their thumbs and fingers and objects they handle in their mouths, they are easily poisoned from chronic ingestion of lead paint chips and house dust or soil that may have lead particles in it.

The Consumer Product Safety Commission (CPSC) banned house paint having more than 0.06 percent lead in 1978. But housing built before then, particularly before 1950, may contain lead paint. The Environmental Protection Agency and Department of Housing and Urban Development require owners of pre-1978 housing to give prospective buyers or renters federally approved information on the risk. Buyers must have 10 days to inspect for lead-based paint before being obligated by a contract.

Improper housing renovation increases exposure. The riskiest practices are sanding, scraping or removing lead paint with a heat gun, which taint the air with lead paint dust. CPSC warns: There is no completely safe method for do-it-yourself removal of lead paint. Only experts should remove lead paint.

Occupational Hazards

Clark Carrington, Ph.D., of FDA's dairy foods and beverages contaminants branch, names workplace exposure as the next major potential source of lead. Besides their own exposures, workers may bring lead dust home on clothes, hands or hair, exposing children in the household.

Occupations that may expose workers to lead include painting, smelters, firearms instruction, automotive repair, brass or copper foundries, and bridge, tunnel and elevated highway construction.

To help protect workers from such exposure, the Occupational Safety and Health Administration calls for removal of workers from the workplace if their blood lead levels reach 50 mcg/dL. EPA limits lead emissions from certain industries.

Keeping Drinking Water Safe

Certain drinking water systems can also pose a lead risk.

Under EPA rules, if lead exceeds 15 parts per billion (ppb) in more than 10 percent of public water taps sampled, the system must undergo a series of corrosion control treatments. The main culprits are corroded lead plumbing, lead solder on copper plumbing, and brass faucets. Lead is highest in water left in pipes for a long time—for example, when the faucet isn't used overnight.

FDA's quality standard for bottled water requires that lead not be present at 5 ppb, the lowest concentration that generally available methods for water analysis can reliably measure. If bottled water contains lead above this level, it is subject to regulatory action, including removal from the marketplace.

Lead in Ceramicware

Some ceramicware has lead in the glaze and may introduce small amounts of lead in the diet, which the body can tolerate, says Carrington. "The major problem with ceramicware is the rare poorly made piece with very high levels of leaching lead."

Bolger adds that even with these pieces, risk varies. "A plate coming in brief contact with food is not an issue," he says, "but storage of food in such a bowl or pitcher is a risk." It's especially wise to avoid storing acidic foods like juice and vinegar in ceramicware, as acids promote lead leaching.

FDA has established maximum levels for leachable lead in ceramicware, and pieces that exceed these levels are subject to recall or other agency enforcement action. The levels are based on how frequently a piece of ceramicware is used, the type and temperature of the food it holds, and how long the food stays in contact with the piece. For example, cups, mugs and pitchers have the most stringent action level, 0.5 parts per million, because they can be expected to hold food longer, allowing more time for lead to leach. Also, a pitcher may be used to hold fruit juice. And a coffee mug is generally used every day to hold a hot acidic beverage, often several times a day.

501

Michael Kashtock, Ph.D., chief of FDA's Office of Plant and Dairy Foods and Beverages enforcement branch, says, "FDA allows use of lead glazes because they're the most durable. But we regulate them tightly to ensure their safety. Commercial manufacturers ... employ extremely strict and effective manufacturing controls that keep the lead from leaching during use." Small potters often can't control the firing of lead glazes as well, he warns, so their ceramics are more likely to leach illegal lead levels, although many do use lead-free glazes. "The best advice is to stick to commercially made products. If you are going to buy something hand-made or hand-painted, get assurance that lead-free glazes were used," he says.

Antique ceramicware may leach high levels of lead. Consumers can use a lead test kit from a hardware store on such pieces and on other hand-painted ceramicware they may already own. Avoid using such items—particularly cups, mugs or pitchers—if the glaze develops a chalky gray residue after washing.

"And you want to make sure," says Rosenthal, "that you know whether an item is for food use, or if it's for decorative use only." FDA requires high-lead-leaching decorative ceramicware to be permanently labeled that it's not for food use and may poison food. Such items bought outside the United States may not be so labeled, potentially posing serious risk if used for food.

Other Lead Sources

Tin-Coated Lead Foil Capsules on Wine Bottles

FDA banned these capsules in 1996 after a study by the Bureau of Alcohol, Tobacco and Firearms found that 3 to 4 percent of wines examined could become contaminated during pouring from lead residues deposited on the mouth of the bottle by the foil capsule.

U.S. winemakers stopped using lead foils before the ban, but older bottles with the foils may still be around. "Remove the entire foil before using such wines," says attorney Martin Stutsman, a consumer safety officer in FDA's dairy foods and beverages enforcement branch. "Then before uncorking the bottle, wipe its neck and rim and the top of the cork with a clean wet cloth."

Lead-Soldered Food Cans

Despite U.S. food canners' voluntary elimination of lead solder and a 1995 FDA ban on lead-soldered cans, requiring their removal from shelves by June 1996, this source of lead in the diet hasn't been fully eliminated. Some countries still use lead-soldered cans for food, and these food items may still occasionally be imported, albeit illegally, into the United States. Also, some small vendors may still stock old inventories of food in lead-soldered cans. In fact, a 1997 FDA investigation found more than 100 such cans in ethnic grocery stores in California alone.

Glassware

Lead crystal glassware may leach lead. "The crystalware industry has established voluntary lead-leaching limits for crystalware," says Kashtock, "that most foreign and domestic manufacturers follow." As a precaution, children and pregnant women should avoid frequent use of crystal glassware. Lead crystal baby bottles should never be used.

Calcium Products

Some people have expressed concern about lead in calcium supplements. Lead is a common contaminant in calcium from such natural sources as dolomitic limestone and oyster shells, but levels vary considerably from trace amounts to higher levels. However, FDA's Carrington says, "Since calcium intakes decrease lead absorption, supplements that correct low calcium intakes may reduce lead absorption, even though they contain small amounts of lead."

Lead is also found in other calcium sources. For example, lead in milk is usually too low to measure, but FDA's yearly Total Diet Study of foods in grocery stores sometimes detects lead in milk, says Carrington.

FDA has been petitioned to establish a tolerance level for lead in calcium sources used in dietary supplements. According to Robert Moore, Ph.D., of the agency's Office of Special Nutritionals regulatory branch, two petitions propose different tolerance levels—one similar to current industry standards and one considerably lower. FDA is reviewing the issues raised in the two documents.

Progressive Hair Dyes

Applied over time to gradually color the hair, these dyes contain lead acetate. After studying information on their safety, FDA found that lead exposure from these dyes was insignificant and that the dyes could be used safely, says John Bailey, Ph.D., director of FDA's Office of Cosmetics and Colors. "But we restricted how much could be in the product, and we required specific labeling instructions, including a warning to keep it out of the reach of children."

Kajal and Surma, or Kohl

These unapproved dyes in certain eye cosmetics from the Middle East contain potentially harmful amounts of lead. A 7-month-old in 1992 had a 39 mcg/dL blood lead level due to surma applied to the lower inner eyelid. Bailey says, "They are sold in stores specializing in Middle East products or brought into the country in personal luggage." He stresses that people using these cosmetics "need to understand the potentially serious health risk."

Foreign Digestive Remedies

Certain unapproved foreign digestive remedies containing lead include Alarcon, Azarcon, Coral, Greta, Liga, Maria Luisa, or Rueda. Greta, for example, is 99 percent lead oxide.

FDA orders the detention at U.S. borders of items known to possibly contain potential harmful levels of lead, including the Middle East eye cosmetics, the foreign digestive remedies, lead crystal baby bottles, and many other prohibited items. Lead sources outside FDA's purview include lead-based artists' paints, lead solder used in electronics work and stained glass, fishing weights, lead toy soldiers, and old painted toys and furniture.

Reflecting that these many lead sources are not all in every family's environment, new CDC screening guidance calls for state lead-poisoning prevention programs to identify communities at risk of high exposure and recommend appropriate screening. To this end, CDC funded 30 state and 10 local programs in 1996.

When announcing the new guidance, Health and Human Services Secretary Donna E. Shalala said, "Lower lead levels for America's children constitute a public health achievement of the first importance. But a significant number of children are still at risk for high lead exposure, and we have to finish the job on their behalf."

Screening and Treatment

Decisions about who needs lead screening should be made by individual doctors as well as state health departments, who can examine local lead hazards and conditions to determine which children are at risk of lead exposure, according to 1997 guidance issued by the national Centers for Disease Control and Prevention.

A new screening test is especially suited for use in isolated U.S. rural areas and in developing countries. In September 1997, FDA approved the LEADCARE In Office Test System, a portable blood lead screening kit for health professionals' use in areas lacking refrigeration and other complex equipment needed with previously approved tests. Manufacturers developed the quick, easy and reliable kit in conjunction with CDC.

FDA has approved three drugs that bind to, or chelate, lead molecules so the body can remove them in urine and stool. Calcium Disodium Versenate (edetate calcium disodium) requires injections or intravenous infusion in the hospital. Along with this drug, BAL (dimercaprol), also injected, may be used. The pediatric oral drug Chemet (succimer) may be taken at home, but it's important to eliminate the lead sources. Like other chelator drugs, Chemet should not substitute for effective environmental assessment and removal of the source of lead exposure.

These drugs may have side effects, however, so doctors closely monitor their patients during treatment.

— by Dixie Farley

Dixie Farley is a staff writer for *FDA Consumer*.

More Information

Centers for Disease Control and Prevention
(888) 232-6789
http://www.cdc.gov/nceh/programs/lead/lead.htm

Consumer Product Safety Commission
(800) 638-CPSC
TDD: (800)-638-8270
http://www.cpsc.gov/

Environmental Protection Agency's Safe Drinking Water Hotline
(800) 426-4791
http://www.epa.gov/opptintr/lead/index.html

National Lead Information Center
(800) LEAD-FYI
clearinghouse: (800) 424-LEAD
TDD: (800) 526-5456
http://www.nsc.org/ehc/lead.htm

Chapter 77

Shaken Baby Syndrome

Description

Shaken baby syndrome is a severe form of head injury that occurs when a baby is shaken forcibly enough to cause the baby's brain to rebound (bounce) against his or her skull. This rebounding may cause bruising, swelling, and bleeding (intracerebral hemorrhage) of the brain, which may lead to permanent, severe brain damage or death. The condition is usually the result of non-accidental trauma or child abuse. In rare instances it may be caused by tossing a baby in the air or jogging with a baby in a backpack. Symptoms may include changes in behavior, irritability, lethargy, loss of consciousness, pale or bluish skin, vomiting, and convulsions. Although there usually are no outward physical signs of trauma, there may be broken, injured, or dislocated bones and injuries to the neck and spine.

Treatment

Immediate emergency treatment is necessary and usually includes life-sustaining measures such as stopping internal bleeding and relieving increased intracranial pressure.

National Institute of Neurological Disorders and Stroke (NINDS), June 1997, updated November 1999.

507

Prognosis

Generally, the prognosis for children with shaken baby syndrome is poor. Most will be left with considerable disability. Retinal damage may cause loss of vision. If the child survives, he or she may require lifelong medical care for brain damage injuries such as mental retardation or cerebral palsy.

Research

The NINDS conducts and supports research on trauma-related disorders, including head injuries. Much of this research focuses on increasing scientific understanding of these disorders and finding ways to prevent and treat them.

Additional Information

These articles, available from a medical library, are sources of in-depth information on shaken baby syndrome:

Alexander, R, et al. "Magnetic Resonance Imaging of Intracranial Injuries from Child Abuse." *Journal of Pediatrics*, 109:6; 975-979 (1986).

Frank, Y, et al. "Neurological Manifestations in Abused Children Who Have Been Shaken." *Developmental Medicine and Child Neurology*, 27; 312-316 (1985).

Joynt, R (ed). *Clinical Neurology*, vol. 3, Chapter 30, J.B. Lippincott Co., Philadelphia, p. 62 (1990).

Spaide, R, et al. "Shaken Baby Syndrome." *American Family Physician*, 41:4; 1145-1152 (April 1990).

Additional information is available from the following organization:

National Institute of Child Health and Human Development
Building 31, Room 2A32
Bethesda, MD 20892-2425
(301) 496-5133

Chapter 78

Infant Cardiopulmonary Resuscitation (CPR)

1. If You Think Your Baby Might Not Be Breathing:

a. Check the baby's color by pulling the lip down and seeing if the inside of the mouth is pink; also the baby's nailbeds should be pink. If these places are pink, just watch the baby. Some babies have long pauses between breaths, even up to 20 seconds, but this is considered normal if there is no color change.

b. Check for breathing by putting your cheek by the baby's mouth and see if you feel the breath coming out. The baby's chest should be gently rising and falling with every breath. Some babies breathe very shallowly. It is easier to see a baby breathe if he/she is lying on his/her back. Look, listen and feel for breathing.

c. If there is no chest movement, and the baby's color is blue, immediately begin stimulation. Stimulate the baby by calling his/her name and rubbing his/her back or feet. Do not shake the baby. If the baby does not start breathing, follow the next step.

Children's Hospital Medical Center (Cincinnati), Patient Education Program, January 1991, revised January 1994. Used with permission of Children's Hospital Medical Center—Cincinnati.

509

2. Open the Baby's Airway

Open the baby's airway by tilting the baby's head back slightly. Check the mouth for any formula, mucus, toys, etc. If you see an object in the baby's mouth, turn the head to the side and clean out the mouth with your fingers. Open baby's airway.

3. Give Two Slow Breaths of Air

Give two slow breaths of air covering the infant's nose and mouth with your own mouth. Place your mouth over the baby's nose and mouth and give 2 slow breaths.

4. Check the Baby's Pulse

Check the baby's pulse (inside of upper arm) with two fingers for about 8 seconds.

a. If pulse is present but baby is not breathing, continue mouth to mouth breathing, one breath every 3 seconds, periodically checking to make sure the pulse is still present.

b. If pulse is not present, put the baby on a hard surface. Begin CPR. Tell someone to call 911 for an ambulance.

5. Begin CPR

Position your index and middle fingers on the breastbone one fingerbreadth below the nipple line and begin CPR using the following sequence:

- 5 chest compressions, 1 breath,
- 5 chest compressions, 1 breath.
- Count to yourself:
    "1, 2, 3, 4, 5, breathe"
    "1, 2, 3, 4, 5, breathe"
as fast as possible. Make sure you are pressing hard enough to make the chest go down 1/2 to 1 inch.

6. Call for Assistance

If you are performing CPR and are alone, take the baby to the phone with you, call 911, then immediately resume CPR until the life squad arrives.

7. Periodically Check Again

Periodically check again for the presence of a pulse.

a. If you feel a pulse, but the baby is not breathing, stop compressions, but continue mouth to mouth breathing, one breath every 3 seconds.

b. If you feel a pulse and the baby also begins breathing on its own, stop compressions and mouth to mouth breathing. Stay with the baby until help arrives.

Chapter 79

Caretaker's Guide to Emergency Illness and Injury Procedures

When parents enroll their child, they should provide you with the contact information and consent that you will need if there is an emergency involving that child. A sample "Child Care Emergency Contact Information and Consent Form" is shown in Figure 79.1. The form includes a statement of parental consent for you to administer first aid and get emergency services for their child. You should request that parents update this form at least once every year.

All parents of children in your care should know your emergency procedures. Let parents know that you are trained in first aid and CPR as taught by the American Red Cross or any other nationally approved first aid training facility. Tell parents how often you take refresher courses. Tell them that in the event of an emergency, you will:

1. quickly assess the child's health,

2. call 911 or other appropriate emergency help as needed,

3. give first aid and CPR, if necessary, and

4. then contact them or the person they have listed to call in an emergency.

At all times, you should:

- Have emergency numbers posted by the phone—police, ambulance (911), and poison control center.

"Emergency Illness and Injury Procedures," Centers for Disease Control and Prevention (CDC), undated.

- Keep parents' consent forms for emergency treatment and numbers for emergency contacts on file.

- Take pediatric CPR and first aid training every year to maintain your American Red Cross certification.

- Post first aid procedures where they can be easily seen. You may want to copy and laminate the list of first aid measures included in this chapter.

- Write up an emergency procedure and evacuation route and make sure you are familiar with it.

- Keep a fully stocked first aid kit in easy reach of all providers, but out of reach of children. Check the first aid kit regularly and restock it as necessary.

- In addition to the supplies listed for your first aid kit, you should also keep ice cubes or ice bags in the freezer to use to reduce swelling of some injuries.

- Place a stocked first aid kit in every vehicle used to transport the children. In addition to the items in your facility first aid kit, your vehicle kit should also include a bottle of water, soap, coins for a pay telephone, and a first aid guide.

- Don't use first aid sprays and ointments. They may cause allergic reactions or skin damage. Use alcohol or antiseptic wipes.

- Wear gloves if you might come in contact with blood.

- Have first aid supplies handy on the playground by keeping a zip-lock plastic bag stocked with disposable gloves, sterile wipes, gauze wrap, and Band-Aids in your pocket.

What Your First Aid Kit Should Include

- Box of nonporous disposable gloves
- Sealed packages of alcohol wipes or antiseptic
- Small scissors
- Tweezers (for removing splinters)
- Thermometer
- Adhesive bandage tape
- Sterile gauze squares (2" and 3")
- Triangular bandages

Figure 79.1. Sample Child Care Emergency Contact Information and Consent Form

Child's Name:_____ Birth date: _____

Parent/Guardian #1 Name: _____

  Telephone: Home_____ Work_____ Beeper/Car_____

Parent/Guardian #2 Name:_____

  Telephone: Home_____ Work_____ Beeper/Car_____

EMERGENCY CONTACTS (to whom child may be released if guardian is unavailable)

Name #1:_____Relationship_____

  Telephone: Home_____ Work_____ Beeper/Car_____

Name #2:_____ Relationship_____

  Telephone: Home_____ Work_____ Beeper/Car_____

CHILD'S PREFERRED SOURCES OF MEDICAL CARE

Physician's Name:_____

Address:_____Telephone:_____

Dentist's Name:_____

Address:_____Telephone:_____

Hospital Name:_____

Address:_____Telephone_____

Ambulance Service: _____Telephone:_____
(Parents are responsible for all emergency transportation charges.)

CHILD'S HEALTH INSURANCE

Insurance Plan:_____ ID#_____

Subscriber's Name (on insurance card):_____

SPECIAL CONDITIONS, DISABILITIES, ALLERGIES, OR MEDICAL EMERGENCY INFORMATION

_____

_____

PARENT/GUARDIAN CONSENT AND AGREEMENT FOR EMERGENCIES

As parent/guardian, I consent to have my child receive first aid by facility staff and, if necessary, be transported to receive emergency care. I will be responsible for all charges not covered by insurance. I give consent for the emergency contact person listed above to act on my behalf until I am available. I agree to review and update this information whenever a change occurs and at least every 6 months.

Parent/Guardian Signature_____ Date_____

Parent/Guardian Signature_____ Date_____

515

- Flexible roller gauze (1" and 2" widths)
- Safety pins
- Eye dressing
- Insect sting preparation
- Pencil and notepad
- Syrup of ipecac
- Cold pack
- Small splints
- Sealable plastic bags for soiled materials

If an injury occurs:

1. Stay calm.

2. Check for life-threatening situations (choking, severe bleeding, or shock). Do not move a seriously injured child.

3. Call 911 or your local emergency number if the child is seriously hurt.

4. Give CPR or first aid, if necessary.

5. Contact the parent/emergency contact.

6. Record all injuries on a standard form developed for that purpose. The form shown in Figure 79.2 is an example of a standard injury report form. You may want to list on the back of the form the names of all of those who witnessed the injury.

First Aid Measures

Note: Wear disposable gloves if coming in contact with blood. Dispose of gloves in a sturdy leakproof plastic bag. Wash hands.

Abdominal Pain (Severe). Notify parents. If the child has been injured and has severe or bloody vomiting and is very pale, call 911. Do not allow child to eat or drink.

Abrasions (Scrapes). Wash abrasion with soap and water. Allow to dry. Cover with a sterile nonstick Band-Aid or dressing. Notify parents.

Asphyxiation (Suffocation). Call 911. If the child is in a closed area filled with toxic fumes, move the child outside into the fresh air. Perform CPR if child is not breathing.

Asthma Attack. Give prescribed medication, if any, as previously agreed to by parents. If attack does not stop after the child is given the medication, and the child is still having difficulty breathing, call 911. If you have no medication and the attack does not subside within a few minutes, call the parents and ask them to come immediately and take the child for medical care. If the child has difficulty breathing, call 911.

Figure 79.2. Sample Injury Report Form

Date of Injury: _____
Time of Injury: _____ _am _pm
Name of Injured_____
Sex: __Male __Female
Age: ___ years

Where injury happened: _____
_____

How injury happened: _____
_____
_____
_____

Part of body injured: _____

Objects involved (if any): _____

What was done to help the injured: _____
_____
_____

Parent/Guardian advised:
        of injury: _yes _no
        to seek medical attention: _yes _no

Supervisor (at time of injury):_____
Person completing form: _____
Date form completed: _____

Bites and Stings

- *Animal:* Wash the wound with soap and water. Notify parents to pick up the child and seek medical advice. If bite is from a bat, fox, raccoon, skunk, or unprovoked cat or dog, or any animal that may have rabies, call the health department, which will contact animal control to catch the animal and observe it for rabies. Do not try to capture the animal yourself. Make note of the description of the animal and any identifying characteristics (whether dog or cat had a collar, for example).

- *Human:* Wash the wound with soap and water. Notify parents. If bite causes bleeding, contact the health department for advice.

- *Insect:* Do not pull out stinger as it may break off; remove the stinger by scraping it out with a fingernail or credit card, then apply a cold cloth. Notify parents. Call 911 if hives, paleness, weakness, nausea, vomiting, difficult breathing, or collapse occurs.

- *Snake:* Call local poison control center. Do not apply ice. Notify parents immediately, then the health department. If the child has difficulty breathing, call 911.

- *Ticks:* Notify parents to seek preferences. If parents approve, try to remove tick with tweezers.

- *Waterlife:* For stingray or catfish stings, submerge affected area in warm water to deactivate the toxin. For other stings, such as from jellyfish, rinse with clean water. Call parents to seek medical care.

Bleeding

- *External:* For small wounds, apply direct pressure with a gauze pad for 10-15 minutes. (Use gloves.) If bleeding continues or is serious, apply a large pressure dressing and call 911 immediately.

- *Internal:* If child has been injured and vomits a large amount of blood or passes blood through the rectum, call 911. Otherwise, contact parents to seek medical care. If a child is a hemophiliac and has injured a joint through a minor bump or fall, call the parents. The child may need an injection of blood factor.

Bruises: Apply cold compresses to fresh bruises for the first 15 to 30 minutes. Note: A child with bruises in unusual locations should be evaluated for child abuse.

Burns and Scalds: Note: A child with burns and scalds should be evaluated for child abuse.

- *No blisters:* Place burned extremity in cold water or cover burned area with cold, wet cloths until pain stops (at least 15 minutes).

- *With blisters:* Same as for no blisters. Do not break blisters. Call parents to take child to get medical care.

- *Deep, extensive burns:* Call 911. Do not apply cold water. Cover child with a clean sheet and then a blanket to keep the child warm.

- *Electrical:* If possible, disconnect power by shutting off wall switch, throwing a breaker in the electrical box, or any other safe way. Do not directly touch child if power is still on. Use wood or thick dry cloth (nonconducting material) to pull child from power source. Call 911. Start CPR if necessary. Notify parents.

Croup and Epiglottitis

- *Croup:* Call parents to pick up child and get medical care.

- *Epiglottitis* (Similar to croup, but with high fever, severe sore throat, drooling, and difficulty breathing): Transport child in upright position to medical care. Call 911 for ambulance if child has severe breathing difficulty.

Dental Injuries

- *Braces (Broken):* Remove appliance, if it can be done easily. If not, cover sharp or protruding portion with cotton balls, gauze, or chewing gum. If a wire is stuck in gums, cheek, or tongue, DO NOT remove it. Call parent to pick up and take the child to the orthodontist immediately. If the appliance is not injuring the child, no immediate emergency attention is needed.

- *Cheek, Lip, Tongue (Cut/Bitten):* Apply ice to bruised areas. If bleeding, apply firm but gentle pressure with a clean gauze or cloth. If bleeding continues after 15 minutes, call the parent to pick up the child and get medical care.

- *Jaw Injury:* Immobilize jaw by having child bite teeth together. Wrap a towel, necktie, or handkerchief around child's head under the chin. Call parent to pick up and take the child to the emergency room.

- *Tooth (Broken):* Rinse dirt from the injured area with warm water. Place cold compresses over the face in the area of the injury. Locate and save any tooth fragments. Call the parent to pick up and take the child and tooth fragments to the dentist IMMEDIATELY.

- *Tooth (Knocked Out):* Find the tooth. Handle tooth by the smooth, white portion (crown), not by the root. Rinse the tooth with water, but DO NOT clean it. Place tooth in a cup of milk or water. Call the parent to pick up and take the child and tooth to the dentist IMMEDIATELY. (Time is critical.)

- *Tooth (Bleeding Due to Loss of Baby Tooth):* Fold and pack clean gauze or cloth over bleeding area. Have child bite on gauze for 15 minutes. Repeat again. If bleeding persists, call parent to pick up and take the child to the dentist.

- *Sores (Cold / Canker):* Tell parent and request physician examination if sore persists for more than a week.

Eye Injuries: If a chemical is splashed in the eye, immediately flush eye with tepid water, with the eyelid held open. Then remove contact lens, if present, and rinse eye with tepid water for at least 15 minutes. Do not press on injured eye. Gently bandage both eyes shut to reduce eye movement. Call parent to pick up and take child to get medical care.

Fractures

- *Arm, Leg, Hand, Foot, Fingers, Toes:* Do not move injured part if swollen, broken, or painful. Call parent to pick up and take child to get medical care.

- *Neck or Back:* Do not move child; keep child still. Call 911 for ambulance.

Frostbite/Freezing: Warm arm, leg, hand, foot, fingers, or toes by holding them in your armpit. Warm ears and noses with a warm palm. For deeper freezing, hold extremity in warm water (105°–110° F) for 20 minutes. Protect involved area from further damage. Apply a sterile gauze and elevate injured area for 40 minutes. Call parents to pick up and take child to get medical care. If child is lethargic, call 911.

Frozen to Metal: Do not allow child to pull away from metal. Blow hot breath onto the stuck area or pour warm (not hot) water onto the object. Gently release child. If bleeding occurs, such as on the tongue, grasp tongue with folded sterile gauze and apply direct pressure. Call parents to pick up and take child to get medical care.

Head Injuries: Keep child lying down. Call parents Call 911 if the child is:

- complaining of severe or persistent headache
- less than 1 year old
- oozing blood or fluid from ears or nose
- twitching or convulsing
- unable to move any body part
- unconscious or drowsy
- vomiting

Nosebleeds: Have child sit up and lean forward. Loosen tight clothing around neck. Pinch lower end of nose close to nostrils (not on bony part of nose).

Poisons: Immediately, BEFORE YOU DO ANYTHING, call the local poison control center, hospital emergency room, or physician. Call parents. If child needs to go to for medical evaluation, bring samples of what was ingested. Bring with you all containers, labels, boxes, and package inserts that came with the material that the child took in. Look carefully for extra containers around the immediate area where the incident occurred. Try to estimate the total amount of material the child might have taken in, and whether the material was swallowed, inhaled, injected, or spilled in the eyes or on the skin. If possible, also bring with you the child's health file, including consent forms and names and telephone numbers of parents/guardians.

Do not make a child vomit if:

- the child is unconscious or sleepy,
- the child has swallowed a corrosive product (acid/drain cleaner/ oven cleaner), or
- the child has swallowed a petroleum product (furniture polish/ kerosene/gasoline).

If instructed by the poison control center to make the child vomit:

- Use ipecac syrup:

    Children 1 year to 10 years old: 1 tablespoon or 3 teaspoons of ipecac and 4 to 8 ounces of water

    Children over 10 years old: 2 tablespoons of ipecac and 4 to 8 ounces of water

- Follow with another 4 to 8 ounces of water.

- Repeat dose ONCE if child has not vomited in 20 minutes.

If a chemical is spilled on someone, dilute it with water and remove any contaminated clothing, using gloves if possible. Place all contaminated clothing and other items in an airtight bag and label the bag. If the chemical has been splashed into he eye, flush immediately with tepid water and follow instructions listed above for "Eye Injuries."

Some poisons have delayed effects, causing moderate or severe illness many hours or even some days after the child takes the poison. Ask whether the child will need to be observed afterward and for how long. Make sure the child's parents/guardians understand the instructions.

Seizures: Remain calm. Protect child from injury. Lie child on his or her side with the head lower than the hips, or on his or her stomach. Loosen clothing. Do not put anything in the child's mouth. Call 911 if seizure lasts more than 5 minutes or if they are the result of a head injury. Notify parents.

Part Seven

Additonal Help and Information

Chapter 80

Glossary of Important Terms

A

abdomen: The area between the chest and the hips. Contains the stomach, small intestine, large intestine, liver, gallbladder, pancreas, and spleen.

abruptio placentae: Premature detachment of a normally situated placenta.

absorption: The way nutrients from food move from the small intestine into the cells in the body.

accessory digestive organs: Organs that help with digestion but are not part of the digestive tract. These organs are the tongue, glands in the mouth that make saliva, pancreas, liver, and gallbladder.

acute: A disorder that is sudden and severe but lasts only a short time.

AIDS (Acquired Immune Deficiency Syndrome): A disease characterized by opportunistic infections (e.g., *Pneumocystis carinii* pneumonia, candidiasis, Kaposi's sarcoma) in immunocompromised

The terms in this glossary have been excerpted from documents produced by the Centers for Disease Control and Prevention (CDC); the National Institutes of Health and its subagencies, including the National Institute of Allergy and Infectious Diseases (NIAID), National Institute of Diabetes and Digestive and Kidney Diseases (NIDDK), National Institute of Mental Health (NIMH), National Institute of Neurological Disorders and Stroke (NINDS); and the U.S. Department of Health and Human Services (DHHS), and the U.S. Food and Drug Administration (FDA).

persons; caused by the human immunodeficiency virus (HIV) and transmitted by exchange of body fluids.

Alagille syndrome: A condition of babies in their first year. The bile ducts in the liver disappear, and the bile ducts outside the liver get very narrow. May lead to a buildup of bile in the liver and damage to liver cells and other organs.

amniocentesis: A procedure whereby fluid is aspirated from the amniotic sac through the abdomen.

anemia: Not enough red blood, red blood cells, or hemoglobin in the body. Hemoglobin is a protein in the blood that contains iron.

antidiarrheals: Medicines that help control diarrhea. An example is loperamide (Imodium®).

antiemetics: Medicines that prevent and control nausea and vomiting. Examples are promethazine (Phenergan®) and prochlorperazine (Compazine®).

antispasmodics: Medicines that help reduce or stop muscle spasms in the intestines. Examples are dicyclomine (Bentyl®) and atropine (Donnatal®).

Asperger's disorder: A disorder marked by repetitive behaviors, severe social problems, and clumsy movements; language and intelligence are usually intact.

autism: A brain disorder that typically affects a person's ability to communicate, form relationships with others, and respond appropriately to the environment.

B

bacteremia: The presence of viable bacteria in the circulating blood.

bile ducts: Tubes that carry bile from the liver to the gallbladder for storage and to the small intestine for use in digestion.

bile: Fluid made by the liver and stored in the gallbladder. Bile helps break down fats and gets rid of wastes in the body.

biliary atresia: A condition present from birth in which the bile ducts inside or outside the liver do not have normal openings. Bile becomes trapped in the liver, causing jaundice and cirrhosis. Without surgery the condition may cause death.

bilirubin: The substance formed when hemoglobin breaks down. Bilirubin gives bile its color. Bilirubin is normally passed in stool. Too much bilirubin causes jaundice.

birth defect: Any defect present when a child is born. Birth defects are disorders of body structure, function, or chemistry which may be inherited or may result from environmental interference during embryonic or fetal life.

blood pressure: Force exerted by the heart in pumping blood from its chambers. The pressure of blood against the walls of a blood vessel or heart chamber. Unless there is reference to another location, such as the pulmonary artery or one of the heart chambers, it refers to the pressure in the systemic arteries, as measured, for example, in the forearm.

C

carbohydrates: A type of food, usually from plants versus animals. Carbohydrates include simple carbohydrates (sugar, fruit) and complex carbohydrates (vegetables, starches).

cholesterol: A fat-like substance in the body. The body makes and needs some cholesterol, which also comes from foods such as butter and egg yolks. Too much cholesterol may cause gallstones. It also may cause fat to build up in the arteries. This may cause a disease that slows or stops blood flow.

chromosomes: Physical structures in the cell's nucleus that house the genes; each human cell has 23 pairs of chromosomes.

chronic: A term that refers to disorders that last a long time, often years.

colic: Attacks of abdominal pain, caused by muscle spasms in the intestines. Colic is common in infants.

common bile duct: The tube that carries bile from the liver to the small intestine.

congenital: Existing at birth. Refers to certain mental or physical traits, anomalies, malformations, or diseases which may be either hereditary or due to an influence occurring during gestation up to the moment of birth.

constipation: A condition in which the stool becomes hard and dry. A person who is constipated usually has fewer than three bowel movements in a week. Bowel movements may be painful.

corticosteroids: A group of hormones produced by adrenal glands.

D

dehydration: Loss of fluids from the body, often caused by diarrhea. May result in loss of important salts and minerals.

diarrhea: Frequent, loose, and watery bowel movements. Common causes include gastrointestinal infections, irritable bowel syndrome, medicines, and malabsorption.

diastolic pressure: The lowest pressure to which blood pressure falls between contractions of the ventricles.

distention: Bloating or swelling of the abdomen.

DNA (deoxyribonucleic acid): A nucleic acid that is found in the cell nucleus and is the carrier of genetic information.

Dubin-Johnson syndrome: An inherited form of chronic jaundice (yellow tint to the skin and eyes) that has no known cause.

dysphagia: Problems in swallowing food or liquid, usually caused by blockage or injury to the esophagus.

dyspnea: Shortness of breath.

dysuria: Difficulty or pain in urination.

E

edema: Swelling of tissue due to injury or disease.

electrolytes: Chemicals such as salts and minerals needed for various functions in the body.

enema: A liquid put into the rectum to clear out the bowel or to administer drugs or food.

esophageal atresia: A birth defect. The esophagus lacks the opening to allow food to pass into the stomach.

esophagus: The organ that connects the mouth to the stomach. Also called gullet.

F

fat: One of six nutrient categories essential for proper growth and development. The others are protein, carbohydrate, water, vitamins, and minerals. At no other age does fat play such an important role as in infancy and early childhood, a period of rapid growth and development.

febrile seizures: Convulsions brought on by a fever in infants or small children. During a febrile seizure, a child often loses consciousness and shakes, moving limbs on both sides of the body.

fiber: A substance in foods that comes from plants. Fiber helps with digestion by keeping stool soft so that it moves smoothly through the colon. Soluble fiber dissolves in water. Soluble fiber is found in beans, fruit, and oat products. Insoluble fiber does not dissolve in water. Insoluble fiber is found in whole-grain products and vegetables.

folliculitis: An inflammation of the hair follicles. The lesions may be papules (small skin elevations) or pustules.

fragile X syndrome: An inherited disorder named for a defective piece of the X-chromosome that appears pinched and fragile when seen under a microscope; people with this syndrome are likely to have mental retardation and many of the same symptoms as autism along with unusual physical features.

G

gastroesophageal reflux disease (GERD): Flow of the stomach's contents back up into the esophagus. Happens when the muscle between the esophagus and the stomach (the lower esophageal sphincter) is weak or relaxes when it shouldn't. May cause esophagitis. Also called esophageal reflux or reflux esophagitis.

gastrointestinal (GI) tract: The large, muscular tube that extends from the mouth to the anus, where the movement of muscles and release of hormones and enzymes digest food. Also called the alimentary canal or digestive tract.

gene: A unit of genetic material (DNA) that occupies a definite locus on a chromosome and contains the plan a cell uses to perform a specific function (e.g., making a given protein).

genitourinary: Pertaining to the organs of reproduction and urination.

gestation: The process, state, or period of pregnancy.

glucose: A simple sugar the body manufactures from carbohydrates in the diet. Glucose is the body's main source of energy.

H

hemangiomas: A congenital anomaly in which a proliferation of vascular endothelium leads to a mass that resembles neoplastic tissue. It can occur anywhere in the body, but is most frequently noticed in the skin and subcutaneous tissue.

hepatitis: Inflammation of the liver, usually from a viral infection, but sometimes from toxic agents.

hereditary traits: Conditions that genetically passed on from parents to children.

hernia: The part of an internal organ that pushes through an opening in the organ's wall. Most hernias occur in the abdominal area.

herniorrhaphy: An operation to repair a hernia.

Hirschsprung's disease: A birth defect in which some nerve cells are lacking in the large intestine. The intestine cannot move stool through, so the intestine gets blocked. Causes the abdomen to swell.

HIV (Human Immunodeficiency Virus): The virus occurring in humans that causes a condition that results in a defective immunological mechanism, opportunistic infections, and eventually in the disease process know as AIDS (acquired immunodeficiency syndrome).

hormone: A chemical substance produced within the body which has a "regulatory" effect on the activity of a certain tissue in the body.

hydrolyzed-protein formula: Formula made from cow's milk in which the protein has been broken up into its component parts; essentially, it's been predigested, which decreases the likelihood of an allergic reaction.

hyperbilirubinemia: Too much bilirubin in the blood. Symptoms include jaundice. This condition occurs when the liver does not work normally.

hyperpnea: Breathing that is deeper and more rapid than is normal at rest.

hyperpyrexia: An abnormally high fever.

hypertension: Abnormally high blood pressure.

hypotonia: Having a lesser degree of tension in any part of the body.

I

icterus: Relating to or marked by jaundice.

impaction: The trapping of an object in a body passage. Examples are stones in the bile duct or hardened stool in the colon.

imperforate anus: A birth defect in which the anal canal fails to develop. The condition is treated with an operation.

indigestion: Poor digestion. Symptoms include heartburn, nausea, bloating, and gas. Also called dyspepsia.

infant: A child under the age of 1 year.

intussusception: A rare disorder. A part of the intestines folds into another part of the intestines, causing blockage. Most common in infants. Can be treated with an operation.

islets of intelligence: Unusual, remarkable abilities sometimes displayed by people with autism; also called savant skills.

J

jaundice: A symptom of many disorders. Jaundice causes the skin and eyes to turn yellow from too much bilirubin in the blood.

L

La Leche League: An international support organization for nursing mothers.

lactase deficiency: Lack of the lactase enzyme. Causes lactose intolerance.

lactase: An enzyme in the small intestine needed to digest milk sugar (lactose).

Lactobacillus bifidus: Beneficial bacteria that prevent the growth of harmful organisms.

lactose intolerance: Being unable to digest lactose, the sugar in milk. This condition occurs because the body does not produce the lactase enzyme.

lactose tolerance test: A test for lactase deficiency. The patient drinks a liquid that contains milk sugar. Then the patient's blood is tested; the test measures the amount of milk sugar in the blood.

lactose: The sugar found in milk. The body breaks lactose down into galactose and glucose.

liver: The largest organ in the body. The liver carries out many important functions, such as making bile, changing food into energy, and cleaning alcohol and poisons from the blood.

M

macrophages: Cells that kill bacteria, fungi, and viruses.

macrosomia: A term meaning "large body." This refers to a baby that is considerably larger than normal. This condition occurs when the mother's blood sugar levels have been higher than normal during the pregnancy. This is a preventable complication of gestational diabetes.

magnetic resonance imaging (MRI): A test that takes pictures of the soft tissues in the body. The pictures are clearer than x-rays.

malabsorption syndromes: Conditions that happen when the small intestine cannot absorb nutrients from foods.

malnutrition: A condition caused by not eating enough food or not eating a balanced diet.

meconium: The first intestinal discharge of the newborn infant.

microcephaly: Pertaining to abnormal smallness of the head.

morbidity: Pertaining to severe illness.

mortality: Pertaining to death.

myoclonic: Spasm or twitching of a muscle.

N

nausea: The feeling of wanting to throw up (vomit).

necrotizing enterocolitis: A condition in which part of the tissue in the intestines is destroyed. Occurs mainly in under-weight newborn babies. A temporary ileostomy may be necessary.

neonatal hepatitis: Irritation of the liver with no known cause. Occurs in newborn babies. Symptoms include jaundice and liver cell changes.

neonatal: Refers to the period directly after birth, up to the first 4 weeks after birth.

neonate: A newborn. Refers to the period immediately following birth and continuing through the first 28 days of life.

nutrients: Proteins, carbohydrates, fats, vitamins, and minerals. These are provided by food and are necessary for growth and the maintenance of life.

O

obstruction: A blockage in the GI tract that prevents the flow of liquids or solids.

occult bleeding: Blood in stool that is not visible to the naked eye. May be a sign of disease such as diverticulosis or colorectal cancer.

oral rehydration therapy (ORT): A simple mixture of water, salts and carbohydrates to prevent dehydration in children with bouts of diarrhea and vomiting (some brand names are: Pedialyte®, Infalyte®, Naturalyte®, and Rehydralyte®).

P

perinatal: Occurring during, or pertaining to, the periods before, during, or after the time of birth, i.e., from the 28th week of gestation through the first seven days after delivery.

pernicious anemia: Anemia caused by a lack of vitamin B_{12}. The body needs B_{12} to make red blood cells.

pertussis: Whooping cough.

Peutz-Jeghers syndrome: An inherited condition. Many polyps grow in the intestine. There is little risk of cancer.

pharynx: The space behind the mouth. Serves as a passage for food from the mouth to the esophagus and for air from the nose and mouth to the larynx.

phenylketonuria: An autosomal recessive aminoacidopathy that leads to severe, irreversible mental retardation (IQ below 50) if it is not treated during infancy.

placenta: A special tissue that joins the mother and fetus. It provides hormones necessary for a successful pregnancy, and supplies the fetus with water and nutrients (food) from the mother's blood.

polyp: Tissue bulging from the surface of an organ. Although these growths are not normal, they often are not cause for concern. However, people who have polyps in the colon may have an increased risk of colorectal cancer.

polyposis: The presence of many polyps.

porphyria: A group of rare, inherited blood disorders. When a person has porphyria, cells fail to change chemicals (porphyrins) to the substance (heme) that gives blood its color. Porphyrins then build up in the body. They show up in large amounts in stool and urine, causing the urine to be colored blue. They cause a number of problems, including strange behavior.

postnatal: Occurring after birth.

prenatal: Occurring before birth.

prophylaxis: To guard against or take precautions that will prevent either disease or a process that can lead to disease.

protein: A substance found in many parts of the body that helps the body to resist disease. Protein often, but not always, comes from animal products. High protein foods include meat, poultry, fish, eggs, hard cheese, cottage cheese, yogurt, and milk. Non-animal sources of protein are nuts and seeds, peanut butter, legumes, whole grains, and tofu.

prune belly syndrome: A condition of newborn babies. The baby has no abdominal muscles, so the stomach looks like a shriveled prune. Also called Eagle-Barrett syndrome.

R

reflux: A condition that occurs when gastric juices or small amounts of food from the stomach flow back into the esophagus and mouth. Also called regurgitation.

Rett's disorder: A progressive brain disease that only affects girls; produces repetitive hand movements and leads to loss of language and social skills.

Reye's syndrome: A rare but serious illness that usually occurs in children between the ages of three and 12 years. It can affect all organs of the body, but most often injures the brain and liver. Several studies have linked the use of aspirin to the development of Reye's syndrome in children recovering from influenza or chickenpox.

rhinoviruses: Viruses associated with the common cold (from the Greek *rhin*, meaning "nose"). Rhinoviruses cause an estimated 30 to 35 percent of all adult colds, and are most active in early fall, spring, and summer. More than 110 distinct rhinovirus types have been identified.

rotaviruses: Wheel-shaped (therefore named rota-) RNA viruses; the most common cause of infectious diarrhea in the United States, especially in children under age 2.

S

saliva: A mixture of water, protein, and salts that makes food easy to swallow and begins digestion.

*Salmonella***:** A bacterium that may cause intestinal infection and diarrhea.

seborrheic dermatitis: Over-activity of the sebaceous glands resulting in a scaly macular eruption that occurs primarily on the face, scalp (dandruff), and pubic and anal areas.

septicemia: Systemic disease caused by the spread of microorganisms and their toxins via the bloodstream.

sudden infant death syndrome (SIDS): The diagnosis given for the sudden death of an infant under one year of age that remains unexplained after a complete investigation, which includes an autopsy, examination of the death scene, and review of the symptoms or illnesses the infant had prior to dying and any other pertinent medical history; commonly known as crib death.

systolic pressure: The highest pressure to which blood pressure rises with the contraction of the ventricles.

T

tachypnea: Rapid breathing.

teratogen: A drug or other agent that causes abnormal fetal development.

thrush: Infection of the oral (mouth) tissues with *Candida albicans*.

toxoplasmosis: Disease caused by protozoan parasite. This prenatally acquired human infection from cat litter boxes can result in an infant with microcephalus or hydrocephalus at birth as well as other abnormalities.

tuberous sclerosis: A genetic condition that causes abnormal tissue growth in the brain and problems in other organs.

V

vaccine: A substance that contains antigenic components from an infectious organism; by stimulating an immune response (but not disease), it protects against subsequent infection by that organism.

VAERS (Vaccine Adverse Event Reporting System): A system for reporting events that are temporally associated with receipt of vaccine. To file a *Vaccine Adverse Event Report* form call 1-800-338-2382.

vas deferens: A duct in the reproductive system of the male. Carries sperm form the testes to the prostate gland.

VATER: A word made from the first letters of a group of birth defects. It is used when all of these birth defects affect the same child. The birth defects are: **V**ertebral defects, **A**nal malformations, **T**racheoesophageal fistula, **E**sophageal atresia, and **R**enal defects.

vitamins: Substances that occur in foods in small amounts and are necessary for the normal functioning of the body.

Chapter 81

Resources for Additional Information

Agency for Healthcare Research and Quality
Publications Clearinghouse
P.O. Box 8547
Silver Spring, MD 20907
Toll Free: (800) 358-9295 or (301) 594-1364
E-Mail: info@ahrq.gov
Web site: www.ahcpr.gov

American Academy of Dermatology
930 N Meacham Rd.
Schaumburg, IL 60173
Phone: (847) 330-0230
Toll Free: (888) 462-3376
Fax: (847) 330-8907
E-Mail: bazzolin@aad.org
Web site: www.aad.org

American Academy of Family Physicians
11400 Tomahawk Creek Parkway
Leawood, KS 66211-2672
Phone: (913) 906-6000
Toll Free: (800) 274-2237
Web site: www.familydoctor.org

Contact information in this chapter was verified and updated in April 2000.

American Academy of Neurology
1080 Montreal Avenue
St. Paul, Minnesota 55116
Phone: (651) 695-1949
Web site: www.aan.com

American Academy of Ophthalmology
P.O. Box 7424
San Francisco, CA 94120-7424
Phone: (415) 561-8500
Fax: (415) 561-8533
E-Mail: comm.@aao.org
Web site: www.eyenet.org

American Academy of Pediatrics
141 Northwest Point Blvd.
Elk Grove Village. IL 60007-1098
Phone: (847) 434-4000
Fax: (847) 434-8000
E-Mail: kidsdocs@aap.org
Web site: www.aap.org

American Medical Association
515 North State Street
Chicago, IL 60610
Phone: (312) 464-5000
Web site: www.ama-assn.org

American Optometric Association
243 N. Lindbergh Blvd.
St. Louis, MO 63141
Phone: (314) 991-4100
Toll Free: (800) 262-2210
Fax: (314) 991-4101
Web site: www.aoanet.org

American Speech-Language-Hearing Association
10801 Rockville Pike
Rockville, MD 20852
ASHA Action Center: (800) 638-8255
TTY: (301) 571-0457
Fax: (887) 541-5035

E-Mail: actioncenter@asha.org
Web site: www.asha.org

Association of SIDS and Infant Mortality Programs
Minnesota SIDS Center, Children's Hospitals and Clinics
2525 Chicago Ave. South
Minneapolis, MN 55404
Phone: (612) 813-6285
E-Mail: Kathleen.Fernbach@childrensch.org
Web site: www.asip1.org

BabyCenter
163 Freelon Street
San Francisco, CA 94107
Phone: (415) 537-0900
Fax: (415) 537-0909
E-Mail: annb@babcenter.com
Web site: www.babycenter.com

BabyWorld
5 The Piazza
Milton Park
Abindgon, OXON
OX14 4RR
UNITED KINGDOM
E-Mail: contactus@babyworld.com
Web site: www.babyworld.com

Centers for Disease Control and Prevention
1600 Clifton Rd.
Atlanta, GA 30333
Phone: (404) 639-3311
Toll Free: (800) 311-3435; Spanish: (800) 232-0233
Toll Free: (800) 232-2522 for Immunization Information
Website: www.cdc.gov

Children's Hospital Research Foundation
Children's Hospital Medical Center—Cincinnati
3333 Burnet Avenue
Cincinnati, OH 45229-3039
Phone: (513) 636-4200
Toll Free: (800) 344-CHMC
Fax: (513) 636-8452
Web site: www.chmcc.org

Drs 4 Kids
37 Stewart Street
Hewlett, NY 11557
Phone: (516) 596-1200
Fax: (516) 599-2229
E-Mail: drsuser@drs4kids.com
Web site: www.drs4kids.com

The Evan B. Donaldson Adoption Institute
120 Wall St., 20th Fl.
New York, NY 10005
Phone: (212) 269-5080
Fax: (212) 269-1962
E-Mail: dlmartin@adoptioninstitute.org
Web site: www.adoptioninstitute.org

Dr. Paula
E-Mail: webmaster@drpaula.com
Web site: www.drpaula.com

Dr. Greene's House Calls
Phone: (650) 358-8883
E-Mail: Cheryl@drgreene.com
Web site: www. drgreene.com

Food Safety Database, (The) National
Web site: www.foodsafety.ufl.edu

Kaiser Permanente
Web site: www.kaiserpermanente.org

KidsDoctor
P.O. Box 1091
Decour, GA 30031
Phone: (770) 234-4141
Web site: www.kidsdoctor.com

La Leche League
1400 N. Meacham Road
PO Box 4079
Schaumburg, IL 60173
Phone: (847) 519-7730
Fax: (847) 519-9585
E-Mail: PRDept@llli.org
Web site: www.lalecheleague.org

National Cancer Institute, Pediatric Branch
Bldg. 10, Room 13N240
10 Center Drive
Bethesda, MD 20892-1928
Phone: (301) 496-4256
Web site: www.nci.nih.gov

National Center for Education in Maternal and Child Health
2000 15th Street North, Suite 701
Arlington, VA 22201-2617
Phone: (703) 524-7802
Fax: (703) 524-9335
E-Mail: brightfutures@ncemch.org
Web site: www.brightfutures.org

National Child Abuse Hotline
(800) 422-4453; TTY: (800) 2-A-CHILD
Web site: www.childhelpusa.org

National Healthy Mothers, Healthy Babies Coalition
121 North Washington St., Suite 300
Alexandria, VA 22314
Phone: (703) 836-6110
Fax: (703) 836-3470
Web site: www.hmhb.org

National Information Center for Children and Youth with Disabilities (NICHCY)
P.O. Box 1492
Washington, DC 20013-1492
Toll Free: (800) 695-0285
TTY: (202) 884-8200; Fax: (202) 884-8441
E-Mail: nichcy@aed.org
Web site: www.nichcy.org

National Institute of Allergy and Infectious Diseases
Bethesda, MD 20892-2520
Web site: www.niaid.nih.gov

National Institute of Child Health and Human Development
Bldg. 31, Room 2A32, MSC 2425
31 Center Drive
Bethesda, MD 20892-2425
Phone: (301) 496-5133
Web site: www.nichd.nih.gov

National Institute of Dental and Craniofacial Research
31 Center Drive
MSC 2290
Bethesda, MD 20892-2290
Phone: (301) 496-4261
Web site: www.nidcr.nih.gov

National Institute of Neurological Disorders and Stroke
Bldg. 31, Room 8A06
31 Center Dr., MSC2540
Bethesda, MD 20892-2540
Toll Free: (800) 352-9424
Phone: (301) 496-5751
Web site: www.ninds.nih.gov

National Institute on Deafness and Other Communication Disorders
31 Center Drive
MSC 2320
Bethesda, MD 20892
Phone: (301) 496-7243
TTY: (301) 402-0252
Fax: (301) 402-0018
Web site: www.nih.gov/nidcd

National Immunization Information Hotline
Toll Free: (800) 232-2522 (English); (800) 232-0233 (Spanish)
Web site: www.cdc.gov/nip

The National Pediatric HIV Resource Center
Toll Free: (800) 362-0071
Web site: www.pedhivaids.org

National Resource Center for Health and Safety in Child Care
University of Colorado
Health Sciences Center at Fitzsimons
Campus Mail Stop F541
P.O. Box 6508
Aurora, CO 80045-0508
Toll Free: (800) 598-KIDS (5437)
E-Mail: Natl.child.res.ctr@UCHSC.edu
Web site: http://nrc.uchsc.edu

National Safe Kids Campaign
1301 Pennsylvania Ave., NW
Suite 1000
Washington, DC 20004-1707
Phone: (202) 662-0600
Fax: (202) 393-2072
E-Mail: Field@safekids.org
Web site: www.safekids.org

National SIDS Resource Center
2070 Chain Bridge Road
Suite 450
Vienna, VA 22181
Phone: (703) 821-8955
Fax: (703) 821-2098
E-Mail: sids@circsol.com
Web site: www.circsol.com/sids/

The Nemours Foundation
1600 Rockland Rd.
Wilmington, DE 19803
Phone: (302) 651-4046
Fax: (302) 651-4077
E-Mail: info@kidshealth.org
Web site: www.kidshealth.org

PARENTING Magazine
P.O. Box 56861
Boulder, CO 80323
Toll Free: (800) 234-0847
Web site: http://www.parenting.com/parenting

The Pediatric AIDS Foundation
2950 31st Street, #125
Santa Monica, CA 90405
Phone: (310) 314-1459
Fax: (310) 314-1469
E-Mail: info@pedAIDS.org
Web site: www.pedaids.org

SIDS Alliance (a national network of SIDS support groups)
1314 Bedford Avenue, Suite 210
Baltimore, MD 21208
Phone: (410) 653-8226
Fax: (410) 653-8709
E-Mail: sidshq@charm.net
Web site: www.sidsalliance.org

University of Virginia Health Sciences Center
Division of Pediatric Gastroenterology and Nutrition
P.O. Box 800386
Charlottesville, VA 22908
Phone: (804) 924-2457
Fax: (804) 924-8798
Web site: www.med.virginia.edu/medicine

U.S. Food and Drug Administration (FDA)
Web site: www.fda.gov

Vaccine Adverse Event Reporting System
(800) 822-7967
Web site: www.fda.gov/cber/vaers/vaers.htm

Vegetarian Society
Parkdale, Dunham Rd.
Altrincham, Cheshire UK WA14 4QG
Phone: 0161 925 2000
Fax: 0161 926 9182
E-Mail: info@vegsoc.org
Web site: www.vegsoc.org

Zero to Three
734 15th St., NW, Suite 1000
Washington, DC 20005
Phone: (202) 638-1144
Toll Free: (800) 899-4301
Web site: www.zerotothree.org

Index

Index

Page numbers followed by 'n' indicate a note. Page numbers in *italics* indicate a table or illustration.

Health Reference Series

COMPLETE CATALOG

AIDS Sourcebook, 1st Edition

Basic Information about AIDS and HIV Infection, Featuring Historical and Statistical Data, Current Research, Prevention, and Other Special Topics of Interest for Persons Living with AIDS

Along with Source Listings for Further Assistance

Edited by Karen Bellenir and Peter D. Dresser. 831 pages. 1995. 0-7808-0031-1. $78.

"One strength of this book is its practical emphasis. The intended audience is the lay reader . . . useful as an educational tool for health care providers who work with AIDS patients. Recommended for public libraries as well as hospital or academic libraries that collect consumer materials."
— *Bulletin of the Medical Library Association, Jan '96*

"This is the most comprehensive volume of its kind on an important medical topic. Highly recommended for all libraries."
— *Reference Book Review, '96*

"Very useful reference for all libraries."
— *Choice, Association of College and Research Libraries, Oct '95*

"There is a wealth of information here that can provide much educational assistance. It is a must book for all libraries and should be on the desk of each and every congressional leader. Highly recommended."
— *AIDS Book Review Journal, Aug '95*

"Recommended for most collections."
— *Library Journal, Jul '95*

AIDS Sourcebook, 2nd Edition

Basic Consumer Health Information about Acquired Immune Deficiency Syndrome (AIDS) and Human Immunodeficiency Virus (HIV) Infection, Featuring Updated Statistical Data, Reports on Recent Research and Prevention Initiatives, and Other Special Topics of Interest for Persons Living with AIDS, Including New Antiretroviral Treatment Options, Strategies for Combating Opportunistic Infections, Information about Clinical Trials, and More

Along with a Glossary of Important Terms and Resource Listings for Further Help and Information

Edited by Karen Bellenir. 751 pages. 1999. 0-7808-0225-X. $78.

"Highly recommended."
— *American Reference Books Annual, 2000*

"Excellent sourcebook. This continues to be a highly recommended book. There is no other book that provides as much information as this book provides."
— *AIDS Book Review Journal, Dec-Jan 2000*

"Recommended reference source."
— *Booklist, American Library Association, Dec '99*

"A solid text for college-level health libraries."
— *The Bookwatch, Aug '99*

Cited in *Reference Sources for Small and Medium-Sized Libraries, American Library Association, 1999*

Alcoholism Sourcebook

Basic Consumer Health Information about the Physical and Mental Consequences of Alcohol Abuse, Including Liver Disease, Pancreatitis, Wernicke-Korsakoff Syndrome (Alcoholic Dementia), Fetal Alcohol Syndrome, Heart Disease, Kidney Disorders, Gastrointestinal Problems, and Immune System Compromise and Featuring Facts about Addiction, Detoxification, Alcohol Withdrawal, Recovery, and the Maintenance of Sobriety

Along with a Glossary and Directories of Resources for Further Help and Information

Edited by Karen Bellenir. 635 pages. 2000. 0-7808-0325-6. $78.

SEE ALSO Drug Abuse Sourcebook, Substance Abuse Sourcebook

Allergies Sourcebook

Basic Information about Major Forms and Mechanisms of Common Allergic Reactions, Sensitivities, and Intolerances, Including Anaphylaxis, Asthma, Hives and Other Dermatologic Symptoms, Rhinitis, and Sinusitis

Along with Their Usual Triggers Like Animal Fur, Chemicals, Drugs, Dust, Foods, Insects, Latex, Pollen, and Poison Ivy, Oak, and Sumac; Plus Information on Prevention, Identification, and Treatment

Edited by Allan R. Cook. 611 pages. 1997. 0-7808-0036-2. $78.

Alternative Medicine Sourcebook

Basic Consumer Health Information about Alternatives to Conventional Medicine, Including Acupressure, Acupuncture, Aromatherapy, Ayurveda, Bioelectromagnetics, Environmental Medicine, Essence Therapy, Food and Nutrition Therapy, Herbal Therapy, Homeopathy, Imaging, Massage, Naturopathy, Reflexology, Relaxation and Meditation, Sound Therapy, Vitamin and Mineral Therapy, and Yoga, and More

Edited by Allan R. Cook. 737 pages. 1999. 0-7808-0200-4. $78.

"Recommended reference source."
— *Booklist, American Library Association, Feb '00*

Alzheimer's, Stroke & 29 Other Neurological Disorders Sourcebook, 1st Edition

Basic Information for the Layperson on 31 Diseases or Disorders Affecting the Brain and Nervous System, First Describing the Illness, Then Listing Symptoms, Diagnostic Methods, and Treatment Options, and Including Statistics on Incidences and Causes

Edited by Frank E. Bair. 579 pages. 1993. 1-55888-748-2. $78.

SEE ALSO Brain Disorders Sourcebook

■

Alzheimer's Disease Sourcebook, 2nd Edition

Basic Consumer Health Information about Alzheimer's Disease, Related Disorders, and Other Dementias, Including Multi-Infarct Dementia, AIDS-Related Dementia, Alcoholic Dementia, Huntington's Disease, Delirium, and Confusional States

Along with Reports Detailing Current Research Efforts in Prevention and Treatment, Long-Term Care Issues, and Listings of Sources for Additional Help and Information

Edited by Karen Bellenir. 524 pages. 1999. 0-7808-0223-3. $78.

Arthritis Sourcebook

Basic Consumer Health Information about Specific Forms of Arthritis and Related Disorders, Including Rheumatoid Arthritis, Osteoarthritis, Gout, Polymyalgia Rheumatica, Psoriatic Arthritis, Spondyloarthropathies, Juvenile Rheumatoid Arthritis, and Juvenile Ankylosing Spondylitis

Along with Information about Medical, Surgical, and Alternative Treatment Options, and Including Strategies for Coping with Pain, Fatigue, and Stress

Edited by Allan R. Cook. 550 pages. 1998. 0-7808-0201-2. $78.

■

Asthma Sourcebook

Basic Consumer Health Information about Asthma, Including Symptoms, Traditional and Nontraditional Remedies, Treatment Advances, Quality-of-Life Aids, Medical Research Updates, and the Role of Allergies, Exercise, Age, the Environment, and Genetics in the Development of Asthma

Along with Statistical Data, a Glossary, and Directories of Support Groups and Other Resources for Further Information

Edited by Annemarie S. Muth. 650 pages. 2000. 0-7808-0381-7. $78.

■

Back & Neck Disorders Sourcebook

Basic Information about Disorders and Injuries of the Spinal Cord and Vertebrae, Including Facts on Chiropractic Treatment, Surgical Interventions, Paralysis, and Rehabilitation

Along with Advice for Preventing Back Trouble

Edited by Karen Bellenir. 548 pages. 1997. 0-7808-0202-0. $78.

■

Blood & Circulatory Disorders Sourcebook

Basic Information about Blood and Its Components, Anemias, Leukemias, Bleeding Disorders, and Circulatory Disorders, Including Aplastic Anemia, Thalassemia, Sickle-Cell Disease, Hemochromatosis, Hemophilia, Von Willebrand Disease, and Vascular Diseases

Along with a Special Section on Blood Transfusions and Blood Supply Safety, a Glossary, and Source Listings for Further Help and Information

Edited by Karen Bellenir and Linda M. Shin. 554 pages. 1998. 0-7808-0203-9. $78.

Brain Disorders Sourcebook

Basic Consumer Health Information about Strokes, Epilepsy, Amyotrophic Lateral Sclerosis (ALS/Lou Gehrig's Disease), Parkinson's Disease, Brain Tumors, Cerebral Palsy, Headache, Tourette Syndrome, and More

Along with Statistical Data, Treatment and Rehabilitation Options, Coping Strategies, Reports on Current Research Initiatives, a Glossary, and Resource Listings for Additional Help and Information

Edited by Karen Bellenir. 481 pages. 1999. 0-7808-0229-2. $78.

SEE ALSO Alzheimer's, Stroke & 29 Other Neurological Disorders Sourcebook, 1st Edition

Breast Cancer Sourcebook

Basic Consumer Health Information about Breast Cancer, Including Diagnostic Methods, Treatment Options, Alternative Therapies, Help and Self-Help Information, Related Health Concerns, Statistical and Demographic Data, and Facts for Men with Breast Cancer

Along with Reports on Current Research Initiatives, a Glossary of Related Medical Terms, and a Directory of Sources for Further Help and Information

Edited by Edward J. Prucha. 600 pages. 2000. 0-7808-0244-6. $78.

SEE ALSO Cancer Sourcebook for Women, 1st and 2nd Editions, Women's Health Concerns Sourcebook

Burns Sourcebook

Basic Consumer Health Information about Various Types of Burns and Scalds, Including Flame, Heat, Cold, Electrical, Chemical, and Sun Burns

Along with Information on Short-Term and Long-Term Treatments, Tissue Reconstruction, Plastic Surgery, Prevention Suggestions, and First Aid

Edited by Allan R. Cook. 604 pages. 1999. 0-7808-0204-7. $78.

SEE ALSO Skin Disorders Sourcebook

Cancer Sourcebook, 1st Edition

Basic Information on Cancer Types, Symptoms, Diagnostic Methods, and Treatments, Including Statistics on Cancer Occurrences Worldwide and the Risks Associated with Known Carcinogens and Activities

Edited by Frank E. Bair. 932 pages. 1990. 1-55888-888-8. $78.

Cited in *Reference Sources for Small and Medium-Sized Libraries, American Library Association, 1999*

New Cancer Sourcebook, 2nd Edition

Basic Information about Major Forms and Stages of Cancer, Featuring Facts about Primary and Secondary Tumors of the Respiratory, Nervous, Lymphatic, Circulatory, Skeletal, and Gastrointestinal Systems, and Specific Organs; Statistical and Demographic Data; Treatment Options; and Strategies for Coping

Edited by Allan R. Cook. 1,313 pages. 1996. 0-7808-0041-9. $78.

"The amount of factual and useful information is extensive. The writing is very clear, geared to general readers. Recommended for all levels."
— *Choice, Association of College and Research Libraries, Jan '97*

Cancer Sourcebook, 3rd Edition

Basic Consumer Health Information about Major Forms and Stages of Cancer, Featuring Facts about Primary and Secondary Tumors of the Respiratory, Nervous, Lymphatic, Circulatory, Skeletal, and Gastrointestinal Systems, and Specific Organs

Along with Statistical and Demographic Data, Treatment Options, Strategies for Coping, a Glossary, and a Directory of Sources for Additional Help and Information

Edited by Edward J. Prucha. 1,069 pages. 2000. 0-7808-0227-6. $78.

Cancer Sourcebook for Women, 1st Edition

Basic Information about Specific Forms of Cancer That Affect Women, Featuring Facts about Breast Cancer, Cervical Cancer, Ovarian Cancer, Cancer of the Uterus and Uterine Sarcoma, Cancer of the Vagina, and Cancer of the Vulva; Statistical and Demographic Data; Treatments, Self-Help Management Suggestions, and Current Research Initiatives

Edited by Allan R. Cook and Peter D. Dresser. 524 pages. 1996. 0-7808-0076-1. $78.

". . . written in easily understandable, non-technical language. Recommended for public libraries or hospital and academic libraries that collect patient education or consumer health materials."
— *Medical Reference Services Quarterly, Spring '97*

"Would be of value in a consumer health library. . . . written with the health care consumer in mind. Medical jargon is at a minimum, and medical terms are explained in clear, understandable sentences."
— *Bulletin of the Medical Library Association, Oct '96*

"The availability under one cover of all these pertinent publications, grouped under cohesive headings, makes this certainly a most useful sourcebook."
— *Choice, Association of College and Research Libraries, Jun '96*

"Presents a comprehensive knowledge base for general readers. Men and women both benefit from the gold mine of information nestled between the two covers of this book. Recommended."
— *Academic Library Book Review, Summer '96*

"This timely book is highly recommended for consumer health and patient education collections in all libraries." — *Library Journal, Apr '96*

SEE ALSO Breast Cancer Sourcebook, Women's Health Concerns Sourcebook

Cancer Sourcebook for Women, 2nd Edition

Basic Consumer Health Information about Specific Forms of Cancer That Affect Women, Including Cervical Cancer, Ovarian Cancer, Endometrial Cancer, Uterine Sarcoma, Vaginal Cancer, Vulvar Cancer, and Gestational Trophoblastic Tumor; and Featuring Statistical Information, Facts about Tests and Treatments, a Glossary of Cancer Terms, and an Extensive List of Additional Resources

Edited by Edward J. Prucha. 600 pages. 2000. 0-7808-0226-8. $78.

SEE ALSO Breast Cancer Sourcebook, Women's Health Concerns Sourcebook

Cardiovascular Diseases & Disorders Sourcebook, 1st Edition

Basic Information about Cardiovascular Diseases and Disorders, Featuring Facts about the Cardiovascular System, Demographic and Statistical Data, Descriptions of Pharmacological and Surgical Interventions, Lifestyle Modifications, and a Special Section Focusing on Heart Disorders in Children

Edited by Karen Bellenir and Peter D. Dresser. 683 pages. 1995. 0-7808-0032-X. $78.

". . . comprehensive format provides an extensive overview on this subject."
— *Choice, Association of College and Research Libraries, Jun '96*

". . . an easily understood, complete, up-to-date resource. This well executed public health tool will make valuable information available to those that need it most, patients and their families. The typeface, sturdy non-reflective paper, and library binding add a feel of quality found wanting in other publications. Highly recommended for academic and general libraries. "
— *Academic Library Book Review, Summer '96*

SEE ALSO Healthy Heart Sourcebook for Women, Heart Diseases & Disorders Sourcebook, 2nd Edition

Communication Disorders Sourcebook

Basic Information about Deafness and Hearing Loss, Speech and Language Disorders, Voice Disorders, Balance and Vestibular Disorders, and Disorders of Smell, Taste, and Touch

Edited by Linda M. Ross. 533 pages. 1996. 0-7808-0077-X. $78.

"This is skillfully edited and is a welcome resource for the layperson. It should be found in every public and medical library." — *Booklist Health Sciences Supplement, American Library Association, Oct '97*

Congenital Disorders Sourcebook

Basic Information about Disorders Acquired during Gestation, Including Spina Bifida, Hydrocephalus, Cerebral Palsy, Heart Defects, Craniofacial Abnormalities, Fetal Alcohol Syndrome, and More

Along with Current Treatment Options and Statistical Data

Edited by Karen Bellenir. 607 pages. 1997. 0-7808-0205-5. $78.

"Recommended reference source."
— *Booklist, American Library Association, Oct '97*

SEE ALSO Pregnancy & Birth Sourcebook

■

Consumer Issues in Health Care Sourcebook

Basic Information about Health Care Fundamentals and Related Consumer Issues, Including Exams and Screening Tests, Physician Specialties, Choosing a Doctor, Using Prescription and Over-the-Counter Medications Safely, Avoiding Health Scams, Managing Common Health Risks in the Home, Care Options for Chronically or Terminally Ill Patients, and a List of Resources for Obtaining Help and Further Information

Edited by Karen Bellenir. 618 pages. 1998. 0-7808-0221-7. $78.

"Both public and academic libraries will want to have a copy in their collection for readers who are interested in self-education on health issues."
— *American Reference Books Annual, 2000*

"The editor has researched the literature from government agencies and others, saving readers the time and effort of having to do the research themselves. Recommended for public libraries."
— *Reference and User Services Quarterly, American Library Association, Spring '99*

"Recommended reference source."
— *Booklist, American Library Association, Dec '98*

■

Contagious & Non-Contagious Infectious Diseases Sourcebook

Basic Information about Contagious Diseases like Measles, Polio, Hepatitis B, and Infectious Mononucleosis, and Non-Contagious Infectious Diseases like Tetanus and Toxic Shock Syndrome, and Diseases Occurring as Secondary Infections Such as Shingles and Reye Syndrome

Along with Vaccination, Prevention, and Treatment Information, and a Section Describing Emerging Infectious Disease Threats

Edited by Karen Bellenir and Peter D. Dresser. 566 pages. 1996. 0-7808-0075-3. $78.

Death & Dying Sourcebook

Basic Consumer Health Information for the Layperson about End-of-Life Care and Related Ethical and Legal Issues, Including Chief Causes of Death, Autopsies, Pain Management for the Terminally Ill, Life Support Systems, Insurance, Euthanasia, Assisted Suicide, Hospice Programs, Living Wills, Funeral Planning, Counseling, Mourning, Organ Donation, and Physician Training

Along with Statistical Data, a Glossary, and Listings of Sources for Further Help and Information

Edited by Annemarie S. Muth. 641 pages. 1999. 0-7808-0230-6. $78.

"This book is a definite must for all those involved in end-of-life care." — *Doody's Review Service, 2000*

■

Diabetes Sourcebook, 1st Edition

Basic Information about Insulin-Dependent and Non-insulin-Dependent Diabetes Mellitus, Gestational Diabetes, and Diabetic Complications, Symptoms, Treatment, and Research Results, Including Statistics on Prevalence, Morbidity, and Mortality

Along with Source Listings for Further Help and Information

Edited by Karen Bellenir and Peter D. Dresser. 827 pages. 1994. 1-55888-751-2. $78.

". . . very informative and understandable for the layperson without being simplistic. It provides a comprehensive overview for laypersons who want a general understanding of the disease or who want to focus on various aspects of the disease."
— *Bulletin of the Medical Library Association, Jan '96*

■

Diabetes Sourcebook, 2nd Edition

Basic Consumer Health Information about Type 1 Diabetes (Insulin-Dependent or Juvenile-Onset Diabetes), Type 2 (Noninsulin-Dependent or Adult-Onset Diabetes), Gestational Diabetes, and Related Disorders, Including Diabetes Prevalence Data, Management Issues, the Role of Diet and Exercise in Controlling Diabetes, Insulin and Other Diabetes Medicines, and Complications of Diabetes Such as Eye Diseases, Periodontal Disease, Amputation, and End-Stage Renal Disease

Along with Reports on Current Research Initiatives, a Glossary, and Resource Listings for Further Help and Information

Edited by Karen Bellenir. 688 pages. 1998. 0-7808-0224-1. $78.

"This comprehensive book is an excellent addition for high school, academic, medical, and public libraries. This volume is highly recommended."
— *American Reference Books Annual, 2000*

"An invaluable reference." — *Library Journal, May '00*

Selected as one of the 250 "Best Health Sciences Books of 1999." — *Doody's Rating Service, Mar-Apr 2000*

"Recommended reference source."
— *Booklist, American Library Association, Feb '99*

". . . provides reliable mainstream medical information . . . belongs on the shelves of any library with a consumer health collection." — *E-Streams, Sep '99*

"Provides useful information for the general public."
— *Healthlines, University of Michigan Health Management Research Center, Sep/Oct '99*

Diet & Nutrition Sourcebook, 1st Edition

Basic Information about Nutrition, Including the Dietary Guidelines for Americans, the Food Guide Pyramid, and Their Applications in Daily Diet, Nutritional Advice for Specific Age Groups, Current Nutritional Issues and Controversies, the New Food Label and How to Use It to Promote Healthy Eating, and Recent Developments in Nutritional Research

Edited by Dan R. Harris. 662 pages. 1996. 0-7808-0084-2. $78.

"Useful reference as a food and nutrition sourcebook for the general consumer." — *Booklist Health Sciences Supplement, American Library Association, Oct '97*

"Recommended for public libraries and medical libraries that receive general information requests on nutrition. It is readable and will appeal to those interested in learning more about healthy dietary practices."
— *Medical Reference Services Quarterly, Fall '97*

"An abundance of medical and social statistics is translated into readable information geared toward the general reader." — *Bookwatch, Mar '97*

"With dozens of questionable diet books on the market, it is so refreshing to find a reliable and factual reference book. Recommended to aspiring professionals, librarians, and others seeking and giving reliable dietary advice. An excellent compilation." — *Choice, Association of College and Research Libraries, Feb '97*

SEE ALSO Digestive Diseases & Disorders Sourcebook, Gastrointestinal Diseases & Disorders Sourcebook

Diet & Nutrition Sourcebook, 2nd Edition

Basic Consumer Health Information about Dietary Guidelines, Recommended Daily Intake Values, Vitamins, Minerals, Fiber, Fat, Weight Control, Dietary Supplements, and Food Additives

Along with Special Sections on Nutrition Needs throughout Life and Nutrition for People with Such Specific Medical Concerns as Allergies, High Blood Cholesterol, Hypertension, Diabetes, Celiac Disease, Seizure Disorders, Phenylketonuria (PKU), Cancer, and Eating Disorders, and Including Reports on Current Nutrition Research and Source Listings for Additional Help and Information

Edited by Karen Bellenir. 650 pages. 1999. 0-7808-0228-4. $78.

"This reference document should be in any public library, but it would be a very good guide for beginning students in the health sciences. If the other books in this publisher's series are as good as this, they should all be in the health sciences collections."
— *American Reference Books Annual, 2000*

"Recommended reference source."
— *Booklist, American Library Association, Dec '99*

SEE ALSO Digestive Diseases & Disorders Sourcebook, Gastrointestinal Diseases & Disorders Sourcebook

Digestive Diseases & Disorders Sourcebook

Basic Consumer Health Information about Diseases and Disorders that Impact the Upper and Lower Digestive System, Including Celiac Disease, Constipation, Crohn's Disease, Cyclic Vomiting Syndrome, Diarrhea, Diverticulosis and Diverticulitis, Gallstones, Heartburn, Hemorrhoids, Hernias, Indigestion (Dyspepsia), Irritable Bowel Syndrome, Lactose Intolerance, Ulcers, and More

Along with Information about Medications and Other Treatments, Tips for Maintaining a Healthy Digestive Tract, a Glossary, and Directory of Digestive Diseases Organizations

Edited by Karen Bellenir. 335 pages. 1999. 0-7808-0327-2. $48.

"Recommended reference source."
— *Booklist, American Library Association, May '00*

SEE ALSO Diet & Nutrition Sourcebook, 1st and 2nd Editions, Gastrointestinal Diseases & Disorders Sourcebook

Disabilities Sourcebook

Basic Consumer Health Information about Physical and Psychiatric Disabilities, Including Descriptions of Major Causes of Disability, Assistive and Adaptive Aids, Workplace Issues, and Accessibility Concerns

Along with Information about the Americans with Disabilities Act, a Glossary, and Resources for Additional Help and Information

Edited by Dawn D. Matthews. 616 pages. 2000. 0-7808-0389-2. $78.

"Recommended reference source."
— *Booklist, American Library Association, Jul '00*

"An involving, invaluable handbook."
— *The Bookwatch, May '00*

Domestic Violence & Child Abuse Sourcebook

Basic Information about Spousal/ Partner, Child, and Elder Physical, Emotional, and Sexual Abuse, Teen Dating Violence, and Stalking, Including Information about Hotlines, Safe Houses, Safety Plans, and Other Resources for Support and Assistance, Community Initiatives, and Reports on Current Directions in Research and Treatment

Along with a Glossary, Sources for Further Reading, and Governmental and Non-Governmental Organizations Contact Information

Edited by Helene Henderson. 600 pages. 2000. 0-7808-0235-7. $78.

Drug Abuse Sourcebook

Basic Consumer Health Information about Illicit Substances of Abuse and the Diversion of Prescription Medications, Including Depressants, Hallucinogens, Inhalants, Marijuana, Narcotics, Stimulants, and Anabolic Steroids

Along with Facts about Related Health Risks, Treatment Issues, and Substance Abuse Prevention Programs, a Glossary of Terms, Statistical Data, and Directories of Hotline Services, Self-Help Groups, and Organizations Able to Provide Further Information

Edited by Karen Bellenir. 629 pages. 2000. 0-7808-0242-X. $78.

SEE ALSO Alcoholism Sourcebook, Substance Abuse Sourcebook

Ear, Nose & Throat Disorders Sourcebook

Basic Information about Disorders of the Ears, Nose, Sinus Cavities, Pharynx, and Larynx, Including Ear Infections, Tinnitus, Vestibular Disorders, Allergic and Non-Allergic Rhinitis, Sore Throats, Tonsillitis, and Cancers That Affect the Ears, Nose, Sinuses, and Throat

Along with Reports on Current Research Initiatives, a Glossary of Related Medical Terms, and a Directory of Sources for Further Help and Information

Edited by Karen Bellenir and Linda M. Shin. 576 pages. 1998. 0-7808-0206-3. $78.

"Overall, this sourcebook is helpful for the consumer seeking information on ENT issues. It is recommended for public libraries."
—American Reference Books Annual, 1999

"Recommended reference source."
—Booklist, American Library Association, Dec '98

Endocrine & Metabolic Disorders Sourcebook

Basic Information for the Layperson about Pancreatic and Insulin-Related Disorders Such as Pancreatitis, Diabetes, and Hypoglycemia; Adrenal Gland Disorders Such as Cushing's Syndrome, Addison's Disease, and Congenital Adrenal Hyperplasia; Pituitary Gland Disorders Such as Growth Hormone Deficiency, Acromegaly, and Pituitary Tumors; Thyroid Disorders Such as Hypothyroidism, Graves' Disease, Hashimoto's Disease, and Goiter; Hyperparathyroidism; and Other Diseases and Syndromes of Hormone Imbalance or Metabolic Dysfunction

Along with Reports on Current Research Initiatives

Edited by Linda M. Shin. 574 pages. 1998. 0-7808-0207-1. $78.

"Omnigraphics has produced another needed resource for health information consumers."
—American Reference Books Annual, 2000

"Recommended reference source."
—Booklist, American Library Association, Dec '98

Environmentally Induced Disorders Sourcebook

Basic Information about Diseases and Syndromes Linked to Exposure to Pollutants and Other Substances in Outdoor and Indoor Environments Such as Lead, Asbestos, Formaldehyde, Mercury, Emissions, Noise, and More

Edited by Allan R. Cook. 620 pages. 1997. 0-7808-0083-4. $78.

"Recommended reference source."
—Booklist, American Library Association, Sep '98

"This book will be a useful addition to anyone's library." *—Choice Health Sciences Supplement, Association of College and Research Libraries, May '98*

". . . a good survey of numerous environmentally induced physical disorders . . . a useful addition to anyone's library."
—Doody's Health Sciences Book Reviews, Jan '98

". . . provide[s] introductory information from the best authorities around. Since this volume covers topics that potentially affect everyone, it will surely be one of the most frequently consulted volumes in the *Health Reference Series*." *—Rettig on Reference, Nov '97*

Family Planning Sourcebook

Basic Consumer Health Information about Planning for Pregnancy and Contraception, Including Traditional Methods, Barrier Methods, Permanent Methods, Future Methods, Emergency Contraception, and Birth Control Choices for Women at Each Stage of Life

Along with Statistics, Glossary, and Sources of Additional Information

Edited by Amy Marcaccio Keyzer. 600 pages. 2000. 0-7808-0379-5. $78.

SEE ALSO Pregnancy & Birth Sourcebook

Fitness & Exercise Sourcebook

Basic Information on Fitness and Exercise, Including Fitness Activities for Specific Age Groups, Exercise for People with Specific Medical Conditions, How to Begin a Fitness Program in Running, Walking, Swimming, Cycling, and Other Athletic Activities, and Recent Research in Fitness and Exercise

Edited by Dan R. Harris. 663 pages. 1996. 0-7808-0186-5. $78.

"A good resource for general readers."
— Choice, Association of College and Research Libraries, Nov '97

"The perennial popularity of the topic . . . make this an appealing selection for public libraries."
— Rettig on Reference, Jun/Jul '97

Food & Animal Borne Diseases Sourcebook

Basic Information about Diseases That Can Be Spread to Humans through the Ingestion of Contaminated Food or Water or by Contact with Infected Animals and Insects, Such as Botulism, E. Coli, Hepatitis A, Trichinosis, Lyme Disease, and Rabies

Along with Information Regarding Prevention and Treatment Methods, and Including a Special Section for International Travelers Describing Diseases Such as Cholera, Malaria, Travelers' Diarrhea, and Yellow Fever, and Offering Recommendations for Avoiding Illness

Edited by Karen Bellenir and Peter D. Dresser. 535 pages. 1995. 0-7808-0033-8. $78.

"Targeting general readers and providing them with a single, comprehensive source of information on selected topics, this book continues, with the excellent caliber of its predecessors, to catalog topical information on health matters of general interest. Readable and thorough, this valuable resource is highly recommended for all libraries."
— Academic Library Book Review, Summer '96

"A comprehensive collection of authoritative information."
— Emergency Medical Services, Oct '95

Food Safety Sourcebook

Basic Consumer Health Information about the Safe Handling of Meat, Poultry, Seafood, Eggs, Fruit Juices, and Other Food Items, and Facts about Pesticides, Drinking Water, Food Safety Overseas, and the Onset, Duration, and Symptoms of Foodborne Illnesses, Including Types of Pathogenic Bacteria, Parasitic Protozoa, Worms, Viruses, and Natural Toxins

Along with the Role of the Consumer, the Food Handler, and the Government in Food Safety; a Glossary, and Resources for Additional Help and Information

Edited by Dawn D. Matthews. 339 pages. 1999. 0-7808-0326-4. $48.

"This book takes the complex issues of food safety and foodborne pathogens and presents them in an easily understood manner. [It does] an excellent job of covering a large and often confusing topic."
— American Reference Books Annual, 2000

"Recommended reference source."
— Booklist, American Library Association, May '00

Forensic Medicine Sourcebook

Basic Consumer Information for the Layperson about Forensic Medicine, Including Crime Scene Investigation, Evidence Collection and Analysis, Expert Testimony, Computer-Aided Criminal Identification, Digital Imaging in the Courtroom, DNA Profiling, Accident Reconstruction, Autopsies, Ballistics, Drugs and Explosives Detection, Latent Fingerprints, Product Tampering, and Questioned Document Examination

Along with Statistical Data, a Glossary of Forensics Terminology, and Listings of Sources for Further Help and Information

Edited by Annemarie S. Muth. 574 pages. 1999. 0-7808-0232-2. $78.

"There are several items that make this book attractive to consumers who are seeking certain forensic data. . . . This is a useful current source for those seeking general forensic medical answers."
— American Reference Books Annual, 2000

"Recommended for public libraries."
— Reference & User Services Quarterly, American Library Association, Spring 2000

"Recommended reference source."
— Booklist, American Library Association, Feb '00

"A wealth of information, useful statistics, references are up-to-date and extremely complete. This wonderful collection of data will help students who are interested in a career in any type of forensic field. It is a great resource for attorneys who need information about types of expert witnesses needed in a particular case. It also offers useful information for fiction and nonfiction writers whose work involves a crime. A fascinating compilation. All levels."
— Choice, Association of College and Research Libraries, Jan 2000

Gastrointestinal Diseases & Disorders Sourcebook

Basic Information about Gastroesophageal Reflux Disease (Heartburn), Ulcers, Diverticulosis, Irritable Bowel Syndrome, Crohn's Disease, Ulcerative Colitis, Diarrhea, Constipation, Lactose Intolerance, Hemorrhoids, Hepatitis, Cirrhosis, and Other Digestive Problems, Featuring Statistics, Descriptions of Symptoms, and Current Treatment Methods of Interest for Persons Living with Upper and Lower Gastrointestinal Maladies

Edited by Linda M. Ross. 413 pages. 1996. 0-7808-0078-8. $78.

"... very readable form. The successful editorial work that brought this material together into a useful and understandable reference makes accessible to all readers information that can help them more effectively understand and obtain help for digestive tract problems."
— *Choice, Association of College and Research Libraries, Feb '97*

SEE ALSO *Diet & Nutrition Sourcebook, 1st and 2nd Editions, Digestive Diseases & Disorders Sourcebook*

Genetic Disorders Sourcebook, 1st Edition

Basic Information about Heritable Diseases and Disorders Such as Down Syndrome, PKU, Hemophilia, Von Willebrand Disease, Gaucher Disease, Tay-Sachs Disease, and Sickle-Cell Disease, Along with Information about Genetic Screening, Gene Therapy, Home Care, and Including Source Listings for Further Help and Information on More Than 300 Disorders

Edited by Karen Bellenir. 642 pages. 1996. 0-7808-0034-6. $78.

"Recommended for undergraduate libraries or libraries that serve the public."
— *Science & Technology Libraries, Vol. 18, No. 1, '99*

"Provides essential medical information to both the general public and those diagnosed with a serious or fatal genetic disease or disorder."
— *Choice, Association of College and Research Libraries, Jan '97*

"Geared toward the lay public. It would be well placed in all public libraries and in those hospital and medical libraries in which access to genetic references is limited." — *Doody's Health Sciences Book Review, Oct '96*

Genetic Disorders Sourcebook, 2nd Edition

Basic Consumer Information about Hereditary Diseases and Disorders, Including Cystic Fibrosis, Down Syndrome, Hemophilia, Huntington's Disease, Sickle Cell Anemia, and More

Along with Facts about Genes, Gene Therapy, Genetic Screening, Ethics of Gene Testing, Genetic Counseling, a Glossary of Genetic Terminology, and a Resource List for Help, Support, and Further Information

Edited by Kathy Massimini. 650 pages. 2000. 0-7808-0241-1. $78.

Head Trauma Sourcebook

Basic Information for the Layperson about Open-Head and Closed-Head Injuries, Treatment Advances, Recovery, and Rehabilitation

Along with Reports on Current Research Initiatives

Edited by Karen Bellenir. 414 pages. 1997. 0-7808-0208-X. $78.

Health Insurance Sourcebook

Basic Information about Managed Care Organizations, Traditional Fee-for-Service Insurance, Insurance Portability and Pre-Existing Conditions Clauses, Medicare, Medicaid, Social Security, and Military Health Care

Along with Information about Insurance Fraud

Edited by Wendy Wilcox. 530 pages. 1997. 0-7808-0222-5. $78.

"Particularly useful because it brings much of this information together in one volume. This book will be a handy reference source in the health sciences library, hospital library, college and university library, and medium to large public library."
— *Medical Reference Services Quarterly, Fall '98*

Awarded "Books of the Year Award"
— *American Journal of Nursing, 1997*

"The layout of the book is particularly helpful as it provides easy access to reference material. A most useful addition to the vast amount of information about health insurance. The use of data from U.S. government agencies is most commendable. Useful in a library or learning center for healthcare professional students."
— *Doody's Health Sciences Book Reviews, Nov '97*

Health Resources Sourcebook

Basic Consumer Health Information about Sources of Medical Assistance, Featuring an Annotated Directory of Private and Public Consumer Health Organizations and Listings of Other Resources, Including Hospitals, Hospices, and State Medical Associations

Along with Guidelines for Locating and Evaluating Health Information

Edited by Dawn D. Matthews. 500 pages. 2000. 0-7808-0328-0. $78.

Healthy Aging Sourcebook

Basic Consumer Health Information about Maintaining Health through the Aging Process, Including Advice on Nutrition, Exercise, and Sleep, Help in Making Decisions about Midlife Issues and Retirement, and Guidance Concerning Practical and Informed Choices in Health Consumerism

Along with Data Concerning the Theories of Aging, Different Experiences in Aging by Minority Groups, and Facts about Aging Now and Aging in the Future; and Featuring a Glossary, a Guide to Consumer Help, Additional Suggested Reading, and Practical Resource Directory

Edited by Jenifer Swanson. 536 pages. 1999. 0-7808-0390-6. $78.

"Recommended reference source."
— *Booklist, American Library Association, Feb '00*

SEE ALSO *Physical & Mental Issues in Aging Sourcebook*

Healthy Heart Sourcebook for Women

Basic Consumer Health Information about Cardiac Issues Specific to Women, Including Facts about Major Risk Factors and Prevention, Treatment and Control Strategies, and Important Dietary Issues

Along with a Special Section Regarding the Pros and Cons of Hormone Replacement Therapy and Its Impact on Heart Health, and Additional Help, Including Recipes, a Glossary, and a Directory of Resources

Edited by Dawn D. Matthews. 336 pages. 2000. 0-7808-0329-9. $48.

SEE ALSO *Cardiovascular Diseases & Disorders Sourcebook, 1st Edition, Heart Diseases & Disorders Sourcebook, 2nd Edition, Women's Health Concerns Sourcebook*

Heart Diseases & Disorders Sourcebook, 2nd Edition

Basic Consumer Health Information about Heart Attacks, Angina, Rhythm Disorders, Heart Failure, Valve Disease, Congenital Heart Disorders, and More, Including Descriptions of Surgical Procedures and Other Interventions, Medications, Cardiac Rehabilitation, Risk Identification, and Prevention Tips

Along with Statistical Data, Reports on Current Research Initiatives, a Glossary of Cardiovascular Terms, and Resource Directory

Edited by Karen Bellenir. 612 pages. 2000. 0-7808-0238-1. $78.

SEE ALSO *Cardiovascular Diseases & Disorders Sourcebook, 1st Edition, Healthy Heart Sourcebook for Women*

Immune System Disorders Sourcebook

Basic Information about Lupus, Multiple Sclerosis, Guillain-Barré Syndrome, Chronic Granulomatous Disease, and More

Along with Statistical and Demographic Data and Reports on Current Research Initiatives

Edited by Allan R. Cook. 608 pages. 1997. 0-7808-0209-8. $78.

Infant & Toddler Health Sourcebook

Basic Consumer Health Information about the Physical and Mental Development of Newborns, Infants, and Toddlers, Including Neonatal Concerns, Nutrition Recommendations, Immunization Schedules, Common Pediatric Disorders, Assessments and Milestones, Safety Tips, and Advice for Parents and Other Caregivers

Along with a Glossary of Terms and Resource Listings for Additional Help

Edited by Jenifer Swanson. 585 pages. 2000. 0-7808-0246-2. $78.

Kidney & Urinary Tract Diseases & Disorders Sourcebook

Basic Information about Kidney Stones, Urinary Incontinence, Bladder Disease, End Stage Renal Disease, Dialysis, and More

Along with Statistical and Demographic Data and Reports on Current Research Initiatives

Edited by Linda M. Ross. 602 pages. 1997. 0-7808-0079-6. $78.

Learning Disabilities Sourcebook

Basic Information about Disorders Such as Dyslexia, Visual and Auditory Processing Deficits, Attention Deficit/Hyperactivity Disorder, and Autism

Along with Statistical and Demographic Data, Reports on Current Research Initiatives, an Explanation of the Assessment Process, and a Special Section for Adults with Learning Disabilities

Edited by Linda M. Shin. 579 pages. 1998. 0-7808-0210-1. $78.

Named "Oustanding Reference Book of 1999."
— *New York Public Library, Feb 2000*

"An excellent candidate for inclusion in a public library reference section. It's a great source of information. Teachers will also find the book useful. Definitely worth reading."
— *Journal of Adolescent & Adult Literacy, Feb 2000*

"Readable . . . provides a solid base of information regarding successful techniques used with individuals who have learning disabilities, as well as practical suggestions for educators and family members. Clear language, concise descriptions, and pertinent information for contacting multiple resources add to the strength of this book as a useful tool."
— *Choice, Association of College and Research Libraries, Feb '99*

"Recommended reference source."
— *Booklist, American Library Association, Sep '98*

"This is a useful resource for libraries and for those who don't have the time to identify and locate the individual publications."
— *Disability Resources Monthly, Sep '98*

Liver Disorders Sourcebook

Basic Consumer Health Information about the Liver and How It Works; Liver Diseases, Including Cancer, Cirrhosis, Hepatitis, and Toxic and Drug Related Diseases; Tips for Maintaining a Healthy Liver; Laboratory Tests, Radiology Tests, and Facts about Liver Transplantation

Along with a Section on Support Groups, a Glossary, and Resource Listings

Edited by Joyce Brennfleck Shannon. 591 pages. 2000. 0-7808-0383-3. $78.

"**Recommended reference source.**"
—*Booklist, American Library Association, Jun '00*

Medical Tests Sourcebook

Basic Consumer Health Information about Medical Tests, Including Periodic Health Exams, General Screening Tests, Tests You Can Do at Home, Findings of the U.S. Preventive Services Task Force, X-ray and Radiology Tests, Electrical Tests, Tests of Blood and Other Body Fluids and Tissues, Scope Tests, Lung Tests, Genetic Tests, Pregnancy Tests, Newborn Screening Tests, Sexually Transmitted Disease Tests, and Computer Aided Diagnoses

Along with a Section on Paying for Medical Tests, a Glossary, and Resource Listings

Edited by Joyce Brennfleck Shannon. 691 pages. 1999. 0-7808-0243-8. $78.

"**A valuable reference guide.**"
—*American Reference Books Annual, 2000*

"**Recommended for hospital and health sciences libraries with consumer health collections.**"
—*E-Streams, Mar '00*

"**This is an overall excellent reference with a wealth of general knowledge that may aid those who are reluctant to get vital tests performed.**"
—*Today's Librarian, Jan 2000*

Men's Health Concerns Sourcebook

Basic Information about Health Issues That Affect Men, Featuring Facts about the Top Causes of Death in Men, Including Heart Disease, Stroke, Cancers, Prostate Disorders, Chronic Obstructive Pulmonary Disease, Pneumonia and Influenza, Human Immunodeficiency Virus and Acquired Immune Deficiency Syndrome, Diabetes Mellitus, Stress, Suicide, Accidents and Homicides; and Facts about Common Concerns for Men, Including Impotence, Contraception, Circumcision, Sleep Disorders, Snoring, Hair Loss, Diet, Nutrition, Exercise, Kidney and Urological Disorders, and Backaches

Edited by Allan R. Cook. 738 pages. 1998. 0-7808-0212-8. $78.

"**This comprehensive resource and the series are highly recommended.**"
—*American Reference Books Annual, 2000*

"**Recommended reference source.**"
—*Booklist, American Library Association, Dec '98*

Mental Health Disorders Sourcebook, 1st Edition

Basic Information about Schizophrenia, Depression, Bipolar Disorder, Panic Disorder, Obsessive-Compulsive Disorder, Phobias and Other Anxiety Disorders, Paranoia and Other Personality Disorders, Eating Disorders, and Sleep Disorders

Along with Information about Treatment and Therapies

Edited by Karen Bellenir. 548 pages. 1995. 0-7808-0040-0. $78.

"**This is an excellent new book . . . written in easy-to-understand language.**" — *Booklist Health Sciences Supplement, American Library Association, Oct '97*

"**. . . useful for public and academic libraries and consumer health collections.**"
—*Medical Reference Services Quarterly, Spring '97*

"**The great strengths of the book are its readability and its inclusion of places to find more information. Especially recommended.**" — *Reference Quarterly, American Library Association, Winter '96*

"**. . . a good resource for a consumer health library.**"
— *Bulletin of the Medical Library Association, Oct '96*

"**The information is data-based and couched in brief, concise language that avoids jargon. . . . a useful reference source.**" — *Readings, Sep '96*

"**The text is well organized and adequately written for its target audience.**" — *Choice, Association of College and Research Libraries, Jun '96*

"**. . . provides information on a wide range of mental disorders, presented in nontechnical language.**"
—*Exceptional Child Education Resources, Spring '96*

"**Recommended for public and academic libraries.**"
—*Reference Book Review, 1996*

Mental Health Disorders Sourcebook, 2nd Edition

Basic Consumer Health Information about Anxiety Disorders, Depression and Other Mood Disorders, Eating Disorders, Personality Disorders, Schizophrenia, and More, Including Disease Descriptions, Treatment Options, and Reports on Current Research Initiatives

Along with Statistical Data, Tips for Maintaining Mental Health, a Glossary, and Directory of Sources for Additional Help and Information

Edited by Karen Bellenir. 605 pages. 2000. 0-7808-0240-3. $78.

Mental Retardation Sourcebook

Basic Consumer Health Information about Mental Retardation and Its Causes, Including Down Syndrome, Fetal Alcohol Syndrome, Fragile X Syndrome, Genetic Conditions, Injury, and Environmental Sources

Along with Preventive Strategies, Parenting Issues, Educational Implications, Health Care Needs, Employment and Economic Matters, Legal Issues, a Glossary, and a Resource Listing for Additional Help and Information

Edited by Joyce Brennfleck Shannon. 642 pages. 2000. 0-7808-0377-9. $78.

"From preventing retardation to parenting and family challenges, this covers health, social and legal issues and will prove an invaluable overview."
— Reviewer's Bookwatch, Jul '00

■

Obesity Sourcebook

Basic Consumer Health Information about Diseases and Other Problems Associated with Obesity, and Including Facts about Risk Factors, Prevention Issues, and Management Approaches

Along with Statistical and Demographic Data, Information about Special Populations, Research Updates, a Glossary, and Source Listings for Further Help and Information

Edited by Wilma Caldwell. 400 pages. 2000. 0-7808-0333-7. $48.

■

Ophthalmic Disorders Sourcebook

Basic Information about Glaucoma, Cataracts, Macular Degeneration, Strabismus, Refractive Disorders, and More

Along with Statistical and Demographic Data and Reports on Current Research Initiatives

Edited by Linda M. Ross. 631 pages. 1996. 0-7808-0081-8. $78.

■

Oral Health Sourcebook

Basic Information about Diseases and Conditions Affecting Oral Health, Including Cavities, Gum Disease, Dry Mouth, Oral Cancers, Fever Blisters, Canker Sores, Oral Thrush, Bad Breath, Temporomandibular Disorders, and other Craniofacial Syndromes

Along with Statistical Data on the Oral Health of Americans, Oral Hygiene, Emergency First Aid, Information on Treatment Procedures and Methods of Replacing Lost Teeth

Edited by Allan R. Cook. 558 pages. 1997. 0-7808-0082-6. $78.

"Unique source which will fill a gap in dental sources for patients and the lay public. A valuable reference tool even in a library with thousands of books on dentistry. Comprehensive, clear, inexpensive, and easy to read and use. It fills an enormous gap in the health care literature." — Reference and User Services Quarterly, American Library Association, Summer '98

"Recommended reference source."
— Booklist, American Library Association, Dec '97

Osteoporosis Sourcebook

Basic Consumer Health Information about Primary and Secondary Osteoporosis, Juvenile Osteoporosis, Related Conditions, and Other Such Bone Disorders as Fibrous Dysplasia, Myeloma, Osteogenesis Imperfecta, Osteopetrosis, and Paget's Disease

Along with Information about Risk Factors, Treatments, Traditional and Non-Traditional Pain Management, and Including a Glossary and Resource Directory

Edited by Allan R. Cook. 600 pages. 2000. 0-7808-0239-X. $78.

SEE ALSO Women's Health Concerns Sourcebook

■

Pain Sourcebook

Basic Information about Specific Forms of Acute and Chronic Pain, Including Headaches, Back Pain, Muscular Pain, Neuralgia, Surgical Pain, and Cancer Pain

Along with Pain Relief Options Such as Analgesics, Narcotics, Nerve Blocks, Transcutaneous Nerve Stimulation, and Alternative Forms of Pain Control, Including Biofeedback, Imaging, Behavior Modification, and Relaxation Techniques

Edited by Allan R. Cook. 667 pages. 1997. 0-7808-0213-6. $78.

"The text is readable, easily understood, and well indexed. This excellent volume belongs in all patient education libraries, consumer health sections of public libraries, and many personal collections."
— American Reference Books Annual, 1999

"A beneficial reference." — Booklist Health Sciences Supplement, American Library Association, Oct '98

"The information is basic in terms of scholarship and is appropriate for general readers. Written in journalistic style ... intended for non-professionals. Quite thorough in its coverage of different pain conditions and summarizes the latest clinical information regarding pain treatment."
— Choice, Association of College and Research Libraries, Jun '98

"Recommended reference source."
— Booklist, American Library Association, Mar '98

■

Pediatric Cancer Sourcebook

Basic Consumer Health Information about Leukemias, Brain Tumors, Sarcomas, Lymphomas, and Other Cancers in Infants, Children, and Adolescents, Including Descriptions of Cancers, Treatments, and Coping Strategies

Along with Suggestions for Parents, Caregivers, and Concerned Relatives, a Glossary of Cancer Terms, and Resource Listings

Edited by Edward J. Prucha. 587 pages. 1999. 0-7808-0245-4. $78.

"A valuable addition to all libraries specializing in health services and many public libraries."
— American Reference Books Annual, 2000

Physical & Mental Issues in Aging Sourcebook

Basic Consumer Health Information on Physical and Mental Disorders Associated with the Aging Process, Including Concerns about Cardiovascular Disease, Pulmonary Disease, Oral Health, Digestive Disorders, Musculoskeletal and Skin Disorders, Metabolic Changes, Sexual and Reproductive Issues, and Changes in Vision, Hearing, and Other Senses

Along with Data about Longevity and Causes of Death, Information on Acute and Chronic Pain, Descriptions of Mental Concerns, a Glossary of Terms, and Resource Listings for Additional Help

Edited by Jenifer Swanson. 660 pages. 1999. 0-7808-0233-0. $78.

"Recommended for public libraries."
—*American Reference Books Annual, 2000*

"This is a treasure of health information for the layperson." — *Choice Health Sciences Supplement, Association of College & Research Libraries, May 2000*

"Recommended reference source."
—*Booklist, American Library Association, Oct '99*

SEE ALSO *Healthy Aging Sourcebook*

Plastic Surgery Sourcebook

Basic Consumer Health Information on Cosmetic and Reconstructive Plastic Surgery, Including Statistical Information about Different Surgical Procedures, Things to Consider Prior to Surgery, Plastic Surgery Techniques and Tools, Emotional and Psychological Considerations, and Procedure-Specific Information

Along with a Glossary of Terms and a Listing of Resources for Additional Help and Information

Edited by M. Lisa Weatherford. 400 pages. 2000. 0-7808-0214-4. $48.

Podiatry Sourcebook

Basic Consumer Health Information about Foot Conditions, Diseases, and Injuries, Including Bunions, Corns, Calluses, Athlete's Foot, Plantar Warts, Hammertoes and Clawtoes, Club Foot, Heel Pain, Gout, and More

Along with Facts about Foot Care, Disease Prevention, Foot Safety, Choosing a Foot Care Specialist, a Glossary of Terms, and Resource Listings for Additional Information

Edited by M. Lisa Weatherford. 600 pages. 2000. 0-7808-0215-2. $78.

Pregnancy & Birth Sourcebook

Basic Information about Planning for Pregnancy, Maternal Health, Fetal Growth and Development, Labor and Delivery, Postpartum and Perinatal Care, Pregnancy in Mothers with Special Concerns, and Disorders of Pregnancy, Including Genetic Counseling, Nutrition and Exercise, Obstetrical Tests, Pregnancy Discomfort, Multiple Births, Cesarean Sections, Medical Testing of Newborns, Breastfeeding, Gestational Diabetes, and Ectopic Pregnancy

Edited by Heather E. Aldred. 737 pages. 1997. 0-7808-0216-0. $78.

"A well-organized handbook. Recommended."
— *Choice, Association of College and Research Libraries, Apr '98*

"Reecommended reference source."
— *Booklist, American Library Association, Mar '98*

"Recommended for public libraries."
— *American Reference Books Annual, 1998*

SEE ALSO *Congenital Disorders Sourcebook, Family Planning Sourcebook*

Public Health Sourcebook

Basic Information about Government Health Agencies, Including National Health Statistics and Trends, Healthy People 2000 Program Goals and Objectives, the Centers for Disease Control and Prevention, the Food and Drug Administration, and the National Institutes of Health

Along with Full Contact Information for Each Agency

Edited by Wendy Wilcox. 698 pages. 1998. 0-7808-0220-9. $78.

"Recommended reference source."
— *Booklist, American Library Association, Sep '98*

"This consumer guide provides welcome assistance in navigating the maze of federal health agencies and their data on public health concerns."
— *SciTech Book News, Sep '98*

Rehabilitation Sourcebook

Basic Consumer Health Information about Rehabilitation for People Recovering from Heart Surgery, Spinal Cord Injury, Stroke, Orthopedic Impairments, Amputation, Pulmonary Impairments, Traumatic Injury, and More, Including Physical Therapy, Occupational Therapy, Speech/ Language Therapy, Massage Therapy, Dance Therapy, Art Therapy, and Recreational Therapy

Along with Information on Assistive and Adaptive Devices, a Glossary, and Resources for Additional Help and Information

Edited by Dawn D. Matthews. 531 pages. 1999. 0-7808-0236-5. $78.

"Recommended reference source."
— *Booklist, American Library Association, May '00*

Respiratory Diseases & Disorders Sourcebook

Basic Information about Respiratory Diseases and Disorders, Including Asthma, Cystic Fibrosis, Pneumonia, the Common Cold, Influenza, and Others, Featuring Facts about the Respiratory System, Statistical and Demographic Data, Treatments, Self-Help Management Suggestions, and Current Research Initiatives

Edited by Allan R. Cook and Peter D. Dresser. 771 pages. 1995. 0-7808-0037-0. $78.

"Designed for the layperson and for patients and their families coping with respiratory illness. . . . an extensive array of information on diagnosis, treatment, management, and prevention of respiratory illnesses for the general reader." — *Choice, Association of College and Research Libraries, Jun '96*

"A highly recommended text for all collections. It is a comforting reminder of the power of knowledge that good books carry between their covers." — *Academic Library Book Review, Spring '96*

"A comprehensive collection of authoritative information presented in a nontechnical, humanitarian style for patients, families, and caregivers." — *Association of Operating Room Nurses, Sep/Oct '95*

Sexually Transmitted Diseases Sourcebook

Basic Information about Herpes, Chlamydia, Gonorrhea, Hepatitis, Nongonoccocal Urethritis, Pelvic Inflammatory Disease, Syphilis, AIDS, and More
Along with Current Data on Treatments and Preventions

Edited by Linda M. Ross. 550 pages. 1997. 0-7808-0217-9. $78.

Skin Disorders Sourcebook

Basic Information about Common Skin and Scalp Conditions Caused by Aging, Allergies, Immune Reactions, Sun Exposure, Infectious Organisms, Parasites, Cosmetics, and Skin Traumas, Including Abrasions, Cuts, and Pressure Sores
Along with Information on Prevention and Treatment

Edited by Allan R. Cook. 647 pages. 1997. 0-7808-0080-X. $78.

". . . comprehensive, easily read reference book." — *Doody's Health Sciences Book Reviews, Oct '97*

SEE ALSO Burns Sourcebook

Sleep Disorders Sourcebook

Basic Consumer Health Information about Sleep and Its Disorders, Including Insomnia, Sleepwalking, Sleep Apnea, Restless Leg Syndrome, and Narcolepsy
Along with Data about Shiftwork and Its Effects, Information on the Societal Costs of Sleep Deprivation, Descriptions of Treatment Options, a Glossary of Terms, and Resource Listings for Additional Help

Edited by Jenifer Swanson. 439 pages. 1998. 0-7808-0234-9. $78.

"This text will complement any home or medical library. It is user-friendly and ideal for the adult reader." — *American Reference Books Annual, 2000*

"Recommended reference source." — *Booklist, American Library Association, Feb '99*

"A useful resource that provides accurate, relevant, and accessible information on sleep to the general public. Health care providers who deal with sleep disorders patients may also find it helpful in being prepared to answer some of the questions patients ask." — *Respiratory Care, Jul '99*

Sports Injuries Sourcebook

Basic Consumer Health Information about Common Sports Injuries, Prevention of Injury in Specific Sports, Tips for Training, and Rehabilitation from Injury
Along with Information about Special Concerns for Children, Young Girls in Athletic Training Programs, Senior Athletes, and Women Athletes, and a Directory of Resources for Further Help and Information

Edited by Heather E. Aldred. 624 pages. 1999. 0-7808-0218-7. $78.

"Public libraries and undergraduate academic libraries will find this book useful for its nontechnical language." — *American Reference Books Annual, 2000*

"While this easy-to-read book is recommended for all libraries, it should prove to be especially useful for public, high school, and academic libraries; certainly it should be on the bookshelf of every school gymnasium." — *E-Streams, Mar '00*

Substance Abuse Sourcebook

Basic Health-Related Information about the Abuse of Legal and Illegal Substances Such as Alcohol, Tobacco, Prescription Drugs, Marijuana, Cocaine, and Heroin; and Including Facts about Substance Abuse Prevention Strategies, Intervention Methods, Treatment and Recovery Programs, and a Section Addressing the Special Problems Related to Substance Abuse during Pregnancy

Edited by Karen Bellenir. 573 pages. 1996. 0-7808-0038-9. $78.

"A valuable addition to any health reference section. Highly recommended." — *The Book Report, Mar/Apr '97*

"... a comprehensive collection of substance abuse information that's both highly readable and compact. Families and caregivers of substance abusers will find the information enlightening and helpful, while teachers, social workers and journalists should benefit from the concise format. Recommended."
—*Drug Abuse Update, Winter '96/'97*

SEE ALSO *Alcoholism Sourcebook, Drug Abuse Sourcebook*

Traveler's Health Sourcebook

Basic Consumer Health Information for Travelers, Including Physical and Medical Preparations, Transportation Health and Safety, Essential Information about Food and Water, Sun Exposure, Insect and Snake Bites, Camping and Wilderness Medicine, and Travel with Physical or Medical Disabilities

Along with International Travel Tips, Vaccination Recommendations, Geographical Health Issues, Disease Risks, a Glossary, and a Listing of Additional Resources

Edited by Joyce Brennfleck Shannon. 613 pages. 2000. 0-7808-0384-1. $78.

Women's Health Concerns Sourcebook

Basic Information about Health Issues That Affect Women, Featuring Facts about Menstruation and Other Gynecological Concerns, Including Endometriosis, Fibroids, Menopause, and Vaginitis; Reproductive Concerns, Including Birth Control, Infertility, and Abortion; and Facts about Additional Physical, Emotional, and Mental Health Concerns Prevalent among Women Such as Osteoporosis, Urinary Tract Disorders, Eating Disorders, and Depression

Along with Tips for Maintaining a Healthy Lifestyle

Edited by Heather E. Aldred. 567 pages. 1997. 0-7808-0219-5. $78.

"Handy compilation. There is an impressive range of diseases, devices, disorders, procedures, and other physical and emotional issues covered ... well organized, illustrated, and indexed." —*Choice, Association of College and Research Libraries, Jan '98*

SEE ALSO *Breast Cancer Sourcebook, Cancer Sourcebook for Women, 1st and 2nd Editions, Healthy Heart Sourcebook for Women, Osteoporosis Sourcebook*

Workplace Health & Safety Sourcebook

Basic Information about Musculoskeletal Injuries, Cumulative Trauma Disorders, Occupational Carcinogens and Other Toxic Materials, Child Labor, Workplace Violence, Histoplasmosis, Transmission of HIV and Hepatitis-B Viruses, and Occupational Hazards Associated with Various Industries, Including Mining, Confined Spaces, Agriculture, Construction, Electrical

Work, and the Medical Professions, with Information on Mortality and Other Statistical Data, Preventative Measures, Reproductive Risks, Reducing Stress for Shiftworkers, Noise Hazards, Industrial Back Belts, Reducing Contamination at Home, Preventing Allergic Reactions to Rubber Latex, and More

Along with Public and Private Programs and Initiatives, a Glossary, and Sources for Additional Help and Information

Edited by Chad Kimball. 600 pages. 2000. 0-7808-0231-4. $78.

Worldwide Health Sourcebook

Basic Information about Global Health Issues, Including Nutrition, Reproductive Health, Disease Dispersion and Prevention, Emerging Diseases, Health Risks, and the Leading Causes of Death

Along with Global Health Concerns for Children, Women, and the Elderly, Mental Health Issues, Research and Technology Advancements, and Economic, Environmental, and Political Health Implications, a Glossary, and a Resource Listing for Additional Help and Information

Edited by Joyce Brennfleck Shannon. 500 pages. 2000. 0-7808-0330-2. $78.

Health Reference Series Cumulative Index 1999

A Comprehensive Index to the Individual Volumes of the Health Reference Series, Including a Subject Index, Name Index, Organization Index, and Publication Index;

Along with a Master List of Acronyms and Abbreviations

Edited by Edward J. Prucha, Anne Holmes, and Robert Rudnick. 990 pages. 2000. 0-7808-0382-5. $78.